THE LAST TREATY

In *The Last Treaty*, Michelle Tusan profoundly reshapes the story of how the First World War ended in the Middle East. Tracing Europe's war with the Ottoman Empire through to the signing of Lausanne, which finally ended the war in 1923, she places the decisive Allied victory over Germany in 1918 in sharp relief against the unrelenting war in the East and reassesses the military operations, humanitarian activities and diplomatic dealings that continued after the signing of Versailles in 1919. She shows how, on the Middle Eastern Front, Britain and France directed Allied war strategy against a resurgent Ottoman Empire to sustain an imperial system that favored Europe's dominance within the nascent international system. The protracted nature of the conflict and ongoing humanitarian crisis proved devastating for the civilian populations caught in its wake and increasingly questioned old certainties about a European-led imperial order and humanitarian intervention. Its consequences would transform the postwar world.

Michelle Tusan is Professor of History at the University of Nevada, Las Vegas. Her previous publications include *The British Empire and the Armenian Genocide* (2017), *Smyrna's Ashes* (2012) and *Women Making News* (2006).

THE LAST TREATY

Lausanne and the End of the First World War in the Middle East

Michelle Tusan

University of Nevada, Las Vegas

CAMBRIDGE
UNIVERSITY PRESS

Shaftesbury Road, Cambridge CB2 8EA, United Kingdom

One Liberty Plaza, 20th Floor, New York, NY 10006, USA

477 Williamstown Road, Port Melbourne, VIC 3207, Australia

314–321, 3rd Floor, Plot 3, Splendor Forum, Jasola District Centre, New Delhi – 110025, India

103 Penang Road, #05–06/07, Visioncrest Commercial, Singapore 238467

Cambridge University Press is part of Cambridge University Press & Assessment, a department of the University of Cambridge.

We share the University's mission to contribute to society through the pursuit of education, learning and research at the highest international levels of excellence.

www.cambridge.org
Information on this title: www.cambridge.org/9781009371087

DOI: 10.1017/9781009371063

First published 2023

A catalogue record for this publication is available from the British Library.

A Cataloging-in-Publication data record for this book is available from the Library of Congress.

ISBN 978-1-009-37108-7 Hardback

For Scott, Nicholas, and Sophia

Contents

Figures

Maps

Acknowledgments

This book was written because of the support of the National Endowment for the Humanities. My fellowship year and a subsequent University of Nevada, Las Vegas sabbatical made it possible to see it through to completion. Along the way, many other people and institutions helped me do this work. It is my privilege to have the opportunity to thank them here.

I had the good fortune to have the benefit of wonderful colleagues and friends during the writing of this book. Tom Laqueur has continued to support my work and talk with me about projects large and small. Antoinette Burton offered intellectual and professional support, many encouragements and always good advice. Alon Confino engaged my work on refugees and gave me a venue to try out ideas at the Institute for Holocaust, Genocide and Memory Studies. Peggy Anderson also encouraged my research. Tammy Proctor, Sue Grayzel, Nadja Durbach, Erika Rappaport, Lisa Cody and Amy Woodson-Boulton kept me writing and thinking and always engaged.

Despite, and sometimes because of, COVID travel restrictions, I had the opportunity to share research with several audiences. I joined the Imperial Afterlives Network led by Jean-Michel Johnson and Anna Ross in Cambridge; The Global 1922, headed by Georgios Giannakopoulos at Kings College London and the online Lausanne Project facilitated by Jonathan Conlin. Presentations at the Armenian Studies Program at the University of Michigan; the Center for Modern Greek Studies at Loyola Marymount University; the Institute for Holocaust, Genocide and Memory Studies at the University of Massachusetts; the Henry Ransom Center at the University of Texas, Austin; Wofford College; the Genocide in the Twentieth Century History conference at the University of

Toronto; the Workshop on Armenian and Turkish Scholarship at the European Academy Berlin; the International Network of Genocide Scholars conference at Hebrew University, Jerusalem and Wiener Holocaust Library, London brought this book into focus. Wendy Lower invited me to give an Athenaeum lecture at Claremont McKenna College, and I discussed the legacies of T. E. Lawrence in the Arab world at the National World War I Museum. Various parts of this project were presented at the North American Conference on British Studies and the Pacific Coast Conference on British Studies. Thanks to Bruno Cabanes for inviting me to write about Smyrna for *L'Histoire* and the *Los Angeles Review of Books* for publishing my work on refugees and film.

Primary research came from archives in North America, Britain and France, and I thank the archivists who opened their collections, both remotely and in person. These included Boris Adjemian at the Nubar Library, Paris; Debbie Usher at the Middle East Center Archives, Oxford; Parliamentary Archives, London; Kings College London: Liddell Hart Military Archive; Imperial War Museum, London; the British Film Institute, London; Friends House, London; Churchill Archives, Cambridge; Hoover Library, Stanford and Huntington Library, San Marino. I would also like to acknowledge my reliance on findings in the secondary literature, especially in the fields of Ottoman, Arab, Jewish, Greek and Armenian studies. This work helped situate my own archival research in a wide and diverse historiography that extends beyond the sometimes parochial focus of British and European studies.

The eighteen months I had away from teaching made all the difference, allowing me to write full time. But it was with my students and in my community where many of the themes and ideas for this book came to life. The Office of Undergraduate Research, led by Levent Atici, funded Victoria Limon's charting of refugee journeys depicted in over fifty Armenian Genocide survivor memoirs. These informed the map made by Hilla Sang of camps, auxiliary services and aid stations used by these refugees in Chapter 3. Serving as a member of the State Board of Education Subcommittee on Holocaust and Other Genocides engaged me in the genocide curriculum of our elementary and high schools.

In addition to the National Endowment for the Humanities, this project received support from a Silas Palmer fellowship at the Hoover Library,

Stanford University and a Mayers fellowship at the Huntington Library. Thanks to Simon Devereaux and Andrea McKenzie for facilitating my very enjoyable time as a Lansdowne Visiting Professor at the University of Victoria. UNLV awarded me a Faculty International Development Award to France and a University Library GIS Development Grant. Librarian Priscilla Finley helped me find material that was difficult to track down. Yuko Shinozaki in interlibrary borrowing never gave up helping me find the sources I needed. Liam Frink expertly facilitated the grant workshop sponsored by Research and Economic Development and the Graduate College. The Faculty Senate approved my sabbatical that the College of Liberal Arts allowed me to take and approved research funds administered by Annette Amdal. Todd Shirley made the two historical maps and Erin Greb made the war fronts map. David Speicher did the index. I thank my chair, Andy Kirk, who supported my leave time and my colleagues Jeff Schauer, Willy Bauer, Paul Werth and Carlos Dimas. Ottoman specialists John Curry, Aimee Genell and Bedross Der Matossian helped me with names and translations as well as the press history of the Ottoman period. Bedross and Melanie S. Tanielian thoughtfully and expertly engaged my work on refugees in the UMass forum, and Melanie later invited me to the University of Michigan to speak. Hans-Lukas Kieser insightfully read and commented on the draft manuscript.

Good friends and colleagues supported me during the research and writing process. The WWWWs were a constant, steady and brilliant source of support. I also thank Elizabeth Fraterrigo, Deb Cohler, Ellen Ross, Jordanna Bailkin, Philippa Levine, Monica Rico and Jena Albert. Maria Jerinic-Pravica and Joanna Kepka and their families have long made this place feel like home. Regular chats with my sister, Christina Tusan, reminded me to keep close what matters. I wish Mom could still be part of our we. I think she would have liked this book. My dad, true to form, asked if I was still working on that project about Armenians.

Thank you to Michael Watson and the team at Cambridge. I also thank *Past and Present* and the *Journal of Modern History* for permission to use versions of articles first published in these journals: "The Concentration Camp as a Site of Refuge: The Rise of the Refugee Camp and the Great War in the Middle East," *Journal of Modern History* 93, no. 4 (December 2021): 824–860 and "Genocide, Famine and Refugees on

Film: Humanitarianism and the Great War," *Past and Present* 237, no. 1 (November 2017): 197–235. While indebted to those mentioned in these acknowledgments, I alone am responsible for what follows.

I've never written anything more purposefully. Sometimes a pleasure and often a strain, as my family will attest, I'll always think of this as my COVID book. No travel, no onsite archives, no engaging colleagues outside of the little Zoom box. My kids necessarily participated by virtue of being stuck at home with me. Every day we'd have lunch in the garden and they'd hear me talk about a place and a people that I hope started to seem a bit more familiar. Nick, intelligently thoughtful, got ready for college, shared his playlists and taught me some chords. Sophia, smart, clever and so much fun, made her own art, helped with images for the book and watched '90s romcoms with me. Our home opened up to a life that felt very full. With my husband, Scott Muelrath, I've shared twenty-five years. He made me believe that this was all possible and for that I will always be grateful. I like to think that this work is a part of him as much as it is of me.

Note on Place Names and Names in the Text

I use historic place names throughout. The modern name is indicated in the first use in parentheses in the text. The maps use mostly the historic names to make the places as they are referenced in the text easier to locate. With apologies to specialists, I have omitted diacritical marks and used common English spellings of Arabic, Armenian, Russian and Ottoman names to correspond with how they are referenced in my source material.

Map 1 First World War fronts in Europe and the Mediterranean

Map 1 (cont.)

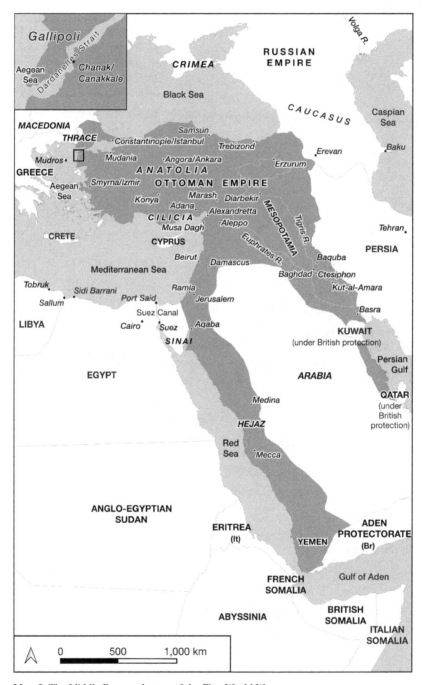

Map 2 The Middle East on the eve of the First World War

Map 3 The Middle East at the end of the First World War

Introduction

❝I AM BISMARCK," TOP OTTOMAN OFFICIAL TALAAT Pasha declared to Armen Garo two days after Archduke Franz Ferdinand's assassination in Sarajevo on June 28, 1914. Garo, an Armenian and former colleague and friend of Talaat, recorded his shock in hearing this embrace of German imperium in a private meeting at the Ottoman Interior Ministry.[1] He had come to Constantinople to protest the forced resettlement of Muslim refugees on Armenian lands but quickly realized that the vision of empire embraced by leaders like Talaat had no room for Christian minorities like himself.[2] The murder of the Archduke in the Balkans sparked a global war that had roots in two recent regional conflicts. The Balkan Wars had raged between 1912 and 1913 and cost the Ottoman Empire most of its territory in Europe while creating a massive refugee crisis.[3]

The ensuing war between the Allies and the Ottoman Empire brought the struggles of the Balkans home to the empires of Europe. Demographic pressure resulting from the Balkan Wars met Talaat's own imperial ambition in a world-shattering moment. On the eve of war in June 1914, Talaat saw a chance to invent a homogeneous ethno-religious empire based on exclusionary nationalism.[4] Bismarck famously created Germany from "iron and blood" by rejecting the boundaries of the Congress of Vienna and liberal pluralism of 1848.[5] Talaat helped forge modern Turkey out of the wartime ruins of the Ottoman Empire by thwarting Allied attempts to partition Asia Minor and enforce minority protection.[6] His "radical nationalism" transformed Asia Minor into a Turkish national homeland under Mustafa Kemal (Atatürk).[7] This process culminated with the end of the war and the signing of the Treaty of Lausanne on July 24, 1923.

The First World War was a war of empires that started in the Balkans and ended in the Middle East.[8] *The Last Treaty* reassesses how and why the Great War ended with the signing of the Treaty of Lausanne between the Allies and the Ottoman Empire.[9] This focuses importance on the Middle Eastern Front, a term I deploy to describe the war in Ottoman territory in the eastern Mediterranean that included the struggle for what was then called Mesopotamia, as well as North Africa and Anatolia. It paralleled the war fought in Europe between the Central Powers led by the German and the Austro-Hungarian empires and the Allies led by the British, French, Russian and American empires. The long war between the Allies and the Ottoman Empire had devastating consequences for civilian populations caught in its wake. To write the history of the First World War from the rear-view mirror of Lausanne requires reassessing military operations, humanitarian activities and diplomatic dealings that continued after the signing of the Treaty of Versailles in 1919.

This book integrates the Ottoman Empire into the war's grand narrative through the study of the Middle Eastern Front from 1914 to 1923. The Ottoman Empire readied itself for war like the whole of Europe after the Archduke's assassination. On August 2, 1914, the Ottoman government signed a secret alliance with Germany that ultimately committed it to a war that lasted nine years and ended in Lausanne.[10] The First World War on the Middle Eastern Front changed the relationship between civilians and combatants; states and international institutions; and humanitarian and military operations that, in turn, transformed modern war making.

That peace did not come with the signing of the Treaty of Versailles in 1919 has broad implications for understanding the history of the First World War as a global war. Peacemaking entailed a protracted and separate set of processes where treaties were negotiated while combat operations continued between belligerent powers.[11] The fallout from the 1915 Armenian Genocide, which resulted in sustained interethnic violence and a massive refugee crisis, further complicated attempts to forge a stable and lasting peace. Greece, though it officially entered the war only in the summer of 1917, played an important role in the final settlement because of the so-called minority question. This came to the fore at the Lausanne negotiations after the burning of the city of Smyrna (Izmir) and the population exchange between Greece and Turkey which made the question of what to do with stateless Christian minority refugees a core issue during the peace process.[12]

The First World War when viewed from the vantage of the last treaty sheds light on violence in the Ottoman Empire after 1918. Conflicts in this period, when discussed at all, are considered part of a separate set of processes that happened in the Caucasus, Cilicia, the Dardanelles Strait and around Smyrna. These battles are variously referred to as part of the Greek-Turkish War or the War of Turkish Independence connecting them to distinct histories linked only to national stories.[13] Clashes between Kemalist-led Ottoman and Allied armies on these battle fronts, however, came out of the larger action of the war and fell in line with Ottoman war aims, namely the protection of the empire and elimination of minorities. The First World War created the axiom that genocide occurs due to the inevitable escalation of violence against civilian populations in total war.[14] This happened in both the First and the Second World Wars and made state-sponsored violence against those marked as enemies from within a reality of the civilian war experience.[15] The destruction of Ottoman Christian minorities continued after the signing of the armistice in late October 1918, despite and sometimes because of military and diplomatic maneuvering between belligerent actors. War-related violence and peacemaking converged around the Armenian Genocide.[16] For the Allied powers – led by Britain, France, Russia and later the United States – ending the war with the Ottoman Empire meant coming to terms with genocide. This required navigating the space between the nation-state and an emergent international system where humanitarianism, international justice and refugee policy found new and uneasy articulation.

War and peacemaking developed as an overlapping set of processes that made continued interethnic and political violence a defining characteristic of the years leading up to the 1923 moment. Rethinking the end of the war in this way represents a descriptive and conceptual problem as much as a chronological one. Simply put, *when* the war ended depended on *where* you were. This book focuses on *how* the First World War ended rather than argues for a new definitive end date to the war. The last treaty marked the end of a set of military and diplomatic actions set in motion by the war. The era after the war remains indelibly marked by its relationship to the war itself, entangling the war and postwar periods. This might explain why historians use the awkward term "interwar" to describe the 1920s and 1930s. The term inscribes the relationality of the period to the experience of the war itself. To understand the significance of the Great War in the Middle East to European history requires studying the blurry borders of the end of the war that gave the "Interwar Years" its seemingly transitional character to yet another world war in 1939.

THE LONG WAR

The Last Treaty employs this wide geographic and chronological lens in order to place the decisive Allied victory over Germany in 1918 in sharp relief against an unrelenting war with the Ottoman Empire. On the Middle Eastern Front, Britain and France directed Allied war strategy to sustain an imperial system that favored Europe's dominance within the nascent international system. Britain played an outsized role on the Middle Eastern Front starting in 1915 and brokered the failed 1920 Treaty of Sèvres that was revised in 1923 at Lausanne. It successfully marginalized its French and Italian allies after the invasion of Baghdad while the 1917 Bolshevik Revolution eventually limited Russian influence. By 1917, Britain used its dominant position on the Middle Eastern Front to guide both military and humanitarian activity.

The resurgence of interest in the aftermath of the First World War has yielded important research on violence in the Middle East, Asia and Africa as part of the "greater war."[17] Historians now understand the war's geographic scope in new ways: a conflict that started in Europe became a truly global war that left a lasting legacy far beyond the West.[18] The long war in the Middle East had its own defining characteristics and meaning just as it did in Europe, Africa and Asia. At the same time, its history remained entwined with and left a lasting legacy on both Europe and the Middle East. The premature war victory celebrations in 1918 in Europe led to disillusionment and the First World War began to be seen as a needless sacrifice that resulted in few permanent gains.[19] In the

Middle East, the settlement with Turkey led to continued violence and uncertainty for religious minorities in the aftermath of the fall of the Ottoman Empire. At the Lausanne Conference, the narrative of an imperfect peace that ended a futile war took full shape.

This book integrates the long and sustained Allied battle against the Ottoman Empire into European historiography on the First World War.[20] European historians typically read fighting in the Middle East after 1918 as an addendum to the war. Their focus instead has been on the mandate system, territories carved out of former Ottoman territory and overseen by the British and the French with the sanction of the League of Nations.[21] This casts the 1920s as a formative period in the making of the modern Middle East through the rise of postwar successor states including modern Turkey. Relegating these developments wholly to the "interwar years," however, has obscured how the ongoing war helped shaped their final form.[22] The First World War operated within its own set of historical contingencies in the Middle East that had consequences including, but not exclusive to, the rise of European-sanctioned successor states.

Far from a neglected subject, studies of civilian sacrifice and military action reveal the complexities and long-term consequences of the war for the Middle East and Europe. Battles in Ottoman territory beyond the story of the Gallipoli campaign, wartime alliances and events including the Armenian Genocide have become part of the narrative of the war and its aftermath.[23] This research provides a deeper understanding of the Ottomans' decision to side with Germany.[24] It also reveals the political, social and economic challenges inherent to fighting a war against the Allies in a massive swath of territory encompassing deserts, mountains and sea.

This work, however, largely has remained the purview of specialists in Ottoman history rather than historians of Europe.[25] With some notable exceptions, this has led to relegating the war in the Middle East to the periphery in European historiography on the war.[26] When telling the story of the Ottoman Empire and the First World War, European historians focus on specific campaigns like Gallipoli, individuals such as T. E. Lawrence and Gertrude Bell, the making of the mandate system and the peace settlement's role in redrawing the regional map and forging imperial alliances.[27] Many of these discussions, especially those related to the Middle East mandates, overlook that war continued as the mandate system came into force.

The periodization of the First World War in the Middle East thus does not make room for the post-1918 Armistice period when the war was far from settled between the Allies and the Ottoman Empire. European historiography on the First World War contributes to neglecting this long war by refusing to give the warfront a name, preserving "Eastern Front" for the battles fought along the Russian and Central European borderlands.[28] This belies the significance of the war in the Ottoman Empire where fighting took place for more than a decade, if we count the Balkan Wars, on lands that extended from the Balkans to the Caucasus to the Arabian Peninsula. The Allied occupation of Constantinople and the Arabian Peninsula extended the war by requiring the further dedication of soldiers and resources in Ottoman lands. These Middle Eastern Fronts, I argue, remain essential sites for understanding the human costs of military conflict and diplomacy in a war incompletely won.

By reorienting the current focus on the outcomes of the Versailles Treaty such as the mandate system and the origins of the Second World War, this book shows how the Middle Eastern Front shaped the military and civilian experience of the war. This approach puts Ottoman and European historiographies in dialogue with official documents and correspondence between state and non-state actors, media and film, and institutional records and diaries of aid workers, refugees and other non-combatants from British, US and French archives. Historians have shown the war's importance to the birth of modern Turkey.[29] Others have focused on the Ottoman home front or the Armenian Genocide.[30] My own previous research analyzes the extent and limits of humanitarian intervention. Since the First World War centenary, these strands have converged to broaden the narrative of the war beyond the trenches of the Western Front to include the consequences of wartime alliances and civilian sacrifices. The next step toward moving the Middle Eastern Front from a peripheral to core consideration involves recasting the period after the signing of the first armistices as the war's final chapter. The period between 1918 and 1923 shaped home and battlefront as well as the contours of the Interwar period. It merits center stage.

HUMANITARIANISM AND WAR

Integrating war making and diplomacy between the Allies and the Ottoman Empire into this story reveals the centrality of violence against civilians and genocide to the narrative arc of the First World War. Here on the Middle Eastern Front, the intertwined relationship between military conquest and humanitarianism had its improbable beginnings.[31] The need to control population movements on the battlefront led the military to fund and support aid to civilians living in a war zone. At the same time, humanitarian missions led and funded mostly by Britain and the United States – though the latter never declared war against the Ottoman Empire – maintained a massive footprint in the region. Together, military and civilian-led humanitarian aid efforts indelibly shaped the conduct of the war.[32]

Britain helped establish new standards for civilian treatment in wartime along racial and ethno-religious lines through the invention of the refugee camp. Ultimately, organized relief work expanded the West's humanitarian presence in the Middle East and supervision of minority populations.[33] Such actions protected and expanded the British Empire while managing US, French and Russian interests beyond the war. *The Last Treaty* reveals the relationship between military and humanitarian operations in the space of the concentration camp set up to manage civilian populations in wartime. The memoirs, reports and diplomatic correspondence read in the following chapters alongside maps of refugee camps and military campaigns render visible the human geography of total war in Mesopotamia during the height of the British-led campaigns there.

The enormous scale of the conflict necessitated a new kind of response on the Middle Eastern Front. Humanitarianism's institutional development relied both on this wartime context and on colonial agendas. Historians agree that the war created new exigencies and institutional frameworks that changed the way humanitarianism operated.[34] The scholarship, however, remains mired in debates over how much this moment represented an actual shift in the practice of humanitarianism. Historians rightly see institutionalization as important for the future of humanitarian practice. Where they disagree is on its aims and effectiveness: did humanitarianism promote human rights and help populations in need or did it simply push colonial agendas?[35] These are important questions that reveal how the institutionalization of humanitarianism contributed to the reconfiguration of geopolitical and imperial alignments.

Reading humanitarianism's development as embedded in wartime Allied agendas, as this book does, further raises the stakes. To fully understand the rise of humanitarianism and its institutionalization, we need to interrogate more deeply its connection to the First World War in the Middle East. Here humanitarianism developed in concert with military and diplomatic concerns. These forces – humanitarian and wartime exigency – did not operate on parallel tracks but rather grew up together. However, this was an uneven process that relied on contemporary conceptions of gender and race that further complicated how aid was delivered. Sometimes humanitarian agendas coincided with war aims, while at other times they resisted the dictates of the military.[36] War, diplomacy and humanitarianism made strange bedfellows, but it was in this moment that they found their modern articulation and took the form that set the script for later developments that extended well beyond the Second World War.

Because of the central role of the British and, to a lesser extent, the French, I have mined diplomatic and humanitarian institutional archives. Scholarship on the Ottoman, Armenian, Jewish, Greek, Assyrian and Arab perspective of the war has made this book possible. It bears underscoring that this book interrogates Europe's understanding of the war in the Middle East. While exploring the inner workings of the official mind that prosecuted the war in the Middle East from London and Paris, it differs from other political histories by uncovering the voices of the people and non-European-based institutions involved in the war: refugees, aid-workers and soldiers.[37]

This act of recovery requires reading the archive differently and paying attention to the moments when diplomatic, humanitarian and military actors met those who told them how this war changed their lives. This is not a story populated by heroes and villains but rather people forced to act in extraordinary circumstances. The impossible conditions of the war for civilians and, in particular, victims of the Armenian

Genocide make it imperative to see why and how those who offered aid did it and in whose name. In the end, the aid itself mattered to those who needed and received it; those stories are embedded in the archive. Historians just have to listen.

THE MIDDLE EASTERN FRONT

I use the term "Middle Eastern Front" rather than "Ottoman Front" to better incorporate this site into the lexicon of the First World War. "Ottoman Front," the term often used by Ottoman historians, denotes the belligerent rather than the geography of a war that was defined as much by location as anything else. Designating fighting that took place among the Allies, Germany and the Ottoman Empire as the "Middle Eastern Front" parallels the use of "Western Front" and "Eastern Front" that, admittedly, are problematic as well. As Map 1 shows, the Western Front refers to fighting in Belgium and France, but the actual area shifted over the course of the war. The same goes for the Eastern Front in relation to fighting along the Russian border. The Balkan Front and the Alpine Front equally lack precise definition. While there are clear geographic problems in seeing the war in accordance with these border-less fronts, such regional designations offer a way of spatially mapping the war that coincides with the political geography as imagined by belligerents at the time. Western Front and Eastern Front continue to be especially meaningful designations that orient the work of war historians. Finally, analyzing multiple fronts – Western, Eastern, Middle Eastern and others – bounded by rough geographical designations further reinforces understandings of the First World War as a war of alliances. The Ottomans fought *with* the Germans on the same front together as allies. To call this the "Ottoman Front" obscures this important relationship.

The use of Middle Eastern Front also draws attention to colonial relationships embedded in the deployment of the term Middle East in the early twentieth century. Not naming this front in European historical accounts of the war has contributed to an act of erasure by using clumsy nomenclature to designate fighting here as a separate set of actions.[38] Denying a geography for this front, however hard to clearly define in terms of territory, renders it less visible to the larger action of the war than the "Western" and "Eastern" fronts that suffer from a not dissimilar lack of precise physical boundaries. Maps, correspondence, film and photography – the representational apparatus used by Europe's generals, strategists, soldiers and diplomats engaged in this theater of war – lend form to this space of engagement.[39] For the British, the idea of the "middle" and "near" East were relational colonial terms that denoted Britain's distance from its empire in India. As I have shown elsewhere, a similar process of imagined geographical definition was at work in the nineteenth century when the British first deployed the term Near East to designate Christian-occupied lands on the borders of Europe as a way of mapping their empire.[40]

I started this project, in part, to understand why there has been comparatively little attention paid to the Ottoman role in the First World War in war historiography. This is particularly surprising since the Middle Eastern and Western Fronts were mirrors of one another in many ways. Trench warfare happened on both fronts at the beginning but, by 1917, gave way to a war of movement in Mesopotamia where quick decisive victories led to the signing of the first armistice with the Ottoman Empire in October 1918. Both fronts also saw the blurring of the relationship between home and battlefront. Civilians helped determine how the war was fought and won on the Middle Eastern Front just as they did on the Western Front.[41] Belligerents mobilized their economies to produce weapons, food and resources to fight the war due to the demands of industrial warfare. This resulted in new ways of seeing civilians in wartime.[42] On the Middle Eastern Front, Ottoman paranoia about enemies from within divided inhabitants into loyal and disloyal camps. Minority Armenian, Assyrian and Greek Ottoman subjects were increasingly viewed with suspicion and subjected, at first, to discriminatory treatment. By spring 1915, they had been targeted for annihilation by their own government.[43]

On the Middle Eastern and Western Fronts, news of the brutal treatment of civilians justified war in Europe. The call to defend civilians targeted by the Armenian Genocide in spring 1915 echoed the Belgian atrocities used by Britain to validate its entry in the war in August 1914.[44] In both cases – the treatment of Christian minorities by their own government in the case of the Ottoman Empire and the treatment of Belgian civilians by the invading German forces – the defense of the rights of others gave the war a just cause. Genocide created a new kind of war victim who solicited a distinct humanitarian response that focused on aid work and, eventually, attempts at resettlement for survivors. This question of the responsibility of warring parties to the security of non-combatants, which had found articulation in the turn-of-the-century Geneva and later Hague conventions, had its first test on the Middle Eastern Front when Ottoman civilians came under the jurisdiction of Allied occupation after 1917. Eventually, humanitarian aid for non-combatants dominated discussions of how to deal with wartime destruction. Private aid organizations coordinated with the Allies to provide care for civilian war victims.[45]

Despite such parallel features, fighting in the Ottoman Empire stubbornly has remained fixed in the language of time: a "sideshow." Politicians, soldiers and even ardent advocates of the importance of this front use this term to describe the Ottoman theater of war. Today, historians debate whether or not it was a sideshow to highlight the sacrifices of the men who fought there.[46] This approach has focused new attention on this front. But why and how the idea of war here as sideshow captured the imagination of the West at the time and historians today needs explanation. The response to the war in the Middle East, in both Europe and the United States, reveals a deep and complicated engagement with the people and history of this region. It is possible to track this response through humanitarian institutions, private donations and volunteer work as well as cultural forms including film, novels and media commentary. These sources both reveal the centrality of the Middle East in Allied thinking about the war and offer new ways of remembering and understanding this front today.

Other factors have contributed to the marginalization of the Middle Eastern Front. The distance between home and battlefront where the fighting happened mattered. The Western Front, a train ride away from home for some of its soldiers, had a geographic nearness that could never be replicated on the Middle Eastern Front, even in the case of the most important and dramatic battles.

As David Lloyd George ruefully remarked about Jerusalem: "the capture by British troops of the most famous city in the world" largely was ignored at home.[47] News of victory came more slowly from foreign news correspondents and communications lagged.[48] During the Gallipoli campaign, a letter took approximately three weeks to travel from the front to Britain with packages taking around five to six weeks.[49]

Who fought in this war also is important. The Middle Eastern Front truly was a global theater.[50] By 1917, the British relied on the Mesopotamian and Indian Expeditionary Forces almost exclusively to fight here. This meant that the majority of soldiers serving here came from the British Empire – Australia, New Zealand and India primarily. The French also relied on soldiers from the empire, mainly North Africa, to fight in the Middle East. Memoirs of those who fought on this front often complain of their forgotten role in the war. Until recently, scholars largely ignored their contribution as fighters and as heads of auxiliary services and their role in humanitarian work in the areas of occupation.[51] While no longer hidden from history, the contribution of colonial soldiers still remains overshadowed by those from Europe and its white settler colonies. Their marginalization as secondary fighters on a forgotten front is evidenced by the separate characterization of non-British troops in the casuality and fighting figures and in commentary by those who led their units. At the same time, precise numbers of colonial soldiers are not as carefully charted in the archives.[52]

New work on colonial soldiers reveals how central the Middle Eastern Front was to the war by tracing the experience of soldiers who served there. Drawn disproportionately from British and French colonies, these men occupied what Anna Maguire calls "contact zones," where colonialism was tested and challenged on the battle front, in the camp and then back at home. In these spaces, colonial relations came under strain and created new ways of understanding empire and imperialism.[53] Here on the Middle Eastern Front, the British and French empires were reimagined by those called up to defend it. In this way and others, as this book shows, race mattered as a factor in how the Middle Eastern Front has been studied and understood.

WAR OF EMPIRES

The signing of the Treaty of Lausanne ended the war of empires. Britain and its imperial military force had led the fight in Mesopotamia. It guarded its imperial and economic interests in Egypt with a special eye to protecting the Suez Canal, while France shored up its empire in North Africa and control of Syria. The Russian Empire had led the war in the Caucasus until the Brest-Litovsk Treaty signed with Germany in 1918 took it out of the war.[54] The United States never declared war on the Ottoman Empire, though it contributed vast amounts of money and resources to the war's humanitarian infrastructure here.

This war of empires was fought to uphold imperialism. Ultimately, wartime alliances contributed to an internationalism that emerged in the name of preserving old European-led colonial relationships.[55] The British Empire's focus on the Middle Eastern Front escalated after Lloyd George took over as Prime Minister in 1916. This expanded the imperial scope of the war. Britain both relied more heavily on colonial troops and stepped up its competition with France and Russia for dominance in the region. While historians now recognize colonial soldiers' contributions, they have shown less interest in how the First World War on the Middle Eastern Front mattered as a war between empires. Part of the reason has to do with the focus on particular battles rather than on shifting strategies. In 1915, British war planners understood war with the Ottomans as an extension of the war with Germany. This was certainly true in the early years, but this changed after 1916.

The Ottomans had their own war aims: to expand and strengthen their empire, a goal that came into increasing focus as the war dragged on. Leaders did not merely follow what the Germans said or serve as fodder in battles, as some writing about Gallipoli has suggested.[56] European historiography still often portrays the Ottoman Empire as a pawn of Germany lacking its own clearly defined war aims.[57] This approach risks uncritically reproducing perceptions of some Allied military leaders of the Ottoman Empire as an appendage of Germany.

Lloyd George, an unapologetic liberal imperialist, clearly understood the war as a battle for the preservation of the British Empire. His version of history defended his own failures to fully realize this aim and his frustration with being thrown out of office in fall 1922. The war as strange defeat makes sense from the vantage of the Lausanne Treaty. President Wilson's rhetoric, sacralized in the "Fourteen Points," that the war was fought to uphold democracy haunts history books that continue to interrogate the ultimate failure of First World War peacemaking.

Like Lloyd George who used nationalist aspirations outside of his own empire to support British imperial aims, Wilson had his own priorities that included weakening European empires in order to increase US power and influence.[58] We know now that the reality of the wartime settlement would serve whichever power emerged as the leading player in the conquered territories, including but not limited to the Middle East. Looking backward from Lausanne shows how the narrative arc of the First World War as a good war gone bad was wrong from the beginning.

***

The Last Treaty begins with the Allied defeats at Gallipoli and Kut-al-Amara and a discussion of how diplomatic agreements, regional alliances and the Armenian Genocide made the Middle East central to the Allied war effort. Chapter 1: "How the First World War Came to the Middle East" explains why failure at Gallipoli in spring 1915 focused attention on fighting the Ottoman Empire. The secret 1916 Sykes–Picot agreement, understood by historians as emblematic of broader British and French imperial ambitions, also provided a blueprint for the prosecution of the war. In this multifront war, what happened on one battlefront had consequences on others and for Allied military and domestic agendas back in Europe.

Chapter 2: "The Middle Eastern Front" analyzes the military progress of the war in Ottoman territory and the diplomatic response. The tide turned with the British capture of Baghdad in March 1917 and the Allied entry into Jerusalem. It resulted in a war strategy that shored up control over the region's natural resources and its peoples using soldiers and personnel largely from the British Empire. Chapter 3: "Civilians at War" argues that the successful prosecution of the war relied on civilians living under Allied occupation. In 1917, refugee camps and social services emerged as tools of humanitarian aid and administration to help secure Allied authority. This chapter analyzes the administration of the camps and auxiliary services alongside the writings of refugees, eyewitnesses and aid workers who learned to live with a war that wreaked havoc on the local economy, social services and regional governance.

Chapter 4: "How War Didn't End" focuses on peacemaking between the Allies and the Ottoman Empire after the signing of the armistice in 1918 and how it relied on the idea of minority protection and humanitarian intervention that dated back to nineteenth-century treaty agreements and diplomatic dealings. Chapter 5: "The Treaty of Sèvres" tells the story of how the Ottoman Empire and the Allies negotiated the blurred line between war and peace that existed from the signing of the Treaty of Sèvres to the Lausanne Peace Conference. Chapter 6: "Humanitarian Crusades" focuses on Europe's response to the ongoing wartime crisis by exploring media-driven humanitarian campaigns. New media fundraising utilized documentary film, memoir, print media and celebrity endorsements to represent this aid as transformative and successfully bolstered interest in the plight of refugees. As a consequence, refugees became a new kind of moral weapon used to bolster support for continued Allied presence in the Ottoman Empire.

Chapter 7: "The Treaty of Lausanne" assesses how extending the war's chronology to include the story of a now little remembered peace treaty broadens our understanding of the global reach and human cost of the First World War. Peacemaking and war making inevitably overlapped as diplomats and humanitarian organizations responded to a conflict that exacerbated already existing ethno-religious tensions. The book's Epilogue explores what it means to read the Allied victory on the Middle Eastern Front as strange defeat. The peace process ultimately reimagined an old imperial system while forging a peace that came at a heavy price for the now former subjects of the Ottoman Empire.

The inglorious end of the war on the Middle Eastern Front exposed notions of unchecked imperial expansion as a chimera. The First World War achieved less than victory. This interpretation has long guided understanding of the interwar years, most especially in the service of seeing the war settlement as responsible for the Second World War. *The Last Treaty* shows the cracks in the war settlement as stemming from the moment of the final peace. By 1923, the Allies had lost the war that they thought they had won in 1918. Lloyd George recognized this in his war memoirs. He called the final two volumes, published in 1938, *The Truth about the Peace Treaties* and dedicated most of the second volume to the settlement with the Ottoman Empire. As he concluded about Lausanne: "No one claims that this Treaty was peace with honour. It is not even peace."[59]

PART ONE

CONFLICT

CHAPTER 1

How the First World War Came to the Middle East

THE OTTOMAN EMPIRE OFFICIALLY ENTERED THE FIRST
World War on the side of the Central Powers in fall 1914. Years of
dilatory diplomatic dealings with the British Empire had failed to bring
the Ottomans onto the Allied side.[1] Joining the German-led coalition
that included Austria-Hungary and later Bulgaria enabled the Ottomans
to pursue national interests while attempting to strengthen their
empire.[2] Talaat Pasha, who would become Grand Vizier in 1917, joined
war minister Enver Pasha and others in leading the Ottoman Empire into
jihad and world war against the Allied Powers led by Britain, France,
Russia, Italy, Japan and eventually the United States.[3]

The Allies initially cast the Middle Eastern Front as a secondary theater
of war. Military strategists believed that the war would be fought and won
on the Western Front.[4] This view dominated Allied thinking well into 1916
and shaped the early course of the war in Anatolia, Mesopotamia, Syria,
North Africa and the Caucasus. Protecting assets such as oil refineries,
shipping routes and key eastern ports proved the first order of business.
Even before officially declaring war on the Ottoman Empire in early
November, the Allies attacked ports in the Red Sea to display their naval
superiority. Meanwhile, the Ottomans planned a naval attack on Russia.
Russia's invasion of the Caucasus commenced after the bombing of its
Black Sea ports.[5] By late November, Britain's Indian Expeditionary Force
(IEF) occupied Basra to protect refineries. Ottoman attempts to conquer
Egypt during the Suez campaign of January and February 1915 ultimately
ended in failure.[6] These successful opening salvos contributed to the
Allied view that they had little to worry about in the fight against the
Ottoman Empire.

Small early victories bolstered Allied confidence and led to the risky and ill-fated invasion of Gallipoli. The plan, as first conceived in late 1914, was supposed to knock the Ottoman Empire out of the war with a swift, decisive blow and provide access to the Dardanelles Strait and Russian grain supplies. This would weaken Germany, deprived of its Ottoman ally and a key waterway, and refocus attention on the Western Front. The battle for the Dardanelles started on the Gallipoli peninsula and ended in disaster for the Allies.

Nine months of relentless trench warfare offered a haunting parallel to the war of attrition taking hold on the Western Front. The Gallipoli withdrawal was followed by a land war in Mesopotamia that went far beyond the initial objective of protecting refineries and ports. These included the Battle of Ctesiphon outside of Baghdad where Allied troops were forced to surrender after a five-month siege at Kut-al-Amara in spring 1916. During this time, the Allies made a new battle plan based on a series of secret agreements between themselves and potential regional allies, including Sykes–Picot and the Anglo-Arab alliance. The Russian-led war in the Caucasus achieved success starting in winter 1916, but the Allies did not fully turn the tide in their favor until the British-led conquest of Baghdad in March 1917.

This chapter traces the strategic and diplomatic maneuverings of war on the Middle Eastern Front before Baghdad. It analyzes the military alliances and humanitarian disasters that shaped the fight between the Allies and the Ottoman Empire and shows the growing importance of this front to the larger war. Here the lines between home front and battle front blurred as easily as they did on the Western Front with civilians suffering terrible loses in an escalating conflict between old imperial rivals.

GALLIPOLI

The Allied landing at Gallipoli on April 25, 1915, came after months of planning. Instead of the anticipated quick victory, however, it marked the beginning of a devastating trench war and sparked a brutal campaign against Ottoman Christian minorities. The night before the Allied invasion, the Ottoman government rounded up an estimated 250 Armenian intellectuals and religious leaders in Constantinople on unnamed charges, an act that would commence the Armenian Genocide.[7] In the wake of the failed Gallipoli campaign, war with the Ottoman Empire turned from easy victory to a series of military and humanitarian crises from the Gallipoli peninsula to Mesopotamia.

First Lord of the Admiralty Winston Churchill argued that opening up the Dardanelles Strait through an invasion of the Gallipoli peninsula would leave Germany unable to fight the Allies in the East and return focus to the Western Front. But as the war plans for Gallipoli took shape, another narrative emerged that cast the fight against Germany and the Ottoman Empire in a different light. As one commentator put it at the end of 1914, "The present war is a war against German militarism and a war of liberation. If it should end in a victory of the Allied Powers, it should not merely lead to the freeing of the subjected and oppressed ... in Europe, but also to the freeing of the nationalities who live under Turkish tyranny in Asia."[8]

These parallel narratives suggest that fighting the Ottoman Empire required both military force and moral justification. Like the decision to go to war with Germany over the so-called "Rape of Belgium," war with the Ottomans needed a just cause. Atrocities committed by invading German soldiers against Belgian civilians on August 4, 1914, gave Britain a reason to enter the war and defend Belgian neutrality under international law.[9] Even before the Armenian Genocide started in the spring of 1915, the British media cast the First World War as a war to defend civilian war victims. In the case of Belgium, this meant defending mostly women and girls from the "Hun."[10] In the Ottoman Empire, it meant protecting Christian minorities from state-sanctioned massacre.[11] On the heels of the British defeat at Gallipoli, moral justifications for war became even more important. In November 1915, widespread reporting of Armenian massacres led another commentator to conclude: "Avowedly one of the chief objects of the present war is to advantage small nationalities. In this war Armenians are playing no unimportant part."[12]

The military justification for the war hinged on imperial concerns; the moral on a commitment to a liberal imperialism that had guided British foreign policy since the late nineteenth century. Defending the rights of Christian minorities against "Ottoman tyranny" began in the aftermath of the Crimean War (1853–1856), a duty later codified in the Berlin Treaty that ended the Russo-Turkish War (1877–1878).[13] French claims in Syria took a similar line by the end of the war, justifying occupation as a way to protect Christian minorities displaced by war and genocide.[14] Gallipoli's military purpose was to defend Egypt, now a British protectorate, as well as divert Ottoman attention from Russia's difficult fight in the Caucasus.[15] The Allies futilely hoped that victory at Gallipoli would prevent Bulgaria from joining the Central Powers, which it did in fall 1915. War planners believed that the ultimate prize, occupying Constantinople after securing the Dardanelles, was worth the risk.[16] Back at home, it was the moral argument of benevolent European empires defending subjects of a tyrannous rival empire that gave the war its purpose. Still relying on an all-volunteer army at this point, these justifications for war had real power especially in Britain and France which represented fighting for the nation as an honor and a duty to uphold democracy.[17]

The scale of a war fought on multiple fronts required centralized planning. In Britain, the war's outbreak resulted in "important alterations … in the methods of conducting business both at the Admiralty and the War Office" and at the Committee of Imperial Defence.[18] Lord Kitchener, appointed Secretary of State for War in 1914, held important sway in this new mostly civilian comprised body. Only in the wake of the Gallipoli disaster did he face accusations of concentrating power in his own hands and not consulting the heads of departments after the War Council replaced the Committee of Imperial Defence. While Kitchener admired the boldness of Churchill's plan to take Constantinople and eventually supported the naval and ground invasion, he saw the Middle Eastern Front as a secondary theater.

The successful bombardment of the outer forts of the Dardanelles between October 31 and November 3 on the eve of the war declarations and the subsequent occupation of Basra led the War Council on November 25 to consider a full-blown naval assault on the Straits. Churchill argued that such an attack would defend Egypt. At the same time, taking the Gallipoli peninsula would secure control of the Dardanelles and "enable us to dictate terms at Constantinople." Intrigued, Kitchener nevertheless rejected proposals to send a large force to achieve these aims believing that it would pull troops away from the Western Front.[19]

Kitchener's attitude began to change in early January. The War Council decided to "make a demonstration against the Turks." Kitchener wanted to draw attention away from military failures on the Western Front and achieve "more decisive results."[20] He began to "regard the possibility of the employment of British Forces in a different theatre of war" as a way to distract both the enemy and his critics at home.[21] Kitchener argued that a limited attack on the Dardanelles would divert Ottoman attention from the Caucasus Front where the Russians had requested British assistance. But his focus remained on home defense, and he made it clear that he was "most unwilling to withdraw a single man from France" to fight the Ottomans.[22] Eastern Mediterranean naval commander Admiral Sackville Carden put together a plan for the invasion approved on January 13.[23]

The reluctance to commit soldiers to the Middle Eastern Front led to the War Council's initial decision to rely entirely on the naval fleet for this operation. This explains Carden's central role in planning. The navy successfully repelled Cemal Pasha's attack on the Suez in early February, bolstering faith in British sea power.[24] Ground troops from across the British Empire eventually were deployed after the mission broadened to include the aim of taking Constantinople. The War Council wanted not just Bulgaria but other neutral nations in the Balkans and Mediterranean to see their interests aligned with Allied strength. As Lord Edward Grey later put it, "Diplomacy was perfectly useless without military success."[25] War planners also believed that victory would open up a corridor to channel munitions and supplies to relieve Russian's precarious position in the Caucasus made more difficult due to a lack of railway access. Kitchener made his position clear: this was a limited operation and under no circumstances would Britain engage in what he called an "Asiatic adventure."[26] In early 1915, the Allies sought to occupy Constantinople and defeat the Ottoman Empire using limited military resources.

Concerns over imperial prestige influenced this strategy. While the British had secured Russian pledges to provide reinforcements after taking Constantinople, they worried about France. The War Council feared that any misstep in this campaign would afford an opportunity to the French. Both claimed status as the most important Muslim power in the region and saw the war as an opportunity to extend their empires.[27] Carden led the naval forces in the assault. His second in command, Vice Admiral J. M. de Robeck, took charge in March after Carden went on medical leave. Kitchener's "vitally important" mission started badly.[28] The first bombardment on February 19 failed to destroy the forts guarding the Straits. The plan, drawn from a parallel strategy in Belgium, did not account for differences in the two battleground landscapes.[29] At the end of March, German commander Otto Liman von Sanders, took charge of operations on the Central Powers side and prepared for the Allies' next move.

Instead of calling off the attack, Kitchener committed ground troops to aid the naval assault. By late February, he dispatched 36,000 Anzac troops, assembled as part of the Mediterranean Expeditionary Force under the leadership of Sir Ian Hamilton. These fighters from Australia and New Zealand joined 10,000 men of the Royal Naval Division stationed in Egypt. The French contributed 18,000 troops from the Corps Expéditionnaire d'Orient, colonial soldiers and Foreign Legionnaires by March.[30] A worried Kitchener followed Hamilton's advice to use ground troops to open up the forty-one-mile stretch of the Dardanelles: "The effect of a defeat in the Orient would be very serious. There could be no going back. The publicity of the announcement had committed us."[31]

The February bombing, however, meant that the Allies lost the element of surprise when they landed at Gallipoli. By late March, the Ottoman army with German assistance began to dig trenches and lay barbed wire which neutralized the effectiveness of Allied ground troops. Mustafa Kemal first made his name at Gallipoli by figuring out the Allied strategy and played a key role in turning the tide for the Central Powers.[32] Allied troops landed on April 25 and faced a trench war that lasted nearly nine months and resulted in over half a million men wounded, killed or taken prisoner.[33]

For those who fought in the trenches at Gallipoli, the war in the Middle East would have seemed not dissimilar to the war in Europe.[34] Protracted battles fought in close proximity to the enemy in trenches dug by the troops themselves resulted in stalemate. The size of the armies engaged in this battle also mirrored battles on the Western Front. An estimated 800,000 men fought this battle which included 410,000 combined British forces; 79,000 combined French forces and 310,000 Ottoman forces.[35] On the Ottoman side, as many as a third of combatants came from predominately Arab provinces.[36] Eventually, the war here was fought by soldiers from all over the world. The Mediterranean Expeditionary Force alone included soldiers from England, Ireland, Scotland, Wales, Canada, Australia, New Zealand and India. The French Foreign Legionnaires forces included troops from Senegal, Guinea, Sudan and the Maghrib.[37]

Gallipoli dashed Kitchener's hope for a victory that would distract attention from the quagmire in Western Europe. He himself did not survive the war, killed on a ship sunk while he was on his way to negotiate with Russia in June 1916. When the Allies finally evacuated the Gallipoli peninsula in December 1915, it came as a relief that there was little resistance from the Ottoman forces. All 77,000 British and imperial soldiers got out alive marking the evacuation as the biggest success of the entire operation. The IEF took the brunt of these errors, making needless sacrifices for poorly conceived missions. Despite their loyalty and efforts on the battlefield, some commanders recorded holding little respect for "native troops."[38]

The strategy of seeking bold, swift victory on the Middle Eastern Front exposed false assumptions about the readiness and willingness of the Ottomans to preserve their empire. At the same time, the moral justification for the war – to defend the rights of innocent civilians – loomed large. Though the Allies continued to see the Western Front as key to winning the war, events in the Ottoman Empire in 1915 and 1916 pulled military resources and public attention eastward.

GENOCIDE

Military disaster at Gallipoli found its moral counterpoint in the Armenian massacres. The Ottoman Empire's minority problem started long before the fateful night of April 24 marked the beginning of both the Gallipoli invasion and what is today called the Armenian Genocide that resulted in the deaths of over 1 million civilians.[39] Periodic massacres against Christian minorities had raged in the cities and provinces of the Empire starting in the second half of the nineteenth century.[40] In 1876, atrocities committed by Ottoman troops against Bulgarian civilians in the lead-up to the Russo-Turkish War received widespread press coverage as did massacres of Ottoman minorities in Crete, Macedonia, Cyprus and Anatolia (Asia Minor). The mid-1890s Hamidian Massacres and the 1909 mass slaughter of Armenians in Adana also captured the attention of the West and sparked an international humanitarian response.[41]

The plan to eliminate Ottoman Christian minorities completely from the Empire came under the cover of war. The genocide targeted Armenians, the largest minority population, as well as the smaller Greek and Assyrian communities. The rise of Turkish ethno-nationalism in the years preceding the war made the position of the Ottoman Empire's non-Muslim Christian population, long subjected to violence and social inequality, more precarious.[42] Armenian nationalism arose, in part, as a reaction to exclusionary policies and resulted in calls for more autonomy and civil rights that were supported by the European powers.[43]

The minority question played an important role in the Ottoman decision to side with Germany in the war.[44] Years of meddling with Ottoman minority policy beginning with the Greek Wars of Independence in the 1820s and continuing with the Crimean War and the Russo-Turkish War had heightened distrust of Britain and France while fueling competition over adjacent lands with Russia.[45] While diplomacy did not improve the status of minorities, it created lasting tensions between Britain, France, Russia and the Ottoman Empire.[46] German support for Ottoman resistance to pressure to improve the treatment of minorities offered the prospect of rebuffing reform and even expanding the Ottoman Empire against imperial rivals.[47]

Talaat Pasha, who had led the Empire as head of the revolutionary Committee of Union and Progress (CUP), embraced both the aggressive German model of nation building and promises of economic investment in the Ottoman Empire.[48] The Young Turk Revolution of 1908 had ushered in the CUP and a brief constitutional period that sparked hope among Armenians like Armen Garo for a pluralistic empire with room for minorities. Under Talaat, a narrowed nationalist vision of "Turkey for the Turks" made constitutionalism impossible to sustain over the long term.[49]

Hardline nationalism took shape under the CUP leadership that by the beginning of the First World War had rejected constitutional reform in favor of autocracy.[50] The regime led the Ottoman Empire to side with Germany to protect it from what leaders increasingly saw as internal threats from minority communities and external threats to its sovereignty. This coupled with territorial losses from the Balkan Wars fed Ottoman fears of imperial decline that created a paranoia about the embrace of constitutionalism by the Empire's minorities after the 1908 Revolution.[51] The elimination of the influence of Christian minority communities in political and civic life soon followed.[52]

The 1915 massacres were the product of this history. They sparked a culture of fear after their start on the eve of Gallipoli.[53] No one knew if the massacres would run their course like they had in the past, allowing those who survived to rebuild their lives after the crisis had passed.[54] Harotune Boyadjian, for example, recalled how the villages of the Armenian region of Musa Dagh set up temporary shelter in the mountains in the ultimately futile hopes of waiting out the violence or fighting back if necessary.[55] Living together in a multi-confessional community, sometimes at war but mostly at peace, was a reality of the minority experience in the Ottoman Empire.[56] This time was different. Those who survived the Armenian Genocide experienced the rest of the war as refugees with most ending up in Mesopotamia where the main action of the war in the Middle East became focused by 1917.[57]

Lloyd George, who would take over as prime minister in December 1916, called Britain "culpable" for the fate of the Armenians: "The action of the British Government led inevitably to the terrible massacres of 1895–6, 1909 and worst of all to the holocausts of 1915." He concluded that this made the Allies "morally bound to . . . redress the wrong we had perpetrated and in so far as it was in our power, to make it impossible to repeat the horrors for which history will always hold us culpable."[58] Viscount James Bryce (1838–1922), in his role as Ambassador to the United States, used the massacres to rally American support for the Allied war effort. He wrote to his colleagues in October 1915: "I am glad to gather from what you say that the general sentiment of the United States is still strongly with us. I should hope it would become even more so after the frightful massacres which have been committed upon innocent Armenian population in Asiatic Turkey in which some half a million persons have perished."[59] He believed defending innocent Armenians made this a just war against a formidable and untrustworthy foe.

Britain blamed Germany for aiding and abetting the massacres. Bryce blasted attempts by the German Ambassador to the United States to explain away the massacres: "There is no foundation whatever for the defense or denial, whichever one is to call it, that [Ambassador] Bernstorff seems to have attempted of these atrocities." According to Bryce, "The Turks were in every case the aggressors, while as to the massacres themselves, the details which have reached me from day to day, are if possible worse than the things which have appeared in the newspaper."[60] Germany's crimes against Belgian civilians and, now, its defense of its Ottoman ally's treatment of Armenians legitimated Britain's "determination to prosecute the war until success is obtained." Arnold Toynbee, who later collaborated with Bryce's investigation of the massacres published as a parliamentary Blue Book, paralleled the situation to "the German incursion into Belgium fourteen months ago ... What she has done is to bring us all back in the Twentieth Century to the condition of the dark ages. **That is the indictment. Let Germany cease to deserve it.**"[61]

These accusations coupled with revelations about the extent of the massacres sparked humanitarian relief campaigns in the United States, France, Russia and Britain. War made relief work on enemy territory impractical but not impossible.[62] The US-based Armenian and Syrian Relief Committee, later known as Near East Relief, led efforts starting in 1915. While the United States never declared war against Turkey, it engaged in a massive humanitarian mission that raised the equivalent of a billion dollars in aid.[63] France had sent aid during the 1909 Adana massacres and aided survivors of genocide during the war starting in 1915. It also welcomed large numbers of Armenian refugees making it an important site of advocacy in Europe.[64]

Russia responded to genocidal violence heightened during its assault on the Caucasus.[65] The Russian imperial government provided humanitarian aid to villagers across the border from the fighting while aiding genocide survivors and those fleeing the battlefront. This work continued until the fall of the Russian Empire in spring 1917.[66] In Britain, new organizations emerged to deal with and, in some cases, coordinate relief efforts.[67] As politician Lord Robert Cecil observed, "This question of Armenian relief is one which excites a great deal of feeling."[68] Cecil was referring to a growing humanitarian ethos that drew on past British and American experiences with massacres and aid in this region. The British public might not be able to do anything about the military failures at Gallipoli and on the battlefields of Belgium and France but aid work could provide a way of mitigating human suffering. The war thus created a "humanitarian narrative" that obliged belligerents to help "distant strangers" suffering from the war's worst effects.[69]

Armenians were represented as both victims and allies in the fight against the Central Powers. France formed the Legion d'Orient in 1916 with Armenian volunteers trained in Cyprus to assist the Allied war effort.[70] Bryce supported the cause of raising Armenian volunteers to fight alongside the Allies on the Russian–Ottoman border. Armenians, however, mostly remained loyal to their respective governments. As Winston Churchill put it, the majority of both Ottoman Armenians and Russian Armenians had pledged to "do their duty" rather than "stake their existence upon the victory of either side."[71] The small number of volunteers who did fight helped support claims that Armenians deserved Allied support. Britain first made the ill-fated pledge to broker a protectorate over Ottoman Armenian lands in fall 1916 during a meeting between Armenian representatives and Mark Sykes and François Georges-Picot. Sykes and Picot believed such promises would shore up regional support for the Sykes–Picot agreement finalized with Russia the previous May.[72]

Ultimately, the response to the Armenian Genocide further committed the Allies to the Middle Eastern Front. In early 1916, as the public call to provide humanitarian aid to this population grew more urgent, the military situation worsened. The unsuccessful beginning of the land war in Mesopotamia that spring at Kut cemented humanitarian aid and the defense of Armenians against massacre as a moral justification for Allied war aims.

KUT

The disaster at Kut-al-Amara tested war strategy and increased public awareness of the Middle Eastern Front. Kut, as it came to be known during the war, showed the folly of thinking that war in the Ottoman Empire demanded fewer sacrifices than the Western Front. Kitchener gave orders to avoid the occupation "of the Asiatic side by military force" during the Gallipoli operation.[73] This strategy proved untenable as the war progressed. The attempt to capture Baghdad by Major General Charles Townshend in late 1915 ended in one of the most dramatic Allied defeats of the war after a nearly six-month-long siege at Kut and resulted in the death of 2,000 Allied soldiers. The 12,000 men taken as prisoners of war (POWs) suffered under brutal conditions widely publicized in Europe.[74]

By spring 1916, the press acknowledged what war planners were reluctant to admit. "We are now committed in Asia Minor . . . which will afford lessons without number," opined the *Saturday Review*. "A war has been evolved on a considerable scale in a sphere where we first embarked for a purpose that we thought would entail but a skirmish."[75] This became clear to others around the time of the Gallipoli evacuation. The mission, to one observer writing in October 1915, was inextricably bound up with a duty to aid the Armenians: "England needs a new gateway into Constantinople; and if Armenia is to be saved, needs it quickly . . . The Gallipoli peninsula is one tangle of barbed wire, one maze of interlocking trenches, while the waterway is fringed with cannon and torpedo tubes that sentinel the straits at every point. If England is to get to the Bosporus in time to exert any saving help on Armenia, she must find another route."[76] "Saving" Armenia thus was for some akin to winning the war.

Kut, a fortified town around 100 miles southeast of Baghdad on the bank of the Tigris River, most likely was not the route imagined by this commentator to achieve Britain's war aims. This first attempt to take Baghdad marked a new phase of the war. It incurred a high human cost and resulted in few gains.[77] Over half a million Indians served on the Middle Eastern Front in combatant and non-combatant roles including as officers, soldiers, porters and in labor corps and paid a high price for their loyalty. The IEF, headquartered in Shimla, India and not the War Office in London at the beginning of the war, fought some of the most dangerous and difficult battles of the war. This included the siege of Kut-al-Amara. Approximately 10,440 of the 12,000 POWs captured after Townshend's surrender on April 29, 1916, were part of the IEF.[78]

Early signs suggested that an invasion of Mesopotamia would fare little better than Gallipoli. The debate over embarking on a land war began in earnest in fall 1915. War planners raised concerns over inadequate railways and ports as well as a lack of knowledge of geography and unreliable intelligence. A relatively easy victory by Townshend's troops in Kut over the forces of Nurettin Bey in late September, however, made it possible to imagine continuing the march north along the Tigris River, first through Ctesiphon and then on to Baghdad. The merits of capturing Baghdad were debated in October. Admiral H.B. Jackson and A.J. Murray, Lt. Gen. Chief of the Imperial General Staff, argued against the advance: "We cannot under present circumstances go to Baghdad without incurring unjustifiable risks. It must be remembered that during the winter the Russians are not likely to be able to make any advance into Armenia and consequently the Turks can very well spare a division or two from the Armenian army at this season to reinforce the Mesopotamian troops."[79]

The inability to "hold Baghdad for any length of time" due to a lack of reserves led to the conclusion that "we must play a safe game and husband our sorely strained military resources."[80] But for some, occupying Baghdad "would reestablish some of the prestige which we have lost by our failure to force the Dardanelles." Gallipoli's failure shadowed war planning: "If, however, we are unable to hold Baghdad . . . our withdrawal from Baghdad might have as great and as unfortunate an effect on the Mohammedan world as our withdrawal from the Gallipoli Peninsula."[81] The invasion thus represented a calculated risk that if successful would restore British imperial prestige and establish military control over Mesopotamia.

General Townshend saw the conquest of Baghdad in terms of his own personal glory. He arrived from India on April 22 and took command of the 6th division under Sir John Nixon. In June, he captured the town of Amara and confidently set his sights on Baghdad promising his superiors

quick victory.[82] He thought success would secure him a military gover-
norship, believing himself destined to help lead a British Empire
inherited from Rome. The War Office took a decidedly less romantic
view. War aims included safeguarding the Indian Frontier; demonstrat-
ing the "power to strike"; checking Turkish "intrigues amongst the
Arabs"; confirming to Arab chiefs their allegiance to Britain; and protecting oil installations.[83] These objectives coupled with Townshend's determination to make a name for himself at any cost drove the mission.
Though the battle in September 1915 resulted in victory, he had not
defeated Nurettin Bey's forces. Townshend instead faced a trench system
constructed between June and September by Ottoman forces that
extended for more than five miles and bordered marshland.[84] This
allowed the Ottoman army to retreat intact and regroup.

Townshend did not engage the enemy again until the end of
November with a force of 14,000 that faced over 18,000 Ottoman
troops. Full of deluded hopes for his own career, Townshend marched
toward Baghdad, confident but ill-prepared. From November 22–25,
the Ottomans repelled Townshend's army at the Battle of Ctesiphon.
This forced a retreat to Kut resulting in a standoff that lasted until
April. To cover his blunders, Townshend conjectured that the
Ottomans had redoubled their efforts. In January he expressed this
unfounded view to his superiors: "I believe Turks are now making
Mesopotamia the principal field in which they are sending their maximum forces."[85]

By this time, the battle for Kut had turned into a siege and Townshend
could do little but wait for reinforcements. He blamed his superiors for
Ctesiphon and the ill-fated retreat to Kut. Historians agree that the
General's own blunders leading the IEF, however, played the biggest
role.[86] While the disaster at Kut unfolded, the Allies engaged the
Ottomans elsewhere. Russia fought the Ottomans in the Caucasus, and
between mid-February and mid-April General Nikolai Yudenich succeeded in driving the Ottoman Third Army out of eastern Anatolia.
Meanwhile, British commander in Egypt, Sir John Maxwell, launched
a campaign to take territory on Egypt's border with Libya. By late
February, Maxwell's Western Frontier Force won the Battle of Aqaqir

and begun the process of securing the Libyan/Egyptian border to neutralize threats against the Allied position in North Africa.[87]

Townshend's defeat overshadowed these victories. After three attempts to break the blockade at Kut, the siege ended in surrender. Months of reduced rations had taken a toll on the soldiers and the townspeople. Townshend requisitioned food from civilians and steadily cut soldiers' rations. Inadequate rations weighed most heavily on the majority of Indian soldiers with religious-based dietary restrictions. The specter of the mass starvation of soldiers and civilians ultimately led Townshend to surrender on April 26 to Halil Bey who was now in charge of operations for the Ottoman army. The futile attempts to relieve Townshend's 13,000 troops resulted in 23,000 casualties.[88] The siege also strained the Ottoman army, forced to fight the Russians in the Caucasus and Townshend at Kut. This required thousands more recruits, which weakened an already depleted Ottoman force.[89]

Worse was to come for the survivors of Kut. The entering Ottoman forces shot or hanged townspeople accused of collaborating with the British.[90] They marched POWs, already in a weakened state, across the desert to Baghdad. Only the officers were spared. Townshend himself spent the remainder of the war in Constantinople in relative luxury and comfort currying the favor of high-ranking Ottoman officials.[91]

NEW STRATEGIES

The failures at Gallipoli and Kut resulted in a reassessment of the war in the Middle East. Britain launched two inquiries in the summer of 1916 to figure out what went wrong: the Dardanelles Commission and the Mesopotamia Commission. The government also commissioned a report on the costs of the war for civilians led by Bryce. *The Treatment of the Armenians in the Ottoman Empire*, like the report on German atrocities against Belgian civilians overseen by him the previous year, exposed the Armenian massacres.[92] Issued as a Parliamentary Blue Book, it chronicled the genocide against the Armenians in the wake of Gallipoli.[93]

These commissions and the Bryce report painted a grim picture. They also paved the way for a new strategy that would take hold after David Lloyd George replaced H. H. Asquith as prime minister in

December 1916. The unusual step of launching not one but two public inquiries into the failures of an ongoing war seemed designed to undermine Asquith's premiership. But criticism of the management of the war began long before the Dardanelles and Mesopotamia Commissions started their work in August 1916. The King's Speech to Parliament the previous February had called for imperial unity to which Asquith responded with an appeal for more money to fight the war and greater economy at home. Mark Sykes used the occasion to accuse the government of "muddling through this war."[94]

Sykes, MP for Hull who had been working under Kitchener and secretly negotiating the Sykes–Picot agreement with France in the preceding months, noted both military defeats and the "extermin(ation)" of the Armenians. "We must face the situation as it is," he told his fellow MPs:

> Take the case of Armenia. The Armenians cannot be replaced, because they have been exterminated. The Gallipoli Peninsula has been left by us. The Suez Canal has been and may be now potentially menaced. In Mesopotamia the situation is not what one might wish. Even in this Island, as we shall hear in the course of the Debates in the next few days, we are menaced by Zeppelin raids. We have to remember that large tracts of France and Russia are occupied by the enemy.[95]

Sykes proposed changes to the chain of command and improvements in communication. His claim that "we are distracted, busy and confused" hit a nerve. Sykes' remarks overshadowed the King's speech and Asquith's response.[96] They also got the attention of Lloyd George who pulled Sykes aside afterwards to request a private meeting for the following day.[97]

By the time the Commissions on the Dardanelles and Mesopotamia met that summer, it was clear that Asquith was in trouble. The calling of these inquiries represented a rebuke to Asquith's leadership, and their publication in 1917 kept the debacles at Gallipoli and Kut in the news. The Dardanelles Commission, led by ten government appointees, released its finding in two phases. The first explained the "origins and inception" of the "attack on the Dardanelles" and questioned First Lord of the Admiralty Churchill's central role as he "was not himself an expert" and the method of conducting business at the Admiralty and the War Office. While less critical of Kitchener who by now had been drowned at sea, the Commission clearly blamed leadership failures.[98] The second report assessed outcomes.[99] Everything from military strategy to the slow speed of communications were investigated to explain the resulting stalemate in rough terrain and against a better prepared enemy. Despite these failings, the report concluded that British "prestige ... remained unimpaired."[100]

The Mesopotamia Commission opened parallel proceedings in August 1916 and held sixty meetings over ten months. It called into question both strategy and the running of the war in the Middle East from India rather than the War Office.[101] Parliament debated the report's findings when it was published a year later.[102] The resignation of Secretary of State for India, Austen Chamberlain, soon followed. The report called the Battle of Ctesiphon "a tactical victory but strategical retreat" and concluded that at best the battle for Kut proved a distraction that "diverted any Turkish movement on Persia and entirely rivetted the attention of the Turks til [sic] later when the Russians were ready to strike both in Armenia and Kurdistan." Others compared Kut to the "retreat from Mons in Flanders" and the Dardanelles.[103] Lord Curzon in June 1917 issued a "very secret and confidential" memorandum with his own assessment of the report: "I regret to have to say that a more shocking exposure of official blundering and incompetence has not in my opinion been made, at any rate since the Crimean War." He considered suppressing the report but, in the end, had it published.[104]

The two reports served as cautionary tales of what could happen in the event of any further leadership failures in the summer of 1917. The capture of Baghdad the previous spring gave Britain, now under the leadership of Lloyd George, the upper hand in Mesopotamia. Lloyd George used the opportunity to lay blame for previous missteps in the Middle East at the feet of Asquith whom the press excoriated along with the generals. The *Irish Times* called the Dardanelles report "a lamentable exposure of the inefficiency and lack of coordination which marked the proceedings of the late Government." It had "doomed a brilliant opportunity to a tragic and impotent conclusion." While criticizing Churchill for his "reckless enthusiasm," *The Times* praised Lloyd George: "We can only be thankful that Mr. Lloyd George has rescued the conduct of the war from the nerveless hands which entrusted great issues to the interfering incapacity of civilians."[105] The *New York Times* had a more cynical take and questioned the timing of the report that it asserted was designed to be a "nail in the coffin of the old gang."[106]

Bryce's Blue Book report offered a further warning against failing to get it right in the Middle East. In it, Bryce represented the British Empire as defender of Armenians ruthlessly targeted for elimination by their own government. The Blue Book condemned the hardline nationalism of the CUP, which it blamed for opportunistically scapegoating the Armenians. The Armenian massacres, like the battles at Gallipoli and Kut, were not the product of what Bryce called "Muslim fanaticism" but of a paranoid and corrupt government that used the idea of a "Holy War" or jihad to further its own ends through the targeting of minorities.[107]

The Armenian Blue Book fed the Allied narrative of the First World War as a war of liberation. Russia, too, wanted the Ottoman Empire held accountable for the massacres. As the largest Orthodox Christian power, it long had challenged Britain's claim as Armenia's protector. In addition to sharing a common faith, significant numbers of Armenians lived on Russia's borderlands in the Caucasus. This was the site of Russia's most significant fighting with the Ottoman Empire in 1915 and 1916.[108] The Blue Book, published at the request of the Foreign Office, bolstered the case for protecting Armenians. In May 1915, the Allies issued the Joint Declaration accusing the Ottoman Empire of "crimes against humanity."[109] The Russian Foreign Minister, Sergey Sazonov, inserted this phrase into the declaration which challenged the Ottoman Empire's treatment of Armenians on the international stage.

The almost thousand-page Bryce Report chronicled atrocities committed against Armenians using eyewitness testimony, charts and maps. Presented to Parliament on November 23, 1916, its timing was important. The report had been ready the previous summer, but Charles Masterman at the War Propaganda Bureau convinced the Foreign Office to present it in the fall when it was more likely to influence public opinion in Allied countries and the still neutral United States where Armenian humanitarian aid campaigns continued to grow. Widely reported in the international press, the Bryce Report gave Britain's allies moral cause to keep fighting.[110]

Together these reports reveal how war with the Ottoman Empire played out in public discourse, Allied rivalries and British politics. The details of the Gallipoli and Kut disasters remain an indelible part of the memory of the war thanks in part to the two Commissions. Gallipoli, in particular, continues as one the most discussed and memorialized battles.[111] Politics clearly influenced the decision to assess the outcome of these operations during the war itself. The Joint Declaration and the Bryce Report reinforced the idea of Armenian protection as a war aim, especially for Russia and Britain. Finally, these reports discredited Asquith's handling of the war and helped deliver the office of prime minister to Lloyd George mere months after the publication of the Blue Book.

"Amateur diplomat" Mark Sykes proved especially useful to Lloyd George's approach to the war.[112] Sykes' response to the Mesopotamia report in July 1917 emphasized the need "to define our objective" instead of relying on what he called "random methods." Regarding Kut, he asserted, "even with victory in our grasp it is easy enough to lose the War by random methods when you have anything but clearcut ideas at the back of your mind."[113] Sykes already had articulated these objectives to the British government in the form of the secret Sykes–Picot agreement that guided war strategy after 1916.

SYKES–PICOT

Sykes–Picot long has been read solely as a diplomatic agreement. But in its earliest conception, it was also a military plan. In a meeting considered the origins of the notorious agreement, Sykes gave evidence to the War Committee which included Prime Minister Asquith, Lloyd George and Kitchener. Lloyd George was the first to suggest Anglo-French cooperation as a "military proposition" to protect Egypt and expand into Mesopotamia in a secret War Committee meeting on December 16, 1915. Kitchener countered that the "diplomatic proposition" needed to be settled first. Asquith agreed, arguing that "a political deal" with the French must be reached. This meant coming to terms "diplomatically" with what the breakup of the Ottoman Empire would mean for the French and British empires before launching an attack.[114] Sykes–Picot was thus touted as a plan to help the Allies win the war. It provided a blueprint for the conquest of Mesopotamia, Syria and parts of Anatolia in the guise of a diplomatic agreement.

Sykes-Picot was only one among many secret agreements negotiated between the Allies. In spring 1915, Britain and France signed the first: the Constantinople agreement with Russia. Never enacted, it promised Russia control over the Straits and Constantinople if it could help secure a British victory at Gallipoli.[115] France and England entered into bilateral negotiations in what would become Sykes–Picot the next fall. France had wanted to open discussions around the time of the Constantinople agreement, but Britain was busy forging an alliance with Sharif Hussein of Mecca. Sykes–Picot, initialed in secret in London on January 3, 1916, had its origins in early strategic failures at Gallipoli and mutual Allied distrust. France's small military presence made it anxious about British ambition. Britain, in turn, worried about France's historical claims over Syria.[116] Eventually, Russia was brought in and negotiations yielded the signed agreement in May 1916.

Sykes–Picot proved important to war planning. The purpose of the agreement, in the context of the war as it was in late 1915, was to turn the tide against the Ottomans. Created by two minor Allied diplomats, it captured the imagination of politicians and strategists who by 1916 had very little to show for wartime sacrifices. The reading of Sykes–Picot only as a postwar plan to divide the spoils of war has blinded historians to the uses of the agreement as a means of moving the war forward in 1916. To be sure, it *was* a plan to claim the Middle East for Britain and France and was criticized at the time for dividing "up the skin of the bear before they had killed it."[117] In 1917, however, it served the more urgent task of readying the way for the Allied invasion of Mesopotamia. Britain used the agreement to better facilitate the movement of its army. In a letter to French diplomat Paul Cambon finalizing Sykes–Picot, Foreign Secretary Edward Grey emphasized that "Great Britain has the right to build, administer, and be the sole owner of a railway connecting Haifa ... and shall have a perpetual right to transport troops along such a line <u>at all times</u> [double underline]."[118]

Statements like this legitimated British military leadership on the Middle Eastern Front. But French concerns over the future of Syria also had to be assuaged. The former French consul in Beirut, François Georges-Picot (1870–1951), was tasked with defending French claims. Born in Paris, Picot studied law and later joined the French Foreign Ministry. A career diplomat, his experience in the Near East as Beirut Consul was followed immediately by a post in London as First Secretary in August 1915. Ambassador Cambon assigned him the task of negotiating the "geographical limits of Syria" with the British that fall.[119] Picot represented the demands of the French clerical/colonial party that understood Syria in its maximalist form to include Palestine and Lebanon.[120] By the time negotiations started, France knew about British discussion with Hussein regarding the boundaries of "Arabia" but not the extent. France worried that these negotiations would result in a smaller Syria. Eventually, they consented to Sykes–Picot based on the belief that the British had made only vague promises regarding a future Arab state.[121]

Though excluded from the bilateral negotiations between France and Britain, Sharif Hussein (c. 1853–1931) was an important player in Sykes–Picot. Born in Constantinople, the head of the Hashemite dynasty grew up in the Hejaz province of Arabia and later returned to the Ottoman imperial capital to raise his four sons, Ali, Abdullah, Feisal and Zayd. Independent minded and politically astute, he successfully navigated prewar attempts to curb his power during the tumultuous Young Turk revolutionary period. Even before the First World War broke out, he saw the British as a possible ally in helping maintain his autonomy in the Hejaz, sending his son Abdullah to meet with Lord Kitchener who was then consul general in Egypt in early 1914.[122]

At a minimum, Hussein's presence as a power broker who promised to deliver Arab support for the Allies sowed distrust between France and Britain. His demands for an independent Arab state loomed large in the context of the French role in a still undefined Syria. Hussein's correspondence with the British High Commissioner in Cairo, Sir Henry McMahon, about the issue ultimately resulted in vague promises that equivocated on the issue of Arab independence but eventually led to the Arab Revolt in summer 1916. The political implications of the so-called

Hussein–McMahon correspondence made the French nervous. While the proposed Arab revolt against the Ottoman Empire boded well for the Allied war effort, the meaning of that alliance was still unclear in late 1915. For France, the question of control over Syria dominated its dealings with both British and Arab interests throughout the war.[123]

Lieutenant Colonel Sir Mark Sykes (1879–1919), played an outsized role in Britain's Middle East strategy that went beyond criticizing British war planning. Born Tatton Benvenuto Mark Sykes to an aristocratic family, he had no formal training in Middle Eastern affairs. In September 1913, he traveled to the Balkans after the Second Balkan War in an unofficial capacity and then began seeking out an official role. In January 1915, he wrote an unanswered letter to Churchill asserting that Britain should take Constantinople. Eventually, his dogged attempts to get involved in war planning captured the attention of Lord Kitchener after he became Secretary of State for War. He served as Kitchener's personal representative on the De Bunsen Committee which in the spring of 1915 had as its brief to define the objectives of war policy in the Middle East.[124] Sykes, an heir to the baronetcy at Sledmere, served as his representative at the War Office until Kitchener's death and later worked for the Imperial War Cabinet, and then as advisor to the Foreign Office. Elected Tory MP for Central Hull in 1913, he advocated British military involvement in the Ottoman Empire. Like many of his contemporaries involved in the First World War, he had fought in the Boer War where he rose to the rank of captain. He came back with a belief that the British Empire should guide global affairs.[125]

Picot's initial limited brief to negotiate the borders of Syria stood in sharp relief to Sykes' ambitions to remake Allied war policy. Sykes traveled regularly to the Middle East during the war and proposed occupying Baghdad after visiting India and Basra on a six-month fact-finding trip.[126] He soon developed a larger vision of what victory in Mesopotamia would mean for the Allies. In early 1916, Sykes went with Picot to Russia to complete negotiations on the agreement that would bear their names and later divide the Ottoman Empire into spheres of influence that eventually included Britain, France, Russia, Italy and an Arab State.[127]

The pair also took care to court non-state interests including the Armenian and Jewish diaspora. Both Sykes and Picot met multiple times with Boghos Nubar Pasha, an influential Armenian leader living in Paris. At one meeting, Picot echoed British claims, reassuring Nubar that France was fighting "a war of liberation of oppressed peoples."[128] Sykes and Picot also met with representatives of the Zionist community about support for a Jewish homeland in Palestine. These discussions intensified before the issuing of the Balfour Declaration in fall 1917. Jewish community leader Chaim Weizmann later called Sykes "one of our greatest finds ... He was not very consistent or logical in his thinking but he was generous and warmhearted. He had conceived the idea of the liberation of the Jews, the Arabs and the Armenians, whom he looked upon as the three downtrodden races par excellence."[129]

But military victory had to happen before help came for "downtrodden" peoples. Sykes convinced his superiors of the importance of finalizing the agreement with France before starting a military offensive in Mesopotamia. In a secret memorandum, Sykes suggested "a statement" to indicate "that dependent on our success the Arabic-speaking people will be under French protection in one area and English protection in another, with the recognition of Arab nationality and of Arab participation in the official administration in both areas." While the eventual administration of the region was important, so too was its conception as a theater of war. Sykes concluded by suggesting mobilizing ground troops in Mesopotamia because "our primal success must ... be derived from military action."[130]

Sykes successfully lobbied the Secretary of the War Committee, Maurice Hankey, for a position as Secretariat member which made him more directly involved in the War Cabinet.[131] After the fall of Baghdad in March 1917, then Secretary of State for India Austen Chamberlain at an Imperial War Cabinet meeting proposed making "the practical destruction of the Turkish Empire" which included conquering "Arabia ... important portions of the Valley of Euphrates and the Tigris" a war aim. He further asserted that "Constantinople and Syria, Armenia and the southern part of Asia Minor" should "fall more or less under" the domination of the Allied Powers.[132]

Sykes refused to see the agreement as a tool to facilitate the annexation of territory. He resisted the labeling of it "Sykes–Picot" in favor of the "Anglo-French Arab agreement," possibly suggesting that he knew that this was exactly how it would be read.[133] Both Sykes and Picot had committed to the idea that defeating the Ottoman Empire would create greater freedom for subject populations even if it meant trading one master for another.[134] The idea of national minorities, as Benjamin White argues, developed out of the war and the term did not necessarily correspond to the actual size of these populations or their locations.[135] The British used the term "small nationalities" to describe subject populations that they believed would accept either military or humanitarian Allied support during the war.[136] This paternalism shaped discussions surrounding Sykes–Picot and its final form.

Sykes worried that "sufficient importance" had not been paid to "the moral side of the question" of fighting a war to liberate small nationalities from the Ottoman yoke. To his mind, the agreement solved this problem. It was "founded on two axioms": "the unalterable friendship of Great Britain and France" and "The duty of Great Britain and France towards oppressed people."[137] Picot spent the war actively involved in Allied affairs in Cairo, Jerusalem and Beirut. Sykes gave public speeches emphasizing the centrality of the war in the Middle East and popularized the term "Middle East" in the process.[138] In 1916 he worked with Admiralty Intelligence on "an atlas of Western Europe and the Middle East." These maps illustrated the geography, history, language and religion of Middle Eastern peoples as closely tied to West. The Atlas he created transposed translucent maps over one another on an illuminated base map that layered the physical and human geography of the region.[139]

This project echoed Victorian ethno-linguistic mapping projects that divided the world into a cosmography of East and West, with the Near and Middle East pulled closer to the western sphere of influence.[140] This manifested itself in wartime discussions in Britain about the administration of Mesopotamia as separate from the administration of India. Here the "Middle East" found expression as a geographical entity defined in relation to the British Empire in

Asia. Sykes suggested that the administration of Basra and Baghdad fall under the Foreign Office, not the Government of India.[141] He argued that Mesopotamia was oriented toward the West rather than the East and therefore should not be administered by the India Office. By March 1917, the War Cabinet had established the Mesopotamian Administration Committee with Lord Curzon as chair and Sykes as unofficial secretary.[142]

Mapping Mesopotamia as belonging to the West was central to Sykes' project. The Sykes–Picot map depicting the Middle East divided into imperial spheres of influence and client states continues to capture the western imagination today. The more well-known map designated the future spheres of influence of Britain and France (see Figure 1.1).[143]

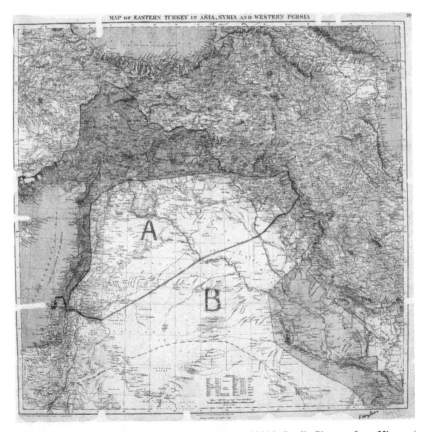

1.1. Sykes–Picot map to Illustrate the Agreements of 1916. Credit: Pictures from History/ Universal Images Group via Getty Images.

This map provided a canvas for T. E. Lawrence to later map ethno-national divisions that he unsuccessfully argued should guide the dividing up of the region (see Figure 1.2).[144] Sykes himself had relied on population maps that showed religious and ethnographic divisions to inform the original Syke–Picot map.[145] Lawrence appears to have marked on the map what already was implicit. Once revealed, Allied-imposed divisions shocked those marginalized by this cosmography, including Hussein. That happened in November 1917 when the Bolsheviks had the Sykes–Picot agreement published in order to discredit now deposed Tsar Nicholas II's wartime policies.[146]

Even before the public knew about Sykes–Picot, the Foreign Office began to make use of the wartime imperial geography.

1.2. Ethnographic Sykes–Picot map created by T. E. Lawrence, 1918. Credit: The National Archives (UK), ref. MPI1/720(1).

The first discussions of the conquest of Baghdad started the same month that Sykes–Picot negotiations began in October 1915. It did not go forward because of the Kut disaster. However, capturing Baghdad from that moment forward symbolized wider ambitions. The mapping of the city within the British sphere of influence in Sykes–Picot happened in January during Townshend's ongoing campaign. It elevated the conquest of Baghdad from a "sideshow" into a strategic war aim. The British saw the French region as ripe for conquest as well. After the capture of Baghdad in March 1917, strategists set their sights on Jerusalem and then the occupation of the entire French zone which was achieved in fall 1918. Before the fall of Jerusalem, the Arabs had driven the Ottomans out of the Hejaz making this move possible.

Ultimately, the conquest of the Ottoman Empire followed the imperial geography of the Sykes–Picot map from the beginning of the Arab Revolt in summer 1916 onwards.[147] Sykes–Picot transformed into an occupation map after Britain's successful Mesopotamian campaigns between 1917 and 1918. A War Office map from 1918 shows the growing extent of the British occupation (see Figure 1.3).[148] By this time, the British in the name of the Allies, had conquered Syria, Palestine and Mesopotamia in the French and British zones that corresponded to the designations on the Sykes–Picot map.

Sykes and Picot continued to wield influence after the tide turned in the Allies favor in Spring 1917. Picot was assigned as Commissaire de la Republique dans les territoires occupés de Palestine et de Syrie. At the time of armistice in October 1918, he served as plenipotentiary with authority to continue negotiating Anglo-French policy.[149] Sykes continued advocating the Sykes–Picot vision. He traveled around the Middle East to make assessments until his death from the Spanish flu on February 16, 1919, while attending the Paris Peace Conference.[150]

Lloyd George used Sykes–Picot to direct Britain's conquest of Mesopotamia. He later distanced himself from the agreement, calling it a "blunder" and disingenuously claiming in his *War Memoirs* that he found it "incomprehensible" that the Arabs were not notified of its

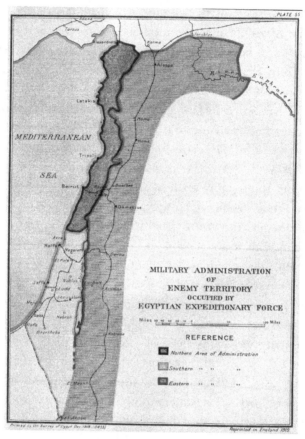

1.3. Allied military occupation map, 1918. Credit: *A Brief Record of the Advance of the Egyptian Expeditionary Force: July 1917–October 1918* (1919), Plate 55.

contents. He went as far as to declare that he was ashamed of the document.[151] LloydGeorge also blamed France for the duplicity and accused it of not contributing enough soldiers and resources to the fight.[152] These statements reflected growing British confidence in the wake of its victories on the Middle Eastern Front. The conquest of Mesopotamia in spring 1917, largely by British forces, had changed the course of the war. But in 1916, the game of secret agreements still mattered especially regarding the Arab alliance. Although they had held up their end of the bargain that summer, the Arabs would not share the advantages of victory over the Ottomans in the Hejaz.[153]

ARAB REVOLT

Indigenous support was important to winning the war for the Allies. Negotiations with Sharif Hussein had stalled repeatedly because of his justifiable distrust of Anglo-France imperial ambitions. Correspondence between Hussein and McMahon on a possible Anglo-Arab alliance continued through the spring of 1916; McMahon promised a "pan-Arab" empire if Hussein would lead a revolt against the Ottomans.[154] During this time, CUP leader Cemal Pasha began a brutal campaign against Arab critics of the regime many of whom were arrested for treason and either exiled or killed. Information on dissidents came from French files Picot left behind in Beirut in October 1914 and later seized by Cemal Pasha's forces.[155]

The campaign against Arab nationalists starting in June 1915 instituted what Eugene Rogan called a "reign of terror" and ultimately influenced Hussein's decision to support the Allied war effort and lead a rebellion against the Ottoman Empire in the Hejaz. The famine in Syria, which began in the spring of 1915, also may have contributed to this decision.[156] Locusts devastated crops for over a year causing widespread starvation.[157] As soldier Ihsan Turjman recorded in his wartime diary: "Locusts are attacking all over the country ... Today it took the locust clouds two hours to pass over the city. God project us from the three plagues: war, locusts and disease ... Pity the poor."[158] Ottoman authorities instituted policies including wartime requisitioning and economic sanctions that actively made things worse and created a "man-made wartime famine" that would claim up to half a million lives in Beirut and its environs.[159]

The Arab Revolt began in June 1916 under the leadership of Hussein and his sons. It ended a long era of not always harmonious relations between the Ottoman Empire and its Arab subjects. Before the war, the government moderated the previous administration's active policy of centralization in response to Arab resistance.[160] Despite promises of limited autonomy and a shared common faith with its Muslim rulers, Hussein continued to fiercely guard his independence from the imperial center. This included resisting the construction of railway lines to link Mecca and Medina to the rest of the country that could lead to closer connections with the Ottoman state.[161]

At the same time, Ottoman Arabs felt tied by language and religion to the estimated 35–40 million Arabs in the larger Islamic World. Growing nationalist consciousness among Arabs in the Hejaz, encouraged by the British for their own ends, threatened to sever historic connections to their Ottoman co-religionists while enforcing bonds with the wider Arab world.[162] This did not happen immediately or easily. When war started, Hussein did not issue a declaration in support of the Sultan's jihad, nor did he initially accept the overtures of Britain.[163]

Eventually, discontent with Ottoman rule and growing nationalism brought Arabs under Hussein's leadership into the war. Hussein had brokered the conditions for the Anglo-Arab alliance after he learned of a plot to overthrow him by the Ottoman government. The unilateral agreement came about in part to counter France's ambitions in Syria. "We rejoice ... that your Highness and your people are of one opinion, that Arab interests are English interests and English Arab," wrote McMahon to Hussein in August 1915.[164] Ultimately, this declaration of mutual interests proved one-sided. McMahon's declaration of mutual interests served only Britain's own imperial ambitions.[165] The final agreement rested on vaguely defined boundaries for the future Arab state and ignored Sykes–Picot. But up to this point, that agreement remained unknown to Hussein and his supporters. The revolt thus took place under the false assumption that Britain would defend Hussein's claims to part of the same region that it had promised to France months earlier.[166] A "disparate crew of irregulars," as one historian characterized the Arab fighters, continued their campaign in the Hejaz for over a year.[167]

After the war, Lloyd George praised Arab efforts and claimed that "the safety of our Arab allies in the Hejaz" had been a top priority.[168] The reality was that Britain offered only uneven assistance to the war in the Hejaz as it focused on fighting the Ottomans elsewhere. The British army advanced into Sinai in the summer of 1916 and all but ended Ottoman threats to Egypt.[169] After a series of initial successes, the Arab Revolt faltered, the result of problematic Hashemite alliances with local tribesmen coupled with a lack of personnel and resources. Britain responded by relying on an old play book used in India. The belief that a network of spies and informants would allow the British to better face adversaries in the Middle East first took shape along the Indian frontier during imperial consolidation efforts in the nineteenth century.[170]

In the Hejaz, this translated into supporting shadowy operations by self-declared experts who promised to infiltrate Arab communities.[171] Lloyd George referenced the usefulness of such informants in recalling his frustration with the War Office which "was strongly opposed to increasing our commitments" in the Middle East. He believed that "capable officers" "with a close knowledge of oriental people and their ways . . . knew how to get the maximum effect with comparatively small forces."[172] Although Lloyd George may have had Sykes in mind, it was T. E. Lawrence who fit this mould best. His presence looms large still today in discussions of the Arab Revolt as a romantic figure who promised to deliver victory through cloak-and-dagger tactics. Lawrence of Arabia, a moniker he took on during the war, took credit for turning the fortunes of the revolt around through cunning and daring exploits.[173] For those fighting in the revolt, he was less fabled. Instead of leading the revolt, some remembered him more as the "paymaster" who deserved minimal credit in the effort to oust the Ottomans from the Hejaz.[174]

CONCLUSION

While historians debate the extent of the effectiveness of the Arab Revolt, the episode had important implications for the course of the First World War.[175] Hussein's entry in the war undermined German attempts to weaken Arab support for the British and diminished the effectiveness of the campaign of the Central Powers in the region. Germany launched a propaganda campaign early in the war to win Muslim loyalty which included both Ottoman Arabs and Indians serving in and alongside the British army. While the Germans failed to incite outright rebellion, the most significant achievement in this effort was to sow the seeds of distrust between British commanders and Indian soldiers.[176] This was apparent at Gallipoli, Kut and in POW camps where active recruiting took place and resulted in limited but highly noticed defections from the Indian army to the Ottoman army.[177]

The Arab Revolt also influenced discussions about future administration and the extent to which the government of India should be
involved in the management of the war.[178] Britain contributed almost
1 million pounds to the success of the revolt but did not commit any of
its already stretched ground troops who, starting in July 1916, were
engaged in the battle of the Somme which would ultimately kill over
a million British, French and German soldiers.[179] No one knew if the
gains made by Hussein and his supporters would last beyond 1916 when
the Ottoman army retreated from the Hejaz. Forcing the Ottoman army
out of Mecca and Medina denied the Central Powers a symbolic victory
in its fight for Arab support and cleared the way for the Allied conquest
of Jerusalem. The ability of the Arabs to hold their ground in the Hejaz
ultimately advantaged the Allies. By spring 1917, the war had taken
a definitive turn in their favor.

CHAPTER 2

The Middle Eastern Front

NOT LONG AFTER WRESTING CONTROL FROM HIS MEN-
tor and fellow Liberal H. H. Asquith in early December 1916,
Punch dubbed David Lloyd George "The New Conductor." The cartoon
accompanying this title depicted the new Prime Minister clutching
a baton raised over his head, directing his orchestra with a determined
stare (Figure 2.1). Lloyd George liked the image so much that he used it
as a frontispiece in his *War Memoirs.*[1]

Lloyd George won the leadership contest by discrediting Prime
Minister Asquith's handling of the war, according to critics.[2] While the
story is certainly more complicated, there is little doubt that mistakes
made by the administration at Gallipoli and Kut as well as in the Somme
contributed to Asquith's downfall. Lloyd George himself called for the
unprecedented appointing of the Dardanelles and Mesopotamia
Commissions in the summer of 1916 immediately after he took over at
the War Office.[3] The seeds of doubt sowed first by military failure and
then by these investigations played an important role in forming the new
National Government – made up of a small group of men from the
Liberal, Conservative and Labour parties – under Lloyd George that
December.[4]

Gallipoli and Kut loomed large in the British psyche and politics. No
inquiries into the terrible failures on the Western Front were launched
during the war or after.[5] The defeat of British forces in Ottoman lands
needed explaining in a way that defeat on the battlefields of France did
not. Damage to British prestige in the East, cited again and again in these
reports, drew on old tropes that played on fears of a lesser civilized
empire defeating the modern British military.[6] In many ways, Lloyd

2.1. David Lloyd George depicted as "The New Conductor" in *Punch Magazine,* December 20, 1916. Credit: "The New Conductor. Opening of the 1917 Overture," by Leonard Raven Hill.

George owed his leadership position to exploiting the failures at Gallipoli and Kut at the hands of the Ottomans.

The new prime minister staked his command of the war on victories in this theater. Lloyd George's focus on the Middle East has been over-shadowed by the view that only winning on the Western Front mattered to war planners.[7] One consequence of this orthodoxy has been reading the Middle Eastern Front as important to narrow imperial wartime objectives that only had consequences for the postwar settlement.[8] This approach has led to an emphasis on the fight against Germany in Europe. But winning in the Middle East mattered particularly to the British. This was especially true after the departure of the Russians and signing of Brest-Litovsk and the rise of a new more cautious strategy by the French in the wake of the Somme. The shifting realities of the war in 1917 gave Britain the opportunity to flex its power in Mesopotamia. While the overall war objective – to defend the British Empire against German conquest and French ambition – did not fundamentally shift under Lloyd George, his premiership brought the war with the Ottoman Empire out from the shadow and shame of Gallipoli and Kut.

Early challenges of war on the Middle Eastern Front threatened Allied unity and resulted in new alliances with indigenous and non-combatant actors from the Arab, Armenian and Zionist communities. With the French retreating into a defensive strategy brought on by devastating loses on the Western Front, the British saw opportunity. During 1917, Britain sought to control the direction of the war by focusing on the breakup of the Ottoman Empire, forging alliances between the so-called "small nationalities" and, ultimately, sidelining the French.[9] These war aims meant renewed focus on the land war in Mesopotamia. In 1917, fighting in this theater offered the one positive piece of news for the Allies.

The conquest of Baghdad that spring and Jerusalem in December proved a turning point. These victories led to an armistice with the Ottoman Empire that came nearly two weeks before the November armistice with Germany. It both sought to end the fighting and hold the Ottoman Empire accountable for war crimes against Armenians. But war was not over. Signed at the end of October 1918 at Mudros on the Greek island of Lemnos, the Ottoman armistice ultimately failed to stop the fighting and the persecution of minorities. Instead, it offered a blueprint for five more years of warfare in the face of uncertain victory.

LLOYD GEORGE'S WAR

By spring 1917, Lloyd George had rearticulated the goals of the war. Calling the war a "struggle of endurance," he believed winning required more resources. As he later put it in his memoirs: "Morale, food, manpower, war material and transport – the belligerent group that failed first in one of these essential elements would lose the War."[10] Four key war aims motivated the new administration. First, to drive the Germans "out of the territories which they have invaded"; second, to promote the "democratization of Europe" which will prevent "military autocracies" from starting wars; third, "the disruption of the Turkish Empire as an Empire" and finally, the "reconstruction of our own country" and the British commonwealth. Lloyd George explicitly included war aims stretching across the Western and Middle Eastern Fronts that served broad domestic and imperial agendas.

The Prime Minister articulated these objectives to the Imperial War Cabinet on March 20, 1917, in the immediate aftermath of the fall of Baghdad. This explains his focus on the future of the Ottoman Empire: "The Turk must never be allowed to misgovern these great lands in the future." Here he included Syria, Palestine, Armenia and Mesopotamia, which the British empire sought to "restore" to their former glory. While the other three goals seemed distant, this aim proved within reach in this moment: "You will hear from the Staff, I hope, how far we have proceeded with this task. I believe we have advanced already about forty or fifty miles beyond Baghdad."[11]

But this focus on winning in Mesopotamia had its costs. He relied at home on a small coalition of mainly Liberals and Conservatives – Arthur Henderson was the only Labour Party representative – to see his plans through and not all shared his enthusiasm for dedicating resources here. There also was the matter of competition with France. Lloyd George disparaged France's contributions repeatedly. He went as far as to call them "almost insignificant compared with that of the British Empire" which contributed 1.4 million men to fighting in Syria and Palestine.[12]

The stalemate on the Western Front further raised the stakes. Lloyd George could not have anticipated how bad things would get in Belgium and France when he took over in late 1916. Conscription started earlier that year and lasted until 1920, initially under pressure from Kitchener who needed more men to grow the ranks of his "new armies." Lloyd George initially tried to "assert political control over his generals" and exercise more control over his massive fighting force.[13] His attempts to direct action on the Western Front, however, created only discord and sowed distrust among Allied generals. Lloyd George decided to create an Imperial War Cabinet and surround himself with a small group of advisors, the first prime minister to do this.[14] While historians argue about whether or not this centralization won the war, this concentration of power mattered to how it was prosecuted.[15] In Europe, Lloyd George tried repeatedly and unsuccessfully to wrest control from General Douglas Haig and General William Robertson who had enormous control over operations. Consolidating authority and surrounding himself with handpicked advisors had the greatest effect on the Middle Eastern Front where he exercised strong control over policy and his generals.

Overall, 1917 promised the Allies little relief from the disasters and miscalculations of the previous year. The United States' entry into the war that spring assured much needed reinforcements but US troop deployment to Europe was still nearly a year away. Two revolutions in Russia effectively ended Russian participation after the takeover of the Bolsheviks late in the year. The settlement at Brest-Litovsk in March 1918 with the Central Powers got Russia out of the war for good and bolstered Ottoman territorial ambitions in the Caucasus. October 1917 saw the Italians routed at Caporetto. This left the British and the French to fight a war now turned to stalemate. These two imperial rivals turned allies now had to work out a way forward.

The coalition with France understandably had come under pressure on the Western Front.[16] The French military and domestic crisis got worse after the failed Somme campaign which ended in November 1916. It sparked strikes, industrial unrest and the threat of mutiny.[17] French President Raymond Poincaré called 1917 the "année trouble," a year that saw four different prime ministers who presided over an anxious parliament.[18] While German submarine warfare wreaked havoc on the domestic economy, the military situation worsened.[19] The Nivelle offensive of April and May 1917 was a failed attempt by the British and the French to break through German lines in northern France. Philippe Pétain subsequently took over as chief of the General Staff, replacing the disgraced Robert Nivelle who launched the disastrous offensive that still bears his name.[20] General Pétain promised to take a more defensive strategy in light of the well over 100,000 casualties in an approximately three-week period under Nivelle's leadership.[21] This approach opened Pétain up to British criticism, but ultimately resulted in stabilizing the French army in the wake of the losses that spring.[22] By the time

Georges Clemenceau was asked by Poincaré to form a government in late November 1917, Allied strategy on the Western Front began to focus on a more limited offensive strategy under Pétain's leadership.

These events forced a reassessment of Allied coordination of the war effort. The Supreme War Council, set up in early November 1917, governed military operations between Britain, France and Italy.[23] It focused on protecting French and Italian territory, preventing an invasion of Britain and making war aims in the "Turkish theater" clear. The Allies sought "to inflict such a crushing series of defeats upon the Turkish armies as would lead to the final collapse of Turkey" and "give effective help to" those resisting German domination in "Roumania [sic] and Southern Russia" and "liberate the Arab regions of the Ottoman Empire."[24] On this last point, Britain led. While the French focused on the Germans in northern France, the Italians worried about possible invasion on the Alpine Front. This allowed Lloyd George to exert influence over the alliance and his war cabinet regarding Middle East objectives. "When I became Premier at the end of 1916," Lloyd George later reflected, "we were still maintaining a defensive attitude on all the Turkish Fronts, although we had overwhelming forces at our disposal in these areas." Even before becoming prime minister he claimed to be "anxious ... to see real pressure being asserted against the Turk" despite strong opposition from the War Office.

In February 1917, Lloyd George asserted his will on General Frederick Stanley Maude who was told to "press on and capture Baghdad" which he did.[25] Lloyd George's view of the importance of the Middle Eastern Front took hold. "The Allies are not in a condition to conduct an offensive on the Western front before the autumn," opined Leopold Amery who would help draft the Balfour Declaration. "Meanwhile the Allies have an opportunity in the Turkish theatre of war, of obtaining military results which ... should change the whole war map, and consequently the peace conference situation, enormously in our favour."[26] Lloyd George appointed his own man, General Edmund Allenby, to finish the job.

The focus on the Middle East was more than the strategy of a man seeking to wrest control from his rivals and lead the alliance. A Gladstonian by heart and inclination, he touted the protection of "small nationalities" as a moral reason for fighting the war.[27] He helped create the idea of a defensive war fought to protect Belgium. A similar tactic was at play in the Middle East. A Welshman who entered parliament in 1890 at age 27, Lloyd George made his name as an anti-Boer War Liberal and held the seat for fifty-five years for Caernarvon Boroughs.[28] He grew up in the Victorian liberal tradition that united imperial and foreign policy and legitimated the exercise of state power abroad as a necessary and even moral enterprise.[29] As prime minister, the war crisis made him embrace an outward-looking foreign policy that strengthened the imperial center and British leadership abroad. Though he claimed to be concerned with Home Rule in the Gladstonian tradition, he had little personal sympathy for Irish nationalism and failed to bring a settlement to the Easter Rising in Ireland in 1916.[30] At the same time, he declared himself "an ardent advocate of the rights of small nationalities" who Britain had pledged to defend since the days of Gladstone.[31]

"Small nationalities" in the Middle East first meant Christian minorities and, later, included both Arabs and Jews. Lloyd George when he used the term was not referencing the size of these populations but rather their subject status and desire for self-determination.[32] He was quick to see the utility of using small nationalities to make the moral argument to continue fighting the war in a place most Britons would have known only through stories in the Bible or the *Arabian Nights.*[33] He described the campaign in Mesopotamia in almost millennialist terms:

> At first they crawled drearily and without purpose across the desert towards the land of the Philistines. But in 1917, the attention of her warriors was drawn to the mountains of Judea beyond ... The redemption of Palestine from the withering aggression of the Turk became like a pillar of flame to lead them on.[34]

The distance of the Middle East from Europe coupled with mythic stories and its distinct role in the history of Christianity made it the ideal canvas to craft new narratives of liberation and heroism.[35] He spoke to his constituents about "Treading on Gladstone's Path" not long after becoming prime minister: "The principle that the rights of nations, however small, are as sacred as the rights of the biggest empire." This meant "expelling" the "Turk ... for his misrule and his massacres," an idea he credited to Gladstone and recalled first reading about as a boy.[36]

Lloyd George began his administration of the Middle Eastern campaign with what he knew: supply chains. Provisioning and supplying massive armies was a problem across all fronts and the alliance itself.[37] As head of the newly created Ministry of Munitions in 1915 and 1916 under the coalition government, he improved arms production and distribution. The failures at Kut prompted the War Office in London to take over the administration of logistics and supplies in February 1916. When Lloyd George became Secretary for War after Kitchener's death, he considered his "first urgent task . . . the mess and muddle of the British Expedition to Mesopotamia."[38] He started extracting resources from the Empire to supply troops rather than sending material from Europe.[39] This increased India's already significant role in the war. It ultimately supplied 460,315 non-combatants to various theaters; 336,890 Indian men went to Middle Eastern Front.[40] The IEF "D" that had captured Basra in 1914 was renamed the Mesopotamian Expeditionary Force (MEF), sometimes referred to as the Egyptian Expeditionary Force (EEF), when London assumed control in 1916. A year later, the force had grown into a well-equipped infantry army with superior artillery; it was also more responsive, mobile and a lot bigger.[41] By November 1918, the MEF was 420,000 strong and required a massive supply of resources that mostly came from India.[42]

The MEF thus evolved from an "imperial constabulary force" in 1914 into a well-supplied professional fighting force by spring 1917.[43] Lloyd George's government set up the Indian Board of Munitions and Industries Board in 1917 under Thomas Holland. This made India the key supplier of both manufactured goods and raw materials.[44] Holland, who previously headed the Geological Survey of India, ran the "central authority for controlling the purchase and manufacture of Government stores and munitions of war" until 1919. It sent Indian materials mainly to Mesopotamia and Egypt. Holland was directly responsible to the Commander-in-Chief in India, Sir Charles Munro, and assisted by four members who oversaw several branches that stretched across India. Together they requisitioned "all kinds of raw material, as well as manufactures of every description."[45]

In late March 1917, Lloyd George initiated the Imperial War Cabinet which included representatives of the Dominions and Indian Empire.

This move acknowledged the central importance of what was then referred to as both the Indian and Egyptian Expeditionary. In characteristically hyperbolic form, his remarks to the inaugural meeting asserted that the Imperial War Cabinet held the "destiny of the Empire" and "the destiny of civilization for many ages to come."[46] Mark Sykes, former advisor to Kitchener, joined Lloyd George's inner circle. This bolstered Sykes status who in this moment proved a much more influential figure than T. E. Lawrence due to his close contact with Downing Street. Lawrence, while useful during the Arab Revolt, sat decidedly outside of the inner circle. Sykes, unlike Lawrence, had a privileged position amongst a small coterie of advisors and influenced policy.[47]

Sykes gave cause to claims that aiding small nationalities would bolster the war effort. He formulated the idea of an Arab, Zionist and Armenian alliance that he put forth in official memoranda and influenced Lloyd George's thinking. Sykes convinced the Prime Minister that together those whose histories remained entwined with that of the region would channel their own interests to serve British war aims. He was emboldened by the seeming ease with which Sykes–Picot came about and Lloyd George's confidence in him. Sykes advocated for a larger role for Britain over France, even before he joined Lloyd George's inner circle. He argued that the "Eastern theatre," as he called it, "must be appraised at its proper importance" and make more efficient or "scientific" use of troops.[48] In 1917, the Prime Minister set his sights on conquering not only Sykes–Picot's British-designated zone in Mesopotamia but also the French-designated zone around Syria as well.

ALLENBY'S ORDERS

General Allenby was Lloyd George's man. After Jan Smuts, commander of Allied forces in East Africa and former Boer War leader, turned down his offer to guide the war in the Middle East, the Prime Minister sought a new general who would deliver a war of movement and rapid victories. Allenby had helped lead the ill-fated campaigns in Belgium and France and lost his own son to fighting here. The second attempt to capture Baghdad had to be a success and, in the mind of Lloyd George, would offer the much-needed boost to morale on the battlefield and support for the war at home. Though few in Europe seemed to notice the capture of Baghdad and then, later, Jerusalem, the campaigns of 1917 turned the tide of the war in a moment when victory seemed far from certain.

Allenby took over operations in Mesopotamia in an auspicious moment. General Maude's capture of Baghdad brought the long-sought victory in Mesopotamia. This second invasion attempt succeeded, in part, due to changes made to the MEF and Lloyd George's focus on the Middle Eastern Front. His limited influence over generals on the Western Front and French strategy which had taken a more defensive stance under Pétain left him eager to score a victory against the Ottoman armies which had routed the British at Kut the previous spring. After progressing up the Tigris River in January, Maude believed he had the upper hand. General William Robertson objected to any further advance, but Lloyd George, who claimed to be "very anxious that Maude should now press on and capture Baghdad," overruled Robertson. When Baghdad fell in early March, Lloyd George called it "a stroke which at once rehabilitated our prestige in the East and cheered our people at home, much in need just then of some bright news, while it was disheartening for the enemy, and cast the first shadows upon the Berlin-Baghdad ambitions of Germany."[49]

The Germans could not help their Ottoman ally stop the British-led advance. Russia, embroiled in revolution at home, could not rally its armies in the Caucasus north of Baghdad to join in the victory. By the time Maude died of cholera in November 1917, Britain had established its authority in Mesopotamia. Baghdad emerged as the epicenter of activity after the invasion. This included military and civilian-focused missions as the British looked to gain the trust of civilians living along the battlefront. Officials immediately commissioned a report on the status of refugees in "our Bagdad colony."[50] Lloyd George's pledge to help refugees earned him comparisons to Gladstone, as Ottoman Christians seeking protection from massacre and aid flooded into the occupied zone.[51]

Lloyd George sought to fully exploit "the opportunities which a campaign in Palestine could offer."[52] Resistance continued to come from Robertson whom he blamed for obstructionism.[53] Refusing to see the campaign as a "sideshow," Lloyd George raised reinforcements to ready the MEF for a massive assault in the fall. This led the French and Italians to contribute what Lloyd George disparagingly referred to as a "token force."[54] Military setbacks that spring led to a change in leadership. After trying to replace General Archibald Murray with Smuts, whom Robertson reportedly advised to turn down the position, he selected General Allenby as Commander-in-Chief of the British Forces in Egypt in June 1917.[55] A month and half after assuming command, his only son Michael was killed on the Western Front.[56] Allenby took direct charge of his forces and commanded operations in Palestine rather than Cairo as Murray had done. Lloyd George claimed to have informed Allenby that "the Cabinet expected 'Jerusalem before Christmas.'"[57] A series of successful assaults forced an Ottoman surrender of Jerusalem on December 9, 1917.

Having led disastrous stalemate battles on the Western Front at Arras and Ypres, Allenby saw an opportunity in the Middle East campaigns to fight a war of movement. Born Edmund Henry Hynman Allenby (1831–1936) in Nottinghamshire, he entered Sandhurst at age nineteen after his father's death. Like many First World War generals, he began his career in South Africa. Later, he trained at the Army Staff College at Camberley alongside Douglas Haig. In 1896, he married above his station to Adelaide Mabel Chapman from the Wiltshire gentry. When the Boer War started, he continued his service as a cavalry expert in the 6th (Inniskilling) Dragoons and impressed Lord Kitchener which ensured his climb through the ranks.[58] He commanded a cavalry division when the First World War broke out and served three years on the Western Front where he was in regular contact with Michael who joined up at age sixteen. Michael's death made winning the war personal. In the midst of Allied setbacks in the spring and summer of 1917, he declared to his wife, whom he called Mabel: "Nevertheless, I believe that we are winning the war, but we must go on winning it ... You and I (by Michael) have paid too big a price for Victory to be content with anything short of a complete victory."[59]

Allenby's victory at Jerusalem allowed Allied armies to steadily push south toward the Sinai Peninsula and north toward Damascus. He achieved this with an army and auxiliary force drawn largely from the British Empire.[60] He also relied on the Arab alliance. "The Sharif of

Mecca is in revolt against the Turks, and is our ally," he wrote to his wife not long after he took up his post.[61] In early October he noted, "The Arab rebellion is spreading well and the Turkish communication will be difficult to guard against their raids." He further noted that he actively recruited Arab fighters to the Allied side by dropping propaganda – along with cigarettes – over enemy lines to exploit the alliance with the Sharif.[62]

The reorganized MEF coupled with Arab cooperation allowed Allenby to avoid fighting a trench war. Instead, he used cavalry divisions. This strategy paid dividends even before Jerusalem. He described the battle for Beersheba to his wife as a "smart little battle, achieved by careful preparation and good staff work. The Cavalry made a 25-mile night march" to "turn the Turks' flank . . . All this was based on water supply and ammunition supply – development of wells and pumps and . . . roads, trams and railways." He reassured Mabel that "All went well . . . . I have another attack tonight, on a smaller scale."[63] In late September 1918, Allenby's forces decisively defeated Ottoman and German forces at the Battle of Megiddo which ultimately led to the seizure of Damascus and armistice with Turkey in October. The army had advanced over 300 miles in five weeks leaving devastation in the surrounding villages in the wake of victory.[64]

Lloyd George made his understanding of Britain's mission in the East clear to Allenby. He arrived with a copy of George Adam Smith's, *Historical Geography of the Holy Land* given to him by the Prime Minister who claimed that this Bible-based history that ended with Napoleon's invasion would prove more useful than War Office surveys.[65] Not long after his arrival at the Front, he wrote to Mabel through an orientalist lens: "all look like biblical characters. Face, dress and everything like pictures from the Bible. Keen, handsome faces; picturesque, Arab dress."[66] Like Maude before him who claimed the conquest of Baghdad had been done to free the population from Ottoman rule, Allenby was anxious to make the case for the British as liberators. Allenby contrasted his entry into Jerusalem on foot with that of German Kaiser who had a hole cut into the gate in order to enter Jerusalem on horseback years earlier.[67]

Allenby managed military and civilian affairs after Jerusalem. He interviewed inhabitants including doctors and police and made speeches in English alongside Arab notables who interpreted.[68] He also took over hospitals and orphanages previously run by Turkish and German authorities while spearheading a humanitarian campaign using British, American and French military and financial resources[69] (see Chapter 3). The Egyptian Labour Corps, whose size grew by a third to 120,000 men under Allenby's command, built communication and transportation infrastructure including railways, roads, military depots and water pipelines that served both military and humanitarian functions.[70] He eventually took over as High Commissioner in Egypt where, among other administrative duties, he continued to oversee the maintenance of hospitals, orphanages, supplies and other civilian relief efforts.

The conquest and occupation of Jerusalem marked a military and strategic triumph. "Jerusalem surrounded on the 9th. I informed the War Office but was not allowed to publish the news before the PM had announced it in the House," Allenby wrote to Mabel.[71] Lloyd George had gotten the victory he wanted. Now the Allies needed to stage a show of unity when they marched into Jerusalem two days later. "Today I entered Jerusalem, on foot," Allenby continued, "with the French and Italian commanders – Lt Col de Piépape and Major D'Agostino – of the detachment in my army and the attachés and a few staff officers." A proclamation declaring the liberation from Ottoman rule was issued at Jerusalem as it had been at Baghdad the previous spring. "We started at Jaffa gate and from the steps of the Citadel" and "issued a proclamation ... (to) the assembled multitude. Great enthusiasm, real or feigned was shown. Then I received the notables and the heads of all the Churches – of which there are many .... After that, we reformed our procession and returned to our horses which we had left outside the walls."[72] Allenby proceeded with his army northward to prevent the Ottomans from retaking Jerusalem.[73] He chose to go to the Church of the Nativity in Bethlehem to mark his victory. Ringing church bells announced his entry and "roused the town." His visit concluded with a tour of the holy sites and a rendition of "God Save the King."[74]

These victories, however, did not direct Europe's attention toward the Middle Eastern Front as Lloyd George had hoped. The capture of Jerusalem failed to distract the public from the loses on the Western Front. In the coming months, the British focused on the land war in Mesopotamia as the best way to defeat the Ottomans and limit French influence. But they also needed to turn public opinion in Europe and the United States more solidly toward the war. To achieve this, the British Empire engaged in a delicate dance to reassert its role as a defender of Ottoman minorities, themselves divided by their own competing interests.

BALFOUR DECLARATION

The minority question shadowed Middle East diplomacy and shaped military decision making. The idea of the "Protection of religious minorities" drew on nineteenth-century precedent when Europe first expanded its presence in the Ottoman Empire using diplomatic and cultural means.[75] The pledge to defend the rights of Christians and Jews provided a reliable way to maintain a consistent foothold in Ottoman affairs.[76] Britain, and to a lesser extent France and Germany, cultivated educational and religious institutional ties with its minorities whom they hoped would see them as allies.[77] This proved an important non-territorial way of exerting influence over Ottoman affairs and secured the Holy Land a permanent place in the European imagination as the center of the Middle East.[78]

British support for Zionism and a Jewish homeland started with Lord Palmerston during the crisis years of the 1840s. The expulsion of Egyptian leader Muhammad Ali by the Ottomans made Palestine central to what was then called the Eastern Question and led to attempts to make Jews, in the words of one historian, "de facto British proteges."[79] France, too, developed its own set of interests in the region. After the British conquest of Egypt in 1882, it focused on Syria, expanding its economic footprint while promising to protect religious shrines and educational institutions. Nascent Zionist thinking represented only one aspect of British engagement with the region which included commercial and tourist-related activities during the second half of the nineteenth century. The "restoration of the Jews to Palestine" after conversion to Christianity also became a strand in popular and political thought. In the late nineteenth century, some went as far as to support colonization schemes based on claims that Jews would steward the land better than the indigenous Arab population.[80]

The Balfour Declaration belongs to this history. Issued on November 2, 1917, by Foreign Secretary Arthur Balfour, the document promised "a national home for the Jewish people" with respect for "civil and religious rights of exiting non-Jewish communities." It came out of a particular brand of liberal idealism characteristic of nineteenth-century imperial thinking supported by Lloyd George and advisors like Mark Sykes. Historians tend to read the Balfour Declaration forward – as part of the story of the founding of Israel – rather than in its wartime context.[81] Some debate its origins and the role played by individual actors in its creation.[82]

The timing and text of the Balfour Declaration made it part of a larger strategy that served the interests of the Allied war machine.[83] Britain's rivalry with France, the entry of the United States on the Allied side and exit of Russia from the war all played an important role in the issuing of the Declaration, which took the form of a letter to Zionist supporter Lord Rothschild. Ultimately, it paralleled other propaganda efforts to bolster support for the war as a fight to defend the rights of small nationalities that, up to this time, had focused on the Armenians.

The issue of minority protection coupled with the Anglo-French rivalry gave the Balfour Declaration its urgency. Cultivating alliances with Ottoman subjects and diaspora interests also played a role. In this way, it paralleled the Bryce Report on Armenian atrocities in terms of purpose and scope. Wartime politicians had individual and political reasons for supporting Zionist aspirations much as they did for Armenians.[84] Lloyd George, though personally not invested in the cause, proposed the idea of a Jewish buffer state in Palestine as early as January 1915. The De Bunsen Committee report, issued that summer, made the case for using military force to occupy the region in order to achieve British war aims.[85] While Asquith showed little interest in Zionism during his premiership, Lord Edward Grey and others began to advocate for a declaration in support of Zionism early in the war.[86]

Grey, who had been instrumental in getting Britain to declare war against Germany after the violation of Belgian neutrality, believed that supporting "Jewish aspirations in Palestine" would help win the war.[87] Kitchener wanted to remove the Mediterranean coast from French control and saw Zionism as a tool that would benefit Britain in the wake of the

Sykes–Picot agreement.[88] Advocates from the Zionist community encouraged these lines of thinking. Chaim Weizmann, an active Zionist from his youth, played an important role in cultivating support among Britain's elite. He helped procure much needed chemicals for munitions production in June 1915, leading Lloyd George to quip, "acetone converted me to Zionism."[89]

The Declaration proved useful to the war in the context of Sykes–Picot. Despite repeated British attempts to sideline the French, the secret agreement had joined them in a marriage of convenience. It defined Allied war aims in the context of the Anglo-French rivalry in the Middle East. As one historian put it, Sykes-Picot "was a temporary wartime measure, designating areas of likely military occupation and control that would avoid disagreements between Britain and France."[90] In Palestine, it meant creating a zone of international control that temporarily kept territorial disagreements at bay. When Sykes proposed raising "an Arab rebellion ... with a view to attacks on the Turkish lines of communication, particularly against the railway between Aleppo and Damascus" in spring 1917, both the Prime Minister and Lord Curzon expressed concerns over upsetting the French.

Sykes-Picot also risked alienating Zionist supporters: "They impressed on Sir Mark Sykes the difficulty of our relations with the French in this region and the importance of not prejudicing the Zionist movement and the possibility of its development under British auspices." Instead, the "PM suggested that the Jews might be able to render us more assistance than the Arabs." Lloyd George went as far as to propose sending Jews living in Britain to Palestine to serve "as motor-drivers and guides" claiming that they could contribute to the war effort "in this theatre."[91] The Balfour Declaration, issued the following November, attempted to fulfill the potential to tilt Zionist support toward the British in ways that direct territorial conquest could not.

The French had their own ideas about gaining the upper hand in Palestine. Rather than actively cultivate ties with the Zionist community, France sought its own alliance with Ottoman Arabs. Col. Edouard Brémond (1868–1948), Chief of French Military Mission to Arabia starting in 1916, was the face of the mission.[92] After the war, he wrote an account of his time commanding French forces in Mesopotamia,

Le Hedjaz dans la Guerre mondiale. His book describes how his force of mostly Muslim Moroccan soldiers participated in the coordination of military and diplomatic missions around Mecca and Medina. The account, written in the third person, provides an important counterpoint to Lloyd George's Anglocentric 2,000 plus pages of writing about the war.[93] It also shows the extent of French engagement with the war in the Middle East in this crucial period. Critical of how T. E. Lawrence treated Arab officers and soldiers, Brémond claimed to have integrated Arab and African ranks and delegated planning to his Muslim officers.[94]

His success worried the British leadership with whom he did not always have the most cordial relations. Brémond's maneuvering may have been behind Mark Sykes' angry declaration in February 1917 about Palestine that "the French have no particular position in Palestine and are not entitled to anything there."[95] This rivalry led to concerns that Brémond would gain momentum and rally others to follow the French. Brémond held this position until December 1917 and later represented French interests in Armenia and Cilicia in 1920. After leaving his post in Arabia, British officials worried that he might be "anxious to obtain command of the Armenian contingent with a view to employment of this body in Palestine in due course."[96]

French claims that they had Muslim support made the British pay closer attention to their relationship with indigenous Arab communities. They also wanted to ensure the loyalty of Indian Muslim soldiers serving in the British army, particularly in light of the Kut disaster. Rather than forging a unilateral alliance, Sykes came up with a plan that he claimed made common cause of rival minority interests discontented with Ottoman rule. By the fall of 1916, Sykes began studying the Zionist question for his periodic updates on Ottoman Arab opinion known as the "Arabian Reports."[97] His move to the Foreign Office a few months later gave him a greater opportunity to shape thinking about Zionist Jews, Arabs and Armenians whom he considered "natural allies of the Entente."[98]

The projection of these assumed loyalties hinged on the impressions of Sykes and other intelligence officers who spoke to select groups deemed representative of these communities. Officials offered freedom from Ottoman rule in exchange for fealty to Britain despite having little authority to do this or any true knowledge of public opinion. This attitude was on display in Lord Robert Cecil's declaration on behalf of the British government at the Zionist demonstration at London's Royal Opera House on December 2, 1917: "We welcome among us not only the many thousands of Jews that I see, but also representatives of the Arabian and Armenian races, who are also in this great struggle to be free. Our wish is that Arabian countries shall be for the Arab, Armenia for the Armenians and Judaea for the Jews."[99]

While easy to dismiss as little more than a smokescreen for British double dealings, connecting the Zionist, Armenian and Arab causes made sense in the context of the Anglo-French rivalry and war situation in 1917. The Foreign Office tied itself up in knots trying to justify its vague and competing promises. Sykes had a dizzying charge when he left for the Middle East as a political advisor in April 1917: secure Palestine as part of the British zone of influence against the French; give no promises to the Arabs about Palestine and do nothing to anger Zionists and turn them against British leadership. The ultimate goal, to occupy Palestine before any peace negotiations, hinged on keeping these interests in play.[100] In the immediate wake of Jerusalem, intelligence officer G. F. Clayton worried in a letter to Sykes that "an Arab Jewish entente can only be brought about by very gradual and cautious action ... We have therefore to consider whether the situation demands out and out support of Zionism at the risk of alienating the Arabs at this crucial moment."[101] Zionist leaders proposed that Sykes establish a commission to study future settlement in Palestine and set up relief work in the occupied area. Sykes believed this would help in the "local administration" of the region, a solution that risked alienating Arabs.[102]

Forging alliances between these groups required manipulation. Sykes reported to Egypt High Commissioner Sir Reginald Wingate that immediately after the Balfour Declaration, Armenians sent "a congratulatory letter" to Zionist leaders for publication. This led Sykes to conclude: "Zionists are prepared to work whole-heartedly for Arab and Armenian liberation." He began efforts to engineer this appearance of unity using Wingate: "It is most urgent to my mind that you get your Arab Committee in Cairo into being once more and impress upon them the vital necessity of Jewish and Armenian good will." For Sykes this was about forging more than an alliance between small nationalities. Winning the war would require the support of the British and American public. As he directed Wingate: "Point out that with Jewish cooperation they have advocates in every country in the world and with Armenian help they have a strong grip on the imagination of British and American Democracy . . . Without cooperation of these two elements there is I think no prospect of their gaining their full desiderata."[103] Sykes proposed a committee be formed in London with representatives from the Zionist, Armenian, Syrian Christian and Arab Muslim community "to act on behalf of the oppressed nationalities in the non-Anatolian provinces of Turkey in Asia."[104]

As untenable as it may seem, the Balfour Declaration gave ideas about cooperation an impetus. The vagueness of territorial commitments made it possible for each side to imagine that it would receive the lion's share. The issuing of the Declaration tapped into a developing shared sense of purpose between Armenians and Zionists. This relationship had been facilitated by James Malcolm, an Armenian Catholic with long-standing ties to the Jewish community. A businessman who attended Oxford and whose family lived in London, he seems to have played a role in introducing Sykes to Weizmann. Malcolm supported connections particularly between Zionism and Armenian self-determination, which he saw as compatible with British patronage.[105]

Like similar public reports and statements, the timing of the Balfour Declaration was important. It served a distinct political purpose for the war in November 1917. Jewish leaders believed that a declaration in support of Zionism was imminent as early as July 1917.[106] That it did not come until November suggests that other factors were still in play. Zionist leaders worried about Sykes' sympathy with the Arab cause and Lloyd George's lack of firm commitment to Zionism as well as the presence of high-ranking anti-Zionist voices including, most notably, Secretary of State for India, Edwin Montagu. The domestic political context improved over the summer and objections to a pro-Zionist stance dissipated.[107]

Although the United States entered the war the previous spring, it had not yet fully mobilized. Support for Zionism, Sykes maintained, had the potential to further strengthen its new ally's commitment by capturing "the imagination of British and American Democracy." Propaganda had been used throughout the war; this included the Balfour Declaration. As

Lloyd George claimed, "the actual time of the declaration was determined by considerations of War policy. It was part of our propagandist strategy for mobilizing every opinion and force throughout the world which would weaken the enemy and improve the Allied chances."[108] Issuing the statement in November rather than during the dog days of summer, much like the timing of the Armenian Blue Book the year before, ensured robust press coverage on both sides of the Atlantic.

Unforeseen events played into the ability to capitalize on publicity surrounding the Declaration. Victory at Beersheba then Gaza and, finally, Jaffa by mid-November meant that Britain had momentum on its side on the battlefield. The Arab victory at Aqaba the previous summer further buoyed Allied efforts.[109] That was also when Greece officially entered the war, adding reinforcement to Allied operations around the Mediterranean.[110] The Declaration, when coupled with increased military support and success on the battlefield, served Britain's aim to occupy Palestine.[111]

At the same time, the public disclosure of Sykes–Picot in the midst of Russia's negotiated exit from the war cast a sinister light on British and French ambition.[112] Brest-Litovsk negotiations, requested by Russia's revolutionary government in early November 1917 and completed the next spring, made Russia agree to large territorial concessions as a condition for exiting the war.[113] Nervous about the effects of these converging forces, the British secretly considered brokering a separate peace with the Ottoman Empire. While these plans fell flat, it is worth considering the objections made in this moment by Sykes and Curzon to such a deal. According to Sykes, "We are pledged to Zionism, Armenian liberation and Arabian independence." He believed these should be Britain's "only desiderata."[114]

Liberal imperial posturing, however, would not win the war. In late 1917, the tide turned toward the Allies because of both Lloyd George's continued insistence on focusing on the Middle Eastern Front and conditions in the Ottoman army. The Third Battle of Gaza from October to December 1917, which culminated with the capture of Jerusalem, succeeded in part because of the Ottoman's "inadequate state of readiness."[115] This was due both to Allied pressure and to a shift in Ottoman strategy. Russia's loss of territory as a condition of its exit from the war emboldened the Ottoman Empire to turn its focus away from Palestine and toward a fight to reclaim land in the Caucasus in Russian-Armenian territory.[116]

This angered Germany, which in vain pressured Enver Pasha to direct his attention to Mesopotamia, Syria and Palestine rather than look to fulfill his imperial ambitions in the Caucasus. In late March, Germany made a breakthrough on the Western Front and needed its Ottoman ally to hold the line in the Middle East before American reinforcements arrived. Though the German offensive did succeed in drawing away British resources, it did not sway Ottoman commanders to renew their commitment to defending southern Ottoman lands. During the final months of the war, the Ottoman Empire focused on the conquest of Russian Armenia rather than engaging the Allied armies advancing along the Mediterranean.[117]

THE ROAD TO ARMISTICE

These circumstances aided the Allied advance through Palestine, Syria and Mesopotamia. Allenby's army would advance 800 kilometers capturing Damascus, Beirut and Aleppo in 1918. While the Transjordan Raids in the spring of 1918 failed to capture Amman and entailed heavy Allied loses, the Ottoman focus on the Caucasus after the signing of Brest-Litovsk strained the Central Power's ability to hold the line in the region. By summer 1918 the Allies, now bolstered by the US army's arrival in Europe, reversed German successes on the Western Front. Enver's conquest of the Caucasus and eventual success in oil-rich Baku had drawn resources eastward. It left a depleted Ottoman army in Palestine that could do little to stop the Allied advance.[118] The Battle of Megiddo at the end of September marked one of the most dramatic and important battles of this phase of the war.[119] Allied forces captured Damascus in early October and then Amman and headed south to join with Arab forces.[120] As a result of this campaign, the British brought under Allied occupation a vast swath of territory that corresponded with the Sykes–Picot vision of conquest (see Figures 2.2, 2.3 and 2.4).[121]

These victories left a broken Ottoman army that could do little to repel Allied cavalry, artillery and airpower.[122] After Megiddo, the Allies

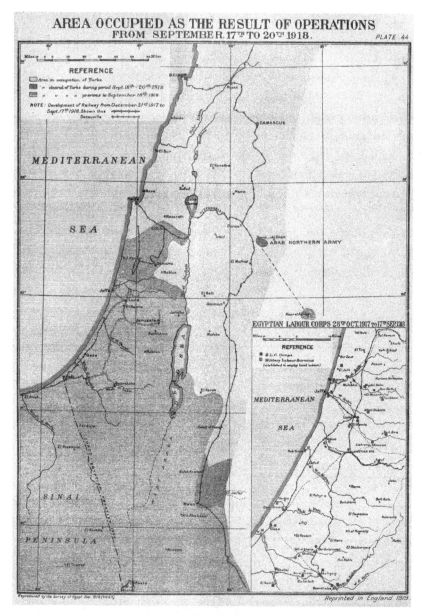

2.2. Progress of Allied occupation, September 17 to September 20, 1918. Credit: *A Brief Record of the Advance of the Egyptian Expeditionary Force: July 1917–October 1918* (1919) [plate 44].

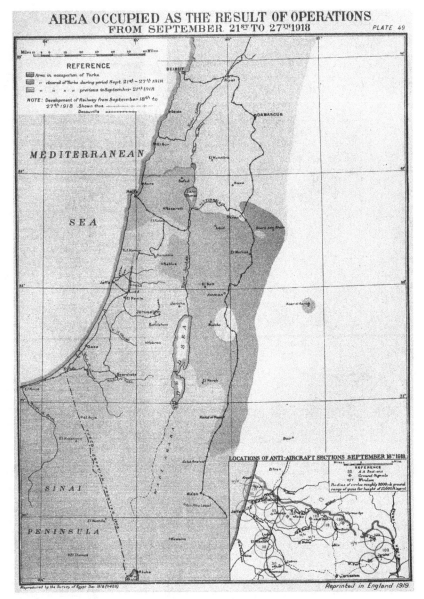

2.3. Progress of Allied occupation, September 21 to September 27, 1918. Credit: *A Brief Record of the Advance of the Egyptian Expeditionary Force: July 1917–October 1918* (1919) [plate 49].

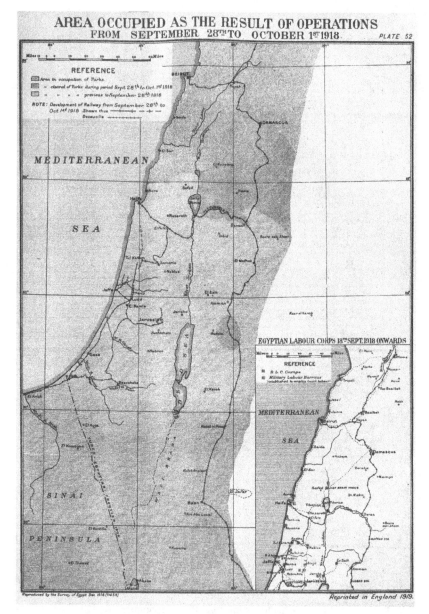

2.4. Progress of Allied occupation, September 28 to October 1, 1918. Credit: *A Brief Record of the Advance of the Egyptian Expeditionary Force: July 1917–October 1918* (1919) [plate 52].

made the 600-kilometer push beyond Aleppo which they captured on October 26. The advance on Mosul in October to secure the oilfields north of Baghdad culminated in the Battle of Sharqat and confirmed that this stage of the war in the Ottoman Empire had come to an end. Nearly 900,000 men had fought in the British armies in the Middle East starting in October 1914 to when the Armistice was signed on October 31, 1918.[123] This sacrifice and the concerted effort to sideline the French led the British to believe that the conditions of the Ottoman surrender would be theirs alone to negotiate.

The Ottoman armistice was one of a series of agreements negotiated with the vanquished Central Powers. The simmering Anglo-French rivalry determined their progress. The French unilaterally negotiated the first armistice of the war with Bulgaria on September 30, 1918, in Salonica, leaving the British out. The Treaty of Neuilly-sur-Seine resulted a little over a year later. The British took part in treaty negotiations which they argued should draw on the precedent of the Russo-Turkish War and the Balkan Wars settlements.[124] Ultimately, it ceded thousands of miles of territory to Greece, Romania and the kingdoms of Serbia, Croatia and Slovenia. Signed on November 27, 1919, the treaty demanded Bulgaria accept culpability for the war, disarm and pay reparations.

The situation was reversed in the case of the Ottoman armistice signed on October 31, 1918. Like the French had done with Bulgaria, the British unilaterally negotiated a ceasefire with the Ottoman Empire at Mudros. Immediately on hearing of the armistice, Lloyd George's top aide reported "hastily" telegraphing "a communique to London to be read out in the House of Commons explaining clearly that the British Admiral had made the Armistice."[125] Peace negotiations with the Ottoman Empire, however, would not follow the relatively smooth course of the Bulgarian precedent with a final settlement coming only in 1923.

Britain intended the armistice to both end the military conflict and settle the minority question. It therefore crafted a document that addressed the conditions of surrender and the end of continued state-sanctioned violence against Armenian, Greek and Assyrian Ottoman subjects. The Armenian Genocide influenced armistice negotiations because of the long-standing question of minority protection. The 1856 Treaty of Paris that ended the Crimean War introduced provisions that protected Ottoman religious minorities as part of the peace. The 1878

Treaty of Berlin extended these protections after the Russo-Turkish War and gave Britain explicit charge to protect Ottoman Christians.[126] Of Berlin's sixty-six articles, eleven dealt with minority civil and political rights as related to Christians and Jews. Ultimately, these provisions did little to benefit either of these populations.[127] The minority protection articles, however, marked a watershed moment regarding the obligation of a state to intervene in the internal affairs of another state on humanitarian grounds.

This history shadowed the Ottoman armistice. Vice Admiral Somerset Gough-Calthorpe negotiated with Ottoman Navy Minister Huseyin Rauf Bey aboard a ship docked in the port of Mudros. In addition to settling the terms of the ceasefire, it called for long-range involvement by the Allies in the internal affairs of the Ottoman government that extended beyond occupying strategic territory. The document also posited a responsibility to protect and defend civilian victims of state-sanctioned violence. One provision called for the pursuit of individuals accused of abusing Allied POWs and massacring Ottoman Christians.[128] On the eve of the signing of the armistice, the War Cabinet reported plans for "the formation of a tribunal" to be put in place to try war crimes and already had contacted the attorney general and key jurors.[129] Other armistice provisions included amnesty for Armenian prisoners, giving Britain charge of Turkish POWs and securing the right to occupy villages in Anatolia to prevent further massacres of Christian minorities. These broad ambitions of the armistice, though agreed to by all parties, ultimately proved untenable.

The Allies accepted the British armistice, agreeing to substitute the word "Allied" for "British" in the final document.[130] Admiral Calthorpe (1865–1937) took charge of the Mediterranean command in fall 1918, a post he held until resigning in July 1919. Remembered as an "organizer and diplomatist," Calthorpe's most significant achievement was his appointment as High Commissioner at Constantinople and negotiating the armistice at Mudros.[131] Lord Curzon praised him for making "better terms even than those expected." Curzon thought that agreement would only be reached on four clauses. In the end, the Ottomans consented to more than six times that number. This included the "right to occupy any strategical points in the event of any situation arising which threatens the security of the Allies."[132] The agreement excluded any Greek man-of-war from participating in the occupation in the vain hope that it would ease tensions between Greece and Turkey. It also included a secret clause. Clause 24 established a British mission "to Armenia to investigate the conditions there." Fear of encouraging "Armenian revolutionaries" left this clause unpublished in the final document. The discussion of the terms of the armistice in the House of Commons caused some concern because it tied Britain to protecting Ottoman subjects as a condition of the peace in an echo of the 1878 Treaty of Berlin.[133]

With over one thousand Allied ships under his command, Calthorpe set about the work of enforcing the armistice. Minesweeping commenced immediately to pave the way for the 6,000 British troops scheduled to land on November 6, 1918. Calthorpe did not anticipate needing the help of French or Italian ships, only the British Aegean squadron.[134] Naming Calthorpe High Commissioner on November 9, Foreign Secretary Balfour informed him that "he would be the official channel of communication with the Turkish Government in regard to the protection of British interests and the execution of the terms of the armistice." Balfour made Calthorpe's involvement in Ottoman internal affairs regarding religious minorities clear: "Turkish domination over subject races should be ended irrevocably."[135]

Calthorpe kept detailed records of his dealings in Constantinople and regularly reported his findings in secret dispatches to the War Cabinet. He sought to eliminate the influence of the CUP in the post-armistice Ottoman government, which was blamed for starting the war and the Armenian massacres. By the end of November, a new but notably weak government made up of "respectable elderly men without pronounced political antecedents" was installed under Ahmed Tevfik Pasha, the last Grand Vizier of the Ottoman Empire.[136] This unpopular regime threatened to delegitimize the peace process and benefit the nationalist agenda of the CUP that had run the war in the name of preserving the Ottoman Empire.[137] Resentment of the Allied presence in Constantinople and "indiscriminate flag-wagging in the Christian quarters, especially by the Greeks" further undermined the government's legitimacy.[138] Calthorpe received reassurances from the Turkish Foreign Minister that "the

Government was doing its utmost to maintain order and to loyally carry out the terms of the armistice."[139] But political intrigue by well-funded and highly visible members of the former CUP government cast doubt on these promises.

The minority issue weighed heavily on Calthorpe and his staff that November. Making little headway with the new government, they focused on humanitarian relief. Admiral Richard Webb, who assisted Calthorpe, entered into discussions with American relief workers to see what could be done for displaced Armenians. Granted the right to return to their homes, they remained "without clothing or food." Their homes in ruins or occupied by "Moslem [sic] emigrants from the Balkans and Syria" meant little possibility for repatriation and opened Armenians up to be further "persecuted." The answer: feed and clothe refugees in temporary accommodation through the winter. Webb concluded by raising the issue of establishing an Armenian state in eastern Anatolia where the "previous Christian inhabitants had been extirpated" and homeless refugees could resettle.[140]

Meanwhile, conditions deteriorated in the countryside. Despite good harvests, prices rose 4,000 percent.[141] People starved in places where food was available due to speculation, corruption and the rising cost of transportation. Distrust of the paper currency caused inflation, further contributing to widespread discontent. In Adana, one of the richest food-producing regions of the country, wartime massacres against Armenian farmers and landowners disrupted the regional economy and produced starvation on a mass scale.[142] These conditions affected the entire community, placing further pressure on a growing internal refugee crisis.

The new Ottoman government had good reason to support the Allied occupation in the beginning. Those in power pledged to uphold the rule of the Sultan and keep the CUP out of government, a position ultimately supported by Britain. The government, however, struggled to maintain its hold over the country in the face of mounting economic and political pressure. Ottoman leaders pursued a policy that placated the British in an attempt to consolidate their own power against the CUP. The government also hoped cooperation would limit territorial losses in the final peace agreement. The situation proved too difficult and threatened further instability. In late January, Calthorpe reported that the cabinet had under-gone yet another reshuffling, making it "slightly more homogeneous than the old one, but almost as weak."[143]

The possibility of immediately forging a lasting peace thus seemed increasingly out of reach. When a top Ottoman official questioned parts of the agreement, the High Commission refused to hear any "complaints ... until the great responsibility lying on the Turks" was "absolutely and completely fulfilled."[144] These included decommission-ing Turkish troops, arresting those accused of war crimes related to civilian massacres and the mistreatment of POWs and stopping the continued harassment of minority populations. The dilatory response to enforcing these terms made the British further consolidate power in Constantinople. The High Commission put increased pressure on the Ottoman government to decommission troops and took over the task of capturing accused war criminals, a duty that fell largely to Calthorpe, Webb and the military officers under his command.[145]

Meanwhile, tensions between France and Britain ran high. The French complained of administrative overreach. Calthorpe broadly inter-preted his power over Ottoman affairs to include everything from policing to public health. He started a commission to clean up Turkish prisons under the category of "sanitary reform," assumed control of the banking system and managed the interests of foreign investors still oper-ating in Constantinople in the name of securing Britain's economic and imperial influence.

CONCLUSION

Amid this increasingly anxious diplomatic and political situation, a humanitarian crisis loomed. High prices, war-damaged infrastructure and the uneven administration of national and local government char-acterized the Allied occupation. This began not long after the occupa-tion of Baghdad when the British and the French began to administer civic functions in the conquered territory. The unsteady peace raised larger issues about the sustainability of occupation. This uncertainty also affected attempts to realize war objectives through military deci-sions that increasingly included the management of civilians living on the battlefront. The question of what to do with civilians under occupation loomed large. Here on the Middle Eastern Front the seemingly incongruous humanitarian and military sides of modern war making first met. The first attempt to negotiate peace in the form of the Treaty of Sèvres began at the crossroads of these competing priorities and political interests.

PART TWO

OCCUPATION

CHAPTER 3

Civilians at War

THE OCCUPATION OF THE OTTOMAN EMPIRE BEGAN
with the fall of Baghdad to Allied forces on March 19, 1917. It
marked the beginning of a period of growing involvement in Ottoman
domestic affairs as the British army increased its footprint across
Mesopotamia. The Baghdad victory reinforced Lloyd George's vision of
what victory over the Ottoman Empire meant. This message was
delivered by Lt. Gen. Sir Stanley Maude who entered the city on horseback shortly after the battle. He issued the now infamous proclamation
that the British came to the city not "as conquerors ... but as liberators."
The Allies, according to this statement, had an unassailable plan for the
region:

> Our military operations have as their object the defeat of the enemy, and
> the driving of him from these territories. In order to complete this task,
> I am charged with absolute and supreme control of all regions in which
> British troops operate; but our armies do not come into your cities and
> lands as conquerors or enemies, but as liberators ... It is the wish not only
> of my King and his peoples, but it is also the wish of great nations with
> whom he is in alliance, that you should prosper.[1]

Read today as a thinly veiled attempt to win Arab support, internal
Foreign Office memos suggest that this declaration had another purpose.
Acknowledging that few in this "stricken deserted city" would hear the
words spoken by Maude in the square that day, the British targeted
a wider audience.[2] The idea of liberation, officials believed, would reson-
ant most powerfully with those diverse ethno-religious Ottoman subjects

living in "Syria, Lebanon and Palestine" displaced by war and genocide who would soon find themselves under Allied control.[3]

The conquest of Baghdad led Britain to create and consolidate a network of camps and auxiliary aid institutions in collaboration with the French and international and regional humanitarian aid organizations. The idea was to secure non-combatant allies in the contest against the Ottoman Empire. At the same time, claims of liberating the oppressed justified the war back in Europe. Civilians had become a new kind of weapon of war who in exchange for humanitarian aid provided conquering forces a potentially docile, grateful and dependent population that would help secure and legitimate Allied hold over the region.

Liberation for those living under military occupation in reality meant relative security in exchange for submission to a new regime of administration and control. No institution represented this devil's bargain more than the refugee camp which emerged as an important tool to manage civilian populations on the Middle Eastern Front. As Allied troops swept across the region, these camps and their auxiliary institutions provided medical, food and clothing aid due to the destruction of vital infrastructure, social services and the local economy. Occupation raised as many questions about future governance as it did about new ways to manage populations during wartime.[4] It also blurred the lines between the needs of civilians and those permanently displaced persons categorized as refugees.

Aid organizations and the military initially focused on victims of the Armenian Genocide.[5] After Baghdad, the plight of Ottoman Christian minorities guided the development of the camp regime but eventually gave way to a broader charge. Diverse local Muslim, Christian and Jewish communities received aid through the vehicle of the camp transforming the humanitarian project into a collaboration between state and non-state actors in the context of emerging international norms and institutions. This had important implications for internally displaced people who needed food, medical assistance and refugees coming from surrounding regions seeking Allied protection in the zone of occupation alike.

The refugee camp in its earliest articulation was the product of negotiations between military, humanitarian and regional actors in the context of total war which blurred the boundaries between the home front and battle front. The First World War made civilians into victims on a mass scale on all battlefronts and they played a central role in the prosecution of the war. In the Middle East, the treatment of civilians in wartime underwent a radical transformation with the invention of the refugee camp as revealed in official documents and archival records and the experiences of refugee and aid workers. The League of Nations would eventually create new protections for minorities and displaced persons predicated on rights-based appeals. Humanitarian aid organizations also supported these claims.[6] Before any of that could take place, the practices and beliefs about the obligation to deliver aid and care for civilians needed to be reimagined.

The concentration camp emerged as a humanitarian institution after Baghdad. In the Middle East, it transformed into a site of refuge intended to temporarily house those displaced by war, genocide and famine while furthering Allied war objectives. Those made homeless by the war experienced the Allied conquest beginning with the capture of Baghdad most profoundly. Hundreds of voluntary camps run and funded by alliances between local, international and regional humanitarian organizations and the military proliferated in its wake and punctuated the landscape from Constantinople to Baghdad to Port Said (Figure 3.1).

The rise of the refugee camp on the Middle Eastern Front shows the interdependent relationship between humanitarianism and geopolitics, which relied on a dynamic of "coercion and care."[7] The "secret solidarity" identified by Giorgio Agamben as existing between humanitarian organizations whose focus is to provide aid and the state which seeks control over subject populations for its own ends needs empirical investigation.[8] This solidarity grew up by design, marrying humanitarian aid with combat operations. It resulted from the wartime crisis and the history of western engagement with relief work in the Middle East. In the First World War refugee camp, the two seemingly incongruent sides of waging modern war – military and humanitarian – first met.

Maude's claim that the British came as liberators thus needs to be taken seriously as a rhetorical strategy that framed perceptions of the Allied invasion and transformed the actual care of civilian populations under occupation as a humanitarian concern. Attributed to Mark Sykes, Maude's statement reflected an imperial positioning that held that aid work would serve British interests, in part, by facilitating indirect rule over the former territories of the Ottoman Empire.[9] It was a strategy that

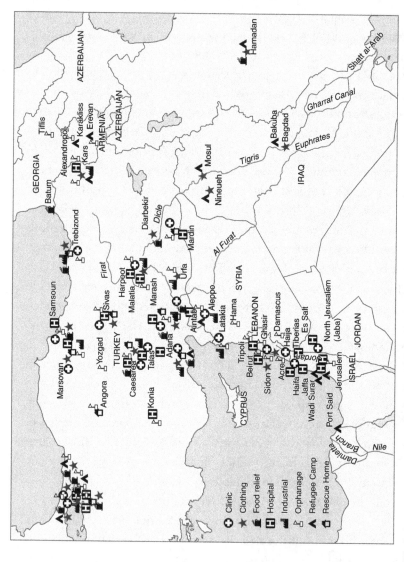

3.1. Map of Allied supported and run refugee camps and auxiliary aid sites in the Middle East during the First World War. Credit: Data mapped by Hilla Sang, Ph.D. ORCID: https://orcid.org/0000-0003-0679-7367.

had long-term consequences for inhabitants, those seeking refuge in newly captured territories and the redrawing of the map of a region where modern humanitarianism found its early articulation and purpose.[10] Secular and missionary relief efforts led to the international-ization of humanitarian aid after the war while remaining rooted in nineteenth-century paternalism and imperial imaginings about the Holy Land. In this way, older forms of humanitarian activism worked alongside imperial and military agendas to create a modern humanitar-ian ethos that eventually included the acknowledgment of the rights and obligations of refugees by the international community.[11] It is worth, then, considering more fully the site where this wartime humanitarian mandate played out in its most recognizable and enduring form.

RISE OF THE REFUGEE CAMP

The concentration camp took shape as an internationalized space of humanitarian relief under British supervision in the Middle East during the First World War. The refugee camp today has been naturalized as a product of failed international idealism and political expediency and serves as a timeless reminder of the plight of displaced peoples. As an institution, it emerged at the crossroads of imperial priorities, wartime crisis and a longer philanthropic tradition that had its roots in the Victorian period.[12] The refugee camp became part of the defining experience of displacement in the British domestic and imperial context.[13] In the Middle East, this form of "refugeedom," in Peter Gatrell's formulation, constituted the conditions under which displaced persons became dependent on British colonial power which both conferred privileges and created exclusions.[14] Politicians, philanthropists and administrators oversaw the ordering of the lives of refugees relocated to camps due to forces deter-mined by political expediency and humanitarian necessity.

Literature on the concentration camp has focused largely on the German experience beginning with Namibia and continuing through to the Holocaust. This work has contributed to understanding the longer history of the camp as a system of control before the Second World War and has led historians to explore how Europeans used concentration camps to manage subject populations starting in the mid -nineteenth century. Most prominently associated with the Boer War (1899–1902), concentration camps first appeared during Cuba's war with Spain (1868–1878). They subsequently were used during the Cuban Independence War (1895), the US War in the Philippines (1899–1902) and as a tool to quell revolt in German Southwest Africa (1904–1907).[15] Considering the refugee camp in the context of the history of the concentration camp reveals the peculiarity and historical specificity of the institution. The First World War created emergency conditions for combatant and non-combatant populations alike, which meant that Middle East refugee camps emerged as part of a larger world of wartime camps established in and around Europe. Studies of the internment of POWs and civilians in concentration camps have shown that states incarcerated and cared for populations because they posed a potential threat to the state, needed protection or served a war-related function.[16]

Camps that concentrated large numbers of non-combatants became known as refugee camps, a term that emerged to explain the conditions of temporary internment of civilians during the Boer War in southern Africa fought between the Boers and the British.[17] Colonial wars and the rise of professional militaries and bureaucratic administrative apparatus subsequently provided the opportunity and means for the internment of large numbers of civilians.[18] Born out of military necessity – controlling the movement of civilian populations in states of emergency – and humanitarian idealism and practice, the refugee camp struck a precarious balance between expediency and assistance. The refugee camp, in this articulation, stood in sharp distinction to concentration camps supported by totalitarian regimes that emerged after the First World War in Germany and Russia that relied on states of emergency to legitimize the indefinite internment of civilians considered either as "undesirables" or "enemies of the state."[19]

The invention of the idea of the refugee camp as a space for the humane treatment of civilians and its association with British practice mattered. Not all Europeans saw the treatment of civilians during war and times of civil unrest in the same way. According to Isabel Hull, Germans labeled missionaries who questioned the treatment of internees in camps in Southwest Africa during the Herero and Nama revolt as "traitors." The British military and government, by contrast, allowed civilian oversight of camps that held civilians even in the midst of war.[20] A free press, parliamentary political debate and public engagement with the humanitarian movement together proved "a brake on documented abuses."[21] The British used the camp in both domestic and imperial settings after the Boer War, which served as a laboratory for how to intern civilian populations.[22] High death rates due to bad conditions in the camp were meticulously recorded by critics. Significantly, authorities paid attention and attempted to address these findings. That Britain looked for models to encourage the humane treatment of civilian populations under pressure does not negate the fact that the refugee camp existed to achieve political ends and could result in the maltreatment of internees. During the First World War, Britain systematized refugee camps as a military response to humanitarian disaster.[23]

In the Middle East, the refugee camp under British supervision manifested itself as a new site of control that responded to wartime conditions. Ottoman authorities had concentrated Christian minorities in camps during the Armenian Genocide to exterminate them.[24] Refugee camps grew up in many of the same locations after the capture of Baghdad. Acknowledging the Ottoman imperial context of the rise of the concentration camp contributes to understandings of the plight of civilians during the First World War.[25] So, too, does studying the ways and locations where aid was delivered to refugees. The refugee camp represented a pragmatic response to changing circumstances on the battlefield after the British and French mission replaced Ottoman and German authority.

Historians have mapped First World War Ottoman concentration camps to provide evidence of the Armenian Genocide and also to show German complicity in the killings because they did not investigate what was happening at camps in jurisdictions where they held influence as the Ottoman Empire's most important ally.[26] The extermination camp turned refugee camp, repurposed as a site of refuge, did not inherit the function of the Ottoman concentration camp as death camp. Camps were, however, administrative spaces where civilians had little choice but to watch and wait for the war to end in the hopes of returning home. Seemingly liberated from the bonds of one empire, those who used the camps consented to disciplinary regimes necessitated by the war and negotiated by humanitarian, political, military actors and refugees themselves.

The refugee camp thus emerged as an ameliorative site, born of modern war, which operated within a set of evolving assumptions about the obligation to protect vulnerable populations seeking aid. In the nascent camp regime, new understandings of the relationship between war and the treatment of civilians took shape. Concentration camps had housed vulnerable populations before but never on this geographic scale and never after genocide. Refugee camps in the Middle East made use of a set of formal and informal practices developed from earlier and contemporary models. The realities of caring for civilians in a war zone determined the character of the refugee camp. Its purpose and scope relied on the wartime situation where the material needs of internees, the war objectives of military personnel and the missions of aid workers and international institutions determined the camp's function.

THE FIRST WORLD WAR AND THE CAMP REGIME

The crisis of world war gave states across Europe increased powers to control combatant and non-combatant populations in designated spaces in an emerging regulatory framework. Though rules set out in the Geneva and, later, Hague Conventions did not deal specifically with civilians, they proved an essential first step in addressing the human cost of total war. These international agreements focused on eliminating violence and destruction not related to military objectives and aims while at the same time defining the status of combatants and guaranteeing equal treatment for POWs.[27] Britain's culture of legalism, press scrutiny and pressure from public opinion led it to embrace these emerging standards set out in the context of the laws of war that, in the case of the Boer War, extended to the colonial context.[28] This, coupled with a growing belief in Britain at this time in the possibility that the welfare state could eliminate social ills, including hunger and disease, by providing ameliorative services, made it possible to imagine a refugee camp run in collaboration by government-run military forces and private aid organizations that delivered assistance to vulnerable populations.[29]

The idea that refugees deserved protection and aid was not new. That the conquering power bore responsibility for their well-being was and resulted in the codification of the category of refugee in this moment.[30] The obligation to provide refuge came from an Enlightenment humanitarian ethos.[31] The camp regime would not have been possible without an already existing set of beliefs that held that refugees deserved some sort of protection. According to Caroline Shaw, Britons saw refugee relief as a "matter of dignity owed to foreigners" and "an act of liberal justice and humanitarianism."[32] First understood along confessional lines, "refugee" entered the English language in reference to French Huguenots whom the British saw as persecuted Protestant co-religionists and believed that they had a duty to defend even if it meant intervening in the affairs of a sovereign state.[33] By the late nineteenth century, the British embraced Orthodox Christians – largely comprising Armenians, Greeks and Assyrians, who were a significant minority in the Ottoman Empire – as oppressed co-religionists like the Huguenots before them.[34] Moralizing rhetoric and pressure to reform, rather than military intervention, historically guided humanitarian engagement and promises of liberation from Ottoman rule.[35] During the war, this same population would find themselves in Middle East refugee camps as the early beneficiaries of aid.

Providing refuge to oppressed Ottoman minorities proved a useful war strategy. It offered a reason to fight the First World War which, by 1917, had turned from heroic struggle to stalemate on the Western Front. Lloyd George's "Great Crusade," as he called a collection of his wartime speeches, found its just cause on the Middle Eastern Front in the defense of small nationalities, most notably the Assyrians and Armenians.[36] Allied promises made to incite the Arab Revolt against the Ottoman Empire in 1916 created new alliances, adding to a growing list of unmet obligations that promised to free populations living under Ottoman rule.[37] These pledges led to the creation of so-called "Arab camps" that though providing aid and assistance were structured along a racialized hierarchy. This contributed to casting Arabs as unequal allies who needed to be managed, sometimes by force.[38] The construction of humanitarianism around religious, racial and political understandings of refuge had its companion in the militarization of the refugee problem which understood civilians as important to wartime objectives. Total war in the East required a new set of strategies and practices that made the humanitarian movement and war machine strange bedfellows.

Refugee camps worked because they controlled the bodies of their subjects. The biopolitical project of the camp came from the need to manage civilian populations in what Foucault called the "game of freedom and security" which led to institutional surveillance constitutive of the systems of control that characterized occupation.[39] While largely ad hoc in its articulation during the war, it would result in the eventual bureaucratization of the humanitarian program reliant on existing military models used to detain combatants.[40] Conversely, the military drew upon decades-long humanitarian practice rooted in a secular paternalism that shaped its new charge to care for civilians. These overlapping missions informed the way the international community subsequently managed populations and embraced the refugee camp as a political and humanitarian tool. In the end, the close association of aid work with war making undermined the humanitarian project by institutionalizing solidarity with the very forces which created the conditions for intervention in the first place.

The extent of the crisis, however, ensured that no single institution, idea or agenda created the refugee camp marking its invention as contested and contingent on the rapidly changing conditions of the war. As the Allied advance into Mesopotamia gained strength after Baghdad, the problem of mass civilian displacement due to combat operations and forced migration became clear. The Armenian Genocide already had created a massive internal refugee crisis after it began in spring 1915. Over 130,000 Armenian refugees still remained in and around Mesopotamia alone.[41] Ottoman concentration camps that marked the deportation routes across Anatolian into the Syrian desert ceased operation after the Allied occupation. Almost immediately, refugee camps, orphanages, hospitals and food and clothing distribution centers sprung up in their place. Formerly sites of horror and fear along the deportation route, this new trail of camps and auxiliary services represented for many the once unthinkable possibility of getting home.

Internment in a refugee camp was voluntary and, not unlike Victorian workhouses, seen for many as a necessary last resort. The material conditions of the war created the camp as a series of accommodations and collaborations intended to sustain "bare life" but also one which required the consent of internees.[42] Agamben's concept of the *soglia* or threshold opens the possibility of reading negotiated space within the camp that challenge the "clear and stable distinction between an inside and an outside."[43] This instability created what human geographers call a "spatial economy" made possible through modern technologies of war, sanitation and ecological mastery over the landscape that determined how refugees interacted with one another, the camp leaders and the institutions within the borders of the enclosure.[44] As the recollections of those who experienced and made decisions about whether to seek aid reveal, participation in the biopolitical project of the camps to manage vulnerable bodies created new obligations and forms of consent that made relief work integral to controlling population movement.

Power over the body could not be totalized in the institution of the voluntary camp organized on a shared axis of power which closely but unevenly governed private and public life. The tension between Foucault's notion of biopolitics as a system of control dispersed across a horizontal axis of power and Agamben's interpretation of the camp as a vertically organized, totalizing biopolitical institution played out in this camp regime.[45] Those who used the camps understood the intimate and evolving relationship between military and humanitarian actors under the colonial conditions which Agamben argues makes the camp possible.[46] Local and regional organizations participated in aid work challenging military and western aid worker dictates and advocating for better material conditions and privileges for internees.

At the same time, strict disciplinary methods ensured control over subject bodies. Aid workers themselves existed within the hierarchies of camp life. The "gendered activity of war" determined how female nurses and supervisors employed in military service enforced discipline and navigated the demands of male administrators.[47] Women workers, despite their subordinate gender status, had important responsibilities which reinforced their authority in the camp. These myriad actors, interests and structures diffused the potential to completely control the lives of refugees and shaped the way camps and auxiliary institutions – orphanages, food distribution centers, hospitals and clinics – functioned up through the end of the combat operations in the early 1920s.

Three well-documented camps located around Baghdad, Jerusalem and Port Said illustrate how populations were managed during the war. They were part of a larger network of camps and auxiliary institutions that housed anywhere from a few hundred to tens of thousands of displaced persons, mostly on the outskirts of towns and settlements. Refugees in the largest, most organized camps lived in tents, while others, in less formal camps housing only a few dozen, took shelter in abandoned hotels or houses under the supervision of aid organizations and or the military.[48] In 1918, the British military set up a camp, in what would become the Iraq mandate thirty miles northeast of Baghdad at Baquba, for Armenian and Assyrian refugees. At Wadi Surar, local Arab populations, displaced during the siege of Jerusalem and supported by the American Red Cross (ARC) and Near East Relief (NER), lived with refugees from across the region. The British opened the longest standing camp at Port Said, initially to house Armenians rescued by the French during the genocide. After Baghdad, they handed it over to the military to be run in association with regional and international humanitarian organizations.

Ultimately, Britain's leadership in combat operations and plan to divide up the southern regions of the Ottoman Empire with its French ally determined how this new regime worked.[49] Together these camps reveal the amalgam of interests and experiments that determined the status and treatment of non-combatants. The portrait of the refugee camp that emerges from these representative examples as a purpose-built tool to manage civilian populations in wartime reveals how the history of internment became tightly bound up with military operations and humanitarianism during the Great War.

SETTING UP CAMP

Amid swift victories and political uncertainty emerged the first refugee camps. The camp at Baquba near Baghdad was the largest and focused on civilians; others at Bahar and Yanghi Khan outside of Hamadan focused on recruiting men to fight on the side of the Allies. Baquba was described by Brigadier General H. H. Austin who commanded the camp as a "tented city" on a nearly two-mile stretch along the uncultivated bank of the Diala River. At its peak, 8 military staff and 3,000 British and Indian personnel and 35 "English ladies" took charge of 50,000 Assyrian and Armenian men, women and children along with their 15,000 animals who had fled to the newly Allied occupied territory.[50]

The Baquba camp was explicitly modeled on turn-of-the-century Boer War camps. But Baquba did not belong to the category of "death camps" memorialized in W. T. Stead's scathing critique.[51] Evidence suggests that the military had learned something from the controversy over these camps where tens of thousands of Afrikaner civilians perished.[52] When Baquba switched from military control to civil administration in late 1919, the Lieutenant in charge justified "the heavy expenditure" at Baquba due to the comparatively low death rate in relation to Boer War camps.[53] Middle East camps did share a similar purpose: to manage vulnerable populations. However, the British were not at war with those who voluntarily interned themselves at these camps. They thus resembled internment camps for "unsettled" civilians operating during this time in Britain.[54] Baquba proved an important model which guided the mission of the refugee camp after Baghdad. The Allies wanted to ensure the loyalty of the Armenians, Assyrians, Arabs and others in the camps while preventing non-combatants from helping the enemy.

There was also the imperative to generate positive news about the war. Austin subtitled his book about Baquba, "An Account of Work on Behalf of the Persecuted Assyrian Christians" and sought "to portray the efforts on the part of Great Britain to afford security and relative comfort to these refugees in Mesopotamia."[55] Foreign Office correspondence shows the desire to "obtain publicity for the very excellent work" at Baquba for public distribution. The *Illustrated London News*, at the behest of the Foreign Office, told readers of "the beneficent results of the British occupation of Mesopotamia" which highlighted work done on behalf of refugees.[56]

Aid flooded in from private and government organizations, which included the Lord Mayor's Fund, Armenian Red Cross and the American Relief Commission during the camp's three-year existence. Access to clean water and rations, arriving weekly by train, led some to compare the camp to a "European town."[57] Schools were set up along with "industrial workshops" and medical and recreation facilities.[58] The camp resembled in some ways western-led relief projects in the Ottoman Empire before the war. Modeled on the Victorian self-help philanthropic tradition, interned residents were required to help run the camp and contribute to their own upkeep through a gendered division of labor.[59] Men not enrolled by the military did construction and maintained the camp while women worked in the workshops sewing, weaving and making lace.[60]

Basic needs and security were guaranteed only if residents stayed in the self-contained world of the camp. Physically divided between an Assyrian and Armenian section, the British believed that separating these populations would ease management and prevent a permanent settlement from forming which could limit military control over the camp's function.[61] The camp was purpose built on the outskirts of Baquba for a similar reason. Inhabitants relied on outside aid for subsistence and needed permission to leave, which kept the population removed from the local economy except for a weekly bazaar staged at the camp. Though it had an appearance of permanence with its city-like functions, institutions and civic life, the camp relied entirely on the yearly budget of 2.3 million pounds provided by the British government.[62] The camp's closed economic system and distance from town meant that residents lived in a marginalized transitional state that ensured their dependence on the military.

Cambridge graduate Lt. Dudley Stafford Northcote was a camp supervisor. Northcote had had no previous experience with relief work. As he wrote to his mother, looking after refugees was "quite a change from soldiering."[63] By spring 1919, the camp housed 45,000 refugees. Northcote took his job seriously, learning Armenian and participating in the daily life and rituals of the refugees. But he knew that ultimately his job would be to "repatriate" his charges. The only question was where. Britain and France still wrangled over the details of administering Syria, Mesopotamia, Lebanon and Palestine as mandates. In August 1920, Northcote got an order to settle refugees in the British mandate of Mesopotamia and moved them to a transitional camp outside of Basra called Nahr Umar.

Residents understood the contradictions embodied in this project. Levon Shahoian was eleven when he arrived at the camp. His family had fled their native village in northwestern Persia, trekked over 700 miles, and ended up first in Baquba, and then Nahr Umar seeking Allied protection.[64] Shahoian remembered the camp as a lifeline where he learned English and waited, trusting that the British would make resettlement possible. Though it did not happen in the way Shahoian and his family expected, he believed the refugee camp had helped heal "deep wounds."[65] After years of uncertainty and exile, many refugees like Shahoian felt secure in the guarded camp despite complaints of boredom, inadequate schools and restrictions on movement. When his brother was arrested for leaving the camp without permission, the family negotiated a way for him to travel to the local village to obtain supplies for a small shop the military allowed him to start.[66] For Shahoian's family, military protection, order and, most importantly, access to resources meant the possibility of starting again.

Others resisted camp mandates. When the military tried to organize an infantry battalion, Armenians refused, worrying that they would be sent to India to fight.[67] While many Assyrians signed up, Armenian resistance led to appeals for help from the exiled Armenian Patriarch Zaven who arrived in Baghdad during the British advance.[68] He had been engaging in aid work supported by the church in the occupied region in collaboration with the British occupying force. Though deeply respected by camp inhabitants, he was unable to change the minds of the 850 men. The Patriarch eventually came to believe that the men were right to resist but nevertheless sent representatives to the camp to prevent "any rupture" with the British.[69] As a result, the alliance between Armenian leaders and the British military along with aid work in the Allied occupied zone continued uninterrupted.

As the occupation wore on, the British began to see these collaborations as expendable. After the Treaty of Sèvres, signed in August 1920, failed to end the war, the British government reevaluated its commitments to civilians under their protection in the Middle East and announced that the camp would close due to cost. Refugees willing to leave voluntarily were promised a small food ration. Northcote successfully lobbied the Colonial Office for more time and launched a public campaign.[70] The Lord Mayor's Fund took charge with the government's consent and hired Northcote to escort the refugees to Erevan in the newly established state of Armenia. Transporting thousands of refugees from the camp in Basra to Erevan, where no infrastructure existed to support such a large influx of people, with few resources tested Northcote's faith in the mission.[71] Though no one expected the temporary camps to continue indefinitely, the conditions of the war strained the uneasy alliance between refugees and the military. Only after peace with the Ottoman Empire was finalized with the signing of the Lausanne Treaty did the responsibility to deliver and manage aid shift more squarely to international institutions and volunteer humanitarian aid organizations.[72]

Military-administered aid to civilian populations all but ended after the fall of the Ottoman Empire and the advent of the mandate system. A failed tool in the attempt at resettlement, camps like Baquba nevertheless provided necessary temporary assistance for those caught in the confusion of the winding down of the war. After the camp closed, Shahoian left for Baghdad on a barge with his family. Though he missed the protection of the camp, freedom of movement, access to the city and aid from the church made integration possible with the Baghdad Arab community who welcomed them, he recalled in his memoir, "as if we were their relatives."[73] In some ways they were. The oppression suffered by Arabs under the Ottomans during the war put tremendous pressure on these populations particularly after the Arab Revolt.[74] Cooperation between different communities that had suffered under Ottoman rule provided a way to start again after aid ended for some. For tens of thousands of others, disbanding the camps and attempted resettlement by humanitarian organizations led to less certain fates in Armenia and the Iraq mandate.[75] Reforging community after the war, however, was possible and took place in the intimate spaces of families like the Shahoians who saw their fate determined in relationship to Allied war objectives.

Humanitarianism thus worked within the confines set up by the military which initially shaped the institutionalization of aid. The world of the camp relied on the investment of both military and humanitarian organizations and created a space for temporary aid to have long-term effects. As Northcote's and Shahoian's experiences suggest, the administration and institutionalization of aid relied on the union between military expediency, humanitarian idealism and accommodations made by the refugees themselves. This model of dealing with non-combatants during wartime would find further definition on the front line near Jerusalem.

"SAND AND TENTS"

"The first impression of Wadi Surar was of sand and tent; tents and sand," reported one Red Cross Nurse assigned to the "hot and cheerless" camp on the outskirts of Jerusalem.[76] For those driven from their homes during the assault on Jerusalem, the "primitive" camp embodied life under occupation. Plans for the camp located along the rail line outside of the city began in the spring of 1918 after reports of the mass displacement caused by Allenby's assault and push to take the Sinai Peninsula, Syria and Palestine reached Allied command. Tens of thousands of people were made homeless while those who remained faced economic hardship and a lack of basic services.

Invited by Allenby now headquartered at Ramleh [Ramla] thirty miles outside of Jerusalem to undertake aid work, the American Red Cross quickly established itself at Wadi Surar. It soon had a network of camps behind the front lines. After the occupation, as had happened around Baghdad, refugees flooded into the occupied zone despite the ongoing conflict. Hospitals, clinics, schools and workrooms were established to employ refugees and initially took charge of the care of the local population. This included mostly Muslim Arabs, many of whom came from the surrounding community, as well as Greeks, Jews and Armenians. Eventually, the camp housed mainly Armenians seeking protection from massacre. ARC managed this mission for the British military with help from local, regional and international organizations. This "quasi-private, quasi-state organization" was part of President Wilson's humanitarian war strategy after the United States entered the war in the spring of 1917.[77] ARC provided aid workers, nurses and funding proving itself an ideal support institution for the Allied mission. Echoing Lloyd George's rhetoric, Wilson cited humanitarianism as a wartime obligation. Between June 1917 and 1919, ARC established a strong presence across Europe and in the Middle East establishing its own "War Council" in Washington DC to coordinate relief work related to Allied operations.[78] ARC ran twelve hospitals and sixteen medical dispensaries to serve refugee and local populations in and around Jerusalem alone and was well integrated into the British model of relief work.[79]

That aid workers immediately followed Allenby's army made a show of a military mission that brought humanitarian relief. Ottoman authorities previously allowed only the Red Crescent Society and the American Committee for Armenian and Syrian Relief to operate under tightly controlled conditions. Allenby enlisted the American Red Cross to work in "the direct service of the British forces" after Jerusalem fell and laid out extensive plans for civilian relief work.[80] ARC joined Near East Relief, the successor to the American Committee for Armenian and Syrian Relief, which stepped up its aid efforts after the invasion. British-run organizations including the Lord Mayor's Fund and those run by the Quakers, the Archbishop of Canterbury and Save the Children joined secular and religious regional aid organizations. The Armenian General Benevolent Union (AGBU), with headquarters in Cairo, was an Armenian-run aid organization that engaged in refugee relief as did the Assyrian Church and Armenian Apostolic Church. The British-based Armenian Red Cross also got involved. While Greeks, Muslim and Christian Arabs, Turks, Jews, Kurds, Maronites, Yazidis and others received aid, it was the Armenians and Assyrians who initially garnered the most visible support because of ongoing massacres and a history of engagement with their plight by western-led philanthropic organizations. Famine conditions and increased fighting in southern Ottoman lands as a result of the Arab Revolt increased the pressure to provide services and aid to those indigenous communities who found themselves in the Allied occupation zone.[81]

In this way, the British military began to reconstruct social services through promoting humanitarian aid supported by ARC and NER. This "British help," as one Armenian refugee called it, facilitated the management of civilian populations and ultimately Allied territorial gains in the face of an uncertain Arab alliance after the defeat of the Ottoman Empire and its German ally in these territories.[82] Populations were divided at camps along ethno-religious lines and learned how to live under occupation while trying to find a way to return home. Refugees adapted to the new regime where English language, traditions and order ruled.

Allenby immediately set about erasing Ottoman and German influence over civilian functions. German-run hospitals, orphanages and missions were handed over to ARC, which renamed buildings, replaced

German language textbooks and reeducated children in the Anglo-American tradition.[83] "Reconstruct[ing] the country" along these lines, one ARC official told a cheering audience, was the best way of "fighting the Hun" in the Middle East.[84] Refugees, it turned out, had the potential to be a new kind of ally who could help maintain a strong Allied presence so long as they did not get in the way.

Running a camp in a war zone necessarily required collaboration between the military and humanitarian organizations. The American-based NER did not have ties to the military. It operated alongside ARC and bolstered the widespread wartime consensus on the importance of US humanitarian intervention. Postwar humanitarianism eventually embraced a secular, apolitical and international mission under the auspices of NER, Save the Children, Quaker Friends Relief, the Lord Mayor's Fund and the League of Nations.[85] But in the midst of ongoing war, the tens of thousands of civilians on the move crisscrossing battle lines required a different kind of solution to ensure that cavalry could move unimpeded by caravans of refugees. ARC alone contributed nearly 6 million dollars to the work.[86]

American dollars coupled with British military infrastructure, ground support and the integration of humanitarianism with Allied strategy made the frontline refugee camp a reality. "In all Jerusalem, the color of war prevails," recalled an ARC nurse, "on the dust-peppered olive trees of the gray and dusty city, in the haze that envelops the lorries, the cavalry, the infantry always on the move northwards."[87] Managing refugees here proved more difficult than around now relatively quiet Baghdad. At the same time, the camp made it possible to better control movements on the front line as well as how the international community understood the war, its purpose and the people upon whose behalf the Allies claimed to be fighting.

The photographic representation of the refugee camp merged military and humanitarian imaginings of aid work. The western public would have been familiar with images of starving and destitute women and children in news media, pamphlets and donor appeals.[88] What Heidi Fehrenbach calls the "humanitarian eye" became trained on the plight of civilians in wartime.[89] Wadi Surar provided a new opportunity to see aid work through the lens of the larger mission of the war. ARC distributed

Colonel Finley standing in a group of Armenian boys, who are about to leave Jerusalem for the refugee encampment at Port Said

3.2. Refugee camp children under American Red Cross supervision at Wadi Surar. Credit: John Finley, "Palestine Just Over the Horizon," *The Red Cross Magazine* 14, no. 1 (January 1919): 61.

3.3. Adults at the refugee camp – "Morning Call of the Sanitary Division," Jerusalem. Credit: John Finley, "The Red Cross in Palestine," *Asia: Journal of the American Asiatic Association* 19, no. 1 (January 1919): 14.

images for publication in newspapers and magazines which included camp supervisors in military uniform taking charge of well-cared-for children (Figure 3.2). The "sanitary division" of the ARC mission in Jerusalem was represented as organizing daily routines under regimented military-style supervision for adults (Figure 3.3). Tents at Wadi Surar appeared clean and orderly sheltering refugees productively engaged in school activities, despite the harsh and desolate surroundings (Figure 3.4). The takeover of German institutions by Allied humanitarian forces was depicted in photographs as a positive outcome of the benevolence and efficiency of occupation (Figure 3.5). In this way, western

3.4. Top: boys outside of Wadi Surar Camp. Bottom: school promotion ceremony for children in a desert refugee camp school. Credit: "The American Red Cross in the 'Land of the Philistines,'" *The Touchstone and the American Art Student Magazine,* January 1919, 282.

3.5. Orphanage for Syrian children previously run by Germans and taken over by the Allies in 1918. Credit: John Finley, "The Red Cross in Palestine," *Asia: Journal of the American Asiatic Association* 19, no. 1 (January 1919): 14.

audiences were asked to see the prosecution of the war as irrevocably tied to humanitarian aid.

Humanitarian relief workers brought their own agendas. Many of the mostly female nurses stationed at the camp had previous experience with relief work in the Middle East as members of missionary and secular aid organizations that had operated in the region starting in the late nineteenth century.[90] As employees of ARC, they understood their job as part of the war effort. "The whole country is a camp and war the main business," observed one nurse.[91] The battalion of largely unmarried American- and British-born nurses found in war work an opportunity to support Allied objectives as trained professionals.[92] Paid substantially less than the men who commanded these units, women ran the day-to-day activities of the camp from sanitation to health care to education and embodied the contradictions of women's service during the war as paid but nevertheless undervalued workers.[93] This incongruity – highly trained professionals relegated to auxiliary status – resulted from gendered assumptions about women's nature as mothers who would care for refugees as they might their own children. As Peter Gatrell argues about women aid workers in Russia in this period, poor remuneration resulted from assumptions that relegated women's public role to an extension of private responsibility to the family.[94]

For the largely well-educated middle-class women nurses, the job little resembled running a household. Many found the demands that came from working in a war zone fulfilling and embraced difficult assignments.[95] "I like my job. It contains great possibilities," commented Rosa Lee who came to the camp as a social worker to seek opportunities not open to her at home.[96] "Only a few days behind the advancing troops," ARC nurses organized social services to stem an outbreak of cholera in Tiberias after Allenby took the city in late September.[97] Those who believed that the business of modern war left them underpaid and under-appreciated had little recourse to challenge the male-dominated hierarchy of the camps. The small number of nurses who questioned their status found sex discrimination and low salaries justified by their male superiors on the grounds that they needed only support themselves while serving as temporary workers during the wartime emergency.[98]

Aid workers brought with them their own racial hierarchies as well. Plans for the expansion of the camp in summer 1918 required money and labor. To transform Wadi Surar from tents and sand, ARC engineers and British "Sanitary Officers" planned a city-like design along the lines of the Baquba camp with well-laid-out segregated sections, fifty tents per block, capable of housing 3,500 refugees organized along ethno-religious lines with a hospital, schools and workrooms.[99] "Disinfecting" refugees was the first order of business, a job given to American and European female nurses who assumed authority over male and female, young and old bodies. A humiliating ordeal for refugees who regardless of their state of health had to strip down together, nurses were reassured that they would not have to touch patients but only get correct names and statistics about their physical condition.[100] Nurses complained about community prac-tices and a lack of discipline among "native" workers and saw it as their duty to impose order in the camp over their charges. The hospital was situated in a barbed-wire enclosure with a guard placed at the entrance to assist in this task and prevent "continuous visiting and mingling of sick and well." The "order" and "efficiency" of the camp, one nurse claimed, remained "a source of amazement and incomprehension to the Oriental mind."[101]

Deeply engrained paternalism and cultural hierarchies shaped per-ceptions of refugees and the purpose of the camp itself.[102] Controlling sandflies, obtaining building materials and the all-important water supply topped concerns. So, too, did access to labor. While women sewed in the workrooms, men worked on the construction and maintenance of the camp. A "refugee force" was needed to "complete the various jobs in the camp" which, although paid, often entailed hard labor.[103] While Armenians were praised for their willingness to work, Arabs were disparaged for not taking assigned jobs and dismissed as lazy by authorities. "All methods to induce the rank and file of the male Arabs to work seem to have failed," commented one supervisor.[104] After the Armenians were transferred to Port Said, ARC leaders considered the possibility of "forced labor" as the only solution.[105] Though the archive does not reveal whether or not "compulsory labor" as it was also called was implemented, the discontent of internees suggests that conditions already had begun to deteriorate.[106] As one child put it: "We do not like it here, we want to go home."[107]

No one understood the spatial economy of the camp better than the refugees themselves. The close collaboration between military authorities and humanitarian workers, in the end, threatened to blur distinctions between civilian non-combatants and POW populations which both lived with camp rations, rules and barbed wire.[108] Refugees, however, had the freedom to complain about conditions and sometimes even prompt change. Those who could left the camp as soon as possible for their homes in local villages but continued to make use of its resources including hospitals and schools. While the "Arab camp" was reduced by half in September 1918, the school lost only one-eighth of its enrollment.[109] Worries about prostitution networks forming in the camp most likely influenced parents' decision to remove their children as residents. As a result, mothers brought their children and waited outside the camp for school to finish each day.[110] Aid workers, in turn, convinced authorities to shift the camp mission to focus on education and health care, two of the most utilized services. They charged a nominal fee to use the school, clinics and hospital that could be earned through performing various tasks at the camp.[111]

For Christian minorities still under pressure from exclusionary Ottoman policies that prevented them from returning home, the camp meant not only social services but also a last resort. When asked when they would return home, one Maronite family from Lebanon informed aid workers of the reality of their situation: "There is nothing there. We had a hotel. One regiment came and took a little; so it went. It is beautiful here compared to what was there."[112] Though the reply of the aid worker is not recorded, the idea that a family chose to stay in the "cheerless" camp recalled the contradiction of a refugee camp on the front line. Offering aid to refugees in a war zone assumed that a state of normalcy would return eventually. But refugees came both from the surrounding regions and hundreds of miles away.

Now under the protection of the occupying force, internees willingly gave up freedom for security upon crossing the threshold of the camp. When opportunities arose, they attempted to reclaim a sense of place, and possibly their independence, by taking part in the rituals of season. At harvest time, for example, "homesick" internees, as aid workers described them, streamed out of the camp to take part. When shelling forced them back, they returned.[113] For those who had no local ties and had suffered the lasting effects of state-sanctioned violence, the reality of refugeedom weighed more heavily. One man from the distant town of Marash in eastern Anatolia and exiled with his family during the genocide understood the control he gave up by entering the camp. "If you kill us," Balthasar Artin told one aid worker, "you kill us. If you save us alive, we live. We are your property."[114]

REFUGE AT PORT SAID

The influx of Armenian refugees like Artin and his family to Wadi Surar in the fall of 1918 revealed another face of relief work that showed the degree of control the occupying army exercised over refugee movement. As the battle lines shifted, Wadi Surar transformed to a transit camp for Armenian refugees targeted for resettlement in regions designated as homelands in Allied treaty agreements. Until that time came, they had to be managed. Pressure from Mustafa Kemal whose forces continued to fight the Allies and commit massacres in Anatolia after the signing of the Armistice prolonged the already slow process.[115] Encouraged to come to Wadi Surar, the military eventually transferred refugees who were willing to go to a well-established and larger camp at Port Said.[116] The camp's central location and expanded mission further internationalized the refugee problem, while imperial ties ensured close British control over administration.

Coming to Port Said refugee camp created expectations of returning home. Founded in the wake of the Armenian Genocide, it would come under the influence of a broad range of humanitarian, military and international actors.[117] After Baghdad, Port Said held increased importance and played an integral part in the refugee camp network. By the time it closed in November 1919, the British military, Egyptian government authorities, French government, American Red Cross, Friends of Armenia, British Quakers, Syrian and Palestine Relief Fund, Armenian General Benevolent Union and Lord Mayors Fund all had contributed to the administration of the camp schools, orphanage, workrooms, hospital, kitchens and bakery.[118] The sight of the rows and rows of tents arranged into blocks punctuated by workrooms, orphanage, kitchens, schools and hospital overwhelmed the landscape. One British soldier said of the camp as viewed from aboard his navy transport ship: "one million Armenians from Turkey settled down under allied supervision on the banks of the canal."[119]

While these numbers were most certainly an exaggeration – the Egyptian government estimated only just over 23,000 refugees including those at Port Said on its soil – the impression that the so-called "remnant" of Armenian Genocide survivors were now under Allied care fit more general perceptions at the time. As another soldier recalled after seeing the camp from his ship as he headed for the Suez Canal: "if you have read the papers at home you will know what the Turks done to the Armenians and we looked after them."[120] These sentiments came from a long-enduring humanitarian connection with Ottoman Christian minorities that started after the massacres of the late nineteenth century. The Allies and aid community focused on Armenians and Assyrians during the war as deserving of heightened sympathy due to the genocide which led to their removal from Anatolia and now, after the armistice, their stateless status.[121] The camp was started after a French naval squadron rescued 4,000 Armenians who were driven from their homes during the standoff at Musa Dagh located along the northern coast of Syria.[122] Immortalized in Franz Werfel's novel *Forty Days of Musa Dagh*, the real-life survivors of the siege landed at the Port Said encampment whose initial cost after the French rescue was born by the Egyptian government and private charities.

On July 31, 1918, Allenby and the Egyptian Expeditionary Force took control.[123] With the military in charge, a familiar pattern emerged. Aid work activities steadily increased as humanitarian organizations helped with administration.[124] Allenby's orders to take Syria, Palestine and the Sinai Peninsula that fall now included taking responsibility for the chain of refugee camps and auxiliary aid services spanning from Anatolia to Mesopotamia to North Africa.

Though under British military administration, the daily management of Port Said fell largely to civilian aid workers. Some of these relationships had been long-standing.[125] The Friends of Armenia supervised industrial work at the camp except for the bakery which was run by a refugee, Mr. Rabinowitz. Local actors played a key role as well. The AGBU set up trade and language schools and, along with the Armenian Patriarch, provided financial support. The Armenian Red Cross ran stores that distributed goods to refugees, "Special Kitchens for Invalids" and paid the wages of refugee hospital workers.[126] Private companies provided the camp with free salt and aid worker transportation. The British Syrian Mission based in Beirut and the American Congregational Mission managed the workrooms while ARC provided funding. Always able to find the business side of relief work which contributed to the sustainability of their projects, Quaker aid workers found markets in Egypt for goods made by the almost 900 refugee workers at the camp.[127] Lace-edged handkerchiefs, woollen rugs, army shirts, garments for camp workers, "fly nets," crochet and needle work, cotton cloth, wooden and bone combs were all produced by refugee workers for sale.[128] As at other camps, British authorities provided "sufficient funds" for rations.[129]

Some aid workers worried that military administration would change the mission of the camp. The planned doubling of its size by transferring refugees from other camps to Port Said also caused concern. A report issued on the eve of the military handover in the summer of 1918 detailed the work done by each aid organization, listing benefits and costs. The bakery was touted as an example of a well-run industry that "cost the Government nothing" providing as many as 40,000 buns and cakes per day for soldiers' canteens.[130] W. C. Hornblower, head of Refugee Administration under the Egyptian Ministry of the Interior, wrote a carefully worded admonition that warned against "exploit(ing) refugee labour for the profit of the Government."[131] He successfully advocated for the continuation of the system where "all profit occurring is allocated to the benefit of the refugees themselves," which mirrored schemes favored by British and American philanthropic organizations since the late nineteenth century.[132]

What did change was an increased vigilance by regional humanitarian organizations. AGBU immediately sought access to refugees. The influx of large numbers of Armenians empowered this Armenian-run organization to make appeals on their behalf.[133] In September, it sent a representative from Cairo to discuss conditions at the camp who suggested several improvements. AGBU proposed that the diet of the orphans include "supplementary foods such as fruit or cakes or cocoa" a few times a week because of insufficient nourishment but also "to make the children happier and so better able to forget the suffering they have been through."[134] A month later, AGBU sent a delegation to seek more control over the orphanage and industrial work and aid from the military.[135] Allenby supported the work of the camp, writing to camp administrators "in his own hand." He also gave Armenian orphans transferred to Port Said the gift of a handkerchief and small money allowance.[136]

Administrative concerns mattered little to refugees who wanted camp authorities to make good on the promise that they would be sent home. Dikran Andreasian who survived the ordeal at Musa Dagh after the French ships were hailed with a crudely fashioned "Red Cross" flag, testified to the "kindness and untiring efforts" on behalf of the Port Said refugees.[137] But four years in a camp took its toll. As they waited for news of surviving relatives, the Musa Dagh refugees began to get restless, accusing those in charge, Armenian and Allied alike, of keeping them in the camp needlessly. Citing unsettled conditions in northern Syria, authorities refused to let them go. Refugees petitioned the French Consul at Port Said.[138] Eventually they received transportation back free of charge in fall 1919, a solution that also served military interests. In November, Egyptian authorities reported to the British government that Port Said "was practically cleared" of inhabitants in accordance with an agreement with the French who received the refugees and camp equipment in the territory they oversaw in the occupied zone.[139] Later that month, Kemalist forces launched an assault on French forces leaving those recently returned as refugees again.

Camps like Port Said provided much needed aid but did little to solve the problem of displacement. The end of 1919 saw an estimated 300,000 refugees on the road. The reverse journey proved dangerous and diffi-cult: "They are to be found all along the roads, in general without money, food shelter or clothing," reported one aid worker assigned to return routes from the camps.[140] Those who found their way back to where their journey began, with or without Allied assistance or sanction, often arrived to find their homes occupied. Life as an internal refugee became harder and more uncertain in the years ahead. In 1930, the Turkish government expelled all remaining 30,000 Armenians. These refugees after having their property seized found their way to Syria with travel documents stamped "not allowed to return."[141]

CONCLUSION

On the Middle Eastern Front, internal refugees were both a military and a humanitarian problem that defied easy solution. Humanitarian organ-izations and the military necessarily and openly collaborated to meet distinct, but not always shared, objectives that unevenly benefited those they were meant to serve. Ultimately, the experience of total war shaped Allied war strategy regarding civilian populations. Humanitarian and military agendas met at the site of the refugee camp where funders, aid workers and refugees contributed to creating the camp as a transitional internment site. It introduced the military to another way of waging war which required taking account of displaced civilians in their care. While guided and shaped by British ideals and practice, the operation of camps and auxiliary institutions – schools, orphanages, cafeterias and hospitals – relied by design on cooperation and funding mainly from the United States, Britain and France as well as local and regional actors.

Camps like Port Said arguably worked best when these interests served as a check on one another, balancing the humanitarian and military interests with conditions on the ground. Humanitarian actors had their own agendas as did local organizations, Allied nations and international institutions. So, too, did the tens of thousands of civilians who found ways to make the most of temporary aid under occupation. The camps proved a useful means of managing populations and preparing those displaced by the war to accept the status of "liberated" subject in a world still being remade by war. As one Port Said refugee argued to secure her return to French-occupied lands as the fighting continued, "We are not Armenian, we are French [dependents] . . . There are French [rulers] on our soil, we will go, we will go."[142]

Failed attempts at peace between the signing of the armistice in 1918 and the final settlement at Lausanne in 1923 redefined what it meant to provide refuge in wartime and who should offer this protection. Eventually, the League of Nations would take over this role in the 1920s and 1930s. But in the no man's land between war and peace, humanitarian relief agencies attempted to fulfill public and private commitments to aid displaced people in the care of the occupying force. In this way, the Armenian Genocide, conditions of total war and the unsteady peace made civilians central actors in the war. Consensus around the idea of refuge coupled with support for small nationalities by humanitarian and political actors during British and French occupation meant that the large-scale and costly project of providing aid to internal refugees received public and private support.[143] For aid to work, new alliances forged the refugee camp into a peculiar institution that served both a population under pressure and a war incompletely won.

The Allied invasion of Baghdad in the spring of 1917 thus created a complex situation. War and massacres against civilians continued. At same time, a network of humanitarian institutions funded by international aid agencies and Allied governments worked to stem the internal refugee crisis. This meant that attempts to forge peace between the Ottoman Empire and the Allies took place in the midst of ongoing humanitarian aid work and military campaigns. Refugees waiting for the war to end would find themselves pushed into limbo as negotiators failed to a create a lasting settlement with the Treaty of Sèvres in the summer of 1920.

CHAPTER 4

How War Didn't End

THE PARIS PEACE CONFERENCE MARKED THE FORMAL beginning of attempts at peacemaking with the Ottoman Empire in 1919. Early discussions at the Paris Conference led to other conferences and resulted in the doomed Treaty of Sèvres that was signed by Ottoman representatives of the Allied-backed government in August 1920. However, efforts to forge a peace based on the armistice agreement that limited the power of a future Turkish state and held the Ottoman Empire accountable for massacres never fully materialized because the Lausanne Treaty replaced Sèvres in 1923. What the Sèvres Treaty did do was create conditions that fueled continued armed conflict and exacerbated an already urgent humanitarian crisis. This chapter traces the road to Sèvres in the period of the Allied occupation and explains why the Treaty failed to put the Allies and the Ottoman Empire on a lasting path to peace.

Treaty making between the Allies and the Ottoman Empire had a long history. The entire peace process, not just the armistice agreement, was guided by the idea of minority protection and humanitarian intervention. Unrelenting violence in and around the Ottoman Empire and the unpopular Allied occupation made peacemaking a slow and deleterious process that challenged the European-led imperial order. War continued on Russia's borderlands and Mustafa Kemal's nationalist movement gained momentum. Peacemakers at Paris watched with alarm at nationalists' subversion of the terms of the 1918 Mudros Armistice. This resistance took hold in the countryside and along the fringes of the Ottoman government as Kemal consolidated power away from Constantinople in Angora (modern Ankara).[1] The thwarting of the Armistice and continued Armenian massacres in Anatolia in early 1920 contributed to the creation of Allied occupation zones and plans to establish an Armenian state.[2] By the time Sèvres was signed in August 1920, demands by Turkish nationalists had gained sufficient strength to make this first peace agreement a dead letter.

First World War peacemaking on the whole was a protracted process controlled by the Allies. Separate treaties resulted from the 1918 armistice agreements between the Allies and Bulgaria, Germany, Hungary, Austria and, finally, the Ottoman Empire. These were the Treaty of Versailles, 1919 (Germany), Treaty of Neuilly, 1919 (Bulgaria); Treaty of Saint-Germain, 1919 (Austria), Treaty of Trianon, 1920 (Hungary) and the Treaties of Sèvres, 1920 and Lausanne, 1923 (Ottoman Empire). Importantly, these treaties did not in and of themselves settle the wartime conflict. Between 1920 and 1923, the Allies hosted twenty-four official peace conferences in addition to numerous ad hoc international meetings.[3] These conferences, treated by historians as discrete events, were in reality part of the same set of conversations about how to end the war.[4] The well-studied Paris Peace Conference started in January 1919 and lasted a year.[5] Other meetings that overlapped with Paris and followed in its wake have received less attention, which has limited understandings of the dynamics of peacemaking. This has served to disconnect the last conference held in Lausanne, Switzerland, from a process that dragged on as wartime conditions continued between 1919 and 1923.

Attempts to end the war took place in the context of continued fighting and constant talking. As Susan Pedersen argues about the role of the League of Nations, these conferences mattered because they created a space for dialogue to consider the adjudication of the war and its aftermath.[6] Importantly, the First World War conference regime was controlled by the victors and cannot be considered a level playing field based on the magnanimous principle of give and take. The Treaty of Sèvres, often considered a footnote in postwar negotiations because of its ultimate failure and replacement with the Lausanne Treaty three years later, was crucial to the peace process. The agreement emerged out of conversations started at the Paris Conference and sustained at regular meetings and conferences culminating in London and San Remo. These debates over the form the Sèvres Treaty should take happened in the context of military conflict and a British imperial-led occupation that ultimately shaped the final peace.

WAR IN PEACE

While the Allies talked about peace at the Paris Peace Conference, war continued along the Middle Eastern Front. The failure of the Allies and Ottoman Empire to negotiate a final peace after the armistice resulted in continued battlefront and intercommunal violence. Diplomatic solutions made few inroads. Ongoing war conditions influenced the series of talks that started immediately after Mudros was signed at the end of October 1918. The final Ottoman settlement happened under conditions that favored Turkish nationalists who challenged the Allied-backed government in Constantinople. Ultimately, the Treaty of Lausanne represented years of negotiations that took place at international peace conferences and on the battlefields of Mesopotamia, Anatolia and the Caucasus.

That fighting raged on outside of Western Europe while diplomats talked belied claims that peace had come between the Allies and the Ottoman Empire. These were not intermittent borderland skirmishes but full-scale military engagements. On the Middle Eastern Front, they claimed tens of thousands of civilian and military casualties. Military confrontations included the Greek invasion of Smyrna and fighting in Cilicia as well as the subsequent reconquest of both regions by Turkish troops led by Mustafa Kemal. Britain fought to protect oil interests in the Caucasus and check its former Russian ally's ambitions and later those of Kemal in eastern Anatolia.[7]

The Paris Peace Conference was unapologetically a victors' conference and denied the vanquished a seat at the table.[8] Negotiations surrounding the Treaty of Sèvres happened largely along these same lines. While the consequences of this approach are well known in the case of Germany, less is known about its effect on peacemaking with the Ottoman Empire. Those present in addition to the Allies included members of delegations from over thirty countries which sent representation to Paris. Some participants came from special interest groups – women, racial, religious and ethnic minorities and labor organizations. They also included in their ranks the "small nationalities" granted observer status. This made Paris, as the first and largest of the peace conferences, an important site for discussions about demands made by those aligned with the Allied cause if not through actual combat, then in principle. Many came inspired by President Wilson's "Fourteen Points" and saw the Paris Conference as an opportunity to make their case on the international stage.[9] While most went home disappointed, the testimony and petitions about what some considered peripheral interests were heard and could have real effect.[10]

Peace negotiations also influenced the way the Allied occupation of the Ottoman Empire worked. The Allies set up institutions and systems of rule meant to legitimize their victory over the Ottoman Empire. Britain's army of occupation enforced armistice dictates upheld at the Paris Peace Conference. With Allenby at the head of operations in Mesopotamia and later serving as High Commissioner of Egypt, occupation functioned as a loosely connected set of dictates. They focused on the security and administration of Ottoman lands, eventually including Constantinople, and were imposed by an ever-dwindling military force.[11] The challenges of occupation included continued armed conflict; clashes between the British, French and Italians over jurisdiction; and the question of how to manage Greek ambition in the region. These military and diplomatic complications coupled with the resurgence of Turkish nationalism under Kemal threatened to delegitimize the occupation. They also undermined Allied peace plans embodied in the Treaty of Sèvres and signed in August 1920.

The Paris Peace Conference first considered the Ottoman peace at the end of January 1919. Discussions primarily focused on Germany, but that did not prevent the delegates from considering the larger roadmap of the peace process. This session dealt with the question of what would come to be known as the mandates, an imperial administrative system set up by the Paris Conference and supervised by the League of Nations that gave Britain and France power over African, Pacific and Middle Eastern territories formerly under German and Ottoman control.[12] Lloyd George argued that the Ottoman Empire's treatment of its minorities, including the attempt to annihilate the Armenians, justified its breakup under Allied supervision.[13] These included the southern lands inhabited mostly by Arabs and eastern Anatolia inhabited by Armenians before the genocide.

The Paris Peace Conference would not settle the mandate question. It would take several more meetings over the course of four years to enact all of the so-called "A" mandates for regions formerly under Ottoman control. Approved in July 1922, the Syrian and Palestine mandates officially commenced in September 1923 after the final settlement with the Ottoman Empire.[14] In the meantime, these territories were administered under Allied occupation. Considerations of governing these territories thus continued as a problem of the peace which in part explains why they found voice at the Paris Conference. Remembered today as a conference focused on peace, it also functioned as a space for dialogue about the ongoing war in Ottoman territory.

How to occupy and rule Ottoman lands emerged as a primary concern. Britain and France had not fully resolved the question of which country would take control of particular territories until the spring of 1920 during a pair of conferences held in London and San Remo, respectively. San Remo opened on April 18, 1920, with a full meeting of the Allied Supreme Council. On that day, Herbert Samuel submitted a memorandum to the British Delegation that included Lloyd George and Curzon regarding the settlement.[15] The Council agreed to put the Balfour Declaration into the Ottoman treaty on April 25 and declare Britain the mandatory power in Palestine and Mesopotamia and the French in Syria.[16] The assigning of the mandates followed the broad outlines of the wartime diplomatic agreements made between Britain and France in Sykes–Picot.

The approval, but not enactment, of the mandates alongside the Ottoman treaty that would become Sèvres in April 1920 at San Remo showed how much and how little things had changed since deliberations began at the Paris Conference. On the one hand, it was now clear that the United States would not be involved in the final settlement with the Ottoman Empire. President Wilson's precarious health and the rejection of the Versailles Treaty by the Senate made it clear that the United States wanted nothing to do with the mandates and the war settlement by the end of 1919. The French and British position followed in the same spirit as it had at the Paris Peace Conference. While the demands for territory had shrunk, the two victorious empires confirmed the partition of the Ottoman Empire under their administration.

No decisions about the fate of the Ottoman Empire took place at the Paris Conference. The delay to settling the treaty with the Ottoman Empire worried diplomats at the time. Balfour sent a memorandum to Lloyd George on June 26, 1919, two days before Germany signed the Versailles Treaty. It expressed his concern that top representatives were leaving Paris before "the outlines of the Turkish settlement are more or less agreed to." Balfour wanted them to wait so the "new arrangement" can be settled which included much of what would be decided the following spring at London and San Remo: determining frontiers and finalizing the mandate system as well as drawing the boundaries of the new Turkish state in Anatolia. As he concluded, only this course of action would settle "all petty jealousies and intrigues between these Allied Nations ... I cannot think that such a consummation is wholly beyond our reach, but if it is to be attained, we should set to work to do it at once."[17]

Paris delegates heard a myriad of voices from representatives of Ottoman ethnic and religious minorities and entertained memoranda from Ottoman representatives themselves. The minority question revolved mostly around considerations of Palestine, the fate of the Armenians and an independent Arab state. Advocates from groups with a vested interest in this process often plead their own case at the Paris Peace Conference.[18] The Ottoman Empire, too, had representation in the form of three memoranda presented to the conference by a delegation that arrived in Paris without an invitation, much to the chagrin of Lloyd George. In sum, well over a thousand delegates passed through Paris between January and June 1919. Each made their case in small and large venues, through petitions and speeches and private meetings with delegates.[19] These discussions shaped the final form of the Treaty of Sèvres, ultimately presented to the Ottomans in May 1920.

THE DELEGATIONS SPEAK

Armenian, Arab and Zionist claims against the Ottoman Empire came up repeatedly at the Paris Conference. The Armenian delegation, headed by Boghos Nubar Pasha and Avedis Aharonian, made the case for the creation of an Armenian state under Allied protection when they appeared before the Supreme Council on February 26. These two men together represented the Armenian diaspora and Ottoman Armenians: Nubar, as the son of a former Egyptian prime minister and based in Paris, represented the former and Aharonian, an Armenian poet from the Caucasus, the latter.[20] Carved out of Anatolia and spanning from the Caucasus to the Mediterranean, the new state they proposed would require just the kind of protection imagined by the mandate system.[21] While the mandate for Armenia was never taken up, in this moment there was a real possibility that Britain or France or, as Nubar, Aharonian and even Lloyd George hoped, the United States would serve as the mandatory power. The shadow of the genocide and belief that this new Armenia could live in peace with its neighbors under the protection of an external power drove these claims.

Zabel Yessayan joined Nubar and Aharonian as an Armenian delegate to the conference. Born Zabel Hovhannisian in 1878 outside of Constantinople, she was educated in Paris and became known as a public intellectual and humanitarian activist.[22] The only woman included on the list of community leaders rounded up by the Ottoman government on the eve of the Armenian Genocide on April 24, 1915, she escaped to Bulgaria with her daughter and eventually found her way back to the Ottoman Empire with the help of the British government who supported her work by giving her shelter in the Legation offices in Tehran.[23] Her reputation as a trusted advisor and voice of war refugees earned Yessayan a seat as an Armenian representative at the Paris Peace Conference. There, she brought women's issues to the international stage.[24]

Yessayan spoke to delegates about two main issues – women's wartime sacrifices and the repatriation of women and children claimed by Turkish families during the war. In January 1919 she delivered an illustrated lecture entitled, "The Role of the Armenian Woman during the War." She spoke on behalf of the Armenian National Delegation (AND) and focused on the devastating effect of the war on women and children. In so doing, she helped shape a gendered discourse around the figure of the war victim. The victims she spoke about were female, young and, perhaps most importantly, moral actors. Women, "in all countries," she asserted had played a "valuable role" in the war in both public and private functions. "The Armenian woman, perhaps more than the men," she argued, kept deep "in her pure and serious soul the sacred traditions of the race." The embrace of European learning and customs among women and girls in urban areas made them adaptive and independently minded. This allowed them to band together to help one another after being "thrown on the road to exile" during the genocide. Those who could bravely fought alongside their husbands and brothers in the war.[25]

In March 1919, she made another contribution to the Paris Conference in the form of a "note" on behalf of AND entitled, "The Liberation of Non-Muslim Women and Children in Turkey." She brought attention to the kidnapping of hundreds of thousands of women and girls from the Armenian, Greek and Assyrian communities and their subsequent conversion to Islam and what was called at the time "absorption" into Muslim families.[26] Starting with the alleged selling of women and child deportees, Yessayan moved to a discussion of collective rape and then to the female victims themselves, many of whom had committed suicide. She concluded with concrete suggestions regarding the repatriation of women and children that centered on establishing "an international commission of women" who would consult with the Allied powers to help those whom she referred to as "slaves." This commission would build orphanages, create work opportunities and set up health and special services for women and children who she saw as the best hope for the renewal of the Armenian nation.[27]

Yessayan's plan placed Ottoman and diaspora Armenian women in a central role. The international commission she proposed would consult "Armenian Ladies of Russian Armenia, Constantinople, Smyrna and European colonies of Egypt and America." The evidence she collected of atrocities committed against women and children during the war from oral testimony, photographs and eyewitness accounts would form the basis of "onsite investigation" into the scope of the problem. Yessayan proposed a very specific program for this team of observers, consultants and investigators who along with the commission would proceed under the protection of the Allied occupation:

> Find minor children who have lost their maternal language the memory of their parents and their nationality, and who have been moreover terrorized by their darkness, and who often renounce being Armenian or Greeks . . .
>
> [Liberate] non-Muslim women and children . . .
>
> [Increase] the number of orphanages . . .
>
> [Create] places for women to return from the house of Muslims until they are repatriated in their birth places.
>
> [Organize] a health service, to examine the women because many are unfortunately contaminated with dangerous and contagious maladies, and to group them as a result.
>
> Create a special service for walled up women.
>
> Organize workers to find work for women and adults.

This program of renewing the Armenian, Greek and Assyrian people by reabsorbing women into the nation through internationally sanctioned aid work had the full support of the Armenian Delegation in Paris.[28]

Nubar offered his endorsement of Yessayan's plan calling her a "woman of letters and one of our most distinguished writers" who "collected herself" testimonies of the women and children she cited in her presentation. Inspired by Yessayan, English feminist activist Emily Robinson suggested to Nubar the formation of a "women's movement . . . to convince the delegation in Paris to take prompt action to deliver these our poor sisters in such terrible distress."[29] Eventually, these ideas would come to fruition in an agency led by the British to repatriate abducted Armenian women and children forcibly converted to Islam during the war.

The Arabs, too, sent a delegation which focused on the political future of an Arab state. Like the Armenians, the Arabs wanted an independent homeland carved out of the former lands of the Ottoman Empire. The Arab delegation, however, did not get the same welcome as the Armenians. Wartime promises ran up against new realities that marginalized Arab claims. Infighting between the

British and French about the administration of Mesopotamia along with promises made to Zionists for a Jewish homeland meant that when Emir Feisal arrived as head of the delegation to make his case for a unified Arab state in January 1919, he had few allies.[30] From the beginning, Feisal was treated as an unequal participant. When he landed at Marseilles on his way to Paris, French officials informed him that he had no official standing at the conference and tried unsuccessfully to delay his trip to Paris.[31]

This treatment resulted in part from the French belief that the British would use Feisal to challenge their claims over Syria. The French could not prevent him from assuming his status as an official delegate but did manage to limit his function as a representative of the Hejaz, which his father ruled.[32] The Hejaz delegation spoke before the Supreme Council on February 6. Feisal made the case for an independent homeland promised by the Allies during the war. His appearance with T. E. Lawrence played into French fears about British ambitions in Syria and led to their continued attempts to weaken Feisal's claims to statehood for the Arab peoples.[33]

This competition between Britain and France for control over Syria undermined the Ottoman settlement from the beginning. Lawrence served as Feisal's liaison officer throughout the war, cementing the Emir's public alignment with the British. The British had no problem using Feisal to get under the skin of the French and tried to control Franco-Arab relations. One officer recalled a meeting between Allenby, Lawrence and Feisal at the Victoria Hotel after the capture of Damascus on October 1, 1918. Feisal had planned a triumphant entry into the city on October 3 but was summoned to the hotel to speak with General Allenby first. Here Allenby informed him that the French would have the upper hand in Syria. Allenby asked Lawrence: "But did you not tell him that the French were to have the Protectorate over Syria?" To which Lawrence replied, "No Sir, I know nothing about it." When further pressed, Allenby admitted that Feisal "was to have nothing to do with the Lebanon."[34] After Allenby informed him that he only had status as Lieutenant-General under Allenby's command, Feisal left the Hotel to reenter the city less triumphantly and with knowledge of his diminished role.[35]

At the Paris Peace Conference, the Council of Four – Wilson, Clemenceau, Lloyd George and Orlando – took up the Arab case. Concerns that the Arabs would not accept a French Mandate were confirmed by Allenby whom Lloyd George summoned in March 1919 from Egypt to advise on the administration of Syria. Allenby claimed to have "not had a moment unoccupied" in Paris where in two days' time he met and talked "with everyone from President Wilson downwards" while fielding interviews.[36] The question of the control of Syria led to more discussion over future administration. A fact-finding commission was suggested to adjudicate the matter, which pleased Feisal. The British and French stalled when it came to appointing representatives. Feisal, who had left for Damascus that May, had little recourse but to protest the inaction.[37] Eventually, this would result in the American-led King-Crane Commission (discussed further below).

For the Zionists, the Paris Peace Conference marked a positive step forward in the realization of the Balfour Declaration. Future High Commissioner for Palestine Herbert Samuel argued on the eve of the Declaration that it would have most power in the context of a "favourable military situation."[38] That occurred starting in late 1917 and 1918 and opened up a space for Zionist claims over Palestine at the Paris Conference. Samuel, a British Liberal Cabinet minister and practicing Jew, was appointed by the British government to administer Palestine as High Commissioner in 1920, two years before the mandate went into effect. According to Leonard Stein, support for the Balfour Declaration had coalesced by the time of the Paris Peace Conference with anti-Zionist voices from within the British government and Jewish community yielding to Zionist claims.[39]

The Zionist delegation had an audience with the Council of Ten on February 27. British Zionists Nahum Sokolow and Chaim Weitzmann were joined by the Russian Zionist leader, Menachem Ussishkin, and French Jewish leaders, Andre Spire and non-Zionist Sylvain Levi. Weitzmann had met with Balfour before the Paris Peace Conference on December 4, 1918, to seek reassurances of support for the Zionist position.[40] Their memorandum asked the Paris Conference to support the claims of the Balfour

Declaration and "recognise the historic title of the Jewish people to Palestine and the right of the Jews to reconstitute in Palestine their national home." It also proposed that "the sovereign possession of Palestine shall be vested in the League of Nations and the government entrusted to Great Britain as Mandatory of the League." Zionist proposals reportedly were well received and led the French to assert that it would not oppose Britain taking the mandate for Palestine under the League.[41] In a meeting with Clemenceau on March 7, Lloyd George made explicit his desire to see the British take Palestine and Mesopotamia as mandates. He also acknowledged French claims over Syria and wanted to see the United States granted control over Armenia and Constantinople.[42]

Here, as in the case of the Armenian and Arab delegation, Zionists' willingness to entertain the mandate regime centered around the idea of protection that they believed the peace settlement would ultimately provide. The British and French empires adjudicated competing claims under this framework between themselves and regional and local interests during the peace process. These different interest groups had their voices heard in Paris and sometimes misheard. While embracing the idea of protection, they did not interpret the mandate system to mean long-term colonial-style rule over former Ottoman lands.[43]

Claims of sovereignty, in this uncertain moment, thus had an almost divisible quality informed by an imperial world view that promised protection as a necessary first step toward independence. Britain's casting of the mandates as a transitional stage met with support by these interest groups who worried about the security of newly proposed states. The mandate regime also received the tacit support of France who hoped to make its own claims of protection over Syria by sidelining the British and convincing Feisal that he needed French protection. While the Paris Conference did not settle the mandate question, these discussions created the framework for a post-Ottoman Middle East. Deteriorating conditions on the ground, however, meant that Allied plans faced the resistance of a growing Ottoman opposition.

OCCUPATION AND ADMINISTRATION IN WARTIME

Deliberations at the Paris Peace Conference about the future of the Ottoman Empire took place in the context of an increasingly tension-filled occupation. Run largely by the British, it increased conflicts with the French and Ottoman civilians living in the occupation zone. These parallel processes – peacemaking and occupation – contributed to the ultimate form of the Treaty of Sèvres, which was signed nearly two years after the first armistice.

The conquest of Baghdad in spring 1917 made the administration of Ottoman territory a primary war concern. As more and more land came under Allied control, the business of occupation settled into a familiar pattern of military oversight, civil administration and collaboration that had long characterized British rule in India and Africa. A system centered in the imperial metropole but managed regionally, British administration of foreign territories relied on local leaders.[44] Allenby explained how occupation worked in Mesopotamia to one of his officers on the eve of the conquest of Damascus at the end of September 1918. While smaller towns like Nazareth, Haifa and Tiberias were given "a spare officer as Military Governor, with an interpreter and a few assistants," a city like Damascus with over 300,000 inhabitants required clear collaboration with local officials. Allenby asked his subordinate, Henry Chauvel, a senior officer in the Australian Imperial Force, to model administration on "what we did at Jerusalem ... Send for the Turkish Wali and tell him to carry on, giving him what extra police he requires."[45]

The British took on the main administrative role in the space between the armistice and the League of Nations' internationalization of the mandates. But the de facto wartime administration of occupied territories needed legitimization. This included regional alliances and military force as well as the setting up of social services and civilian infrastructure in towns as well as the concentration camps discussed in Chapter 3. After France took over the administration of Cilicia and Syria in early 1919, it managed affairs along much the same lines as had the British.[46]

The Eastern Committee, set up by the War Cabinet in March 1918, was tasked with sorting out Britain's commitments in the Ottoman Empire.[47] Britain considered regional administration as part of its larger war plan long before the armistice. The Arab Bureau, created early in the war under the influence of Mark Sykes and centered in Cairo, covertly collected information on local politics that influenced Sykes–Picot. Intelligence gathering by British agents, as Priya Satia argues, often "shaded into administration."[48] Britain's desire to manage and control Arab interests influenced discussions in late 1915 and early 1916 on the question of the future governance of Ottoman lands. Some wanted India at the center, while others favored a more regionally focused structure separate from Indian administrative. In the Eastern Committee, Lord Curzon, Robert Cecil, Gen. Smuts, Sir Louis Mallet and others coordinated British policy on the Middle Eastern Front. In addition to questions of future governance, the Committee focused on "enemy movement or action in the Black Sea, the Caucasus, and Trans Caucasus, Armenia, Persia, the Caspian, Transcaspia, Turkestan, Afghanistan, Sinai, Palestine, Syria, the Hejaz, Arabia, Mesopotamia, the Persian Gulf."[49] This joining of political and military priorities shaped the way occupation worked.

While Sykes–Picot continued to influence questions of administration, armistice terms also played a role. Curzon opened the Eastern Committee's December meeting citing Britain's obligation to Christian minorities in the Treaty of Berlin. He proposed creating an Armenian state in Cilicia out of both concerns over the treatment of minorities and strategic considerations which focused on stopping nationalist-driven "Pan-Turanism" that would spread under Kemal's leadership.[50] Other committee members wanted a bigger Armenian state set up in Eastern Turkey that would include more territory beyond that of the historically Armenian-dominated vilayets in Anatolia for these same reasons.[51] The influence the United States also came into play. Robert Cecil's support for an American proposal for humanitarian aid that he claimed "can do no harm" met with immediate objections. This aid, some argued, would lead to a US-run "commercial enterprise" in the region that would challenge British trade interests.

Considerations of borders and US power eventually turned to the question of occupying Constantinople. Curzon struck a familiar orientalist refrain in the December meeting: "If we could get rid of them, if we could agree on the 'bag and baggage' policy of Mr. Gladstone and remove them to the other side, we should all feel that a kind of miasma had disappeared from the atmosphere of Europe."[52] The status of

Constantinople was not easily resolved, however. Admiral Calthorpe, as High Commissioner at Constantinople, guided the early months of the occupation ostensibly in collaboration with the French and Italians.[53]

An ever-weakening Ottoman government centered in the capital made Allied control of government affairs relatively smooth at first. The Ottoman officials who had signed the armistice tolerated a strong Allied presence in Constantinople to protect their own tenuous hold on power. Formal occupation commenced on March 16, 1920, in the name of law and order. In reality, the Allies had decided to occupy Constantinople as a show of strength after Kemal's military reconquest of Anatolia in the preceding months. Formal occupation led to more unrest including the arrest of Allied officials by Turkish nationalists, which weakened British and French stature.[54] But Britain did not need to run the occupation from Constantinople. Egypt proved a much more practical imperial center.

EGYPT

Rivalries between nationalists and amongst the Allies themselves meant that administration never fully centered in Constantinople. Rather, Britain guided Ottoman affairs from Egypt. On the outbreak of the war, Britain declared Egypt a protectorate. It deposed the Ottoman-appointed khedive and replaced him with Egyptian prince Hussein Kamil and forced the secession of Egypt from the Ottoman Empire in December 1914. Egypt's "semi-colonial" status bred resentment and a growing nationalist movement. Nevertheless, it remained crucial to Britain's ability to occupy Ottoman lands.[55]

General Allenby led the administration as High Commissioner from 1919 to 1925. Allenby's entry into Aleppo on October 27, 1918, symbolized the final defeat of the Ottoman Empire and made him the hero of the Middle Eastern theater.[56] The creation of three regional "occupied enemy territories" that encompassed the southern lands of the Ottoman Empire led to a system of indirect rule divided between the French and British. Allenby ran British administration. "The concern is with Administration rather than fighting," he acknowledged on November 11, 1918, just as

Germany signed the Armistice. "Under martial law, my territory is wide; as I am supreme in Egypt, Palestine and Syria."[57]

This "temporary military fiefdom," as his biographer called it, led to constant travel between Egypt and the occupied territories.[58] His appointment as High Commissioner for Egypt and Sudan on March 20, 1919 meant that Cairo emerged as a central hub of activity for administrators, dignitaries and those seeking influence under the occupation regime. His wife, whom he called "a perfect hostess," worked endlessly entertaining dignitaries who sought Allenby's council.[59] This included Admiral Calthorpe, Emir Feisal, Herbert Samuel, Winston Churchill, Robert Cecil and T. E. Lawrence. On tour, he sought out local dignitaries, missionaries and diplomats including Sykes and Picot whom Allenby characterized as "trying to get what they want for each side."[60] Allenby, while technically in charge of only British administered regions, took on the role with the sanction of the Foreign Office of power broker and became involved with the overall scheme of administration.[61] He did not trust the French. They wanted to put Syria under Picot who did not want to cede control of Arab lands to Feisal.

The Allies could not sustain their authority under military occupation alone. The 400,000 British troops in Egypt at the end of 1918 fell to 150,000 by April 1919.[62] In the early days, Allenby ran a sort of negotiated occupation from his position in Egypt. Here he remained subject to various interests at Whitehall and the Quai d'Orsay. The League of Nations, still in its infancy, also played a role, if only to remind the British and French of the guiding principles of self-determination in Wilson's "Fourteen Points," which held sway among nationalist interests in the occupied territories.[63] Allenby soon made his command over the occupation felt. In early February 1919, he joined Calthorpe in Constantinople to assert British authority and enforce the armistice. He received the Ottoman Ministers of Foreign Affairs and War in the presence of Calthrope to demand collaboration and inform them that he would personally oversee the implementation of armistice provisions. This included the disarming and demobilization of Turkish forces and the general population; removal of recalcitrant Turkish officials; the repatriation of Armenians and restitution; the arrest of those charged with crimes and "likely to cause agitation and disquiet";

control over the railways, telegraphs and telephones in the occupation zone. Allenby wanted this "carried out at once in areas under the command of my force" and refused to entertain any "argument or discussion" by the Ottoman ministers. His final command made no mistake about who was in charge: "It must be understood that I have the power to occupy any place I wish."[64]

Allenby navigated his role as head of the occupation through a combination of military threats and collaboration. This included managing the French and Italians. During his February visit to Constantinople, he expressed relief at having spoken with Gen. d'Espèrey who, Allenby worried, might have believed that he "was trying to steal a march on him. I told him and the Italian[s] exactly why I had come, and what I had done."[65] Allenby openly confronted resistance in Egypt. This included nationalists who rejected Egypt's protectorate status under the British Empire. He returned from Paris in his new official role of High Commissioner just as protests against British rule grew around Cairo. At the conference, he spoke to delegates and the press about the Ottoman occupation that he would run from Egypt. As he wrote to his mother, "I return to a restless Egypt with full power as High Commissioner and tackle a difficult problem. This in addition to military duties. I was brought here to discuss purely military matters connected with the Peace Negotiations. This Egyptian complication is a new one ... I think that my return, as special High Commissioner will have a calming effect, but ... there will be hard work to do."[66]

In Egypt, Allenby inherited from the previous High Commissioner, Sir Reginald Wingate, an unsustainable occupation regime. Egypt had proved central to the war effort in the Middle East despite growing nationalist protest. It long served as a center of British influence in the region, first with the opening of Suez in 1869 and then, after the 1882 British invasion. The conquest of Egypt resulted from both economic interests –Britain controlled the majority of shipping through Suez – and political expediency. Egypt's economy suffered during the war under requisitioning and Britain's decision to keep Egyptian cotton prices artificially low.[67] This coupled with censorship and martial law fueled resentment culminating in a sustained anti-colonial and anti-missionary movement.[68] Saad Zaghlul, a former Egyptian cabinet minister and friend of the former Consul General of Egypt, Lord Cromer, led the nationalist movement. The rebellion against British rule in 1919 brought ordinary Egyptian men and women out into the street to protest colonialism.[69] In March, British authorities faced the "ladies protest" led by Huda Shaarawi and started in the name of mobilizing Egyptian women on behalf of the nation.[70]

Allenby, as High Commissioner, understood Egyptian nationalism in the context of the British Empire's expanding footprint in the Middle East.[71] He resolved the situation in part by negotiating an end to the protectorate and Egyptian independence under more limited British influence in 1922.[72] Eventually, he had Zaghlul released from exile in the Seychelles who returned to campaign for elections.[73] The process of negotiating this nominal independence made it possible for Egypt to remain at the center of British imperial interests in the Middle East as the peace process with the Ottoman Empire continued.

PALESTINE AND SYRIA

The wartime occupation of southern Ottoman lands began with Baghdad and grew in the wake of Allenby's victories in Palestine. The British attempted to manage French and Arab interests in Anatolia and Syria and secure their own claims in Mesopotamia. They also pledged to protect and repatriate Armenians. Achieving these aims relied on creating a workable administrative structure. In Palestine, this meant creating a civil service directed from London and run in collaboration with local leaders. This included facilitating public works that built on Ottoman-led projects undertaken during the war.[74] Palestine came to exist as "administratively part of the British imperial world."[75] The San Remo Conference in April 1920 assigned Britain control over Palestine and France over Syria.

Attempts to legitimate British and French authority began well before San Remo. The American-led King-Crane Commission started its survey of public opinion in Palestine regarding future governance in June 1919. This fact-finding commission was proposed as part of the consultative apparatus of the Paris Peace Conference but would not have happened without pressure from Arab leaders.[76] Feisal issued the following protest upon hearing rumors that the commission might not be sent: "The Peace Conference may treat its enemies in any way it pleases but not its friends. The Arabs have fought with the Allies against the Turks and consequently they ask to be justly and equitably treated."[77]

The Commission interviewed residents and collected petitions in order to gauge local views on the occupation and future administration. One petition written by the "Muslims and Christians of Tripoli" pleaded against French occupation in Syria. Instead, they proposed "complete independence for Syria" under Feisal's leadership.[78] The commission's final findings, reported to the American delegation at the Paris Conference, showed that the population was "practically unanimous" in support of a united Syria and "practically unanimous against Zionism." The report, as it did not serve the administrative interests of the assumed mandatory powers, was not made public for three years.[79]

This period of transition put pressure on indigenous communities and intercommunal relations, further blurring the line between imperial rule and the nascent nation-state.[80] Herbert Samuel arrived in Palestine as governor at the end of June 1920. His appointment ended just over thirty months of military rule and placed civilian administration firmly in British hands.[81] A Liberal politician cut from the Gladstonian cloth, he governed the territory first under occupation and later under the British mandate until 1925. He attempted to balance his own support for Zionism as High Commissioner with his role as head of the British occupation.[82] Allenby worried that Samuel's own Jewish roots would make it difficult to navigate Arab-Jewish politics but thought him "the best choice they could have made" after his nomination as Civil Governor of Palestine was announced.[83] Samuel regularly traveled to the region and discussed matters with Allenby. Allenby watched "events in Syria very closely as they (nearly) affect the politics of Palestine." He noted in spring 1919 that "Dr. Weizmann has come out again; and goes to Jerusalem shortly. He, like all the Zionists, is anxious as to the effect of Feisal's camp on the feeling of the Arabs towards Zionism. Herbert Samuel's still out here."[84]

The assigning of Samuel as head of civil affairs in Palestine did little to smooth the transition to mandatory rule. The war already had strained relations among indigenous communities in Palestine regarding governance, administration and national identity.[85] Allenby, while supporting

Samuel's tenure, expressed worry about his ability to manage Zionist, Christian and Arab interests.[86] Not able to rely on the popular fiat of the Arab population, the British consolidated rule by stoking internal regional rivalries.[87] Eventually, Britain further centralized control under a specialized Middle East-focused structure. In 1921, the Foreign Office ceded administrative control to the newly created Middle East Department in the Colonial Office. The Colonial Office was run by Winston Churchill who appointed former India Office administrator John Shuckburgh as head.[88] This move formally incorporated the mandate system into Britain's imperial administrative structure.

In Syria, the short period of Arab rule from October 1918 to July 1920 came to an end after Feisal had difficulty gaining widespread support from Arab nationalists. France took quick advantage of the situation.[89] On March 8, 1920, Feisal had himself declared King of Palestine, Lebanon and Syria by the Syrian congress in Damascus. One month later, the San Remo Conference confirmed that France would be given the mandate over Syria.[90] That summer, French troops marched into Damascus deposing and sending Feisal into exile and leaving an unpopular French occupation in its wake. Robert de Caix, a strategist and advocate of French colonization of Syria, had plotted Feisal's demise in the wake of San Remo after securing Britain's pledge not to interfere in Syria.[91]

"Feisal [arrives] to me today," Allenby recorded on the eve of the French invasion. "He has conceded all the French demands but . . . they are still [amassing] a hostile attitude."[92] Days later, Allenby observed: "Feisal and the French are at war . . . after much fighting the French have entered Damascus. We have no details yet. I fear that this will be only the beginning of a lot of trouble. It is very disappointing to some; but I had not much hope for a peaceful outcome of the quarrel."[93] France administered Syria and Lebanon starting in 1920 under a series of high commissioners, drawing on its colonial experiences in North Africa. However, it failed to understand the power of growing Syrian nationalism in the countryside. France instead trusted urban elites to help them rule the region, much as the Ottoman Empire had done.[94] Like the British, the French put little stock in the discontent with colonial rule recorded so clearly in the stillborn King-Crane Commission report.[95]

MESOPOTAMIA

Occupation followed not dissimilar lines in Mesopotamia. The tangle of British, French, Arab and other regional interests overlapped with what was happening in Palestine and Syria. Britain and France wanted to move quickly from an army of occupation to legitimate control over former Ottoman territory. At the same time, Arab leaders insisted that the Allies make good on promises of "native" government and full-fledged independence. Britain responded by creating a civil administration structure that employed lower-level Arab administrators to run regional affairs in Mesopotamia.[96] The Anglo-French Declaration of November 1918 was an attempt to show unity between the Allies on the question of the administration of Ottoman territories. The agreement, while paying lip service to Wilsonian ideals of self-determination, did not result in self-rule for the Arab provinces and instead facilitated French and British administration.[97] Allenby and others somewhat naively believed that T. E. Lawrence, who acted as Feisal's liaison, would mitigate any Arab objections to Britain and France overseeing the government in what the Declaration called the "liberated territories."[98]

Britain wanted to make the Mesopotamian occupation pay. It raised the customs tax from 11 percent to 15 percent in April 1919. Concerns over the Arab response to raising taxes led the British to proceed with caution.[99] The new British-run administration turned toward exploiting natural resources. This included making claims over oilfields recently discovered in and around Mosul.[100] France and Britain went back and forth over who would claim Mosul. Britain published an extensive "Mesopotamia Handbook" in February 1919 that included demographic, geographic and historical information. The main part of the study, however, centered on natural resources. It was used to support claims that Britain's role as victor and, now, administrator entitled it to profit from control over the land and its people: "The development of the resources of this country should someday help the British Empire greatly to meet the financial obligations imposed by the war."[101] This further muted Arab demands for self-government. Curzon asserted that the ideal form of government for "Arabia" "at their present stage of development" would consist of "a benevolent patriarchate, which consults and is to a certain extent dependent on public opinion, but which retains executive control."[102] This included judicial administration complete with a British-run court system in Baghdad.[103]

Administering a region that resisted long-term occupation meant conflict. Little attempt was made to understand the internal rivalries exacerbated by the British occupation and few Arabs served in senior administrative positions.[104] A report to the Civil Commissioner in Baghdad in the spring of 1919 described "atrocities committed in Mosul" by Kurds between the regions of Urmia and Van. Information came from American missionaries sent through Arab Bureau intelligence officer Gertrude Bell and up through the channels of the Foreign Office, eventually reaching the British Delegation in Paris.[105] Britain, as the occupying force, had failed in its assumed responsibility for security. The inability to keep the peace fueled further discontent among Arab leaders and challenged the legitimacy of the occupation.

So, too, did the rivalry with France. Feisal repeatedly warned Allenby of the danger of ceding Syria to the French. In May 1919, he asserted that if the French increased their forces "even by one soldier," he could not be "held responsible for the consequences." Feisal also confronted Allenby about a rumor that "that the Mission has been stopped; and that British troops are to be withdrawn from Syria." If true, "a great upheaval must be expected in all Arabian countries" and "the responsibility of shedding innocent blood must rest with the Peace Conference." Allenby called this "an extremely grave situation" and worried that Feisal would "raise the Arabs against the French and ourselves." War with the Bedouins would jeopardize "the whole situation in Palestine and Syria."[106] Feisal demanded that he be "officially reassured" of the promise made to him in Paris that the Allies would send a fact-finding mission "to decide the future of the country." The ill-fated King-Crane Commission provided the temporary reassurances that kept Feisal's threats at bay.

Conflicts with Feisal revealed the precariously shifting state of the occupation. The ultimate betrayal of Feisal and the short-lived independent Arab kingdom in Syria had undermined the peace process. Infighting between Britain and France at the Paris Peace Conference over administration made things worse. Britain's withdrawal from Syria and Lebanon at the end of 1919 and transfer of authority to the French military did not renew trust between the Allies. Brémond went as far as to accuse the British of believing that the Hejaz was their mandated territory.[107] The awarding of the mandates at San Remo led to the 1920 uprising in Mesopotamia against colonial rule in late summer and early fall.[108] Britain put down the revolt and now saw threats everywhere, including with former Arab allies. In December, one official suggested threatening Feisal that his father's subsidy would be stopped if he refused to "leave Mesopotamia alone."[109]

In the end, the British realized that they needed Feisal to formalize indirect rule over Mesopotamia. In March 1921, the Middle East Department arranged the Cairo Conference to affirm Feisal as head of the new kingdom of Iraq in front of British and Arab officials. He was crowned King of Iraq on August 23, 1921.[110] In the name of Iraqi security and to police the activities of purported Arab allies, the Conference approved a controversial and terror-inducing system of air bombing and surveillance run by the Royal Air Force.[111]

ARMENIA

Competition between the British and French for control over Ottoman lands extended into southern Anatolia. Allenby eventually handed over Cilicia, considered by the Allies as part of a future Armenian homeland, to French command. General Henri Gouraud, who had fought in North Africa and was gravely injured during the Gallipoli campaign, took charge from the British in a moment when Turkish nationalists had started gaining ground in Anatolia.[112] He had led the campaign to depose Feisal and became High Commissioner and Commander in Chief in Syria with headquarters in Beirut. Ultimately, his aim was to consolidate French rule over the occupied territories. By the time Damascus fell to his forces on July 25, 1920, Gouraud's campaign was well underway. He faced intense nationalist resistance that led to Lloyd George's smug conclusion that Gouraud along with other French generals had "failed to reconcile the inhabitants of Syria to French rule."[113]

While Arab nationalists challenged the French in Syria, Turkish nationalists challenged them in Cilicia. In January 1920, violence broke out around Marash (modern Kahramanmaraş), the center of historic Armenia and of Allied repatriation efforts. At the same time, Reouf Bey challenged France's right to Cilicia in the Ottoman Chamber of Deputies because it was not part of the Armistice. By the middle of February, the Grand Vizier and Minister of Foreign Affairs launched a formal protest that asked the Allies to limit the area of the French occupation in consultation with the Ottoman delegation and adhere to the principle of majority rule.[114] The Allies responded to the violence in Marash by "taking action ... to protect the Armenians in Turkey." The French sent reinforcements from Beirut while the British "demanded the immediate dismissal by the Ottoman Government of Mustapha Kemal, Governor of Erzerum" and ordered "the occupation of Constantinople by Allied troops ... . Until the terms of the Peace have been accepted and put into force."[115] This response further escalated fighting in Anatolia and led to the conflict that would culminate in the Turkish nationalist's reconquest of Cilicia the following year.

As the French found in Cilicia, military occupation did not smooth the way for peace. The stateless status of Armenians, still suffering periodic massacres at the hands of CUP-inspired operatives, heightened tensions.[116] This affected the peace process. After the massacres in Cilicia, the Allies "informed the Turkish Gov't that unless the persecution of the Armenians immediately ceases the terms of Peace will inevitably be rendered more severe and the concessions already made will be withdrawn."[117] Armenians had taken matters into their own hands and fought the Turkish army in the Caucasus to create the small 11,500 square mile state of Armenia on the borders of eastern Anatolia in 1918. The product of the battle over boundaries in the wake of the Brest-Litovsk agreement, the Republic survived until 1922 when it became a Soviet republic.

Armenia's precarious existence led to debates over making Anatolian lands historically inhabited by Armenians part of their homeland.[118] These discussions had taken place at the Paris Peace Conference as a "mandate for Armenia" under US supervision. The massacres in Cilicia made the Armenian issue more urgent. The Allies asked the United States "to cooperate with them in the steps now being taken and any further steps which may be thought necessary ... to protect the

Armenians."[119] While the US mandate for Armenia never came to pass, the conversation emboldened the British and French to attempt to secure minority protection provisions and repatriation of Armenians to Cilicia in peace treaty negotiations with the Ottoman Empire.

The experiences of two consular officials offer a perspective on how the British defined the responsibility of minority protection. Andrew Ryan and Robert Graves came of age in the early days of the Levant Consular Service. Graves, a member of a prominent Anglo-Irish family, was part of a first generation of Levant trainees. Ryan, the son of a Cork candle maker, entered the Consular service twenty years later attending Queen's College in Cork and Kings College London before being sent by the Foreign Office to Cambridge in 1897 for further language training.[120] Their wartime service centered in Constantinople in a period of flux. As Ryan remembered it, "There were large numbers of Allied warships in the port. The presence of so many authorities was all the more confusing as their position in relation to each other and to the Turkish Government had still to be defined."[121] He was assigned to a special section of the High Commission to "deal with the affairs of Armenian and Greek victims of persecution."[122]

Upon his arrival in 1919, Graves joined the Armenian and Greek Section (AGS) as a military attaché with special responsibilities that included the "rescue of Armenian and Greek women and children who had been forcibly converted to Islam from the Turkish houses and institutions into which they had been taken." He was also tasked with obtaining restitution "for owners of Christian properties which had been arbitrarily confiscated." The AGS also employed "Relief Officers with knowledge of the country and the languages" to report "on the condition of the native Christians who had remained in the interior, and in ministering to their needs as far as they were able."[123] Ryan took part in similar efforts; corresponding with relief workers and aiding British and American efforts to repatriate Armenian girls.[124]

Repatriation was not the only issue related to Armenia. The Allies also pledged in the Mudros armistice to prosecute those responsible for the Armenian massacres. The arrest of key CUP figures for "crimes against humanity" began in the spring of 1919. Admiral Calthorpe and others involved themselves in the hunt for and capture of accused war criminals.[125] In May 1919, the British "arrested and deported to Malta ... leading members of the Committee of Union and Progress."[126] Eventually, a handful of trials were held as part of the Constantinople War Crimes tribunals.[127] The proceedings, however, became increasingly unpopular especially in the countryside where Admiral Webb, who also took part, believed "people were still in absolute ignorance of the Entente victory."[128]

The uneven course of the occupation after the armistice threatened to delegitimize Allied authority during ongoing peace negotiations. Resistance from diplomats, leaders and civilians in the occupied territories coupled with infighting between the British and the French made attempts to forge peace with the Ottoman Empire difficult at best. The Treaty of Sèvres came out of the uncertainties of this period as well as long-held assumptions that shaped Allied perceptions of the Ottoman Empire and its peoples. At the end of 1919, the Allied Supreme Council rejected sending relief funds in the wake of new massacres in Cilicia. As Graves recalled, "The year 1919 had ended with the rejection by the Supreme Council of the Allies of an appeal from the Armenian and Greek Patriarchates for an advance of funds for their distressed communities, and I began the New Year with a sense of depression and the fear that the hopes which I had founded on our victory in the War were in danger of being disappointed."[129] The Sèvres negotiations did not offer much hope of countering Graves' disillusionment.

CONCLUSION

Delegates began departing Paris in summer 1919 without reaching an agreement on peace with the Ottoman Empire. The Interallied Conference tasked with finishing the job opened in London on February 12, 1920, without the United States. By this time, Lord Curzon had taken over from Balfour in the Foreign Office and Alexandre Millerand had replaced Clemenceau. Tensions between the French and British continued to run high.[130] Millerand did not want to compromise on Syria and attempted to undo the Lloyd George–Clemenceau agreement of December 1918 on the mandates. France challenged Britain at every turn, leading one historian to call the discussion about the Palestine Mandate "confused and rambling."[131] Conditions on the ground also had changed.

By the time the Allies handed the Treaty to the Ottoman delegation in May 1920, nationalists had mounted a serious resistance to the occupation. The problem of administering occupied territories under wartime conditions would prove a key factor for the failure of the Treaty of Sèvres.

The blurred line between war and peace that existed from the signing of the armistice in late October 1918 led to the signing of the Sèvres Treaty in a porcelain factory on the outskirts of Paris in the summer of 1920. It came out of the ongoing dialogue about the Ottoman Empire started at the Paris Peace Conference. These conversations happened within the context of an unpopular Allied occupation and debates over the details of the mandate system. The mandates proved a wartime tool that facilitated occupation. To read the Treaty of Versailles and the institutions it spawned as part of the ongoing war cedes center stage to the various interests that shaped peacemaking with the Ottoman Empire. At the same time, the journey to Sèvres reveals how the peace process that started in earnest at Paris shaped the late course of the war.

PART THREE

MAKING PEACE

CHAPTER 5

The Treaty of Sèvres

I N LATE OCTOBER 1919, Admiral de Robeck, High Commissioner at Constantinople, sent a photograph of a cartoon published in the Turkish daily paper, *Tasvir-i-Efkiar* [*sic*] to Lord Curzon (Figure 5.1). It had been almost exactly a year since the signing of the armistice and explained, to his mind, the current state of affairs. "Your Lordship will observe," he wrote:

> The very large and undefeated Turk reclining on the map has his feet well planted in Thrace, Constantinople and the Bosporus lie snug beneath his garter. The mid-portion of his manly frame reposes comfortably in Central Anatolia while his drawn sabre is ready to sweep Konia, Adalia and Smyrna clear of the invaders, and his left arm stretches over potential Armenia and Kurdistan with Van between the thumb and forefinger. His shadow lies black on Diarbekir, and extends southward into Syria. Azerbaijan ... is marked on the map and stretches from the Persian frontier to the Black Sea. His scabbard lies across Cilicia, and his menacing glance is evidently fixed on the further distance of Mesopotamia.

This cartoon from the large-circulating CUP-affiliated paper represented for de Robeck "the spirit of the ideals of the 'national movement' ... with whom the Peace Conference will have to reckon, should they presume to affect any superiority in their dealings with Turkey."[1]

The image suggests that out of the ashes of the Ottoman defeat would rise a reconstituted empire that harkened back to the greatness of an earlier time. Under the watchful eye of an orientalized warrior Turk, reemerges an Ottoman-led empire stretching from Europe and across the Mediterranean into Asia, Mesopotamia and the Caucasus. The British

5.1. *Tasvir-i-Efkiar* cartoon sent by Admiral de Robeck to Lord Curzon to explain his understandings of the state of the Turkish nationalist movement. Credit: *Tasvir-i-Efkiar* cartoon included in Constantinople dispatch [no. 1929] sent October 19, 1919.

and the French were busy with their own imperial imaginings during this time. The problem was that each of these empires – Ottoman, British and French – sought to lay claim to the same territory. So, too, did the Russians who looked to assert their influence in the region and regain territory lost under Brest-Litovsk.[2] The failure to settle the peace at Sèvres meant that this war between empires persisted.

This chapter continues the story of the making and unmaking of the Treaty of Sèvres. It bridges the diplomatic and humanitarian sides of peacemaking in the context of the longer treaty process from Versailles to Lausanne in which Sèvres played an intermediary role. The diplomatic stops and starts happened alongside international and imperial anxieties that intersected with the politics of humanitarianism and relief work in regions under occupation. The consequences of this process had long-term implications for the settlement of the war and the civilians who found themselves in the crosshairs of the reconfiguration of empires.

DRAFTING SÈVRES

The Treaty of Sèvres was meant to secure the peace terms laid out in the armistice between the Ottoman Empire and Allied governments. The final agreement built on discussions at the Paris Peace Conference, and later, the London and San Remo conferences in 1920. The treaty sought to undo Ottoman imperial power through partition. At the same time, it codified in international law the protection of minorities as consistent with Allied war aims that claimed to defend their rights.[3] The Paris Peace Conference provided the early space to air considerations over how to remake the Ottoman Empire as a series of ethno-religiously defined states. Meanwhile, the Allied occupation altered conditions on the ground by establishing military and civilian administrative and social infrastructure to govern these regions. By the time the London and San Remo conferences finalized peace terms for signature at Sèvres, the Allied occupation started to falter making the treaty less likely to succeed. Nationalist push back against Allied dictates, however, only made Britain and France more determined to enforce the terms that they had spent the last year and a half discussing.

The Treaty of Sèvres thus came out of an evolving set of diplomatic policy concerns that shaped the final document. Some of these dated back to the Treaty of Berlin (1878), including minority protection and freedom of the Straits, while others addressed more contemporary concerns, such as stopping the spread of Bolshevism by creating buffer states between Western Europe and Russia. The broken promises of Allied wartime agreements, most notably Sykes–Picot, does not satisfactorily explain why peace failed. By the time the Treaty of Sèvres was finalized, Sykes–Picot was in the process of being disavowed, altered and condemned by those on the inside of negotiations.[4] This challenges its solitary importance as a blueprint for carving up the Ottoman Empire. Sèvres was a product of the Paris peace process. The series of earlier agreements, made sometimes in secret and sometimes in the open to win the war, together influenced but did not wholly determine its outcome.

Just as the Versailles Treaty did with Germany, the Treaty of Sèvres imposed a harsh peace on the Ottoman Empire. But unlike the Germans, the Ottomans pushed back. Three memoranda submitted by Ottoman representatives at the Paris Peace Conference made the case for returning the Ottoman Empire to its prewar boundaries.[5] These memoranda had little effect on the final treaty. Their reception, however, shows the strongly consistent position put forward by the Ottoman delegation, led by Damad

Ferid Pasha, to resist partition and helps explain why the Sèvres Treaty took so long to negotiate. On June 23, the Ottoman delegation submitted a "memorandum concerning the new organization of the Ottoman Empire" as requested by the Allied Supreme Council the previous week.[6] While the Council initially seemed to attach little consequence to this exchange, it offered a glimpse of what lay ahead for the peace negotiations.

The Ottoman case rested on maintaining the Empire's "unity and independence," and it refused to "accept the dismemberment of the Empire or its division under different mandates."[7] This position fell in line with nationalist aims to maintain and even grow the Ottoman Empire after the war. The "Answer" approved by the Council that same day rejected claims in the memorandum that the Ottoman government did not bear responsibility for the conduct of the war which included "crimes" committed against minority populations and that "its territories should be restored undiminished, as they existed when war broke out."[8]

This statement, published alongside the Allied response as part of the Paris Peace Conference proceedings, made any quick resolution impossible. Two days later, Lloyd George "asked that Turkey might be considered" shortly before President Wilson's departure from Paris with the heads of the French, British, Italian and Japanese delegations.[9] Anxious "to agree on some Peace Terms which would put Turkey out of her misery," Lloyd George wanted to know if the United States would accept the mandate for Armenia.[10] Continued war with Turkish nationalists in the Caucasus and the refugee crisis threatened to overwhelm the fledging republic.[11] The ultimate decision to postpone peace negotiations dismayed all but Wilson who did not commit to the mandate, instead insisting on a partition plan that "cleared out" the Turks from Europe. He believed that "the amputations would involve Mesopotamia, Syria and Armenia" and suggested that the delegates continue the discussion without him since his representatives "knew his mind."[12] The months of waiting and watching that followed this episode revealed the significance of the minority question to the settlement.

The dividing of the Ottoman Empire into a series of ethno-national states complicated proceedings in a way that the dividing of the great

European land-based empires in the earlier Paris Peace Conference negotiations did not. In the case of Austria-Hungary, the treaty system gave way to a series of weak nation-states unable to pose a strategic threat or economic rival to the British or the French.[13] The status of Russia still remained to be determined as a result of the continued civil war and rise of the Soviet Union that would ultimately define its borders.[14] The case of the Ottoman Empire meant reconciling promises made to Arabs, Zionists and Armenians; agreements between the French and the British and the enshrinement of the League of Nations Covenant. While Wilson supported the "amputations" of Mesopotamia, Syria and Armenia from the Ottoman Empire, there was no consensus on how to do this when the Paris Peace Conference ended. This drawn-out process made the transition to what has come to be known as the Paris system far from easy or certain.[15]

This "anxiety" producing situation, a word repeatedly used by diplomats, military men and negotiators during this episode, did little to push the Ottoman treaty forward. In the foyer of the Versailles Senate Chamber immediately after the signing of the Treaty with Germany on June 28, the Ottoman delegation was handed a letter that stated that treaty negotiations with the Ottoman Empire would be delayed and dismissed them from Paris. Damad Ferid Pasha replied before departing that the Ottoman Government remained "aware of the serious disadvantage of the current uncertainty" and "desired to return to a state of peace ... without delay."[16] The Ottoman delegation had little to show for their efforts and soon after embarked on a humiliating journey home where, according to one source, they "felt they had been unceremoniously bundled out" due to a lack of arrangements made for their journey.[17] They would carry the memory of this slight with them as they prepared for the Allied occupation and worked to appease Turkish nationalist sentiment. Damad Ferid insisted on maintaining prewar borders and that the Allies "restore on a rational basis the boundaries of the Ottoman Empire."[18]

In Constantinople, the unsettled peace weighed heavily on those charged with leading the occupation. The boundary question clearly remained tied up with the question of minorities. Admiral Calthorpe admitted to feeling "considerable anxiety" the day after the dismissal of the Ottoman delegation from Paris. He faced claims of atrocities by both the Greek High Commissioner and Ottoman government during the Greek occupation of Smyrna and its environs which started in spring 1919. Calthorpe believed that the only way to "avert threatening dangers" was the "the very early declaration of terms upon which Peace will be (secured) to Turkey."[19] Admiral Webb reported on the "increase of friction out here between Greeks and Turks" that he attributed to the "indefiniteness of the situation." Economic and political instability threatened the legitimacy of the occupation and could undo efforts on behalf of "thousands of Christians whose welfare we have so much at heart, and concerning which we have made so many protestations."[20] As Admiral de Robeck concluded in a letter to Lord Curzon in October 1919, "Every week that the Peace terms are delayed, sees further acquisition of the power of resistance."[21]

Both sides continued to express dismay at the inability to resolve the peace as the occupation came under increasing pressure. Not even the unsettled question of oil concessions and control over natural resources could force the negotiations forward. The still unsettled question of the status of Mosul complicated US, British and French claims over its newly discovered oilfields.[22] Britain sought to replace the United States with the Middle East as its primary supplier of oil. The United States wanted to secure the future of its own supply and France also wanted its share. But gaining access to Mesopotamian oil was still years away because of the lack of a pipeline.[23] In the end, competition for natural resources and access to trade contributed to a climate of distrust between the wartime allies with Britain accusing "American Relief Expeditions in Asia Minor" of "being used to advertise and push American trade."[24] Economic rivalries spilled over into politics. Britain and France accused the United States of needlessly holding up Ottoman treaty negotiations by not committing to take the mandate for Armenia.[25] In reality, much of the blame for the delay rested with the muddled Allied policy that shaped the post-armistice moment. Together, economic and political conflicts between the French, British, and the Americans and wartime promises to minorities and Wilson's "Fourteen Points" contributed to the protracted process.

The competition sparked by Sykes–Picot also played a role in the context of other wartime diplomatic arrangements. Sykes–Picot was only one of five main agreements that shaped the peace with the Ottoman Empire and Allied diplomacy in this moment. Balfour's August 1919 memorandum on Syria, Palestine and Mesopotamia began with his "considerable anxiety" over the "Syrian question" on "Anglo-French relations." Considered the clearest statement of the British position on the Ottoman Empire in the summer of 1919, it sought an "economic and ethnographic" solution rather than a strategic one, since he believed that Britain and France would likely never go to war over the settlement.[26]

While Ottoman representatives stood firm on what they wanted out the peace settlement – a reconstituted empire that respected prewar boundaries – the Allies showed less unity. Balfour described the five wartime documents that guided Anglo-French policy as follows: "promises to ruler of Hedjaz in 1915"; Sykes Picot 1916; Anglo-French declaration of November 1918; the Covenant of the League of Nations and the American-led Commission sent "to examine the Arab problem on the spot." This list, which included secret agreements and promises, public declarations and the suppressed King-Crane Commission report, spoke to the maze of interests that governed the execution of Allied policy. At the same time, Balfour understood the obligation of Britain to follow the dictates of the peace process. He acknowledged that in cases where interallied agreements contradicted the League Covenant, that the Covenant "must be held to represent our policy."[27] As Balfour concluded: "These documents are not consistent with each other; they represent no clear-cut policy; the policy which they confusedly adumbrate is not really the policy of the Allied and Associated Powers." This posed a problem for Allied peacemaking in 1919: "so far as I can see, none of them have wholly lost their validity or can be treated in all respects as of merely historic interest."[28]

In addition to unsettled diplomatic agendas, fighting continued to create an "anxious situation" in regions that extended from the Black Sea to the Caucasus to northern Persia.[29] This state of uncertainty continued through the fall of 1919 and into the early months of 1920. On the eve of the London Conference, convened in early February 1920 to continue treaty negotiations, security broke down in both the old and the newly occupied zones in the Ottoman Empire. Ottoman complaints about the Greek occupation of the area around Smyrna continued and conditions deteriorated around Aleppo and in Cilicia. On February 4, Admiral de Robeck received a notice that General Henri Gourand, who oversaw the French occupation zone, believed that the "situation was such that it could no longer be called armistice and that there was in effect a [? state] of hostilities between forces and the Turks." At the same time, British intelligence received information that "nationalists are concentrating around Smyrna to attack the Greeks."[30] Around Adana in Cilicia, according to aid worker Harold Buxton, several towns and villages had risen in revolt against the French occupation. The French restored order but not before the town of Marash was burned to the ground and the "inhabitants of some seven Armenian villages in the vicinity were massacred" along with two American aid workers, leaving 1,500 survivors.[31]

The London Conference sat from February 12 until April 10, 1920. Early sessions focused on the recent massacres, Greek presence in and around Smyrna and discontent with the Allied occupation. The massacres at Marash, according to Lord Curzon, constituted "a very serious situation." He believed that "public opinion in Great Britain and France would be very gravely excited" and "undoubtedly ask where the responsibility lay." Lloyd George "considered the matter to be of such grave importance" that he immediately called a meeting of the Supreme Council to consider the situation.[32] Admiral de Robeck had earlier expressed concern that "recent events in Marash" represented a "definite forward movement on the part of Nationalists."[33]

Worries over the so-called Marash incident led to claims that the Ottoman government had broken the armistice and that the Allies need no longer to bind themselves to its terms. Bilateral meetings between the French and British in the months leading up to the London conference produced treaty drafts that were presented to delegates in London and debated.[34] These early drafts declared that the Ottoman government's violation of the terms of the armistice freed "the Allied powers from every other obligation other than respect for the guiding principles of justice." Long memoranda laid out possible solutions to the four key issues to be addressed by the peace: the status of Constantinople and the Straits; the boundaries of Anatolia and Asia Minor; the future of Armenia and the status of Syria, Mesopotamia and Arabia.[35]

Past interactions between Europe and the Ottoman Empire guided the resolution of these issues in the final treaty. The ghost of the Treaty of Berlin haunted discussions of Sèvres. Damad Ferid insisted that the Ottoman Empire "did not hesitate to adopt a series of reforms" when previously urged by the Great Powers and thus required no more interference from the Allies.[36] His claim that Muslim and Christian populations suffered equally in the war in the memorandum issued in Paris outraged Allied delegates who cited the Armenian massacres as an example of a long-standing policy against minorities.[37] This defiant insistence by the Ottoman delegation that things should return to their prewar status contributed to the protracted peace process because it flew in the face of both Allied war aims and previous agreements with the Ottomans. In this way, London, San Remo and the Treaty of Sèvres continued a decades-long conversation about the status of minorities made urgent by the war. This issue defined European–Ottoman relations after the armistice and led to the rejection of the Ottoman memoranda at the Paris Peace Conference.

The London and San Remo conferences, held successively from February to April 1920, settled the conditions presented to the Turkish delegation at Sèvres later that summer. While these two conferences worked out the details of the peace initially discussed in the bilateral French-British negotiations in December 1919, their conclusions remained contingent and subject to continued negotiation. Members of the British delegation worked on reconciling draft after draft, a process started in earnest in December 1919, which looked to "harmonize" decision making. Two weeks after San Remo, negotiators anticipated having to reconcile the "notes and protests" of the Turkish delegation to "our data and statistics."[38] Ultimately, the Supreme Council remained beholden to conversations started at the Paris Peace Conference that further exacerbated French-Anglo tensions. These came to a head in bilateral negotiations that continued up to the eve of the London Conference. The French sought to preserve the partial integrity of the Ottoman Empire while imposing stringent controls to guarantee security for French investments.[39] British objectives were less clear. Though agreement came on the opening of the Straits, diplomats disagreed on how to divide Anatolia into a series of minority-run states for Armenian and Kurdish populations.

The Supreme Council drafted the initial terms in London under the watchful eye of Lloyd George who controlled the proceedings to the chagrin of both the French and the Italian premier: Alexandre Millerand and Francesco Nitti respectively. Britain wanted to oversee the Straits as part of an "International Control Commission" as revenge for Gallipoli, while the French, under military pressure in Anatolia from the Kemalists, expressed a willingness to abandon Cilicia to get prewar commercial concessions restored. Italy, seeing its own ambitions sidelined, objected to the proceedings. It felt betrayed, having entered the war in 1915 under the Secret Treaty of London that promised it control of lands in southern Anatolia.[40] These internal disagreements resulted in a "Tripartite Agreement" that divided the Ottoman Empire into zones controlled by the three powers. Still, key territorial questions remained. This included the status of Smyrna, currently precariously occupied by the Greeks.[41]

The San Remo conference took place at the end of April to settle remaining questions. The French wanted negotiations held in France, but Lloyd George trusted the French less than the Italians and made sure that the Supreme Council reassembled in San Remo on April 19. Initial plans to use the conference to talk about German reparations gave way to a focus on the Ottoman Empire which included the mandates. This resulted in part from military setbacks suffered by the French at the hands of Turkish nationalist forces that February in Cilicia.[42] The Allies retaliated for violence against the Armenians by occupying Constantinople while acknowledging what the occupation authorities had recognized all along: without a treaty, war continued. Rather than directly confront Kemal, the Allies agreed to "enforce the treaty in those areas where they were themselves directly involved."[43] Lloyd George refused to commit more divisions to secure the Allied position. This created a weak enforcement system where each side defended only the territory over which they held authority. The British later experienced the problem with this system at Chanak in September 1922 when they defended the freedom of the Straits without French or Italian help.[44]

Ultimately, the San Remo conference approved the terms of the Ottoman treaty laid out in London. The short length of the conference – it lasted only eight days – belied its importance to the peace process as a venue for codifying Allied priorities and voicing disagreements about the status of minorities.[45] While the United States tried to exercise influence through arm's-length diplomatic dealings, Turkish and Armenian interests vied for attention. President Wilson sent a note read at the first session outlining US policy and sent the American Ambassador in Rome to attend five conference sessions as an observer. This suited Lloyd George who asserted, "the smaller the conference was, the better."[46] Delegates replied to Wilson that his absence signaled a willingness to let the treaty conclude without US input.[47] They then invited Nubar and Aharonian to give testimony about Armenia. Signor Nitti, representing Italy, commented that past and current massacres meant that "the conference had been much preoccupied with the question of Armenia."[48]

While Lloyd George believed that there was little hope in fully resolving the issue of minority protection, the Supreme Council decided to make Armenia a signatory of the treaty. This had to do in part with the ongoing violence in Cilicia.[49] Here in the troubled heart of historic Armenia, the treaty carved out an Armenian state. It also included considerations for a future Kurdish state.[50] Turkish nationalists rejected this move and on the eve of the conference, Ahmed Riza Bey, former President of the Chamber and Senator of the Ottoman Empire, sent a letter to San Remo conference delegates. Though exiled by the Damad Ferid Ministry and therefore not the official voice of the Ottoman government, he assumed an authoritative stance that revealed a hardening of the nationalist position:

> The Turks cannot in any way, in this age of liberty and democracy, acknowledge a peace that would lower them to the level of an inferior race and would treat them worse than the Hungarians or Bulgarians, who have lost comparatively small territories, whereas Turkey is to be utterly crippled. We want to be treated as a vanquished people, not as an inferior people or a people in tutelage. The victors may have a right to take from us the territories they conquered by force of arms; they have no right to intrude into our home affairs .... In respect of the crimes and atrocities against Armenia and Greece which the Turks are charged with, we deny them earnestly and indignantly.[51]

The statement echoed the Ottoman delegation's Paris Peace Conference memorandum. But it went further by denying responsibility for the "crimes and atrocities" committed against Armenians and Greeks which were to justify the carving out of an Armenian state in Anatolia, the "home" of the Turkish peoples.

Competing Armenian and Turkish claims led to controversy. Lord Montagu defended the "political principles underlying Turkish Peace Terms" in a memorandum. This was later followed by the publication of "The Allied Case for the Turkish Treaty" which addressed Ottoman resistance to the direction of negotiations. Together, these documents defended the treaty in the context of war aims and minority protection:

> It has been urged in some quarters that the terms of peace now given to the Turks are in violation of the professed aims of the Allies and the principles applied in the case of the other treaties of peace with our late enemies. In this connection it is well to remember first, that the only Allied declaration in regard to Turkey was that of January 1917, in which the expulsion of the Turk from Europe was declared an allied war aim and secondly that the principle applied by the Peace conference throughout its deliberations, namely that of nationality, has been faithfully observed by the Peace Conference in its proposals for the Turkish peace ... This being the case can there be any question as to the clear duty of the Peace Conference to liberate substantial majorities of non-Turkish nationalities form Turkish rule, and join them to their own national States? If this has been the principle applied throughout Europe are not the reasons doubly strong for applying it in the case of the Turks?[52]

The statement denied any "religious prejudice" or "anti-Islamic" feelings and claimed that it applied "the same principles to Turkey as it has applied throughout Europe." But in this case, the "principles" had roots in the minority protection provisions of the Treaty of Berlin.[53] Montagu cited as a reason for the harsh terms of the treaty the "massacre of 800,000 of its subjects" and the driving of "200,000 more from their homes."[54] Like Germany, Turkey would be punished – not for starting the war but for the treatment of minorities. In the end, despite these admonitions and support for minority claims over historic homelands, the Treaty of Sèvres left the major part of Anatolia to Turkey, including Constantinople.

The signing of the Treaty of Sèvres happened without the grandeur or pomp and circumstance of the Treaty of Versailles. Even the choice of the suburban venue reflected attempts to avoid further controversy by not drawing attention to the proceedings. The San Remo conference stipulated that the Ottoman plenipotentiaries be summoned to Paris on May 10. Worries over backlash voiced in Montagu's defense, cited above, contributed to the decision to avoid the ceremonial flourishes of Versailles. On May 11, 1920, the 433 articles of the Treaty of Sèvres were handed to the Ottoman delegation, who were given a month to consider terms. After taking a look at the treaty, delegates requested an extension, leaving Paris for Constantinople on June 10. Damad Ferid arrived back in Paris on June 17 to present Turkish counterproposals. These included territorial readjustments and the proposal for a special autonomous regime for Smyrna similar to that of the free city of Hamburg along with the desire to preserve the Ottoman Caliphate.[55]

Calling the delegates together for a signing on July 28 in Paris proved premature. The Allied rejection of the counterproposals hardened the stance of the group of senators and former ministers who made up the delegation – Hadi Pasha, Reiza Tewfik Bey and Reshid Haliss Bey. Hadi Pasha requested further changes on August 1. Though these counter-proposals proved a dead letter, one concession was achieved: the demand to not let Nubar Pasha, who had been the face of the Armenian cause during the war, sign the Treaty. Instead, Avadis Aharonian, an important but lesser known figure, signed on Armenia's behalf. The Ottoman delegation signed the Treaty of Sèvres on August 10, 1920, under what Lord Curzon referred to as "considerable pressure."[56]

RESPONSES TO THE PEACE PROCESS

The Allies remained keenly aware of the growing unpopularity of the provisions of the Treaty of Sèvres in Turkey. Despite arguing against partition in its final conference memorandum, the Ottoman delegation was blamed for the harsh terms of the treaty which added fuel to nation-alist discontent. This, coupled with a growing lack of Allied resolve to back up the terms of the armistice with military force, threatened the legitimacy of the Sèvres Treaty. While the Allies maintained a significant military presence during this period, a drawdown of troops began in summer 1919 when the British reduced its force from 1 million to 320,000.[57] Kemal's army continued to challenge Allied occupation in Anatolia which nationalists saw as the heart of the new Turkish state. The British responded by further tightening administrative control. This strengthened resistance to peacemaking by both the Allied-backed government and Kemalist-led nationalists. By the time of the signing of the Treaty of Sèvres in summer 1920, it was clear that any attempt to enforce the treaty provisions would require military force.

In Downing Street, consensus emerged around four key principles: ending "Turkish militarism"; internationalization of the Straits; freeing the Armenians "from Turkish domination"; and not returning Arab and Syrian populations to "the domination of the Turk."[58] At the same time, Britain noticed growing criticism in India of the settlement. This included the question of the freedom of the Straits for commercial and military purposes, capitulations (a system that historically maintained European privileges in the Ottoman Empire), war debt and the status of the Sultan.[59] The latter would prove most significant in the face of Indian nationalists' questioning of British dealings with the Ottomans.[60] Some in the British cabinet argued that elevating the Ottoman Sultan as Caliphate for all Muslims and promising a rapid end to the occupation would make the Treaty of Sèvres' provisions more palatable and win over Indian public opinion.

Rising nationalism shaped this line of thinking.[61] Ultimately, the Kemalist-led government of Turkey abolished the Caliphate in 1924.[62] But in 1920, the British took seriously the possibility of heeding Damad Ferid's demand to support the Ottoman Sultan as a symbol of unity in the Muslim world. According to "secret information," dismantling the Ottoman Empire and removing the Sultan from Constantinople threatened a full nationalist assault on British rule.[63] War in Ireland and unrest in Egypt further added to imperial insecurity and uncertainty.[64] The massacre at Amritsar on April 13, 1919, of unarmed civilians by British troops heightened tensions further. Understood by historians as a key event in the lead-up to Indian independence, it served as a catalyst for Gandhi's non-cooperation movement and represented an important moment in the delegitimization of British imperial power.[65] Gandhi and highly respected Muslim leaders agitated against the Treaty of

Sèvres as an affront to Indian Muslims, a move that they hoped would unite the nationalist cause against British rule in India. Gandhi connected Amritsar with the treatment of the Ottoman Empire. "The wrongs done at Amritsar and the infamous Treaty of Sèvres," he argued, required "repentance on the part of the British government."[66]

Some believed agitation against Sèvres would result in full-scale revolt against the British Empire. "From the moment this Treaty was signed," warned one official, "we should have for the first time a movement, comparable to the Sinn Fein movement, breaking out in India, in favour of complete separation from England."[67] British Indian officials believed that enforcing the Treaty of Sèvres would cause the "boycott of British goods and a general refusal of all Government measures."[68] Britain relied disproportionately on Indian troops to fight on the Middle Eastern Front.[69] The risk of alienating Indian Muslims who loyally fought for the British Empire and now had the support of Gandhi's nationalist movement had the potential to ignite anti-British protest in India *and* undermine the Ottoman peace. If Britain removed the Sultan from Constantinople, some believed, it would "add one more spark to the spreading conflagration" that included growing Bolshevik threats to Indian security in relation to Afghanistan. The start of the Third Afghan War in 1919 further added to tensions.[70]

Opinion, however, was far from unified, and it remains unclear how much the issue of the future governance of Turkey represented an actual threat to the British Empire in India. Many still maintained that the greatest risk to the Allies was "Turkish militarism," which also threatened the Armenians, Arabs and Assyrians. Lord Curzon and Admiral Calthorpe most clearly represented this view. Curzon put on record his dissent from the majority view that the Sultan should stay in Constantinople. Calling the claim that such a move would "avoid trouble in India" and "render our task in Egypt less difficult" "largely manufactured" and "ephemeral," he argued that such a policy would fly in the face of Allied war aims.[71] Others joined Curzon, calling concerns over a rebellion in India and Egypt an illusion. The real threat was not placating Muslim opinion in India, but eliminating the military threat of Mustafa Kemal.[72]

The issue of war crimes clouded matters further. Officials sought to enforce armistice terms that promised justice for prisoners of war and massacred civilians. Evidence gathering began in December 1918. By early March 1919, Balfour ordered an official inquiry that resulted in a report entitled "Turco-German Outrages on Armenians and British Prisoners."[73] Dozens of pages of detailed evidence were organized in a manner that recalled Bryce's Blue Book. This report, however, went further and listed the names of perpetrators and described individual crimes in order to make "the case against offenders who are to be prosecuted."[74] The report was presented to the Paris Peace Conference on April 22 but never received a full hearing as news of the massacre at Amritsar reached delegates. That spring, the Constantinople War Crimes trials limped along, succeeding only in further feeding nationalist anger.[75] Indeed, by the time the Treaty of Sèvres was signed, the question of prosecuting individuals for war crimes had completely faded from view. As one British official put it upon receiving the report on April 25: "No action can be taken at present. These lists must be put by until the treaty with Turkey takes shape and comes into force. If it contains provisions for the list of punishment of these individuals, the appropriate steps must then be taken."[76]

Negotiations surrounding the Treaty of Sèvres were also overshadowed by fighting between Allied forces and Kemal's nationalist army. This added to the tension that resulted from the Greek occupation. While the French faced defeat in Cilicia at Marash, the British had their own difficulties attempting to secure a foothold in the Caucasus. The Italians were also unable to make inroads against the Kemalists. After the terms of the Treaty of Sèvres had been decided, Churchill learned that it would take a strong force of arms to enforce the treaty. The War Office estimated that twenty-seven divisions would be needed to support Greek forces which represented "a formidable stumbling block," standing in the way of "the question of the protection of minorities" and the "definition of frontiers."[77]

MP Aneurin Williams visited the War Office about this time to find out how Churchill planned to protect minorities. Williams wanted the British to occupy Trebizond (modern Trabzon) to stave off the still looming threat of massacre. He was told in no uncertain terms that it was "hardly possible to dump two to three battalions in Trebizond and leave them there all alone to face any troops that Mustapha Kemal might detach to attack them."[78] News of continued massacres appeared daily in the press. The issue that brought Williams to the War Office now had a broader hearing among the British public. Massacres committed in the Caucasus in the winter of 1920 by Kemalist troops killed an estimated 50,000 Armenians; the autumn of the following year news arrived of large numbers of Greeks deported from Trebizond and Samsun.[79] In 1921, as a result of the Angora Agreement signed between the Turkish nationalist government and France, the French withdrew 70,000 troops from Anatolia.[80]

HUMANITARIAN CRISIS

The diplomatic crisis over the Treaty of Sèvres paralleled the humanitarian crisis in the Ottoman Empire that only continued to worsen. The drawdown of troops raised the question of what to do with the increasing number of civilians who had come to rely on Allied protection. In the Caucasus, the war exacerbated the refugee crisis and led to more massacres. "It is a terrible situation that I write you this letter," Zabel Yessayan wrote to Boghos Nubar a month before the signing of the armistice about the deteriorating situation in the Caucasus. "Battles in the street continue ... There is not precise information on the situation of the inhabitants of the city who are certainly between the fire and the sword." This meant more human and environmental disaster: "There is to also arrive 3000 refugees and orphans ... The oil wells ... of Bibi, Eybat and Balakhaiut [sic] are on fire and it is in this infernal and hideous situation that probably live the large part of the population." News of the impending Allied victory did little to raise Yessayan's hopes: "It is a great deception for us that the [Europeans] are just victors at the moment."[81]

This grim view from Baku and its environs presaged the experience of others. In early January 1920, Lord Curzon, worried about the ongoing situation in the Caucasus, asked his colleagues "whether any interallied action is possible for relief of situation."[82] The Marash incident proved the most dramatic humanitarian disaster in the period between the armistice and signing of the Treaty of Sèvres. "Last night was another night of burning and bombing," reported American NER aid worker Stanley Kerr in late January 1920. "Still the massacring goes on, and the

French admit they are powerless to stop it."[83] The fires set by the nation-alist army continued to burn through February. Another eyewitness working in Marash for the YMCA wrote in his diary as he watched the French retreat from the city: "As the column moved away from the city it was a blaze of splendor. The great barracks just evacuated by the French was on fire, silhouetted against the sky."[84]

These conflagrations proved effective terror tactics against the Allied occupation in the face of an unsettled peace and ongoing civil war in Russia. Yessayan, who had traveled to southern Anatolia to help with repatriation efforts, sent an urgent plea to 10 Downing Street at the end of February 1920: "Alarming situation in Cilicia. Any Armenian population is in danger of massacre. 20,000 are already massacred in the Marash region evacuated by the troops ... Please take urgent and energetic steps to save the population by all means."[85] By April, the few remaining Armenian churches that served as centers of communal life in Marash not burnt to the ground were used to house displaced fire victims. Instead of celebrating the Easter ritual, Armenians sought food and assistance from Kerr and other aid workers who initially came to the village to assist resettlement efforts.[86]

Burning cities to the ground proved an effective way for the Kemalists to interrupt the resettlement of Armenians and reclaim Allied occupied territory in Anatolia. The difficulty of resolving the problem of refugees fleeing war and the threat of massacre in the midst of a worsening economic crisis influenced the peace process. "Public opinion in America, Great Britain and France wants to save Armenia," Balfour wrote to Curzon during the planning stages of the Treaty of Sèvres.[87] The Allies responded by shuffling top diplomatic posts in Constantinople in the futile hope of regaining influence.[88] The London Conference in February 1921 between the Turkish nationalist government at Angora and Allied representatives did not resolve the situation. The maze of political and humanitarian interests governing the peace settlement generated confusion as the Treaty of Sèvres unraveled. In a letter to Lord Curzon, Montagu at the Foreign Office admitted in the spring of 1921 to feeling "so very much at sea as to what exactly is the position with regard to the Turkish treaty that I do not know how to answer it ... Are we to allow fighting to go on forever? What is the end of this business?"[89] In the end, the aim to protect minorities failed to sustain peace with the Ottoman Empire.

This did not mean that the minority question went away. MP T. P. O'Conner wrote Curzon on Christmas Eve 1921 that he believed that despite signs of waning interest, public opinion remained "unanimous" in favor of the liberation of Armenians and every Christian race from the dominion of Turkey."[90] The failure of the Treaty of Sèvres to end the war affected advocacy work. At the end of 1921, the AGS, which oversaw resettlement operations and adjudicated victim claims, was disbanded.[91] Private efforts filled in the void sometimes using the same personnel. Former AGS official Robert Graves worked on behalf of the advocacy arm of the Lord Mayor's Fund and later joined Quaker Ann Mary Burgess on the island of Corfu where, along with his sons, he supported her work with Armenian and Greek refugees.[92] This movement of personnel between government and private aid and advocacy work characterized this moment. Graves later served on the League of Nations Greek Refugee Settlement Commission.[93]

Others like Andrew Ryan remained a steady presence in peace negotiations through to the Lausanne Conference. His role as a delegate made him "mostly occupied with questions concerning minorities and the position of foreigners and their interests in Turkey." As previous head of the AGS, he exercised influence over responses to President Wilson's scheme for Armenia and Kurdistan. Graves worked closely with Ryan and together they influenced minority policy first at the Paris Peace Conference and later in negotiations leading to the Treaty of Sèvres.[94] As Ryan claimed of his own motivations regarding the minority issue: "We were dealing with a country which, under its then rulers, had stabbed us in the back in 1914 which had shown hostility to foreign interests, which seemed unlikely to be able to work out its own financial and economic salvation, and which above all (in my view) could not be trusted with the fate of its minorities, to judge by the merciless persecution of the Armenians during the war." He concluded, "Rightly or wrongly, these were the ideas which inspired all discussions in responsible Allied circles."[95]

The Allied occupation's focus on ameliorating the condition for Ottoman minorities had a lasting impact on how humanitarian aid worked.[96] Humanitarian organizations focused on those deemed the most vulnerable victims of the war: women and children.[97] Before establishing herself at Corfu, Ann Mary Burgess founded the Friends' Constantinople Mission. Burgess' network of philanthropists, businessmen, government consuls, and workers created a thriving industry that supported over 700 women workers.[98] The British Consul in Constantinople helped defray start-up costs at the mission and supported it throughout its nearly three decades of existence.[99] Burgess' Constantinople Mission bridged the roles of political advocate and spiritual guide, helping "prisoners in obtaining their release, in visiting and caring for the sick, in clothing the naked and in feeding the starving ones around us."[100]

Burgess had served the Armenian community for nearly thirty years when news of the signing of the 1918 Mudros Armistice came. Initially, she believed she could continue her mission uninterrupted while the Allies sorted out the final peace. On the eve of the signing of Sèvres, she worried about the "political storm" over the treaty which led to an increase in the numbers of refugees at the mission and an attempt by nationalists to burn down her rug factory.[101] She wrote one supporter a year later that "All these great upheavals are the results of the war which still continues in this unhappy land."[102] In February 1921, she claimed that 20,000 refugees had converged in Constantinople, fleeing the Greek invasion, the Red Army and Kemalist forces. "Hatred and desire for revenge is found on all sides," she lamented. "Hunger, cold, sickness and inadequate clothing in this period of cold weather is horrible."[103]

This "life of strange cares" she attributed to the French withdrawal from Cilicia in the winter of 1921, which exacerbated the refugee crisis. It forced her to acknowledge that she could no longer continue her work in Turkey: "Here everything is against us ... Strife is the order of the day."[104] By the time the British Embassy informed her that she had to leave Constantinople for her own safety in November 1922, she had already decided to move the mission and her charges to Corfu. On this small island where thousands of refugees took shelter, the Greek bishop who visited Burgess' factory called it a "sacred place." She kept the factory going with the labor of refugees who received both a small wage and support from the mission funded by profits from rug sales.[105]

Burgess' experience mirrored that of Zabel Yessayan who, too, understood the limits and risks of aid work during the later years of the war. As a woman and an Armenian, she found her work politicized and her efforts interrupted by both local leadership and the League of Nations. The Armenian Red Cross, based in Britain, relied on Yessayan for reports on the humanitarian emergency in the Caucasus in the summer of 1918. Aid money went through Tehran where Yessayan used it to fund her projects. The Armenian National Delegation, headquartered in Paris, supported her work in French-occupied Cilicia. Her advocacy work supported Armenian causes and set up orphanages and schools, while she also continued to write about her experiences.[106] As Emily Robinson of the Armenian Red Cross explained, "We do not send help through missionaries or through any political committee: our object is to help Armenians to help themselves." Funding Yessayan's schools and industrial work programs along with her advocacy work were presumably ways to achieve this objective.[107]

Yessayan worked with prominent members of the philanthropic community including Rev. Harold Buxton and made requests of the British government for support for Armenian causes supported by Aneurin Williams, chair of the British Armenia Committee in Parliament.[108] Emboldened by her growing stature in the aid community, she embarked on a campaign to set up schools and orphanages in Cilicia in 1920 before the nationalist reconquest.[109] On the international stage, the League of Nations commissioned a committee to oversee the work that Yessayan argued was so necessary to help women in 1921. But Yessayan was not selected for the committee, most likely due to waning support for Armenia.[110] In the early 1920s, after the death of her husband, she returned to Paris and later accepted an invitation from the USSR to settle in Soviet Armenia where she wrote and lectured on French literature. In 1937 she was sent into exile to Siberia by Stalin where she presumably died in the early 1940s.[111]

By making relief work their business, women like Burgess and Yessayan squarely focused the humanitarian movement's attention on the costs of war on women and children. After visiting, with a Turkish doctor, a Turkish refugee camp that housed over 4,000 women and children, Burgess wondered how nations could support the "terrible bloodshed" by continuing the war.[112] In this way, humanitarian advocacy shadowed diplomatic efforts to forge a lasting peace by focusing on the war's most vulnerable victims. The battle to determine the postwar makeup of the Ottoman Empire included the future protection of minorities in relation to the war's effects on civilian populations.[113]

CILICIA

Cilicia marked a turning point in Allied thinking about minority protection. While other minorities including the Kurds made claims to Anatolia, Armenians had a strong a connection to both Cilicia in southern Anatolia and the area bordering the Caucasus in eastern Anatolia. Armenians had inhabited Cilicia uninterrupted since the thirteenth century BCE and still today refer to Cilicia or "Giligia" as a homeland. The Allies legitimated the occupation of this region after the Mudros Armistice based on these claims. The French oversaw the occupation and encouraged the repatriation of around 170,000 Armenians to Cilicia.[114] The occupation of eastern Anatolia was also facilitated earlier by the Russians, who conquered and occupied the eastern Anatolian borderlands in the Caucasus, and then by the British who fought to hold it after the armistice.[115]

The Marash incident showed the difficulty of protecting minorities through occupation.[116] The truce between Kemalists and France came on May 28 and entailed the temporary surrender of Anatolian lands under French occupation.[117] While nationalists could not reverse territorial loses in Mesopotamia and Arabia, Anatolia was a different story. The Turks claimed Anatolia as their homeland and it was on this basis that the nationalists kept fighting: to preserve Anatolia, including Cilicia and the borderlands in the Caucasus, for the postwar Turkish state. The image of the Ottoman warrior reclining across all of Anatolia that so worried de Robeck in late 1919 reflected a vision of postwar Turkey first put forth by Damad Farid in Paris and then enforced by Kemal's army. The defeat of what remained of the British army in the Caucasus and the Russian Civil War made the defense of eastern Anatolia as part of the proposed Armenian state impossible by the summer of 1920. Fighting between Kemalists and the Armenian state established around Erevan began in September and lasted for four months.[118] By the time the French departed Cilicia for good in November 1921, nationalists had laid clear claim to the entirety of Anatolia as a Turkish homeland.

France's decision to unilaterally end the occupation of Cilicia showed the fragility of its alliance with Britain. It also revealed the futility of humanitarian diplomacy in the face of growing Turkish nationalism. The French had believed that repatriating Armenians would secure its long-term presence in Cilicia by creating a grateful ally. Britain saw it in its best interest to embrace this policy. Allenby, who did not like the idea of handing over the territory to the French, appointed Col. Brémond as chief administrator and provided a military force to assist the under-staffed French army from February to November 1919.[119] The British at first dedicated resources to aid repatriation, which included efforts to return "absorbed" women and orphan children to Armenian homes. Initially under the supervision of the AGS, this "rescue work" ended up in the hands of local, regional and international relief committees including mostly NER.

Admiral Webb worried that stopping the military's support of repatriation efforts already underway was tantamount to "massacre" since it would result in the deaths of those suddenly abandoned without any resources.[120] The maze of interests involved in relief work centered on repatriation came under increasing strain. In Adana alone, 60,000 refugees who were part of the repatriation program, according to one historian, "posed a serious problem to the French administration, as most lived in miserable conditions and required food, clothing and medical care."[121] These realities exposed the inconsistencies of an Allied policy that sought to use tools like repatriation and private aid to avoid the long-term burden of caring for refugees.[122]

Administration proved a serious problem for the French throughout the occupation. In the face of personnel shortages, the French enlisted local gendarmerie units under the command of former Ottoman officer Col. Hashim Bey who subverted Allied dictates.[123] They also relied on colonial soldiers from Algeria and formed an Armenian-led Legion d'Orient.[124] Tensions between these different units eventually flared up during the Marash incident. Curzon blamed the violence on the racial composition of the force rather than nationalist aggression and asked if the French had any "white" soldiers to bring order.[125] The inability to control events in Cilicia led the French Parliament to express interest in ending the war as early as June 1920. After one aborted peace attempt with the nationalist leadership in Ankara in the spring of 1921, a bilateral agreement was reached in October under French envoy Henry Franklin-Bouillon who brokered a French withdrawal by December.[126]

News of the French departure from Cilicia in November 1921 exacerbated the ongoing humanitarian crisis. But the French ultimately did not abandon the newly repatriated Armenians, staging a hasty evacuation. During the occupation they had relied on local Armenian-led organizations to help with refugees, required Ottoman administrators to provide spaces for relief work and established the government-run "French Agency for Repatriation and Public Welfare."[127] Gouraud issued a proclamation in early November imploring residents to stay and asserting that France had done what it could to "safeguard the rights of minorities." This did not reassure nervous residents who wanted to leave.

Public and private support for an evacuation, mostly to French-occupied Beirut, and Aleppo, forced the issue. As one French official put it, there was a choice to be made "between organizing the emigration . . . or washing our hands of the Christians determined to leave the territories handed back to the Turks, which is morally impossible."[128] As Benjamin White has argued in his history of this incident, the decision to evacuate those who wanted to leave before the French withdrew, "remained beholden, if not to immediate military necessity, then certainly to wider strategic and diplomatic imperatives."[129] The two-week-long evacuation happened under the full sanction of the French government which issued *laissez-passer* to the 39,377, mostly Armenian, evacuees.[130]

The French evacuation of civilians from Cilicia mirrored British thinking about refugees. Britain supported camps in the aftermath of Baghdad but did not want to take responsibility for the mass of people made stateless by the war. In the end, both governments did very little to support resettlement while paying lip service to treaty commitments. The strain of a disastrous war and the slow, shaky peace process started to weigh on those charged with negotiating and implementing the peace. Curzon faced accusations by critics that he had failed to make good on promises to protect Armenians massacred at Cilicia, the region he had earlier proposed as home of the Armenian state, when the French withdrew in 1921. "What would you have us do?" he angrily replied in a heated exchange with Aneurin Williams who wanted aid for refugees. "It is a practical impossibility to accommodate them in Cyprus, Egypt, Mesopotamia or Palestine." He made it clear that: "there is no money to defray accommodation were it available."[131]

Britain laid the failure of the French occupation and Armenian mandate at the feet of the United States. Churchill claimed he always doubted that America would follow through with its pledges. "It seemed inconceivable that the five great Allies would not be able to make their will effective," Churchill observed, but, in the end, "no power would take a mandate for Armenia." The French failed to carve out a small autonomous region in Cilicia after their defeat. America, however, deserved most of the blame: "The atrocities committed by the Turks during this campaign upon the Armenians and the moral responsibility for these disasters which the American people are considered in some quarter to bear, owing to their refusal to accept a mandate in this part of the world."[132]

For those stuck in the chaos of the cycle of conquest, occupation and reconquest, the situation meant one thing: more war. One eyewitness to the evacuation concluded in assessing its aftermath: "I don't know what people think elsewhere, but in Adana, everyone is unanimous in saying that life is untenable for indigenous Christians." He believed that even if peace did not "remedy the situation" it meant little to Europeans who had "only to go away" and thus wash their hands of the situation.[133]

The reconquest of Cilicia further legitimated Kemal's stature and showed him firmly in charge. Suffering from a nervous breakdown in the wake of attempts to negotiate with Kemal, Damad Ferid, the European-educated commoner who had married Sultan Abdul Hamid's sister, would be remembered as the man who helped bring about the fall of the Ottoman Empire. His attempt to placate Allied demands while serving both as Grand Vizier and a plenipotentiary at the Paris Conference did little to preserve the old regime. The government's futile attempt to argue for the maintenance of the Ottoman Empire by agreeing to try CUP officials as war criminals ultimately contributed to his downfall. In February 1920, a parliamentary commission made up of nationalists and former CUP members discussed the impeachment of Damad Ferid on account of his inability to prevent the Greek landing at Smyrna and the ordering of "a large number of illegal arrests." Though he continued in politics until 1921, he remained little more than the face of a doomed government. He died at Cap d'Ail on the southern coast of France in October 1923.[134]

Kemalist forces seriously threatened the Greek and Allied position in the wake of the French withdrawal. Reports of massacres of Muslim civilians by occupying Greek troops further strengthened nationalist resolve.[135] In early September 1922, Lord Curzon proposed the "Complete evacuation of Asia Minor" as the strength of the Kemalist army grew. "His Majesty's Government are ... anxious to terminate disastrous warfare and to avoid further shedding of blood," wrote Curzon to his counterpart in Constantinople, and "will gladly take any steps in conjunction with their allies to secure these objects." Curzon cautioned that the government must also "consider political conditions" under which the evacuation would take place, including the "protection of Christian populations."[136]

One week later, Kemalist's forces entered Smyrna chasing a retreating Greek army and around 50,000 refugees.[137] Many suspected that the violence would get worse but few anticipated that the nationalist army would set fire to the city. Eyewitnesses reported Kemal's army deliberately starting the fires that would leave the city in ruins. The burning of the Armenian and Greek quarters and passing over of the Turkish quarter led to the conclusion that the fire was started in order to rid the city of Ottoman Christians.[138] The fire destroyed the Ottoman Empire's key commercial Mediterranean port city, killing and displacing its entire population of non-Muslim inhabitants.

CONCLUSION

Reflecting on the significance of the burning of Smyrna years later, Churchill wrote that it marked the "final act" in the "tragedy" of the war in the East.[139] Within weeks of the Smyrna conflagration, the British were driven back from what turned out to be the military's last stand on the Dardanelles Straits at Chanak (modern Çanakkale). By late fall 1922, Kemalists fully controlled Anatolia and the Allies began preparations to negotiate a new treaty. The Lausanne Conference, called to revise the

Treaty of Sèvres, began in the immediate aftermath of Smyrna and crisis at Chanak near where the war had had its inauspicious beginning at Gallipoli. Negotiations at Lausanne started in November 1922 and resulted in a signed final agreement on July 24, 1923.

Diplomacy and humanitarianism continued to play a dual role in this final chapter of the war. Even before the nationalists set fire to Smyrna, the humanitarian crisis across the Ottoman Empire had garnered the attention of the international aid community. Western-based organizations tapped into a global aid network supported by individuals, national governments and the League of Nations. Large-scale fundraising campaigns took place mainly in the United States and Britain and relied on the human stories of the war to raise awareness and money to help victims. As war and peacemaking continued, these efforts offered a glimpse of a conflict many thousands of miles away fought to protect distant strangers under the protection of the victorious Western powers. The humanitarian response to the crisis found renewed purpose in a moment when new media brought home the faces of those on whose behalf the war ostensibly had been fought. As the next chapter shows, the reality of a war depicted in the press, in photographs and on film created a lasting legacy of relief work's undeniable connection to wartime diplomacy.

CHAPTER 6

Humanitarian Crusades

THE WAR IN THE EAST HAD AN UNDENIABLE EFFECT ON the business of relief work.[1] At the same time, the humanitarian movement indelibly shaped public perceptions of the war. The false peace at Mudros, the failed Treaty of Sevrès and the fallout from Russia's exit from the war resulted in the largest humanitarian crisis to date. New media brought home to western audiences the brutal effects of the First World War on vulnerable civilians as war and peacemaking continued. Films made by humanitarian organizations between 1919 and 1923 portrayed the war in and around the Ottoman Empire as a protracted but solvable human tragedy. Images of transformative aid projects further justified Allied control over Ottoman administrative functions and activities in Bolshevik Russia. Such depictions idealized aid as a neutral and apolitical form of humanitarian diplomacy. This had a lasting effect on how the West understood and, ultimately, forgot what happened on the Middle Eastern Front.

Films produced about victims of genocide, famine and fighting along the Russian border, the Anatolian frontier and the Arabian Peninsula depicted attempts to mitigate the cost of war for those still living under siege. This "humanitarian imaginary," in Lilie Chouliaraki's formulation, was shaped by the experience of total war that made civilians into victims and the belief that waging war required a massive humanitarian aid apparatus.[2] A product of Victorian understandings of philanthropy's importance to the *Pax Britannica*, it showed that the way to empathize with suffering subjects and improve their condition was through giving.[3] These imaginings relied on film's visual storytelling medium to document need and transform humanitarian disaster into the possibility for renewal.

Before viewers' eyes, refugees turned into healthy bodies after receiving care from relief workers. They stood as a new kind of moral symbol of the importance of Allied long-term presence in the East.

The Anglo-American humanitarian movement dominated the aid work landscape in the First World War.[4] While rooted in older forms of humanitarian practice, wartime humanitarianism embraced documentary film, memoir, print media and celebrity endorsements that conveyed in dramatic visual and literary form an optimism about the effects of western-led emergency assistance. Media representations of humanitarianism were about both how aid organizations wanted their mission seen by the public and how they understood the Allied role in the war.[5] These films narrated the healing experience of making peace and, by extension, offered a view of what a western-led postwar order would mean.

Humanitarianism promised to make amends by bringing order to the refugee emergency and alleviating distant suffering through aid work. Film emerged as a "theatre" to produce these "imaginations of solidarity" that scripted how viewers responded to the profound needs of civilians trapped on the battlefront.[6] New media helped facilitate the delivery of much needed assistance to war victims by forging a universal solidarity with suffering subjects. At the same time, these representations elided the root causes of wartime suffering, namely the rise of exclusionary nationalism, the civil war in Russia and imperial competition.

This chapter assesses the popular cultural forms that generated sustained interest in the human costs of the protracted war in the East. The fragmented records of aid organizations, filmmakers, audience responses and the films themselves make this as much an act of reconstruction of the moment in which these films were made and watched as a study of their effects. Viewing the experience of war and the response through the filmmaker's lens offers a way to understand why and how humanitarian organizations focused on particular agendas and raised funds for specific groups: Orthodox Christians after the Armenian Genocide, in particular, and children, in general.[7] During the war, the issue of who deserved aid along with the objectives of that aid became diffuse in the face of the ongoing political crisis.

Leaving the question of justice for victims of genocide and mass violence aside in favor of universal humanitarian posturing around "saving the children" or "saving the remnant" of minority Christian communities, these films projected what one advocate called a "new order of philanthropy" to support "British prestige" in the postwar order.[8] As important cultural artifacts of the wartime moment, film embodied the humanitarian movement's belief in the transformative and even utopian potential of this new technology to document the war's effects on civilians, especially children. But a narrative of saving suffering bodies, which had relied on campaigns that targeted specific needs, became increasingly difficult to sustain as the scale of the crisis began to overwhelm the response by 1923. The rise of the humanitarian film is thus also a story about the limits of the belief in the possibility of redemption during a brutal war where empathetic victors had turned from antagonists into liberators.

THE RISE OF HUMANITARIAN FILM

Silent film promised the humanitarian movement broader reach, greater visibility and the power to transform cultural attitudes about civilians in wartime. The notion that all effective "campaigns must begin" first with "a film" spread in relief circles around the time of the war.[9] "To my mind there is no greater force for educative propaganda in the world today," enthused one activist:

> The language of the cinematograph is universal, it has no limitations of language, and its message is equally clear to every nationality ... It will create a deeper and more lasting impression upon the mind of the witness than any other medium ... I am confident that its possibilities are limitless.[10]

US and British-based humanitarian organizations were in the forefront of using film to mitigate human suffering and promote peace.[11] Depictions of atrocity on film against communities affected by the ongoing genocide in the Ottoman Empire and starvation conditions in Russia during the 1921–1922 famine dramatically scripted the framing of the wartime humanitarian response in the East. About twenty humanitarian films focused on victims of the Armenian Genocide, the Russian famine and conflicts between Turkish nationalists and the Greek army were produced for Anglo-American audiences to support emergency aid work between 1919 and 1923.[12]

Aid organizations embraced the idea that film provided the best medium for creating communities of solidarity. Film was called "a far more influential instrument even than the press." If these organizations successfully harnessed the power of film to tell their stories, "The opportunities for good are unlimited."[13] Moving images were believed to have an advantage over still photography. On screen, the transformative effect of aid was brought to life by privileging the action of relief work and the aid worker doing something to help.[14] Others believed that film had the unique ability to unite once belligerent nations in a common cause. Directors produced a montage of moving images that showed viewers that those on the "other side" were not unlike themselves as they engaged in everyday tasks, worked and cared for their children. For one aid worker, "relief work cinema" demonstrated to audiences the importance of "not merely material help" but also participating in the larger work of "the healing of nations."[15] The peace movement embraced this view, touting film's ability to create an "international fellowship,"[16] while the League of Nations praised its "highly humanitarian mission."[17]

This belief in the power of film to foster good will and promote a common cause emerged amidst growing geopolitical uncertainty surrounding the failed peace with the Ottoman Empire. Aid organizations reassured donors that relief agencies could help mitigate the ongoing crisis. NER, the Society of Friends and Save the Children all supported and produced films depicting the costs of the war through the eyes of civilians after the armistice. They joined organizations like the International Committee of the Red Cross (ICRC) which, by 1921, had produced over sixty films on the wartime crisis.[18] The widespread screening of these films to English-speaking audiences in theaters, churches and schools meant that they witnessed emergency aid as a necessary response to world war.

NER would grow into the largest humanitarian aid organization of its kind at the time, with branches all over the globe thanks in part to its history of aid work after the Armenian Genocide. British Quakers, in addition to supporting the work of Ann Mary Burgess, founded a number of country-specific aid projects including the Armenian Committee that raised money through the Friends' Emergency and War Victims' Relief Committee.[19] The Quakers developed "a strong Utopian strain which grew stronger as the war went on" believing that emergency aid would help victims while ushering in a period of profound "social change."[20]

Founded in 1919, Save the Children took an immediate interest in the Ottoman refugee crisis.[21] It eventually absorbed other British relief organizations including the Armenian Refugees Lord Mayor's Fund and the Russian Famine Relief Fund and took the lead in fundraising and administering aid throughout the region during this period.[22] Unlike the American Relief Administration (ARA)[23] which raised money for Russian famine relief and had an explicit anti-Bolshevik political agenda, these organizations proclaimed neutrality from political or national interests in the administration of aid and collaborated on a number of humanitarian relief projects for what one advocate called "relief and rehabilitation."[24]

On screen, audiences saw what was happening on the Middle Eastern Front as a humanitarian emergency. The stewardship of Britain and its empire as "guardians" was cast as necessary to restore order.[25] This echoed Lloyd George's "Great Crusade" that promised to usher in an era of unprecedented peace after Britain and its empire defeated the Central Powers.[26] Understandings of the war's purpose as a fight for the liberation of ethnic and religious minorities, however, was undermined in the face of forced civilian displacements, the product of genocide and, later, population exchanges mandated by the Lausanne Treaty that transferred Greek Muslim minorities to Turkey and Ottoman Christian minorities to Greece in 1923[27] (see Chapter 7). Starvation conditions in Eastern Europe, the Russian civil war and famine further challenged the story of the Great War as a heroic struggle.

These realities, coupled with the return home of maimed and injured men from the battlefield, made the protracted peace process with the Ottoman Empire difficult to grasp. The characterization of Britain as a war-weary nation after the First World War stands up when you look at popular entertainment. According to one theater critic, "wartime audiences wanted anything but to be reminded of the grim realities of warfare." Expressionist nightmares that exposed the "human cost" of "imperialist wars," depicted in plays like the *Silver Tassie*, initially did not appeal to audiences.[28] This assessment applied to the entire war film genre which did not gain popularity until the late 1920s. A survey of the *British Film Catalogue* for these years shows a preponderance of comedy, drama, romance and, to a lesser extent, crime films.[29] Only in the late 1920s did films showing the realistic and negative side of war get produced, including one that reconstructed the Battle of the Somme.[30] Depictions of war before this time came not from feature films but from Pathé newsreels shown in theaters before the main feature.[31]

As war dragged on, audiences needed more than news briefs or a temporary escape from the fighting when they went to the cinema. Post-armistice films reflected a desire to recreate a more familiar prewar order that softened the harsh reality of continued war depicted on the newsreel. Audiences flocked to the movie theater for both entertainment and information.[32] Twenty million mainly middle-class and working-class viewers in Britain went to the cinema every week and film magazines encouraged viewers to experience movie-going as both a reflection of everyday life and a pleasure of the imagination.[33] Some critics, however, rejected film as part of a frivolous prewar culture and called cinema a "new form of illusion."[34] But the experience of war had changed tastes and the cinema itself.[35] Film audiences did want an escape. At the same time, their own experiences and the realities of the war challenged the film industry to make movies that served a new kind of male and female viewer who had known real tragedy on the battlefield and at home.[36]

A "great drive for respectability" defined the movie-going experience in Britain and the United States during this period.[37] Going to the cinema still carried a stigma. With three-quarters of the audiences made up of women, charges that movie-watching promoted immorality, whether stemming from the fictions depicted on screen or the viewing conditions in the dark theaters themselves, had real power. "Women only" matinees allayed some fears as did the availability of films with a purpose which did not challenge traditional values.[38] Ministers writing in the cinema trade press conceded that film could serve as a useful tool for "imparting knowledge" and filling congregations by promising "clean" entertainment in well-chaperoned church halls that offered an alternative to commercial theaters.[39]

Out of this cultural moment emerged the humanitarian film. Often shown in church social halls and community centers, it provided suitable viewing for mixed audiences. While acknowledging war's brutality, these films offered a vision of hope that peace would return order and certainty by depicting scenes of unmet followed by met need. This juxtaposition conformed well to the silent film genre. Audiences expected "continuous action" and readily accepted "causal connections" in a "hectic montage" of images in film.[40] The shared experience of witnessing scenes of suffering followed by the ameliorative results of aid repeated on screen implicated the viewer as participant. These films' philanthropic focus further enforced Victorian ideas about women's central role in charity campaigns while opening up cinema culture to women, albeit in a highly circumscribed way.[41] With more women than ever participating in the humanitarian movement in both professional and non-professional capacities, these films projected an acceptable message and role for women viewers and society more generally.[42] Like other genres of educational and political films, the humanitarian film served a multiplicity of purposes which included fundraising and education while providing a modern form of entertainment.[43]

Participating in the experience of the humanitarian film offered a way of squaring audiences' desire for both normalcy and purposefulness in entertainment. Part live-action theater and part film-centered drama, attending a humanitarian film was anything but silent. The experience engaged viewers as participant in contrast to aid appeals that relied on still images, pamphlets and lectures.[44] Multimedia performances made Victorian forms of philanthropic appeals like the lantern slide lecture seem old-fashioned. They certainly were less interactive. Audiences typically entered the theater where a moderator introduced the film followed by the live performance of a "prologue" on stage.[45] After viewing the film, performers or ushers would take up a collection. In some cases, the cost of admission was a food donation and a pledge of financial support. Films thus created a sense of possibility through collective action.

Sympathetic representations of non-western victims dominated media depictions of the war.[46] Representing the Middle Eastern Front as a humanitarian disaster rather than political stalemate both explained why suffering continued and allowed for the possibility of caring for suffering subjects at a safe distance. Humanitarian films made for Anglo-American audiences portrayed the East as an especially significant geographic center of unmet material need and hunger. Refugees fleeing the burning city of Smyrna, for example, lent an immediacy to the crisis. Film was the ideal medium to document this crisis. The humanitarian movement learned how to harness the desire for a return to normalcy through representations that brought to life the war's forgotten victims.

HUMANITARIANISM AND GENOCIDE

The first widely circulated film used to raise awareness about war in the Ottoman Empire was about the Armenian Genocide. Between 1915 and 1923, it killed over one million Armenian, Greek and Assyrian Ottoman minorities and displaced almost as many others.[47] Released in 1919, *Ravished Armenia*, or *Auction of Souls*[48] recounted the "true narrative of the life of Aurora Mardiganian, a young Armenian girl held in captivity by the Turks" (Figure 6.1).

The depiction of the Armenian Genocide on film promised viewers a "vivid picture of almost unbelievable barbarism, persecution and inhumanity such as the world has never before known."[49] It was produced in Hollywood and based on Mardiganian's widely read memoir.[50] For audiences who read about massacres against Ottoman Christian minorities in the press, the film brought home the cost of continued war in an accessible though, ultimately, problematic form.[51]

Auction of Souls stands out as a radical departure in both the history of film making and humanitarian campaigning.[52] Considered the world's first atrocity film, it pushed the boundaries of prewar humanitarian fundraising strategies which largely relied on decontextualized still photos of starving bodies, live lectures and print. Humanitarian organizations promoted their mission together with the film studio which saw the advantages of "respectable citizens" supporting what some labeled pornographic representation of genocide and war in this highly political and commercial film. Unlike in photographs, unmet need was not juxtaposed with met need. Rather, scenes of violence appeared repeatedly alongside the result: dead or maimed victims. With little experience of film as a genre, humanitarian organizations saw only an opportunity to

Aurora Mardiganian

*in the Film founded
on the book*

"RAVISHED ARMENIA"

("Auction of Souls.")

6.1. *Ravished Armenia/Auction of Souls* film promotional material featuring Aurora Mardiganian. Credit: Undated leaflet (author's collection).

raise funds to support relief work and raise awareness about the massacres. These organizations had a lot to learn about controlling the message of a movie like *Auction of Souls* which dramatically politicized the humanitarian message. Ultimately, the film courted controversy by raising unanswerable questions about how to provide justice for victims due to its uncompromising representation of Turkish culpability for atrocities against Armenians.

The film opened in private screenings sponsored by humanitarian organizations on both sides of the Atlantic in 1919.[53] NER used the film to bolster fundraising to help refugees as did pro-Armenian organizations in Britain and the British Empire.[54] The League of Nations Union (LNU), an advocacy organization set up to promote the League of Nations, sponsored *Auction of Souls* as an educational film on the horrors of war that supported the League's internationalist principles.[55] The *Daily Mail* called it "a terrible lesson on the defenseless position of a small nation if it falls foul of a cruel overlord ... it should be seen by all those who desire to avert a repetition of the war in its ugliest aspect."[56]

The film's theme – the persecution of the Ottoman Empire's Armenian Christian minority population – had resonance in 1919 as peace conference delegates in Paris considered the Armenian case. The film contained graphic violence, rape and sexual assault that advocates justified on account of its "nobility of purpose." "These are not things to be shown for recreation or amusement," admonished Viscount Gladstone in an interview. One reviewer asserted: "Those who would learn how a small nation was nearly exterminated even though their hearts are wrung when they are gaining the knowledge should see it."[57] Activists used *Auction of Souls* as a platform to focus public attention on the Armenian issue. Bryce and his Blue Book, *The Treatment of Armenians in the Ottoman Empire*, were cited as the authority in the verification of the film.[58] The humanitarian movement joined forces with peace advocates to promote *Auction of Souls*. The LNU funded screenings hoping the "vivid representation of the horrors of war" would also make audiences aware of the plight of "racial minorities in Turkey."[59]

Plans for the film's release in fifty theaters throughout Britain, however, met with objections and undermined the humanitarian and anti-war messages. The government put pressure on the LNU through the British Board of Film Censors (BBFC), a voluntary organization of industry experts set up to police film content.[60] Scotland Yard visited the LNU and the film's distributor and informed both that *Auction of Souls* constituted an "Indecent exhibition" and temporarily interrupted LNU plans to show the film at Albert Hall.[61] Concerned that withholding the BBFC certificate and charges of indecency would not prevent "the indiscriminate public exhibition of the film," the case was sent to the Foreign Office. Officials concluded that the film "as it stands is calculated to offend the religious feelings of any Moslem."[62]

The film's visual representation of atrocity thus was not, as supporters thought, a transparent lesson in the evils of the ongoing war. The crucifixion scene, showing young naked women nailed to crosses lined up in a row, generated the loudest objection. The depiction of tortured bodies was read as religiously insensitive and obscene. The image of young women nailed to crosses fed negative depictions of Muslim rule over Christians.[63] It also challenged social mores. Officials worried about the effects that ostensibly nude female actresses and rape scenes would have on some audiences.[64] Obscenity charges most likely were behind the initial banning of the film in some parts of the United States as well.[65] To mitigate these concerns, theaters sponsored special "women-only" matinees and raised the price of tickets out of the reach of working-class patrons. Mardiganian, or a look-a-like, sometimes appeared demurely dressed at matinee showings to add to the air of respectability.

The controversy revealed the difficulty of controlling audience responses to representations of the war. The uncertain peace with the Ottoman Empire complicated attempts by the humanitarian movement to mobilize obscene images of suffering to provoke moral outrage. Eventually, US authorities allowed the film to be shown. In Britain, the indecency charge used in conjunction with worries over the film's effect on the peace process was understood as exacerbating religious hatred and promoting obscenity. In the wake of the April 1919 Amritsar Massacre, a film depicting violence by Muslims against Christians led Lord Curzon to argue *Auction of Souls* would stoke anti-British sentiment in India. That spring also saw the beginning of the Constantinople War Crimes Tribunals against Ottoman officials accused of "crimes against humanity" against Armenians.[66]

Auction of Souls failed to support the case for justice for Armenians as Turkish nationalists challenged Greece, Britain and France on the battle-field in Anatolia. A censored version of *Auction of Souls* stayed in theaters despite some continued objections.[67] One trade journal reported in 1922 that it made "more money last year than any other single feature ever drew."[68] The popularity of *Auction of Souls* among the movie-going public as entertainment, however, did not necessarily make it useful to the humanitarian movement. In addition to removing the crucifixion scene, officials excised all "Christian" references in intertitles and changed the original last line of the film from, "The lone survivor of a million Christian girls" to the trite sentiment: "Give them your moral support, help them hope for a new day."[69]

For the LNU, graphic portrayals of atrocity on film failed to guarantee the effective spread of its pro-minority, anti-war message, and the executive came to see its sponsorship of the film as a waste of its limited resources.[70] NER, the Quakers and Save the Children took an entirely different lesson from the episode: to focus the hearts and minds of the public on its mission the message, not the medium, would have to change.

ALICE IN HUNGERLAND AND NEAR EAST RELIEF

The illegibility of rape, murder and sectarian violence on screen, when put in the context of the war and domestic and imperial concerns, made Anglo-American humanitarian organizations rethink the film-based charity appeal. After *Auction of Souls*, humanitarian organizations turned to making their own films in an attempt to redefine atrocity in terms of unmet material need and hunger.

The 1921 film *Alice in Hungerland* was emblematic of this approach. It cultivated the humanitarian imaginary in traditional ways by showing viewers aid recipients in their most desperate hour juxtaposed with their moment of recovery. But it also introduced a sense of agency by empowering aid workers, aid organizations and, by association, donors. No image was more powerful than the one of helping the needy child. "These children are the hope of the Armenian people," read a promotion for the film, "the seed corn of a great race."[71]

Silent film's unique storytelling form took the viewer from the moment of acute depravation to receiving aid to wellness. Aid organizations long had exploited images of starving children in news media, pamphlets and donor appeals.[72] The "humanitarian eye" became trained on the plight of the hungry child as a "common denominator" which promised to unite postwar Europe and forge lasting peace.[73] Unlike in a still image, the horror of seeing a desperate child was blunted by the animated appearance of the healthy child in a subsequent frame. Films made by Save the Children, Near East Relief and the Quakers asked audiences to see a world that could get back to normal through the eyes of children benefiting from their care.[74]

NER produced around two dozen films to promote its highly successful "Hunger Knows No Armistice" campaign (Figure 6.2), the film *Alice in*

6.2. "Hunger Knows No Armistice," Near East Relief fundraising poster created by Leone M. Bracker. Credit: Library of Congress First World War poster collection (www.loc.gov/pictures/item/2002708879/).

Hungerland depicted a "true life" drama of hunger and depravation (Figure 6.3). Audiences easily recognized this reworking of Lewis Carroll's book. The use of the story represented atrocity in a familiar and evocative visual frame. At least four film versions of *Alice in Wonderland* had been made before the NER appropriation and provided a touchstone for audiences. "Lewis Carroll's Alice," one review of the NER film began, "experienced many emotions. Some of them were pleasant ... But Alice sees many things that were disconcerting to her child mind and gave her and her readers great distress." NER's Alice stows away on a boat stocked with supplies headed for the Ottoman Empire to meet her father who is an aid worker. Here she sees need firsthand: "When Alice alighted from trains she saw children many of them a great deal younger than herself, parentless, homeless, ragged, starving and ill." Alice, we are told, "did all she could to help."[75]

NER wanted the purpose and meaning behind the film made clear: audiences should "see the sights Alice saw, the frightful incongruities of humans living in the country where war seems perpetual and humanity of little account" as well as the transformative effect of aid. Only fragments of the film exist alongside movie stills and narrative accounts in NER's magazine, the *New Near East.* The film starts with Alice's experiences with

6.3. Alice feeding hungry orphans in a scene from the film *Alice in Hungerland.* Credit: Still image from *New Near East,* November 1921, p. 5.

children outside the gates of the orphanage. Inside, "She saw hundreds of healthy children at long tables eating. She saw children in classrooms and workshops industrious and happy." This was the effect of aid: creating a safe haven from the war-torn world. These contrasting scenes implored the viewer to bring those outsides of the gates inside. Ending with a quote from Carroll, the viewer is given the hope that "all the sadness, and the sin, that darkened life on this little earth shall be forgotten like the dreams of a night that is past!"[76] Audiences viewed this promise rather than images of starving children before being asked to offer a donation to extend the work of the "feeding stations" and orphanages.

NER enlisted clergy and aid workers to take the film around the world and to use it to found international relief branches. Technological advances made it possible to show films almost anywhere with a power source and a portable projector.[77] The humanitarian press printed information on how to set up a film showing.[78] Screenings often were accompanied by a live program and sometimes followed by the barebones meal given to orphan children. At one cinema in Sydney, Australia the price of admission was a tin of milk and a pledge that the viewer would make sacrifices at their tables at home for the orphans.[79] The film quickly earned a spot in *Moving Picture Age's* list of "suitable films for church use."[80]

Alice in Hungerland broke the taboo of exposing western child audiences to hardship.[81] The film used a child actor and appealed directly to children to make sacrifices for other children. Esther Razon had been handpicked from a Jewish orphanage in the Ottoman Empire to play Alice in the film. Similar to Mardiganian's case, Razon played the part of the refugee from real-life experience. Unlike Mardiganian, however, "Alice" was the victim turned heroic aid worker. The campaign to promote the film by NER featured an image of a well-fed, well-dressed Razon who once had been a "waif and refugee" with US Ambassador to the Ottoman Empire, Henry Morganthau, and his family. Audiences accepted images of dead children and deplorable living conditions, NER believed, because of the familiar frame of the "Alice" story and the film's purpose to redeem hundreds and thousands of orphans like Razon.[82] Donations contributed to feeding over 200,000 people and thousands of children who ate at the more than twenty-four miles of "mess tables" funded by NER (Figure 6.4).

The Power of Children

|More than one hundred thousand children are fed daily |by Near East Relief.

6.4. A feeding table sponsored by Near East Relief. Credit: "The Power of Children," *New Near East*, December 1921, p. 14.

None of the controversy that surrounded *Auction of Souls* touched this film. "I wish to pay tribute to your splendid moving picture, *Alice in Hungerland*," wrote one film industry insider to the *New Near East*. "I have never seen anything more stimulating or more dramatic. It makes me feel proud that I belong to a profession which possesses the power to convey to the public, in a graphic, irresistible way, such a magnificent message as yours."[83] The adoption of Razon by a Christian family did lead to some protest by the American Jewish community, which insisted she be raised in the Jewish faith.[84] The limited amount of publicity generated over Esther's religion, however, suggests that the issue was overshadowed by her usefulness as a symbol of NER's larger mission.

The film's success was mirrored in other productions, most notably *Jackie in the Near East* (1921) which used a child celebrity to publicize the hunger issue.[85] It starred five-year-old Jackie Coogan, called the "most talked about child-actor in the world." The film launched an international appeal for donations that Coogan took, with camera crew in tow, to Greece to feed child victims of the war on "the greatest crusade the modern world has known, the Children's Crusade ... to raise funds for the Near East Relief."[86] He reportedly raised a "million dollar cargo of foodstuffs and clothing for the orphans of the stricken Near East" which earned him recognition by the Greek government and an audience with the Pope.[87] When Coogan arrived in London to promote the film and his campaign, "the London dailies kept him on the front page the entire week – something that had never happened before."[88]

DOCUMENTING HUMANITARIANISM

Save the Children and the Quakers admired the "success" of NER "in arousing and sustaining interest, by means of film, placard and platform advocacy." Their own films adapted the American model to project the importance of eliminating want through large-scale charity enterprise. Rejecting "self-interest" as "inhuman" and warning that "the future of Europe" was "morally doomed" if they failed to act, these organizations used film to visually record the wartime crises.[89] This included extending relief work's reach to the Russian borderlands now in the throes of famine exacerbated by the terms of Brest-Litovsk and the civil war.[90]

Wartime relief culture focused on a twofold task: documenting need and providing aid on a large scale. It also united givers and aid recipients under the banner of international cooperation and Anglo-American benevolence. Along with NER, the Society of Friends and Save the Children were the largest relief organizations working in the region at the time. Like *Alice in Hungerland* and *Jackie in the Near East*, films made by these organizations eschewed politics in favor of representing humanitarian relief work as neutral. The crisis in Russia revealed a different side of the horrors of war. These films did not use Hollywood actors or characters from children's literature and instead documented the effects of mass starvation.

Authenticity mattered in humanitarian filmmaking and the documentary offered a new claim on that authority. Mardiganian's story was believable because it was her published life story reenacted on film. *Alice in Hungerland* cast a former orphan in the lead role. The introduction of the documentary filmmaking approach by British aid organizations prized realism first and foremost. This "documentary work" that stressed authenticity in filmmaking gained credibility as early as 1914.[91] No stages were constructed, celebrities engaged or actors hired. Instead, aid organizations dispatched a filmmaker with his camera and crew to the site of need. These scenes were connected by intertitles and, during screenings, accompanied by lectures or testimonies from relief workers that further authenticated the filmmaker's story.

In 1921, Save the Children promoted the first of two documentary films about relief work among the 20 million people living in the Russian Volga called *The Soviet Appeal*. Russia's exit from the alliance in 1918 did not preclude aid workers from focusing attention there when famine hit. The short film "prepared by the Soviet authorities" and produced by Save the Children launched an initial charity appeal to English-language audiences. The next year, Save the Children released a longer film, *The Russian Famine*, which specifically focused on aid work in the hard-hit and relatively densely populated lands situated around the Volga River.[92] Millions of Russian peasants devastated by failing harvests, Soviet food requisition programs and the ongoing civil war in the bread-basket of Russia faced starvation.[93]

The film contained scenes of relief work overseen by League of Nations representatives and funded by Save the Children, the *Manchester Guardian* and other organizations. Titles interspersed between scenes of a desolate Russian landscape and starving children appealed to viewers to help stop the famine that would kill as many as 3 million people.[94] Described as a film "so moving that when shown in Britain and the Dominions it brought tears to the eyes not only of the audiences, but also of the lectures who went with it," the film succeeded in raising awareness and funds.[95] Shown regularly through 1923, *The Russian Famine* reportedly brought in 60,000 British pounds to the organization during its 300 showings in that year alone.[96]

Save the Children founder, Eglantyne Jebb, commissioned the Russian films to raise money for famine relief. While worries about the threats of Bolshevism shadowed diplomatic relations between the two former allies, the extent of the crisis made cooperation between Vladimir Lenin's government and western-run aid projects possible.[97] Jebb hired G. H. Mewes, a photojournalist based in Russia for the *Daily Mirror*, to make *The Russian Famine*. Most of the filming took place over a period of three weeks in the Saratov district. He started in the town of Riga where he and a group of Englishmen accompanied a "food train of twenty-eight wagons" to the famine-struck district. The crew delivered and distributed the food under armed guard in between filming.[98] Relief workers used the films as the centerpiece of fund-raising efforts when they spoke to audiences and collected money for relief projects.[99] The campaign sparked a debate over who deserved aid. American Friends working in Russia had to maneuver the anti-Bolshevik politics of the ARA that had its own agenda.[100] In Britain, the issue revolved around helping needy Britons first.[101]

In "Filming the Famine," Mews raised the question of why help Russians while English children went hungry: "On my return to England I find a section of the Press conducting a campaign against sending food to Russia, while it is needed at home ... None will deny that we have much distress in this country of ours, but of this I am sure, that it would be impossible in England for children to reach such a starved state as the poor kiddies I have seen in Russia."[102] The Rev. W. E. Orchard, an English Presbyterian also ordained in the Eastern Orthodox Church, had another answer after viewing the film: the close connection between the Orthodox and Anglican Churches made Russians deserving recipients of aid. "I am tortured by the vision burning in my brain of what is going on out there: suffering, misery and death, and all relievable and preventable. What has happened to Christendom that it can allow this appalling horror in its midst and lift no more than a little finger to save?"[103]

For those like the Rev. Orchard, humanitarian diplomacy through aid work could heal the bond between nations broken by the war and promote empathy and universal social responsibility. "The imagination of Europe has been scarred and seared by the suffering in recent years. The result is that people can either bear no more or they can no longer feel suffering." He connected the cause of ameliorating hunger with saving humanity from the ravages of war: "we shall be killing our own humanity within us, and we shall soon show the signs of it in increasing brutality, in social misery and in personal desolation [if we do not help] 'TWENTY SHILLINGS WILL SAVE A LIFE.'" "If everyone did this," he told his war-weary audience, "the terror would be broken."[104]

Mewes produced other films "depicting the work done and the results achieved" by Save the Children around the world. Two surviving films from 1922, *Salvage in Austria* and *Salvage in Poland* documented humanitarian relief work in Europe's eastern borderlands. Another film, which has not survived, reportedly documented work done in Armenia. According to one advertisement, these films represented the Society of Friends' mission: "to bring order out of chaos, to bring a new chance of life to those who have been overwhelmed in the problems of the postwar tragedy."[105]

Aid appeal for Soviet Russia emphasized famine relief's universal purpose and neutral character. Scenes of starving bodies in *The Russian Famine*, including a final flashback at the end of mass graves, provided a dramatic look at famine's toll on the human body. Feeding stations, kitchens, trains filled with supplies and images of adults and children alike helping build shelter for themselves, working at handicrafts and industrial pursuits are repeatedly juxtaposed with scenes of utter depravation. While in reality the United States and Britain supplied and facilitated this aid, League of Nations' High Commissioner for Refugees, Fridtjof Nansen, was filmed inspecting relief work and watching women making bread from substitute ingredients. This both legitimated the humanitarian project and affirmed the necessary role of Britain and the United States in working with the League to support a new international order of emergency relief in wartime.[106]

MAKING PEACE

Quakers fully embraced film as a tool to document need and provide aid to the East during the war. In 1923, British Friends produced *New Worlds for Old* to chronicle and promote the work of the Friends' Emergency and

War Victims' Relief Committee. In the hands of the Australian naturalist filmmaker G. H. Wilkins, who had recently filmed Sir Ernest Shackleton's last voyage on the *Quest* to Antarctica, the stark landscape of the frozen tundra was placed in contrast with the activity of homebuilding and aid work to peasants and city dwellers alike. Wilkins, a veteran of the film industry and Royal Geographical Society fellow, was not a Quaker.[107] His experience as a cameraman familiar with harsh, natural environments and reputation as a frontline photographer during the war led to his being given 300 British pounds to travel to Russia to make the film in November 1922.[108] He filmed aid recipients "paying" for help by making items for sale or providing labor to facilitate relief projects. "Our policy is not one of pauperizing relief but of helping folks help themselves," one intertitle reassured donors. The press praised this approach to emergency aid, calling the film, "A wonderful record of humane undertaking."[109]

Raising money was only one purpose of the film. "Friends Relief Cinema" would, simply put, banish fear in a moment of uncertain peace. As the lecturer who introduced the film to an audience in February 1923 put it, "The nations, because of their suspicions and fear of one another, are all quakers with a small 'q' but you have got to make them anti-quakers and into real Quakers." Calling it "entirely devoid of sensationalism," the film was likened to the work of an objective reporter: "Just as an able journalist can make even a Blue Book interesting, so Mr. Wilkins, with many a little touch, stimulates our attention with humorous or moving incidents."[110]

The intertitle, "Relief is but a step on the road to reconstruction – we seek new worlds for old," emphasized the longing for an end to the years of conflict.[111] Without the viewer's pledge of support, another intertitle read, 250,000 more would starve. Emergency aid promised to mitigate the humanitarian disaster and lend a chance at normalcy for civilian war victims. For one viewer, the focus on the promise of the "new world" over the tragedy of the "old world" "acts like a tonic" instilling hope for the future.[112] The film eventually became a platform for arguing against the "fundamental immorality" of the Treaty of Versailles, which failed to "relieve the common sufferings of the people."[113]

The Friends' Relief Committee believed *New Worlds for Old* would serve the cause of making peace through a message of hope. It made two different versions of the film: one suitable for showing in a hall and the other in the cinema.[114] By early 1923, the film raised enough to cover production costs and satisfy demand for copies of the film in Britain and the United States.[115] Almost 1,000 people packed into the New Gallery Cinema in Regents Street in London to see the film. "Immediately after the film had been shown a minute's silence served to impress on the mind more vividly the cumulative evidence of the whole," reported the *Friend*, urging "our many helpers to rally to our support in this new method of propaganda."[116] In Aberdeen, Scotland Friends rented a theater, gave away free tickets and took up a collection.[117] The film buoyed a massive fundraising campaign that already raised nearly 500,000 pounds for relief work.[118]

Perhaps the filmmaker, now Sir George Hubert Wilkins, understood the motivations behind documenting humanitarian disaster on film best when he later reflected: "It took us ten days to photograph the film, and each day was like the other. We had ten days of frozen roads, of frozen forests, of frozen lakes, of peasant tragedies, of narrow escapes ... This picture was to go over the world, and tell the world of our refugees and how they could be helped if people were generous."[119] Wilkins, a "bearded, tall, young and enthusiastic" filmmaker, rejected any "purely unselfish motives" for relief work. Nevertheless, he like those who had commissioned the work, believed that this film would help those whom he called "our refugees."

THE TRAGEDY OF THE NEAR EAST

The destruction of Smyrna created a new wave of refugees. Private organizations, led by Save the Children and NER, began administering aid soon after the city burned in September 1922. The subsequent population exchange under the Lausanne Treaty forced 1.2 million Ottoman Greeks to move to Greece and 400,000 Greek Muslims to move to Turkey exacerbated the crisis.[120] The fire meant ameliorating the condition of more than 1 million additional refugees. Greece faced the reality that nearly a quarter of its population held refugee status by the mid-1920s.[121] This was the subject of the *Tragedy of the Near East* made by Save the Children in 1923. The film supported the "All British Appeal for the

Near East" that included the Imperial War Relief Fund, the Friends Relief Committee, the ICRC and other relief organizations. This thirty-one-minute silent film depicted the "appalling sufferings" of "at least a million, mainly women and children" refugees who made up the "homeless and hopeless" who needed immediate aid.

The film opened with an image of the British flag flying above a soup kitchen in Greece labeled, "A Symbol of Help." For Save the Children, the success of the Russian campaign proved a model for Greece. Called an "outstanding feat in international cooperation," it relied on Anglo-American leadership, a media campaign and documentary film.[122] Though little is known about the making of the film, it has been attributed to G. H. Mewes and is consistent with his realist style. Refugees queuing for food under a Union Jack and British-run soup kitchens, the film suggests, would make weak bodies strong and ready to face a new life in a foreign land. After a shot of a shivering boy next to a crying mother and older sister huddled around a soup pot, the intertitle read, "Destitute and homeless without food, warm clothing or covering, these unhappy people are easy victims of the dread diseases of the East." Britain's Queen Alexandra led the cause to help "save them from starvation."[123]

This film, "depicting the conditions of refugee life in the Near East following the burning of Smyrna," in the words of Save the Children promoters, raised funds by documenting need efficiently met. Lectures by distinguished speakers, including the Bishop of London and relief workers recently returned from the field, preceded film screenings. The press wrote approvingly of the film's mission to serve the "thousands of hapless refugees whom the war has left as a legacy to the human and large-hearted." It described "a wonderful new series of films by Save the Children" which depicted economically run kitchens to serve Greek, Assyrian and Armenian children and responded with "many generous gifts and subscriptions."[124] "It was really cheering," one columnist reported after viewing *Tragedy of the Near East*, "to see the anxious little faces light up with joy as the steaming soup was ladled out and the generous chunks of bread distributed."[125]

Tragedy targeted children and was shown at Westminster School where a collection was taken up for the Greek refugees among the boys in attendance. The campaign spread to boys' and girls' schools from both "the well-to-do" and the "poorest." School children were encouraged to deprive themselves of luxuries like sweets, much as they had been in the *Alice in Hungerland* campaigns, and write to refugee children.[126] In return, school children were praised for their "spirit of self-denial" and received handmade buttons and letters of thanks. These exchanges linked donors and recipients and allowed children to give from a safe vantage point as sympathetic yet privileged participants. Children were told that "they were not merely giving to a fund they are actually helping boys and girls of their own age, possessing many of the qualities they possess with the same love of fun and games and childish pursuits (alas, so often denied) the same desire for knowledge, the same need for affection and loving care." For observers, the campaign represented for England's youth an object lesson in responsibility and benevolent engagement in the world: "Long may our boys and girls continue to show their sympathy and friendly interest in these children."[127]

Victorian imperial models of leadership, cooperation and self-help philanthropy inspired relief work.[128] The Society of Friends was satisfied to "leave the work in the hands of the many societies giving active help" in the Near East but extended their own "All British Appeal" for the Near East to raise funds for Save the Children to administer.[129] A Canadian who had served as an administrator of the Armenian Refugees (Lord Mayor's) Fund in Constantinople and in Greece for the Imperial War Relief Fund, Dr. W. A. Kennedy led the efforts on behalf of the 1.2 million Smyrna refugees now living in Greece.[130] Kennedy "promoted the self-help principle" and set up workshops where refugees were employed knitting, making carpets and weaving fabrics that Save the Children sold to support relief efforts.[131]

But *Tragedy* did not depict the workshops or very many healthy bodies. This lent a much darker mood to the film than ones where refugees were shown, sometimes smiling, mending boots, making handicrafts and returning to health over the course of the film. One explanation may be that this film was made relatively quickly after the burning of Smyrna, as early as December 1922. This was most likely before workshops were fully in operation and the response to the massive influx of refugees from Turkey still was being formed.

Despite best efforts to keep up with the need, the campaign faltered. The crisis had grown dramatically and quickly overwhelmed aid
efforts. The public's interest began to wane as well. When the film was
shown in Derby, England, the *Telegraph* called the attendance "dis-
tinctly disappointing" despite support from local government and
civic organizations. "The film was pathetic enough to move any
heart," one aid worker in attendance remarked, but expressed surprise that the film did not comment on the political reasons behind
the tragedy which resulted in the "exodus" of "the entire Christian
populace of Asia Minor."[132] In Aberdeen, the local paper called it
a "striking film." It raised over 4,000 pounds in Scotland to "feed the
Smyrna refugees" which "among the 400,000 refugees" included 3,000
British nationals. These little-known British refugees made up the
large Anglo-Turkish community, many of whom had lived in Smyrna
for generations. Asking Britons to help their own may have served to
quiet charges that international humanitarian aid work ignored needy
Britishers. Their inclusion in the appeal also contributed to the
uncomfortable truth that the war in the East had indeed hit close to
home.

CONCLUSION

Humanitarian filmmaking by American and British aid organizations all
but ceased after the signing of the Treaty of Lausanne. Why did film
appeals dwindle despite having a positive effect on fundraising? Years of
sustained crisis and the seemingly unending flow of refugees effectively
challenged the utopian ideal that had animated how advocacy organizations represented their mission to audiences. It had stemmed from
a prewar sensibility no longer sustained by compelling stories told on
screen and brokered by imperial politics.

The final peace at Lausanne hastened the end of these efforts. These
films depicted an immediate wartime crisis. The refocusing of humanitarian efforts after Lausanne to resettling war refugees rather than providing emergency relief in the Middle East and the Caucasus explains in
part the disappearance of film appeals. Aid organizations raised considerable funds for resettlement campaigns in the mid-1920s, but the slow,

pain-staking drama of moving refugees and building communities in Syria, Lebanon, Palestine, Iraq and Armenia that took years to realize were more easily represented in still images, lectures and print media campaigns than through scenes of sudden transformation on film.[133] This opened a new chapter in aid work which centered on the League of Nations' role in remaking the mandated territories of the Middle East as a patchwork of nations populated by millions of displaced peoples. In the end, film's utopian promise failed to deliver the "new world" of a common humanity living in peace envisioned by activists.

The rise and fall of humanitarian filmmaking marked a hinge moment in the practice of humanitarianism. Many activists had grown up in a Victorian frame of mind that understood the plight of Ottoman Christians as an Anglo-American responsibility. This helped them to imagine the possibility of saving lives through humanitarian intervention even in the face of faltering Allied diplomacy.[134] Attempts to eliminate hunger during the war, when genocide, mass atrocity and famine proved to be the root causes of suffering, overwhelmed efforts to offer neutral aid and "save the remnant" of minority Christian communities. The representation of aid as apolitical provided a possible though imperfect way forward. For Save the Children, NER and the Society of Friends, the massive population exchanges at Lausanne, discussed in the next chapter, marked the end of the last great emergency of the war. Those survivors of mass atrocity which their work helped sustain now became stateless refugees.[135]

Understanding the depiction of civilian victims on film, like tracing the humanitarian uses of the concentration camp in the Middle East in Chapter 3, offers a way of seeing how the Allies dealt with the reality of civilian and military casualties on a mass scale during a relentless war. Helping suffering subjects from a safe distance arguably was easier than negotiating a workable political settlement to stem the overwhelming demographic, economic and cultural effects of genocide and the refugee crisis that would worsen after the peace at Lausanne. Initially, representing war in the East as a solvable humanitarian disaster allowed Britain to cope with the human costs of the First World War. It also reaffirmed a moral and global leadership role in the face of rising US hegemony and in a moment when international institutions were still in their infancy.

Humanitarian organizations successfully used film to raise money for relief work, but making amends for the crimes against the war's civilian victims was left for another generation. On film, humanitarian action meant help for survivors not the burden of guilt or responsibility for prosecuting perpetrators of mass atrocity and commemorating the dead. This is a strange sort of solidarity that eliminates the question of justice and demands only limited engagement with suffering subjects and why, as Didier Fassin has shown, "people often prefer to speak about suffering and compassion than about interests or justice" in the face of atrocity.[136] It is no wonder that the annihilation of the Armenians became most easily remembered as a humanitarian disaster rather than a wartime genocide. Out of the crucible of war emerged a narrative of suffering that made it possible for the causes and consequences of the crisis to vanish from the historical record. The Lausanne Conference would write the war's final chapter in the Middle East as an inglorious end to a part of the war that Europe wanted to forget.

CHAPTER 7

The Treaty of Lausanne

"WE TOOK HOME PEACE WITHOUT GREAT HONOUR," reflected Andrew Ryan upon witnessing the signing of Lausanne. "Still it was peace, after close on five years of armistice."[1] Harold Nicolson, who attended the conference as Lord Curzon's personal secretary, came away from his experience at Lausanne disenchanted as well. He recalled that by October 1922 the cloud of the Ottoman settlement, "had swollen into a typhoon- submerging Asia Minor in blood and ashes, wrecking the coalition of the victorious Powers, and raising in England a tidal wave beneath which Mr. Lloyd George and his Government were overwhelmed."[2]

Such foreboding contrasted with Nicolson's mood at Paris four years earlier. He had gone to the Paris Peace Conference with the other peacemakers hoping "to found a new order" and make "not Peace only, but Eternal Peace." Nicolson's subsequent disillusionment has become emblematic of the misguided failure of the First World War peace process: "There was about us the halo of some divine mission. We must be alert, stern, righteous and ascetic. For we were bent on doing great, permanent and noble things."[3] He hoped that the Treaty of Versailles could avoid the mistakes of the Congress of Vienna and focus on "the self-determination of peoples" rather than "compensations." Nicolson rejected this once "passionately sincere" belief when recalling the peacemaking process in his memoirs as a mere "exuberance of fancy."[4]

At Lausanne, the idea of a peaceful new world order led by Europe collapsed under the weight of nearly a decade of uninterrupted war. Peacemaking at the Lausanne Conference has received scant attention when compared to the Paris Peace Conference. The peacemakers have faded from history as well. After Lausanne, Ryan, a career diplomat who participated in the Conference and had spent the better part of his career in Constantinople, finished his service in a series of obscure posts. Nicolson, a Balkan and Middle East expert at both the Paris Peace Conference and the Lausanne Conference, was demoted. He eventually abandoned his diplomatic career and focused on his writing.[5] Curzon, who had taken over from Balfour as foreign secretary in October 1919, believed that his role as head of the British delegation at the Lausanne Conference had cost him what he desired most. "I do not think that I shall ever be Prime Minister," he wrote despairingly to Lady Curzon from Lausanne. "The chances against a success here are so great that my shares will go down."[6]

There may be good reason for casting aside both the Lausanne Conference and its negotiators. Seven months of negotiating at Lausanne failed to adequately resolve key outstanding issues around sovereignty, minority protection and the refugee problem, all of which had consequences well beyond the signing of the treaty. The powerful position of the newly legitimated Kemalist government on the heels of its victory over Greek forces meant that the Allies occupied a much weaker position than at any time after the 1918 armistice and thus could not fully dictate peace terms.

When viewed from the vantage of the Treaty of Lausanne, the First World War takes on its full dystopian mantle. The slow motion ending of the war between 1918 to 1923 reveals gradual disappointment with a carefully planned peace process that looked to undo the mistakes of previous generations of peacemakers through preparation, deliberation and lots and lots of talking. But the main innovation that the peace process yielded at the Lausanne Conference was the reimagining of empire in an anti-imperial age. The disenchantment captured so clearly by Nicolson, the writer, was a product of the experiences of Nicolson, the diplomat, and others like him. The trope of the war as a meaningless tragedy with a fatally flawed peace was a product in part of the prolonging of the settlement. At the Lausanne Conference, the utopian ideals of the Wilsonian moment met the dystopian realities of pragmatically ending a war that Europe and the United States no longer wanted to fight.

Studies of the Lausanne Conference tend to focus on either its political or its demographic legacies. This separate treatment centers on the treaty itself and the agreement's influence on international diplomacy, in the case of the former, or humanitarian practice, in the latter.[7] This chapter focuses on the peace process and treats these two sides of peacemaking together. It uses diplomatic correspondence, memoirs and media responses to highlight the disconnect between high-minded diplomatic and humanitarian ideals and the peace settlement, and pays special attention to the consequences of debates that would affect those living under the dictates of the Treaty and especially refugees. This approach to the Lausanne Conference and final peace settlement embeds anti-colonialism, state-sponsored violence and the refugee crisis in the war itself rather than the interwar period. This wide geographic and chronological lens that includes the Middle Eastern Front after 1918 shows war and peacemaking as an overlapping set of processes that ultimately determined how the Great War ended.

CRISIS AT SMYRNA AND CHANAK

"Fire has broken out in the Armenian quarter of the town, aided by strong wind, is spreading rapidly" recorded a British sailor stationed in Smyrna on September 13, 1922.[8] The fire spread westwards to the Greek and European quarters making it to the American settlement of "Paradise" leaving only the Turkish quarter untouched. "The stench of human flesh burning was appalling and the streets were stacked with dead, men, women, children and dogs," wrote another. Commander, Sir John de Brook, concluded: "The spectacle was magnificently terrible."[9] Smyrna, one of the most cosmopolitan and multiethnic cities of the Ottoman Empire, disappeared from the map within a matter of days.

The burning of Smyrna represented more than a tragic chapter in the ongoing conflict between Turkey and Greece. It signified the beginning of the end of the settlement of the war in the Middle East.[10] Allied ships patrolling the Smyrna harbor in early September included American, French, Italian and British destroyers, battleships and aid vessels with orders of strict neutrality. "Our duty is to watch the pier and landing places for refugees, and if British to bring them off," one sailor recorded in his diary.[11] The British Consul at Smyrna, Sir Henry Lamb, initially sounded the alarm, requesting that evacuation ships be sent as soon as word of the Greek defeat in the interior at the hands of Turkish nationalist forces under Mustafa Kemal had reached him. Reports of Greek atrocities against Muslim subjects during the occupation fueled an already tense situation made worse when victorious Turkish nationalist forces replaced the retreating Greek army.[12]

September 1922 marked the lowest point for the Allies in nearly four years of clumsy military and diplomatic maneuvering that had failed to bring peace. Fear of continued sectarian violence and costly military operations eroded trust and fueled conflict. Problems started during the Paris Peace Conference when the Allies decided that Greece, as an Orthodox Christian nation, should take command over the Christian Orthodox-dominated region around Smyrna.[13] On May 11, 1919, Foreign Secretary Balfour sent a secret dispatch from Paris outlining Allied plans for the protection of Smyrna's Christian inhabitants: "with a view to avoiding disorders and massacres of Christians and its environs, the occupation of the town and forts by Allied Forces has been decided upon by President, P.M. and M. Clemenceau. Greek troops are on their way to Smyrna and Turks will be summoned to hand over forts to a landing party." The United States, Britain and France put this plan into action within forty-eight hours without informing the Turkish or Italian delegation.[14] Lloyd George's support of the invasion had at its core the belief that leaving the administration of Christian minorities to the Greeks would best serve British national interests.[15] For the French, the Greek invasion did not require additional resources and also prevented more territory from falling directly into the hands of Britain.

Smyrna was part of a wider drama unfolding around the collapse of the 1920 Sèvres settlement. The 1919 Greek occupation had emboldened Turkish nationalists who blocked the implementation of the Treaty of Sèvres and started separate negotiations with the Allies. The secret Franklin–Bouillon agreement brokered in October 1921 between France and Kemalist forces put pressure on already frayed Anglo-French relations. It led to a conference in March 1922 in Paris that acknowledged the willingness of the Allies to abandon the Treaty of Sèvres and renegotiate terms with the Kemalists.[16] In August 1922, a confident Turkish nationalist army began the campaign to drive Greek forces out of Anatolia. General Charles Harington, head of Allied occupied forces in Constantinople, reported in early September on the "utterly demoralized" refugees streaming into Smyrna to escape Kemal's army.[17] The Greek army continued to withdraw "in good order," but the refugee situation worsened.[18] Harington wrote to the War Office anticipating an armistice "to avoid further bloodshed."[19] By September 8, "A proposal for an immediate armistice" was "made by the Allied High Commissioners to the Turkish Nationalists."[20] On September 9, Kemal's forces entered the city. Harington refused to send in troops to calm what had grown into a very tense situation.[21]

Kemal had little interest in the armistice proposal or the evacuation of Greek troops already underway by the time he entered the city. On September 13, Kemal announced to British Consul Lamb that he considered his forces in a state of war with Britain.[22] Kemal's army made his point using a familiar terror tactic. By the next day, the entire city was in flames. Fire, used by the Kemalist army against civilians in the reconquest of Cilicia, proved effective on the battlefield. The burning of Smyrna, as had happened with the burning of the city of Marash, finished the job of ridding Anatolia of the Greeks by destroying all non-Turkish neighborhoods. After the war, Smyrna was rebuilt with a new name, Izmir, which erased all traces of its multiracial, religious and ethnic past.[23]

The Allies had already commenced a hasty evacuation of their own nationals. Kemal's forces, operating without the sanction of the Ottoman government at Constantinople, fully controlled the city by mid-September. The inability of the "Greek army to defend the town from invasion," according to a Foreign Office telegram, prompted orders for the "Evacuation of the British Colony at Smyrna" on September 2. Curzon proposed the "complete evacuation of Asia Minor" the next day. "His Majesty's Government are ... anxious to terminate disastrous warfare and to avoid further shedding of blood," wrote Curzon to the occupation force in Constantinople, and "will gladly take any steps in conjunction with their allies to secure these objects."[24] On September 4, the Foreign Office asked the "American Relief Association to do what they can to provision Smyrna."[25]

By the time nationalists engulfed the city in flames in the middle of September, the die had been cast. The British Cabinet acknowledged that Kemal was "de facto in control at Smyrna." The "Greek retreat was now complete," and it "left behind them a trail of bloodshed." Kemal, when he confronted Consul Lamb on the street on September 13, had "told him that he could not recognise him as he was at war with Great Britain, and he threated to intern the British colony." That night, nationalists set fire to the Armenian quarter.[26] Two days later, as Smyrna burned, Kemal softened his tone and expressed a desire to "establish political relations in accordance with the usual procedure." No matter, the reality of Smyrna in flames was enough to make the British Cabinet begin discussing the defense of the Allied position around Constantinople and in Mesopotamia.[27]

Confrontations with Kemalist forces over the evacuation sent a clear message to the Allies that they were no longer in charge. It foreshadowed how relatively little say they would have in dictating peace terms after Smyrna. But the Allies were not prepared to concede quite yet. As they readied for a second armistice, the British prepared for military confrontation with the Kemalists at Chanak. The defense of Chanak and Scutari, the gateway to the Dardanelles Straits and thus to Constantinople, came to a head at the end of September.[28] Britain decided it would protect its position with or without French help.[29] It also worried about Kemal making "at any moment some formidable demand" and attacking Palestine and Mesopotamia.[30] Concerns over Feisal's ability to hold "extremists" at bay in the British mandated territory of Iraq were raised in August. Kurdish nationalism also started to regain force due to the lack of progress with the Kurdistan question after the signing of the Treaty of Sèvres. The British wanted to draw down troops and limit expenses, but some leaders worried that Kemal could put Britain out of Mosul "in a fortnight."[31] The Secretary of State for India, Viscount Peel, expressed concern that it would look very bad in India if the British lost a fight with Kemal in Mesopotamia. Closer to home, others worried about the ongoing Irish Civil War and whether or not Britain would have troops available to send to Ireland if needed.[32]

In this context of growing uncertainty, the British readied plans to move more troops to the fort at Chanak. Debates took place in a series of

Cabinet meetings in September and October before receiving approval. One official raised the question of approaching the United States for help, given its "large missionary interests in Turkey," but the Cabinet deemed this unlikely to yield results. Instead, Curzon – "anxious about the movement of troops, which might possibly precipitate action by the Turks" – went to Paris. He hoped that Poincaré would support British efforts to hold Chanak. Some expressed doubt "as to whether the existence of a small Inter-Allied force would deter Mustapha Kemal who was flushed with victory, from sweeping the Allies into the sea," while others believed that he would not commit "such an act of folly."[33] Many of those attending this mid-September meeting would have remembered seven years earlier at Gallipoli when arguments in favor of establishing British dominance over the Straits resulted in disaster. This time they justified defending the Straits to gain the upper hand in the anticipated renegotiation of the Treaty of Sèvres. Discussion quickly turned to the anticipated new treaty where only "those States ... that were specially [sic] concerned" would attend because to invite all those who signed Sèvres would "render the procedure very difficult."[34] This excluded, most notably, Armenia, which had a huge stake in the Sèvres treaty but would have no say in negotiations at the Lausanne Conference.

Other factors influenced this line of thinking. Atrocities committed against civilians at Smyrna affected faltering Allied diplomacy. Refugees fleeing the fire overwhelmed the surrounding regions and brought with them stories of terrible carnage. As one survivor put it, Kemal was responsible for "butchering thousands of Christians, after robbing and ruining this rich city" and subjecting "hundreds of thousands of people to an untold misery."[35] In early October, High Commissioner at Constantinople Sir Horace Rumbold reported that "Turks have started arresting Christians here especially in Asiatic suburbs where Kemalist influence is strong. I consider this intolerable while the allied occupation lasts. I have sent a very strong message to Grand Vizier and will see him myself tomorrow."

Rumbold, however, was not optimistic. As he concluded: "Diplomatic pressure alone, however, will produce little result."[36] On October 7, he wrote in a "very urgent" telegram to the Foreign Office, "I am fully alive to danger to Christian populations." Lloyd George's copy of this telegram had this statement underlined twice in red pencil.[37] The British, even before the fire started, proposed getting the Red Cross "to establish a commission to enquire into the atrocities committed by the Kemalists against the Greek population."[38] The issue only drove a further wedge between Britain and France. The British accused the French of throwing obstacles in the way of the inquiry by refusing to contribute funds to the investigation because of Henry Franklin-Bouillon's earlier bilateral agreement with Kemal.[39]

This lack of cooperation eroded commitments to minority protection. Kemal's resistance to Allied humanitarian dictates also played a role. After he invaded Smyrna in September, the Allies requested allowance to remove around 15,000 refugees fleeing the city. The British ended up referring the case to the League of Nations. This left Balfour to sort things out in Geneva. Back in Britain, public opinion began to turn against troop mobilizations at Chanak.[40] At a Trades Union Congress meeting members "made very extreme speeches threatening strikes and labour difficulties if the Government's policy should lead to war."[41] The Cabinet, understanding that the British public believed the war over despite the ongoing crisis, decided to couch the deployment in terms of defense and prevention, refusing to admit that the military buildup amounted to the planning of a new offensive. The official line held that this action would protect the freedom of the Straits and thus prevent the prolonging of the war.[42]

While, Kemal fortified his position at Chanak, his soldiers taunted British troops through the barbed wire that separated the two sides.[43] On the brink of military confrontation, the Allies asked Kemal to discuss a settlement. The invitation to Kemal included two main issues to be decided at a proposed conference in Venice: freedom of the Straits and protection of racial minorities.[44] The British, however, were eager to avoid any "moral responsibility" for civilian casualties and blamed the failure to protect minorities on French intrigue and the Greek defeat.[45] Nevertheless, the Allies together participated in the evacuation of refugees to nearby Greek islands and dedicated funds to refugee relief.[46] The United States played an important role in the evacuation and provided relief services for refugees but kept its distance from diplomatic negotiations.[47] The mostly Greek and Armenian refugees evacuated from Smyrna avoided Constantinople so as not to anger Kemalists who, like the British, continued fortifications at Chanak. Together these actions upped the stakes. As a meeting of the Conference of Ministers concluded at the end of September: "Apart from its military importance, Chanak had now become a point of great moral significance to the prestige of the Empire."[48]

Fear of attack motivated the buildup at Chanak as did the desire to prevent Kemalists from controlling the Straits.[49] Diplomacy also was engaged. A conference eventually took place at Mudania in Kemalist home territory, not Venice, as originally proposed. General Harington who commanded troops at Chanak reported having one eye on the battlefield and one on the negotiating table at Mudania. "Practically threatened" by Kemalist negotiators that their army was ready to "resume operations" unless an agreement was reached, Harington kept his troops on alert at Scutari and Chanak.[50] After a series of difficult starts and stops, the two sides came to an agreement on October 11, sometimes referred to as the second armistice. This set the wheels in motion for a new peace conference to settle the main questions surrounding the status of Thrace, Mosul and the Straits.

Meanwhile, tensions heightened in domestic Greek politics. Greek public opinion expressed anger with the Allies, and "newspapers of all shades" denounced negotiations with "Kemalists as a betrayal of promises made to Christians in Turkey."[51] Turmoil over the Greek army in Anatolia pitted Eleftherios Venizelos, who had been in and out of power starting in 1917, against King Constantine.[52] It eventually resulted in the overthrow of the Greek government by a military dictatorship in late September. Greece would be back at the table at the Lausanne Conference with Venizelos at the head of the delegation but with little bargaining power.[53] This laid bare the reality that the war in Anatolia, which had long been cast as a fight between only Turkey and Greece, was truly the final chapter of the Allied war against the Ottoman Empire.[54]

British preparations for military confrontation flew in the face of public opinion at home and in the Empire and eventually backfired. The government sought Canada's and New Zealand's support for a military action that it denied would prolong the war. Lloyd George's coalition, however, failed to withstand criticism over Chanak, and tensions over the crisis helped usher in a new Conservative government under Bonar Law in October that was anxious to the put war behind them.[55] Lloyd George expressed no regret and instead blamed the failure of his policy on Conservative support for Turkish control over "subject races." "It was not a bluff," he wrote in his memoirs. "I certainly meant to fight and I was certain we should win. Had the Turks been checked in their victorious chase of a broken and a broken-spirited army, they would have been easier to deal with." But, as even he acknowledged, "the average Briton had had enough of fighting, and he was not prepared to fire another shot for any cause."[56]

Winston Churchill, then head of the Colonial Office and a strong supporter of the Chanak plan, titled his chapter on the episode in his memoirs, "Greek Tragedy." In characteristically bombastic style, he went so far as to claim Chanak as a victory: "Considering the limited resources available, the public fatigue, the precarious position of the Administration and its declining authority at home and abroad, the achievement of 'Peace with Honour' was memorable." For Churchill, the near confrontation with Kemal's troops at Chanak, "prevented the renewal of the war in Europe and enabled all the Allies to escape without utter shame from the consequences of their lamentable and divided policies."[57]

But Chanak was no British (or Allied) victory. Rather, it represented a final standoff at the site where it all began: the entrance to the Straits across from the Gallipoli battlefields. The response to Smyrna and the subsequent ill-conceived standoff with Kemalist troops at Chanak sealed the Allied fate at the Lausanne Conference. Before Smyrna, Kemal's rise had challenged peace negotiations with Ottoman representatives in Constantinople. Conditions deteriorated further for the Allies in its aftermath. The destruction of the city represented an emblematic retaking of Anatolia in the name of the Turkish nation. This was the strongest repudiation yet of the claims of the empires of Europe over Ottoman lands as the prize for winning the war. Continued harassment of Consul Lamb by Turkish soldiers meant that by the end of November only a handful of Europeans who had refused to leave remained in Smyrna. High Commissioner Rumbold informed Curzon in early November: "Military attitude increasingly aggressive ... seriously considering both advising British subjects to leave Smyrna and preventing others landing."[58]

Nationalist diplomatic and military victories made a new treaty inevit-able. The process of renegotiating the Treaty of Sèvres had languished until after the destruction of Smyrna and standoff at Chanak. Less than two months after the last fires died out, the Allies were back at the table with a nationalist-led Turkish government that had replaced the Allied-backed government in Constantinople and ready to make the necessary concessions for peace.[59] The final agreement reflected a new reality. "Though Turkey had shared the final defeat of the Central Powers, the nationalists had never ceased fighting," one British commentator observed. "In peace conferences there should be a victor and a vanquished, but at Lausanne the vanquished had become victorious and the partner of the former victors had been woefully defeated."[60] The powerful position of the new Kemalist government on the heels of its victory over Greek forces meant that Britain occupied a much weaker position than it had at the time of the 1918 Mudros armistice. As Bonar Law put it to Curzon, "we shall not by ourselves fight the Turks to enforce what is left of the Treaty of Sèvres."[61]

Over the seven months of negotiations at Lausanne, the entire Sèvres agreement came under scrutiny, including the minority protection art-icles, the ending of the Allied occupation of Constantinople and the freedom of the Straits. On the eve of the opening of the Lausanne Conference, one newspaper headline summed up the British position: "Constantinople must not be allowed to be a second Smyrna."[62] The accompanying photo showed refugees packed into overfilled boats flee-ing a smoldering Smyrna quayside (Figure 7.1).

DRAFTING PEACE AT LAUSANNE

Lausanne opened on November 20, 1922, at the elegant Casino de Montbenon near the city center. The Allies chose the neutral Swiss site after rejecting Kemal's push to hold preliminary proceedings in Smyrna amid the ruins wrought by his army.[63] Swiss President Robert Haab read a welcome address that received replies from Lord Curzon and Turkish nationalist negotiator Ismet Pasha and set the tone for what was to come. Haab anticipated that the conference would "put an end to the conflict in the Near East" and "the terrible tragedy which for ten years past has laid

7.1. Photo accompanying headline in the *Sphere* from November 18, 1922, "Constantinople must not be allowed to be a second Smyrna." Credit: *The Sphere,* November 18, 1922.

waste to Europe and a portion of Asia." Curzon, less sanguine, showed his own exhaustion with peacemaking: "We meet here today for the latest – and let it be hoped, the last of the various conferences that have been held during the past four years to conclude peace and to throw into the background, soon to be forgotten, the memories of the cruel and devastating war."[64]

Ismet struck an entirely different tone. He framed negotiations in terms of compensations for the wartime sacrifice of his people, concluding that "more than a million innocent Turks are wandering homeless and hungry amidst the ruins on the plains and table lands of Asia Minor." Curzon immediately sent a telegram to the Foreign Office protesting Ismet's "truculent remarks" and warned that "His attitude today was indicative of the spirit in which the Turkish delegation are approaching the Conference and foreshadows trouble at every turn."[65]

Curzon quickly took hold of the Lausanne Conference and claimed the position of president, a role typically performed by the leader of the host country. The Swiss, however, had agreed to serve as hosts on the condition that they not preside over the potentially tension-filled proceedings. Curzon did not bother with plenary sessions – he held only one – and instead split delegates into three committees on territorial matters, capitulations, and financial and economic issues. He headed the territorial committee, which by far met the most frequently.[66] Under Curzon's leadership, diplomacy at Lausanne took on his own imperious and anxious attitude. The "strained but absentminded" arguments of the Lausanne Conference, as one historian characterized the negotiations, continued until the signing of the Treaty in late July 1923.[67] The new treaty not only replaced the Treaty of Sèvres but rewrote the end of the war. Bonar Law's more cautious sensibility and desire to put a stop to his predecessor Lloyd George's pro-Greek policies hamstrung British diplomacy. Curzon had little room to maneuver in the face of Ismet Pasha's demands that both minority protection and the partition of Anatolia not be part of the new treaty.[68] The Turkish delegation, consisting of Ismet Pasha, Riza Nur and Hasan Saka, made this crystal clear. When confronted with Armenian claims early in the conference, Riza Nur stormed out of the room.[69]

This rocky start chipped away at the hard-won military victory over the Central Powers. But the Allies were in no position to enforce demands through force. Britain, France and Italy already had refused to dedicate soldiers to help the Greeks continue fighting Kemalist forces in a war increasingly unpopular in Europe. War-weariness contributed to the dilatory way in which the treaty negotiations proceeded. So, too, did the unsettled state of the British Parliament led by three different prime ministers. This unstable leadership situation made it difficult for career diplomats to chart a clear course. The fall of the Liberals under Lloyd George and the subsequent struggle of the Conservatives to hold power in the face of the rising Labour Party contributed to uncertainty in the war settlement negotiations. These circumstances led one historian to characterize, the Lausanne Treaty as "the greatest diplomatic victory" in Turkish history.[70]

Lausanne was really two conferences. The first, physically presided over by Lord Curzon lasted from November 1922 until January 1923. It failed to resolve the key outstanding issues around sovereignty and the refugee problem.[71] This resulted from an impatience on the part of the British to put the war behind them. It also had to do with the unified position of the Ottoman delegation.[72] Curzon's frustration with not turning the negotiations his way led to his own dramatic exit from the conference after issuing an ultimatum to Turkey to sign the treaty or risk the end of the possibility of a settlement. He consented to give the Ottoman delegates one more week beyond his original deadline. When that failed to yield results, he and his delegates again briefly delayed their departure and then called a cab for the train station and left for London on the Orient Express.[73]

The conference resumed later that spring; this time without Curzon. High Commissioner and Ambassador at Constantinople, Sir Horace Rumbold, and his consular staff were charged with restarting negotiations.[74] At this second session, the Treaty of Lausanne took its final form as an agreement that Allied diplomats found a bitter but necessary pill to swallow. Internal correspondence between the Lausanne delegation, the High Commissioner's Office at Constantinople and the Foreign Office reveal the precarious nature of negotiations in what they referred to as "the armistice period."[75] Curzon continued to play a behind-the-scenes role while in London, leaving Rumbold and the consular staff to negotiate the details. Some in the press expressed doubt over whether a military solution would succeed in enforcing the Treaty of Sèvres and wanted negotiations reopened.[76] The Foreign Office again worried that the protracted negotiations pitted Indian Muslim interests against the principle of protecting Ottoman Christians and that the British Empire could potentially lose on both fronts.[77] "It is not reasonable to solve the Near Eastern question in terms of Christianity," argued one official.[78]

The Ottoman Empire, the British delegation at the Lausanne Conference believed, remained "ready to fight rather than submit to any interreference" in internal affairs.[79] Between the two sessions, the Greek army had regained its strength and threatened to launch a major offensive against Kemalist troops. A combination of instability in the Greek government, brought on in part by the massive influx of refugees and a lack of British military support, meant that renewed armed conflict never materialized.[80] But the tensions that resulted from the threat of continued violence were palpable throughout the Lausanne negotiations. Delegates faced pressure from both the Foreign Office and public opinion. A flood of international journalists attending the conference reported on proceedings.[81] The British media described attempts to grab oil-rich Mesopotamia to shore up the Empire's hold over the Mediterranean and safeguard India as well as the minority question which diplomats cast as a strategic and humanitarian issue.[82]

During his tenure as conference president, Curzon provided the moral argument to "unmix" populations, a term deployed by League Refugee Commissioner, Dr. Fridtjof Nansen, when he addressed the conference in December. Often attributed wholly to Nansen, the idea to "exchange" populations came from his knowledge that the Turkish nationalist government already had planned a compulsory removal of all remaining Ottoman Christians. In November 1922, Turkey's Lausanne delegates were given explicit instructions from the parliament in Angora to "exchange all minorities" as a condition of the peace.[83] The idea for the exchange thus started with the Turkish delegation's demands to remove all non-Muslims from postwar Turkey not the Allies. Nansen's support for the population exchange in his address to Lausanne's delegates represented a response to very real threats made as part of a consistent and long-standing policy that started with CUP attempts to rid Anatolia of non-Muslims dating back to the Balkan Wars.[84] The nationalist vision brought by the Turkish delegates to Lausanne was one that limited citizenship for non-Muslim minority populations.[85]

Curzon had invited Nansen to garner support for the League's scheme, which was enacted as the Lausanne Convention on January 30, 1923.[86] Though he later tried to distance himself from the agreement due to the tremendous human cost of compulsory relocation for both Christian minorities and Muslims, Curzon supported the idea of "unmixing" as part of Lausanne's mandate at the first conference session.[87] This challenged multiethnic and religious state formation in principle and practice. Instead, the notion of an unmixed population supported the impossible dream of homogeneous nation-states defined by race and religion. Curzon also supported this idea via proxy during the second session arguing that states divided along religious lines would offer the best answer to the "changed conditions in the Near East."[88] He dedicated three sittings of the first conference to the problem of minorities. He fully realized, however, that Turkish negotiators would not agree to outside interference on how it dealt with the remaining Christian population in the new Turkey.[89]

Given these circumstances, conversations around religious minorities shifted from the principle of protection to separation. Multiethnic empires already had been replaced by more homogeneous nation-states in Europe under Versailles and other treaties. New borders and notions of self-determination shifted the meaning of the nation-state and eventually gave way to the idea of partition as a solution.[90] The same issue was at play at the Lausanne conference, but here, instead of using the category of ethnicity to divide groups, national identity was defined by religion. It resulted in a subtle but important difference in how to describe minorities. In the Treaty of Lausanne, the category of "Moslem and non-Moslem" replaced the Treaty of Sèvres' more diverse characterization of minority communities.

The Treaty of Sèvres had used the terms "racial minorities" and "non-Turkish" instead of overt religious distinctions.[91] These old and new categories drew upon nineteenth-century understandings of a world divided along ethnographic and religious lines. These divisions increasingly codified a vision of a Christian West and Muslim East divided by religion.[92] While this categorization appealed to forms of nationhood, states divided along ethno-religious lines had roots in an imperial model that used religious categories to govern populations and keep them separate. Adherence to this principle would plague later British imperial decolonization schemes in Ireland and India along with the fate of Palestine.[93]

The Treaty of Lausanne further refined the focus on religion as distinct from ethnicity and race. This meant that religion played an outsized role in defining nationalist politics in the settlement.[94] British leadership was eventually supplanted by the League of Nations on the issue of minority protection. The reifying of minorities as a religious category made nationhood a matter of religion first and rewrote how the nation-state was understood in the context of the destruction of multi-confessional Russian, Austro-Hungarian and Ottoman empires.[95] Understanding new forms of nationhood in terms of Muslim versus non-Muslim populations hardened the religious divisions between so-called "cross and crescent" politics that had animated liberal humanitarian calls for the protection of Christian minorities since the Crimean War. In the Treaty of Lausanne, the Armenians, Assyrians and Greeks all became part of a catchall category of Christian minorities defined in opposition to Islam.

This shift in thinking helped fuel continued intercommunal violence. As Mark Levene has argued, the Treaty of Lausanne codified a nationalist solution in international law and practice for the first time.[96] The idea that different religions could not live side by side despite ethnic and cultural affinity was embodied in the provisions of a treaty driven by Turkish nationalist politics in a newly reconfigured imperial world that had to accommodate the nation. Defining the status of minorities and then sorting out their claims in a post-Ottoman world remained a sticking point at the Lausanne Conference because it fundamentally dealt with this question of belonging. National solutions previously based on non-religious categorizations, codified in the Treaty of Sèvres, were now deemed unworkable. Simply put, as Turkish delegates were told by their parliament before they arrived in Lausanne, religion defined national belonging.[97]

The Treaty of Lausanne did not include provisions that protected Ottoman minorities. It also did not carve out independent states for Armenians, Assyrians or Kurds in former Ottoman lands. Instead, the mandated population exchange between Muslims and non-Muslims fostered the hope of peace through separation. Nansen proposed that European Muslims living in Greece switch places with Ottoman Christians living in Anatolia to stave off threats from nationalists in Angora. He, like Curzon, publicly worried about the effects of displacement on an already vulnerable population. At the same time, Nansen understood and accepted how neatly this fit with an historic geopolitical and ethnographic world view that had been given new life in the hands of Turkish nationalism.[98]

The exchange sparked widespread protests and suffering among the over 1 million Orthodox Christians and nearly half a million Muslims who switched places with one another after the Convention was enacted at the end of January 1923.[99] Christian minorities sent to Greece included Armenians, Greeks and Assyrians, while Muslim minorities who had lived in Greece for generations were forced to go to Turkey.[100] Rather than learn from the mistakes of this ill-fated "demographic engineering," the principle of the separation of religious minorities later animated thinking about decolonization with equally disastrous results.[101]

Populations were on the move all around Europe, Asia and the Middle East in this troubled moment.[102] The mandated population exchange made an already difficult refugee situation worse. For Lausanne's negotiators, the exchange agreement hung over discussions that spring. Nansen's report on Greece and Asia Minor revealed that the condition of "refugees [has] become steadily and universally worse in spite of the efforts of the Government and the relief agencies." The report went on to cite the "vast number of refugees" fed on "famine rations." They found themselves "without adequate shelter . . . still living in railway stations, in tents, in old dug outs and unrepaired hutments . . . many were still in the open air." The cold Macedonian winter killed at least 30,000 women and children.[103] The American and International Red Cross attempted to serve all refugees and distributed tons of flour, administered vaccinations and established "feeding camps." In winter 1922, the situation was grim. Ten thousand refugees relied on rations predicted to last two months.

As Sir Horace Rumbold prepared to take over from Curzon at the Lausanne Conference that spring, his wife, Lady Rumbold, organized a relief fund to provide a hospital of 120 beds for refugees in Constantinople.[104] While the British did help coordinate relief efforts between national, international and private aid organizations, the 1923 budget provided no more money for aid. Furthermore, the refugees wanted to return home. The British Consul in Athens wrote to Curzon, "The terrors of the Smyrna flames would appear to be short lived."[105] Mass meetings and protests by those swept up in the population exchange did little good. Refugees were not allowed to return and instead they spent that spring trying to survive under an unevenly funded international aid regime.

The Lausanne Conference itself in this moment was on its own precarious footing. Lord Curzon's abrupt departure in January had left peace negotiations in limbo. While matters like the population exchange threatened further instability and strife, the terms of the treaty languished. Calmer heads eventually prevailed under Rumbold and his staff. When it finally came to signing the treaty at the end of July 1923, Curzon did not bother coming to Lausanne.[106] He defended this decision as a clever diplomatic ploy, claiming that the conference "had succeeded and not failed" to protect the interests of the British Empire.[107] In this way, the architect of Lausanne washed his hands of the final settlement and any future consequences.

LAUSANNE'S LEGACY

But what exactly had the Lausanne Conference accomplished? Responses to the treaty, unsurprisingly, revealed both diplomatic wins and losses for both sides. They also reflected a changing view of Europe in the world. While empire persisted under the guise of internationalism, as Mark Mazower has argued, it did not have the same nineteenth-century swagger and confidence.[108] The rivalry between the British and French revealed deep fissures in what increasingly came to look like a marriage of convenience. Europe's broken promises to those whom they pledged to free from the "Ottoman yoke" had weakened the foundational logic of liberal imperialism and liberalism itself. The First World War, when viewed from the perspective of the last treaty, looks less like a moral and political victory for the Allies than a cautionary tale of British, French and Turkish imperial hubris.

Lausanne defended European economic and political interests while keeping rising US power temporarily in check, despite giving lip service to national self-determination and minority protection.[109] Empire, in the case of Britain, had lost the moral argument that had sustained liberal imperialism since the time of Gladstone. France's *mission civilisatrice* hardly looked more justified. For both countries, resistance to the mandates in former southern Ottoman land, first by Feisal's forces and then others, showed a tangible resistance to empire in the shadow of a war fought supposedly for the liberation of small nationalities.

Diplomatically, Europeans mostly got what they wanted in terms of war aims and territory. Britain won the freedom of the Straits under international supervision and put the question of the disputed territory of Mosul back to the League.[110] The League eventually made it part of the British-run Iraq mandate.[111] Curzon succeeded in driving a wedge between Angora and Moscow that helped restore Britain's economic and political status in the East.[112] France secured its mandate over Syria but was less successful in achieving other wartime financial and economic goals.[113]

The peace process also came with important costs and finalized what Nicolson called the "divorce" between Britain and France.[114] Bilateral French negotiations with the Kemalists, which led to concessions ultimately sought by France, sowed distrust during the Lausanne Conference. France's own precarious military position in the Ruhr and fear that the Greeks would launch an attack to hold Thrace in January 1923 made them desperate for a settlement. Curzon's theatrics made French negotiator M. Camille Barrère leave the conference with a nervous breakdown. The British called his actions a "disgraceful" ploy to secure France's earlier agreement with Turkey.[115]

The Greeks found themselves on the outside looking in at Lausanne. Initially cast aside because of Lloyd George's distrust of King Constantine, the September 1922 revolution ushered in military rule and further marginalized Greece.[116] The Greek army's resurgence in Thrace along its eastern frontier with Turkey in late 1922 led to fears that Greece would reject the peace process. The Foreign Office warned of a "possible renewal of war by Greece" because of the Turkish expulsions of Greek civilians and expressed the unwillingness of Britain to make "extreme concessions" to Venizelos.[117] Nicolson responded to Venizelos's charges that delegates at the conference intended to "humiliate Greece in the eyes of Europe" with the explanation that British public opinion was opposed to any further military action against Turkey.[118]

Allied reluctance to support the Greek military at Smyrna coupled with the negative effects of the population exchange agreement on the Greek economy emboldened Kemalists. This left Greece with a worsening refugee crisis and little clout at the Lausanne Conference. Greece's population grew by 25 percent over a two-year period due to the influx of refugees and the treaty provisions.[119] Charges of atrocities in Thrace also continued to pile up on both sides while talks continued at Lausanne.[120]

For Italy, with a new leader in Benito Mussolini, the conference yielded few territorial gains. Mussolini's complaints were met with little more than a shrug from Curzon who viewed him positively but found him both naïve and ill-informed.[121] The situation with Russia was more complicated. The Russians, still recovering from civil war, sought admission to Lausanne on equal terms but never achieved this due to the failure of the Allies to recognize the new Soviet government. Complaints that they were unfairly shut out of negotiations led to their inclusion in Straits discussions. In the end, Russian delegate Georgy Vasilyevich Chicherin felt overlooked, believing his opinions unheard.[122] Nicolson's memos from the Lausanne Conference recalled the ways in which both Italy and Russia were treated because of their marginal status. Mussolini's involvement with pre-conference negotiations and Russia's eventual inclusion on the Straits discussion did not negate the fact that Britain and France considered both countries bit players in the peace process.[123]

Lausanne had little to offer the small nationalities. The new treaty undid the Treaty of Sèvres' minority protections and promises of territory for Armenians, Assyrians and Kurds. The Ligue Internationale Philarmenienne petitioned unsuccessfully for a seat at the table to advocate for an Armenian homeland. British advocates of the Armenian cause – Harold Buxton, Arnold Toynbee and Aneurin Williams – all sat on the executive committee.[124] Buxton presented information to the conference on both this question and the protection of minorities, arguing that the promises of the Treaty of Sèvres should not be forgotten. Bonar Law, however, actively sought to distance the British from a pro-Armenian stance for fear of risking "military disaster."[125] The Assyrians, 35,000 of whom had taken refuge in Iraq and then risen up against the Ottoman government at the urging of Britain, also found themselves disappointed.[126] Assyrian representative Agha Peros Ellow unsuccessfully lobbied the Lausanne Conference as Britain's "smallest ally" for a national homeland and included a map of the new state located around the British mandated zone.[127]

For the Kurds, Sèvres promised the formation of autonomous Kurdish provinces in southeastern Anatolia, which northern Iraqi Kurds were free to join. The desire to contain Bolshevism on this Russian borderland, however, undid this promise at the Lausanne Conference, leaving Kurdish populations divided between Turkey, Iraq and Syria.[128] Representatives from the mandated territories in Syria, Mesopotamia and Palestine came to "demand recognition for their independence."[129]

The only territory, however, that received sustained attention was Mosul, which remained in play not to fulfill a promise to the Assyrians but due to Britain's control of 75 percent of the shares in Turkish Petroleum.[130] Even with the oil, Bonar Law had reservations about Mosul and argued against any fight for the territory. As he admonished Curzon, "We cannot go to war for Mosul ... I would not accept responsibility for any other policy."[131]

The Turkish delegation came to Lausanne with a clear set of objectives intended to preserve as much of the Ottoman Empire as possible known as the National Pact. Drafted at Erzurum and published on January 28, 1920 by "dissident deputies to the Constantinople Parliament," the Pact was adopted by the National Assembly at Angora in 1921 and provided a blueprint for Turkey's Lausanne delegation. It called for the total repudiation of the Treaty of Sèvres, a plebiscite to determine the territorial affiliation of Western Thrace; the reclaiming of Mosul; freedom of the Straits; the elimination of military restrictions and minority protection provisions; no financial or economic control and the end of European privileges known as the capitulations.[132]

Turkish delegates had reason to feel optimistic about the likelihood of success on these points. In early October, a British General Staff memorandum conceded: "the creation of a national spirit in Turkey ... has resulted in the success of the Turkish Army, with the result that we can no longer treat the Turks as a conquered nation to whom it is possible to dictate any terms we wish."[133] To further ensure no more meddling by the Allied-backed government in Constantinople, Kemal had Sultan Mehmet VI deposed and abolished the sultanate on November 1. While not achieving everything stated in the National Pact, Turkey regained control of Eastern Thrace, Smyrna and the Aegean islands of Imbros and Tenedos along with other concessions.[134]

This was a far cry from the situation when the conference started. Curzon had opened Lausanne with a public challenge to Ismet Pasha on the minorities question. He accused Turkey of standing in the way of the Allied aim to ensure "the protection and, where possible, liberation of Christian minorities existing in large numbers in Asia Minor." Curzon went on to support establishing an Armenian homeland in addition to the Erevan [Yerevan] republic and invited the Turkish delegation to respond. Ismet Pasha claimed that the history of Turkey and minorities had always been peaceful and that Russian propaganda was responsible for any current problems. Curzon angrily asked "how was it that the 3 million Armenians formerly in Asia Minor had been reduced to 130,000? Had they killed themselves, or had they voluntarily run away? By what pressure had this reduction been accomplished?"[135]

He then brought up the case of the French in Cilicia and wondered why

60–80,000 of these happy, contented people fled ... to live in misery elsewhere, leaving their homes and families behind? Why were hundreds of thousands of Armenians now fugitives in every country in the world, when all they had to do was to return to the cordial embraces of the Turkish government? Why was this Armenian question one of the great scandals of the world?

Curzon concluded sardonically that "he was delighted to hear that the Turkish gov't were willing to live on terms of amity with the Armenians; but it was easy to live on good terms with a minority reduced to a miserable remnant."[136]

This line of argument stretching back to the early days of the Paris Peace Conference, and Curzon's explicit and heated references to what is today recognized as the Armenian Genocide, suggests that the minorities issue was always more than a cover for economic and political issues as some historians have claimed.[137] Talk of war aims and past promises to Armenians, however, were not enough to counter Turkish demands that the treaty include no mention of minority protections. The Turkish delegation won on this point, undermining the moral argument that once sustained the war for the Allies. Curzon understood the stakes in relinquishing the claim of imperial protector:

This conference has one purpose only. My object and that of my Allies has always been to remove barriers in the way of attaining that purpose; the object of the Turkish delegation is apparently to create barriers. This cannot go on indefinitely. Europe has other things to do. The minorities problem excites more attention throughout the world than anything else, and by the manner in which it is solved will this conference be judged.[138]

Rumbold was more circumspect when the conference came to its final conclusion seven months later. In a letter to King George V, he remarked that "we have obtained the least unsatisfactory terms possible."[139] What else could Rumbold do but defend a diplomatic act that, as Curzon put it, made it possible for Europe to move on from the war.

A WAR WON AND LOST

"All was set for the signature of the Treaty and the many other texts," recalled Andrew Ryan. "The President of the Swiss Republic entertained us all at dinner the evening before, and presided next day at a great gathering at the Palais de Rumine to witness the ceremony of the signature. We left for London the same evening."[140] The Allied evacuation began as soon as the Turkish government ratified the Treaty of Lausanne on August 24. The last Allied ship left the Straits on December 15, 1923 (Figure 7.2). The First World War, at long last, was over by Christmas.

The Allies got what they wanted at Lausanne for the most part: a true diplomatic end to the war and a belief that European dominance in the East had been restored. This was manifest through the eventual

7.2. The last British navy ships leaving the Bosporus. Credit: Photo by Keystone-France /Gamma-Keystone via Getty Images.

enacting of the League of Nations-sanctioned mandates that ceded control over former Ottoman territories to Britain and France.[141] Both had divested themselves of the minority question, which now belonged to the League, and abandoned the moral argument that had justified the First World War as a war of liberation. For some, the conference succeeded because it closed an important chapter in history: "The world does not perhaps realise that now, for the first time, the Great War has been brought to an end, so that really for the first time since 1914, to put it in other words, the doors of the temple of Janus are shut."[142]

As it turned out, not many people *had* realized that the war was finally over. Peace with Turkey excited little interest in Europe. At Lausanne, the First World War became an event that many wanted to forget, not simply assign to history. This sentiment found its way into the representation of the final settlement.

"The Woman of No Importance" cartoon published in the *Daily Express* on the eve of the signing of Lausanne took its title from the Oscar Wilde play of the same name about a bastard boy who refuses to acknowledge his paternity. The Treaty, like the play, had the air of Victorian satire.[143] Peace, represented as a woman holding a caged and crying dove in one hand and an olive branch in the other, looks perplexed as to why she has not captured the attention of a room full of men more interested in golf and cricket than the end of the war. It depicts a public that already had moved on from the war and to more trivial pursuits (Figure 7.3).

Acknowledging the Lausanne Conference and Treaty as a victory for peace would have required admitting the defeat of the heady vision of men like Nicolson who at the Paris Peace Conference had sought to create a new world order. The disillusionment with the Lausanne Treaty reflected a more general attitude about the end of the First World War on the Middle Eastern Front. That peace had not fulfilled those war aims that had relied on a narrative of liberation to justify the huge sacrifice left those involved in the peace process pessimistic about the future. For Ryan, the Treaty of Lausanne dealt the "final death-blow" to the possibility of coexistence between Muslims and Christians in the Near East.[144]

7.3. "The Woman of No Importance" cartoon from the cover of the *Daily Express*, July 23, 1924. Credit: *Daily Express*, July 23, 1923. Strube/Daily Express/Reach Licensing.

Eager for a return to normalcy, victory in the East seemed as remote as the deserts where the war had been waged. Europe wanted to get back to a seemingly more familiar prewar world of fewer cares. The demands of a public anxious to put the war behind them also helped shape the contours of the Lausanne Conference.[145] Disappointment with the outcome of treaty negotiations led one official to assert: "no criticism would be just that did not ascribe the blame not to an individual or a government but to the British nation as a whole. It is the British public which is responsible for a treaty which is probably in many respects the most degrading we have ever signed."[146]

It was little wonder, then, that Britain refused to claim Lausanne as its child. When documents from the peace process were published in their entirety in the 1950s, one reviewer in the *Manchester Guardian* asked why anyone need bother trying to sort out the failure of this final episode of the Great War.[147] It was a sentiment with which Lausanne's delegates would not have disagreed.

Epilogue

"DURING THE DAYS FOLLOWING THE ARMISTICE . . .
all those black days . . . I could not free myself of my
nightmare," recalled Armenian Genocide survivor Grigoris Balakian in
his memoir.[1] For those stuck in the no-man's-land between war and
peace in the Ottoman Empire, the First World War did not end with
the signing of the 1918 armistices or the 1919 Treaty of Versailles. It
continued for nearly five more years on the Middle Eastern Front and
produced the world's largest refugee crisis to date. For survivors like
Balakian, the peacemakers at the Lausanne Conference failed to bring
an end to their nightmares. His fate and that of others was in their hands,
but negotiators had wearied of diplomatic dealings and a previously
unimaginable humanitarian crisis. In place of a clear end to the trauma
of the First World War emerged the triumph of exclusionary nationalism
and imperial hubris.

The First World War came to its final, uneasy settlement at the
Lausanne Conference. The Allied prosecution of the war on the
Middle Eastern Front drew on deep imperial institutions and attitudes
rooted in the idea of minority protection and humanitarian intervention.
While it might seem counterintuitive to insist on a wartime chronology
that ends with the signing of a treaty Europeans wanted to forget, this
extended timeline reveals how fundamentally the process of making
peace indelibly shapes war making. The road to Lausanne entangled
humanitarianism, internationalism and refugee policy with battlefield
considerations and had lasting effects on how states wage war. The Treaty
of Lausanne concluded an imperial war that spelled the ostensible end of
some empires and the eventual undoing of others.

Understanding 1918 to 1923 as part of the war itself rather than the postwar or greater war era reveals the extent to which the First World War blurred the lines between home and battle front in both East and West. The refugee crisis, often relegated to the interwar years, was not caused wholly by intractable differences between religions and internecine conflict but by actions taken during the final years of the war. Population transfer and repatriation campaigns were worked out by state actors, aid organizations and the international community under the conditions of war where military campaigns determined particular humanitarian solutions and outcomes.[2] The extended process of making peace also transformed international justice by exposing its imperial pedigree. The inability to prosecute perpetrators of the Armenian Genocide came not from a lack of will, sympathy or resources but from questions about the survival of the British Empire in the face of rising nationalism and the transition to a post-imperial internationalism.[3]

In the end, imperial, domestic and internationalist priorities shaped the peace process and the Lausanne Treaty. The treaty system that ended the First World War was the product of a diplomacy of empire that forged new ties between the nation-state and an emerging international system. Overlapping imperial entanglements meant that Allied leaders often found themselves at odds. This undermined the common cause of winning the war and resulted in a strategy dependent on secret diplomatic agreements and double dealings. Sykes–Picot alongside other wartime agreements laid bare jealous rivalries emblematic of broader British and French imperial ambitions. They also provided a blueprint for the prosecution of the war which led to a new strategy that moved the Middle Eastern Front from the war's periphery to the center under the leadership of David Lloyd George. As the head of military operations in this theater after 1917, Britain focused on securing control over the region's natural resources and its peoples using soldiers and personnel largely from its empire. It also forged an alliance with Ottoman Arabs, Zionists and promised to liberate Ottoman Christians persecuted during the 1915 Armenian Genocide using the rhetoric of minority protection to bolster support for the war at home.

The final years of the First World War were important to the forging of modern Turkey. They also had far-reaching implications for Europe and the international order. The war's successful prosecution depended on managing civilian responses and movement. On the Middle Eastern Front, the Allies created the refugee camp to help administer humanitarian aid and secure their authority. New media represented humanitarian aid as transformative and successfully bolstered interest in Europe and the United States in helping war victims. Supporting refugees through donations and aid work justified the war and the long-term Allied presence in Ottoman lands. The humanitarian uses of the concentration camp in the Middle East coupled with graphic representations of want cast civilians in the war zone as the responsibility of the occupying power. This obligation extended to dealing with the fallout from nationalist-led campaigns against minorities that resulted in internationally-sanctioned population policies purportedly created to protect persecuted groups. Lausanne's dictates influenced the principle of population transfers in the Middle East well past 1948.[4]

The long war also had lessons for European politics and Europe's new empire builders in Germany and Italy.[5] Lloyd George's "Greek disaster" relegated him to a voice in the wilderness of a Liberal Party left in disarray after the war. A pariah in the Liberal Party, he had the unenviable distinction of serving as the party's last prime minister.[6] The French appeared to get what they wanted in Syria, yet unilateral negotiations with Turkey left the European alliance in shambles. Germany and Italy looked to rebuild their own empires under fascism, a move that Britain and France were in no position to resist after the Lausanne Conference.[7] The United States, in keeping an arm's length distance from the peace negotiations focused on shoring up its own economic influence in the region. Finally, the Lausanne Treaty reinforced an internationalism based on the principles of national sovereignty that privileged European authority under the mandates. This old colonial system in new bottles proclaimed itself in defense of self-determination. In the end, it desperately sought to maintain western supremacy over human and environmental resources, the movement of peoples and the prosecution of justice.

No states end war with peace treaties like the ones that ended the First World War anymore. But in the early twentieth century, these protracted, multilateral negotiations led by Britain, France and the United States mattered. In its modern form, the peace treaty was a vestige of the

Napoleonic War settlement made at the Congress of Vienna. It represented for generations of statesmen an almost sacred institution that promised sustained peace after a period of disastrous war.[8] It had worked for Europe. The 1815 settlement signed at Vienna brought lasting peace for Europeans who, with the exception of the Crimean War, chose to fight proxy colonial wars rather than each other during the long nineteenth century. This was particularly true for Britain, which fought wars to expand the Empire throughout Asia and Africa.[9] War continued in the name of imperial expansion while Europeans slept easy, believing themselves protected by the harmonious Concert of Europe.

If the peace treaty system offered the comfortable illusion of lasting peace for Europeans, why the rush to disown the First World War's last treaty? Cracks in the vengeful and short-sighted Versailles Treaty barely had begun to show by the time of the Lausanne Conference, though, the signs were certainly there. Ignoring the Treaty of Lausanne was not about a rejection of treaty making as a form of diplomacy. Rather, the agreement signed between the Ottoman Empire and the Allies in the summer of 1923 marked the end of a part of the war that many Europeans had tried not to notice. Eager for a return to normalcy, ignoring victory in the East meant the possibility of recapturing a prewar world where imperial concerns seemed remote and separate from Europe. But this view shielded a stark reality. By 1917, the Middle East had emerged as a central, if less visible, front that shaped the Allied conduct of the war against the Central Powers. The costs of the war on the Middle Eastern Front on civilian populations and soldiers shaped the politics and economies of Europe and the experiences of the generation who would fight the next world war.

First World War peace settlements had long afterlives that shaped domestic and international politics. The moments when these agreements found articulation lay bare the reality of peacemaking as process. The practical matter of how to end a protracted conflict happened in the fog of war and alongside discussions about what each side hoped to achieve once it was all over. Peacemaking, as evidenced in the lead-up to Lausanne, was contingent on the way individual actors responded to events on the ground – massacres, military conflict, humanitarian crisis. We often think of the high-minded principles of the First World War's peace conferences as a betrayal of liberal values or, by contrast, showing their true colors.[10] But there is also the matter of how individual actors built this house of cards in the context of circumstances that had taken shape from the nineteenth century onwards. Peacemaking required grinding out immediate responses to evolving military and diplomatic circumstances alongside historical and future concerns.

Not taking Lausanne seriously as the final episode of the First World War has blinded historians to the moment when Great Power politics faced its biggest challenge to date. Lausanne marked the beginning of the end of the old European order. Turkey emerged out of the war under Atatürk's leadership as a strong regional power. The British and French empires were bigger than ever after the war. The mandate system put them in control of vast new territories and peoples. But imperialism, arguably, as an idea and practice had never been weaker. Nine years of unrelenting war had taken their toll on the economy and frayed the social and political fabric of Europe. Meanwhile, nationalism across the Empires of Britain and France gained ground during the First World War in Ireland, India, Asia and North Africa. The story of the Treaty of Lausanne shows war in the Ottoman Empire as crucial to the reconfiguration of imperial alignments in postwar Europe and the Middle East in the twilight of formal empire.

Books on European relations with the Ottoman Empire in this period often end with an assessment of how the West made the Middle East. *The Last Treaty* instead ends where it began with a focus on the human costs of prolonging the First World War on the Middle Eastern Front. The final years of the First World War were a story of humanitarian and political crisis that hinged on the decisions of local, regional and international players. Today's struggles in the Middle East remain associated with this period, but they were not predetermined by the war. Decisions made in the midst of this brutal global conflict by diplomats, military men and local actors on all sides created new worlds not just in the Middle East but in Europe as well. The reality of the nightmare of total war was determined by where you were when the Great War ended.

Notes

INTRODUCTION

1. *Bank Ottoman: Memoirs of Armen Garo*, trans. Haig Partizian Boghos (Detroit: Topouzian, 1990), 187–190. Others made this connection as well, referring to him as the "Turkish Bismarck." Hans-Lukas Kieser, *Talaat Pasha: Father of Modern Turkey, Architect of Genocide* (Princeton: Princeton University Press, 2018), 286, 404.

2. I use "Constantinople" for "Istanbul" because this now superseded designation for the city was used exclusively during the period covered in this book and in all of the primary sources cited. I also use the terms "Ottomans," "Ottoman officials" and "Ottoman government" when discussing the leadership of the Ottoman Empire during this period. For a nuanced discussion of the use of these designations, see Mustafa Aksakal, *The Ottoman Road to War in 1914: The Ottoman Empire and the First World War* (Cambridge: Cambridge University Press, 2008), x–xi.

3. The Ottoman Empire fought the First Balkan War against Bulgaria, Greece, Montenegro and Serbia from October 1912 until the signing of the peace agreement in London on May 30, 1913. Bulgaria fought the Second Balkan War against Greece, Montenegro, Serbia, Romania and the Ottoman Empire. It began in June 1913, and ended with two peace agreements, one signed in Bucharest in August 1913 and the other in Constantinople in September 1913. Edward Erickson, *Defeat in Detail: The Ottoman Army in the Balkans, 1912–1913* (London: Praeger, 2003); Richard Hall, *The Balkan Wars 1912–1913: Prelude to the First World War* (London: Taylor & Francis, 2000); Ernst Helmreich, *The Diplomacy of the Balkan War, 1912–1913* (New York: Russell and Russell, 1969), 3.

4. Taner Akçam, *From Empire to Republic: Turkish Nationalism and the Armenian Genocide* (London: Zed Books, 2004).

5. Otto von Bismarck, "Blood and Iron Speech," September 30, 1862.

6. Stefan Ihrig argues that ideological and political connections between Germany and the Ottoman Empire started under Bismarck when he adopted a policy to defend the Ottomans against British pressure in regard to the Armenian question. *Justifying Genocide: Germany and the Armenians from Bismarck to Hitler* (Cambridge, MA: Harvard University Press, 2016), 19–30.

7. Kieser, *Talaat Pasha*, xiv. Ryan Gingeras shows the continuities between prewar, wartime and postwar regimes in *Eternal Dawn: Turkey in the Age of Atatürk* (Oxford: Oxford University Press, 2019).

8. I use the term "Middle East" rather than "Levant" or "Eastern Mediterranean" to designate territories controlled by the Ottoman Empire and, later, the British and French empires. The use of the term in this study designates the relationship of the region to the other fronts of the war – the Eastern and Western – as discussed further below. I acknowledge that this term does not adequately define this region as a place and that this problematic geographic designation remains embedded in colonial ideology and practice. On the history of the naming of this region, see Osamah F. Khalil, "The Crossroads of the World," *Diplomatic History* 38, no. 2 (2014): 299–344; Daniel-Joseph MacArthur-Seal, *Britain's Levantine Empire, 1914–1923* (Oxford: Oxford University Press, 2021); and Keith Watenpaugh, *Being Modern in the Middle East* (Princeton: Princeton University Press, 2006).

9. Both the beginning and end of the First World War has come under scrutiny by scholars. Christopher Clark calls it "the Third Balkan War." *The Sleepwalkers: How Europe Went to War in 1914* (New York: Harper Collins, 2013), 242. Robert Gerwarth shows how the war failed to end in Russia and Eastern Europe after the signing of the Versailles Treaty. *The Vanquished: Why the First World War Failed to End* (London: Penguin Books, 2017).

10. Dogachan Dagi argues that the Ottomans joined Germany as the result of alliance politics. "Balance of Power or Balance of Threat," *Open Political Science* 1 (2018): 143–152.

11. Leonard Smith analyzes the peacemaking process in relation to the problem of sovereignty from the perspective of International Relations theory. *Sovereignty at the Paris Peace Conference of 1919* (Oxford: Oxford University Press, 2018). For the Ottoman case, see Rodric Davison, "Turkish Diplomacy from Mudros to Lausanne," in Gordon Craig and Felix Gilbert, eds., *The Diplomats* (Princeton: Princeton University Press, 1953), 172–209 and Briton Busch, *Mudros to Lausanne: Britain's Frontier in West Asia* (Albany: State University of New York Press, 1976).

12. Bruce Clark, *Twice a Stranger* (Cambridge, MA: Harvard University Press, 2006); Ramazan Erhan Gullu, "Ottoman Rums and the Venizelos: Constantine Conflict after the Armistice of Mudros," *Middle Eastern Studies* 57, no. 4 (2021): 499–515; Paschalis M. Kitromilides, *Eleftherios Venizelos: The Trials of Statesmanship* (Edinburgh: Edinburgh University Press, 2006); Richard Clogg, *A Concise History of Greece* (Cambridge: Cambridge University Press, 2013).

13. On categorizations of these battles as part of Greek and Turkish histories, see Stephen Evans, *The Slow Rapprochement: Britain and Turkey in the Age of Kemal Ataturk, 1919–38* (Tallahassee, FL: Eothen Press, 1982); Michael M. Finefrock, "Atatürk, Lloyd George and the Megali Idea," *Journal of Modern History* 52, no. 1 (1980): 1047–1066; Ryan Gingeras, *Fall of the Sultanate* (Oxford: Oxford University Press, 2016); Şükrü Hanioğlu, *Atatürk: An Intellectual Biography* (Princeton: Princeton University Press, 2017); Renee Hirschon, *Heirs of the Greek Catastrophe* (Oxford: Clarendon, 1989); Peter J. Kincaid, "The Greco-Turkish War, 1920–1922," *International Journal of Middle East Studies* 10, no. 4 (1979); Konstantinos Travlos, ed., *Salvation and Catastrophe: The Greek Turkish War, 1919–1922* (New York: Lexington Books, 2020); Eric-Jan Zürcher, *Young Turk Legacy*

and Nation Building: From the Ottoman Empire to Atatürk's Turkey (London: I. B. Tauris, 2014). On Armenia, see the essays in Richard Hovannisian and Simon Payaslian, eds., *Armenian Cilicia* (Costa Mesa, CA: Mazda Publishers, 2008).

14. Understandings of genocide now extend beyond the confines of the total war framework to include crimes committed by the state in peacetime and during times of civil unrest. A. Dirk Moses, *The Problems of Genocide* (Cambridge: Cambridge University Press, 2021).

15. Andrea Graziosi and Frank Sysyn, eds., *Genocide: The Power and Problems of a Legal and Ethical-Political Concept* (Montreal: McGill-Queen's University Press, 2022); Berel Lang, *Genocide: The Act as Idea* (Philadelphia: University of Pennsylvania Press, 2017).

16. Ihrig, *Justifying Genocide*; Michelle Tusan "'Crimes against Humanity': Human Rights, the British Empire, and the Origins of the Response to the Armenian Genocide," *American Historical Review* 119, no. 1 (2014): 47–77; Jay Winter, ed., *America and the Armenian Genocide* (Cambridge: Cambridge University Press, 2003).

17. Gerwarth, *The Vanquished.*

18. See Santanu Das, ed., *Race, Empire and First World War Writing* (Cambridge: Cambridge University Press, 2011); Robert Gerwarth and Erez Manela, eds., *Empires at War: 1911–1923* (Oxford: Oxford University Press, 2014); Xu Guoqi, *Asia and the Great War* (Oxford: Oxford University Press, 2016); Richard Fogarty, *Race and War in France: Colonial Subjects in the French Army* (Baltimore: Johns Hopkins University Press, 2008); Michele Moyd, *Violent Intermediaries: African Soldiers, Conquest and Everyday Colonialism in German East Africa* (Athens: Ohio University Press, 2014); Bill Nasson, *Springboks on the Somme: South Africa in the Great War* (New York: Penguin, 2008); Christopher Pusgley, *The Anzac Experience: New Zealand, Australia and Empire in the First World War* (Auckland: Reed Publishing, 2004); Priya Satia, *Spies in Arabia: The Great War and the Cultural Foundations of Britain's Covert Empire in the Middle East* (Oxford: Oxford University Press, 2018); Timothy Winegard, *Indigenous Peoples of the British Dominions and the First World War* (Cambridge, Cambridge University Press, 2012).

19. Previous studies argue that this disillusionment only took hold in the late 1920s and 1930s. Paul Fussell, *The Great War and Modern Memory* (New York: Oxford University Press, 2013); Stephen Heathorn, *Haig and Kitchener in Twentieth-Century Britain: Remembrance, Representation and Appropriation* (London: Routledge, 2016).

20. Eugene Rogan masterfully tells this story up until the signing of the 1918 Armistice of Mudros in *Fall of the Ottomans* (New York: Basic Books, 2015).

21. The Supreme Council at the Paris Peace Conference labeled former Ottoman territories "A" mandates – a category meant to indicate their readiness for self-rule. The transition from Ottoman to European rule and indigenous responses to occupation and eventual statehood has received increasing attention by scholars. Laura Robson, *States of Separation: Transfer, Partition, and the Making of the Modern Middle East* (Berkeley: University of California Press, 2017); T. G. Fraser, ed., *The First World War and Its Aftermath: The Shaping of the Middle East* (London: Gingko Library, 2015); Elizabeth Thompson, *Colonial Citizens: Republican Rights, Paternal Privilege and Gender in French Syria and Lebanon* (New York: Columbia University Press, 2000); Ziad Fahmy, *Ordinary Egyptians Creating the Modern Nation through Popular Culture* (Stanford: Stanford

University Press, 2011); Rashid Khalidi, *The Iron Cage: The Story of the Palestinian Struggle for Statehood* (Boston: Beacon Press, 2006); Abigail Jacobson, *From Empire to Empire: Jerusalem between Ottoman and British Rule* (Syracuse: Syracuse University Press, 2011); Michelle Campos, *Ottoman Brothers Muslims, Christians, and Jews in Early Twentieth-Century Palestine* (Stanford: Stanford University Press, 2011); Peter Sluglett, *Britain in Iraq: Contriving King and Country*, 2nd edn (London: I. B. Tauris, 2007); James L Gelvin, *Divided Loyalties: Nationalism and Mass Politics in Syria at the Close of Empire* (Berkeley: University of California Press, 1998). For a recent history of peacemaking and the mandate system, see Susan Pedersen, *The Guardians: The League of Nations and the Crisis of Empire* (Oxford: Oxford University Press, 2015). On the Ottoman experience, see Rogan, *Fall of the Ottomans*; Stefan Ihrig, *Ataturk in the Nazi Imagination* (Cambridge, MA: Harvard University Press, 2014); Gingeras, *Fall of the Sultanate*; Hasan Kayali, "The Ottoman Experience of World War I," *Journal of Modern History* 89, no. 4 (December 2017): 875–907.

22. Gerwarth, whose work remains central in "greater war" studies, shows the importance of continued violence after the signing of the armistice, questioning the validity of the characterization of this period as the "interwar years" (*The Vanquished*, 4).

23. Rogan, *Fall of the Ottomans*; Michelle Tusan, *The British Empire and the Armenian Genocide: Humanitarianism and Imperial Politics from Gladstone to Churchill* (London: I. B. Tauris, 2017).

24. Aksakal, *Ottoman Road to War in 1914*.

25. Yiğit Akin, *When the War Came Home: The Ottomans' Great War and the Devastation of an Empire* (Stanford: Stanford University Press, 2018); Leila Fawaz, *A Land of Aching Hearts: The Middle East in the Great War* (Cambridge, MA: Harvard University Press, 2014); Melanie Tanielian, *The Charity of War: Famine, Humanitarian Aid and World War I in the Middle East* (Stanford: Stanford University Press, 2017); Thompson, *Colonial Citizens*.

26. Exceptions include Satia, *Spies in Arabia* and Pedersen, *The Guardians*.

27. On Gallipoli and other battles, see Peter Hart, *Gallipoli* (Oxford: Oxford University Press, 2014); Nigel Steel and Peter Hart, *Defeat at Gallipoli* (London: Papermac, 1995); David Woodward, *Hell in the Holy Land: World War I in the Middle East* (Lexington: University of Kentucky Press, 2006); Brad Faught, *Allenby: Making the Modern Middle East* (London: I. B. Tauris, 2020). On Lawrence see Jeremy Wilson, *Lawrence of Arabia: The Authorized Biography of T. E. Lawrence* (London: Heinemann, 1989); Phillip Knightly and Colin Simpson, *The Secret Lives of Lawrence of Arabia* (London: Nelson, 1969); John Mack, *A Prince of Our Disorder: The Life of T. E. Lawrence* (Boston: Little Brown 1976). On Bell see Janet Wallach, *Desert Queen: The Extraordinary Life of Gertrude Bell* (New York: Doubleday, 1996); Heather S. Gregg, *The Grand Strategy of Gertrude Bell* (Carlisle: US Army War College Press, 2022). On the peace settlement and borders, see Margaret Macmillan, *Peacemakers: The Paris Conference of 1919 and Its Attempt to End War* (London: John Murray, 2001); Michael D. Berdine, *Redrawing the Middle East: Sir Mark Sykes, Imperialism and the Sykes–Picot Agreement* (London: Bloomsbury, 2018); Busch, *Mudros to Lausanne*.

28. Eugene Rogan refers to the "Ottoman fronts" or "Middle Eastern fronts" in *Fall of the Ottomans.*

29. Rogan, *Fall of the Ottomans*; Gingeras, *Fall of the Sultanate* and Kieser, *Talaat Pasha.*

30. Akin, *When the War Came Home*; Fawaz, *Land of Aching Hearts*; Ronald Suny, *"They Can Live in the Desert but Nowhere Else": A History of the Armenian Genocide* (Princeton: Princeton University Press, 2017); Taner Akçam, *The Young Turks Crime against Humanity: The Armenian Genocide and Ethnic Cleansing in the Ottoman Empire* (Princeton: Princeton University Press, 2012).

31. Keith Watenpaugh, *Bread from Stones: The Middle East and the Making of Modern Humanitarianism* (Berkeley: California University Press, 2015); Benjamin White, "A Grudging Rescue: France, the Armenians of Cilicia, and the History of Humanitarian Evacuations," *Humanity* 10, no. 1 (2019): 1–27.

32. Watenpaugh, *Bread from Stones*; Davide Rodogno, *Night on Earth: A History of International Humanitarianism in the Near East* (Cambridge: Cambridge University Press, 2021).

33. Michelle Tusan, "The Concentration Camp as Site of Refuge," *Journal of Modern History* (December 2020).

34. Watenpaugh, *Bread from Stones*; Tanielian, *Charity of War*; Bruno Cabanes, *The Great War and the Origins of Humanitarianism, 1918–1924* (Cambridge: Cambridge University Press, 2014); Rodogno, *Night on Earth*; Andrekos Varnava and Trevor Harris, "It Is Quite Impossible to Receive Them," *Journal of Modern History* 90, no. 4 (December 2018): 834–862; Rebecca Jinks, "'Marks Hard to Erase': The Troubled Reclamation of 'Absorbed' Armenian Women, 1919–1927," *American Historical Review* 123, no. 1 (February 1, 2018): 86–123.

35. The issue of motive can reduce debates about humanitarianism to a question of good and bad actors. For a nuanced discussion of this problem in contemporary culture and the historical literature, see Michael N. Barnett, *The Empire of Humanity: A History of Humanitarianism* (Ithaca, NY: Cornell University Press, 2011), 7–18.

36. White, "A Grudging Rescue."

37. European historians still largely rely on David Fromkin's military history, *A Peace to End all Peace: Creating the Modern Middle East, 1914–1922* (New York: Henry Holt, 1989). More recent works on Allied war strategy and the Middle East include Robert Johnson and James E. Kitchen, eds., *The Great War in the Middle East: A Clash of Empires* (London: Routledge, 2019) and Kristian Ulrichsen, *The First World War in the Middle East* (London: Hurst, 2014).

38. This happens in the case of fighting in Africa as well. For example, Jörn Leonhard's comprehensive history of the war uses "The War in the Near and Middle East" and "The War in Africa" as titles for maps that appear alongside maps of "Western, Eastern, Balkan, and Alpine" fronts. See the front matter in *Pandora's Box: A History of the First World War* (Cambridge, MA: Belknap, 2018).

39. The debate over establishing the Middle East Department by the British government in 1921 to oversee the governance of the region between India and the Mediterranean reveals the stakes in codifying this geography as an imperial category during the war

and why the designation Middle East was seen in strategic terms in the early twentieth century. Khalil, "Crossroads of the World," 299–344.

40. Michelle Tusan, *Smyrna's Ashes: Humanitarianism, Genocide, and the Birth of the Middle East* (Berkeley: University of California Press, 2012), 40–75.

41. On the importance of the home front in the First World War, see Susan Grayzel, *Women's Identities at War: Gender, Motherhood, and Politics in Britain and France During the First World War* (Chapel Hill: University of North Carolina Press, 1999); Nicoletta Gullace, *"The Blood of Our Sons": Men, Women and the Renegotiation of British Citizenship during the Great War* (London: Palgrave, 2004).

42. Tammy Proctor, *Civilians in a World at War, 1914–1918* (New York: New York University Press, 2010).

43. Suny, *"They Can Live in the Desert."*

44. Nicoletta Gullace, "Sexual Violence and Family Honor: British Propaganda and International Law During the First World War," *American Historical Review* 102, no. 3 (1997): 714–747.

45. Emily Baughan, *Saving the Children: Humanitarianism, Internationalism and Empire* (Berkeley: University of California Press, 2022); Tanielian, *Charity of War*; Watenpaugh, *Bread from Stones*; Bertrand Patenaude, *The Big Show in Bololand: The American Relief Expedition to Soviet Russia in the Famine of 1921* (Stanford: Stanford University Press, 2002); Elisabeth Piller, "American War Relief, Cultural Mobilization and the Myth of Impartial Humanitarianism, 1914–17," *The Journal of the Gilded Age and Progressive Era* 17, no. 4 (2018): 619–635; Jaclyn Granick, *International Jewish Humanitarianism in the Age of the Great War* (Cambridge: Cambridge University Press, 2021); Julia Irwin, *Making the World Safe: The American Red Cross and the Nation's Humanitarian Awakening* (Oxford: Oxford University Press, 2013); Stephen R. Porter, *Benevolent Empire: US Power, Humanitarianism and the World's Dispossessed* (Philadelphia: University of Pennsylvania Press, 2016).

46. Johnson and Kitchen, eds., *The Great War in the Middle East.*

47. Lloyd George, *War Memoirs*, vol. IV (London: Ivor, Nicholson and Watson, 1933), 1939.

48. This was the dawning of the era of the foreign news correspondents and international reporting. Angela John, *War and Journalism and the Shaping of the Twentieth Century* (London: I. B. Tauris, 2006); Deborah Cohen, *Last Call at the Hotel Imperial: The Reporters Who Took on a World at War* (New York: Random House, 2022).

49. "The Final Report of the Dardanelles Commission," Cmd 371, *Parliamentary Papers* (London: HMSO, 1919), 170.

50. According to Eugene Rogan, "No battlefield in the Great War would prove more global than Gallipoli" (*Fall of the Ottomans*, 143). See also Jenny Macleod, *Gallipoli: Great Battles* (Oxford: Oxford University Press, 2015).

51. India supplied one in ten soldiers to the war effort, outnumbering those from Australia and Canada. Most of these soldiers were stationed in the East. Tarak Barkawi, *Soldiers of Empire: Indian and British Armies in World War II* (Cambridge: Cambridge University Press, 2017), 7, 84. They served in segregated units as officers and in other ranks as well as in non-combatant roles such as porter and service in the labor corps which included work in

refugee camps. Santanu Das, *India, Empire, and First World War Culture: Writings, Images, and Songs* (Cambridge: Cambridge University Press, 2018), 239–273; Kate Imy, *Faithful Fighters: Identity and Power in the British Army* (Stanford: Stanford University Press, 2019), 9. Soldiers from the West Indies also served disproportionately in the Middle East theater rather than on the Western Front. Scholars have attributed racialized constructions of colonial service as contributing to the makeup of the military in the Middle East in both combatant and non-combatant roles, which contributed to a growing sense of nationalism among some of those who served. Anna Maguire, "'I Felt Like a Man': West Indian Troops Under Fire during the First World War," *Slavery & Abolition* 39, no. 3 (2018): 602–621; Andrew Davies, *Geographies of Anticolonialism: Political Networks Across and Beyond South India, c. 1900–1930* (Hoboken, NJ: Wiley, 2020).

52. Santanu Das, "'Subalterns' at Mesopotamia," in Roger Long and Ian Talbot, eds., *India and World War I: A Centennial Assessment* (London: Routledge, 2018), 134–149.

53. Anna Maguire, *Contact Zones of the First World War: Cultural Encounters across the British Empire* (Cambridge: Cambridge University Press, 2021), 1–4. See also Santanu et al., eds., *Colonial Encounters in a Time of Global Conflict, 1914–1918* (Milton Park: Routledge, 2022).

54. Gerwarth and Manela, eds., *Empires at War*.

55. Mark Mazower, *No Enchanted Palace* (Princeton: Princeton University Press, 2013).

56. Ottoman soldiers appear in these accounts as formidable adversaries under the leadership of German high command. Recent Ottoman historiography offers a more complex view. See Rogan, *Fall of the Ottomans*; Akın, *When the War Came Home* and Fawaz, *A Land of Aching Hearts*.

57. This view has been challenged by Ottoman scholars including, most notably, Aksakal, *Ottoman Road to War in 1914*.

58. Erez Manela, *The Wilsonian Moment: Self-Determination and the International Origins of Anticolonial Nationalism* (Oxford: Oxford University Press, 2007); Larry Wolff, *Woodrow Wilson and the Reimagining of Eastern Europe* (Stanford: Stanford University Press, 2020); Tosh Minohara and Evan Dawley, eds., *Beyond Versailles: The 1919 Moment and a New Order in East Asia* (New York: Lexington Books, 2021).

59. Lloyd George, *The Truth about the Peace Treaties*, vol. II (London: Gollancz, 1938), 1361.

CHAPTER 1 HOW THE FIRST WORLD WAR CAME TO THE MIDDLE EAST

1. Warren Dockter, *Churchill and the Islamic World: Orientalism, Empire and Diplomacy in the Middle East* (London: I. B. Tauris, 2015).

2. Aksakal describes the conditions that led to the strengthening of the German–Ottoman Alliance between the signing of the secret pact on August 2, 1914, to the time of the war declarations (*Ottoman Road to War*, 2–5, 17–18, 53–156).

3. Jihad was declared by Sultan-Caliph Mehmed V Reshad in November 1914 to mobilize the fight against the Allies at home and abroad. Erik-Jan Zürcher, ed., *Jihad and Islam in World War I: Studies on the Ottoman Jihad on the Centenary of Snouck Hurgronje's "Holy War*

Made in Germany" (Leiden: Leiden University Press, 2016), 13; Mustafa Aksakal, "The Ottoman Proclamation of Jihad," in Zürcher, ed., *Jihad and Islam in World War I*, 53–65.

4. "Final Report of the Dardanelles Commission."

5. The Ottoman attack on Russian positions was based on a manufactured claim by the government that Russia acted first. Aksakal, *Ottoman Road to War*, 171–172, 181, 186.

6. When war broke out, Britain declared Egypt a protectorate. It forced succession from the Ottoman Empire in December 1914. Rogan, *Fall of the Ottomans*, 115–124.

7. Peter Balakian cites the number of 250, in Grigoris Balakian, *Armenian Golgotha: A Memoir of the Armenian Genocide* (New York: Knopf, 2009), xiii. Literature on the origins of the Armenian Genocide now includes studies of Armenian, Greek and Assyrian victims. See Ronald Suny et al., eds., *A Question of Genocide: Armenians and Turks at the End of the Ottoman Empire* (New York: Oxford University Press, 2011); Vahakn N. Dadrian, *The History of the Armenian Genocide: Ethnic Conflict from the Balkans to Anatolia to the Caucasus*, 6th edn (New York: Berghahn Books, 2008); Taner Akçam, *A Shameful Act: The Armenian Genocide and the Question of Turkish Responsibility* (New York: Holt, 2006); Donald Bloxham, *The Great Game of Genocide: Imperialism, Nationalism, and the Destruction of the Ottoman Armenians* (Oxford: Oxford University Press, 2005); Peter Balakian, *The Burning Tigris: The Armenian Genocide and America's Response* (New York: Perennial, 2003); Winter, ed., *America and the Armenian Genocide*; Richard Hovannisian, ed., *The Armenian Genocide: History, Politics, Ethics* (New York: St. Martin's Press, 1992); Erik Sjöberg, *The Making of the Greek Genocide: Contested Memories of the Ottoman Greek Catastrophe* (New York: Berghahn Books, 2017).

8. J. Ellis Barker, "Menace in the Near East," *Fortnightly Review*, December 1914, 994–1014.

9. Gullace, *"The Blood of Our Sons,"* 17–34; H. A. L. Fisher, *James Bryce* (New York: Macmillan, 1927), vol. II, 132–136. John Horne and Alan Kramer, *German Atrocities: A History of Denial* (New Haven: Yale University Press, 2001), 237.

10. Nicoletta Gullace, "Sexual Violence and Family Honor," *American Historical Review* 102, no. 3 (1997): 714.

11. Bloxham puts the number of Assyrian victims at between 20,000 and 30,000. Greek deportations are estimated at around 150,000 (*Game of Genocide*, 98–99). Evidence of the wholesale deportation of towns with a majority of Greek and Assyrian residents before and during the war suggests that these populations were victims of the anti-Armenian fervor due to their status as part of the Ottoman Empire's remaining Christian minority population. For the Greek case, see Ioannis K. Hassiotis, "The Armenian Genocide and the Greeks," in Hovannisian, ed., *The Armenian Genocide*, 129–151 and Thea Halo, *Not Even My Name: A True Story* (New York: Picador, 2000).

12. W. Williams, "Armenia and the Partition of Asia Minor," *Fortnightly Review* (November 1915).

13. Tusan, *Smyrna's Ashes*, 27–30.

14. Philip Khoury, *Syria and the French Mandate: The Politics of Arab Nationalism, 1920–1945* (Princeton: Princeton University Press, 1987); Benjamin White, *The Emergence of Minorities in the Middle East* (Edinburgh: Edinburgh University Press, 2012); Thompson, *Colonial Citizens*.

15. Russia prevailed against the Ottoman army at the battle of Sarikamish by mid-January 1915 and no longer needed British assistance in the Caucasus. Russian troops would continue to advance and, after setbacks in spring 1915, prevailed at Van in September 1915. By mid-February 1916, Erzurum was also under Russian control. W. Allen and P. Muratoff, eds., *Caucasian Battlefields: A History of the Wars on the Turco-Caucasian Border, 1828–1921* (New York: Cambridge University Press, 1953); Michael Reynolds, *Shattering Empires: The Clash and Collapse of the Ottoman and Russian Empires, 1908–1918* (Cambridge: Cambridge University Press, 2011).

16. "The First Report of the Dardanelles Commission," *Parliamentary Papers* (London: HMSO, 1917), 19.

17. This was not the case in the Ottoman Empire where unpopular conscription programs came into full force after Gallipoli where the army suffered tens of thousands of casualties. Akin, *When the War Came Home*, 87; 100–101.

18. "First Report of the Dardanelles Commission," 12.

19. Ibid., 14.

20. Kitchener dispatch to John French, January 9, 1915. "Final Report of the Dardanelles Commission," 6.

21. Ibid.

22. "First Report of the Dardanelles Commission," 15–16.

23. Rogan, *Fall of the Ottomans*, 132.

24. Ibid., 122–23.

25. Grey, quoted in "First Report of the Dardanelles Commission," 19.

26. "Final Report of the Dardanelles Commission," 10.

27. As the French Foreign ministry put it on February 5, 1919, "la France, grande puissane Muselmane." As quoted in F. W. Brecher. "French Policy toward the Levant 1914–18," *Middle Eastern Studies* 29, no. 4 (1993): 641–663.

28. Kitchener, quoted in "First Report of the Dardanelles Commission," 26.

29. "First Report of the Dardanelles Commission," 31.

30. Rogan, *Fall of the Ottomans*, 134.

31. "First Report of the Dardanelles Commission," 32.

32. M. Şükrü Hanioğlu, *Atatürk: An Intellectual Biography* (Princeton: Princeton University Press, 2017); Rogan, *Fall of the Ottomans*, 154–156.

33. Rogan, *Fall of the Ottomans*, 214.

34. Fawaz, *Land of Aching Hearts*, 51; Rogan, *Fall of the Ottomans*, 144. British soldiers who fought on the Middle Eastern Front often complained that people at home did not see it this way and thought deployment in this theater was easier. Woodward, *Hell in the Holy Land* 208.

35. Rogan, *Fall of the Ottomans*, 214.

36. Kayali, "The Ottoman Experience of World War I," 889.

37. Rogan, *Fall of the Ottomans*, 143.

38. Lt. Gen. Sir William Raine Marshall regularly complained about the "quality" of Indian troops under his command in his letters home. Letter to Jack dated July 4, 1915, quoted here. See also letters from October 22, 1916, and November 14, 1916. Papers of Lt. Gen.

Sir William Raine Marshall, Kings College London: Liddell Hart Military Archives (KCLMA). On the separate treatment of Indian troops during the war, see Memorandum on "Officers of British Units having Indian Personnel." Gen. Sir John Stuart Mackenzie Shea Papers (KCLMA). On Indian experiences at Gallipoli, see Das, *India, Empire, and First World War Culture*; Imy, *Faithful Fighters*, 56–58; Rogan, *Fall of the Ottomans*, 211–212.

39. Suny, *"They Can Live in the Desert,"* 347.

40. I use the term "massacre" according to Bedross Der Matossian's definition as it has come to relate to violence against minority Christian communities in the Ottoman Empire. *The Horrors of Adana: Revolution and Violence in the Early Twentieth Century* (Stanford: Stanford University Press, 2022), 6–7.

41. Der Matossian, *Horrors of Adana*, 153, 159. On the very different German response to the massacres that often ignored, explained away or defended the Ottoman Empire, see Ihrig, *Justifying Genocide* and Margaret Anderson, "Down in Turkey, Far Away: Human Rights, the Armenian Massacres, and Orientalism in Wilhelmine Germany," *Journal of Modern History* 79 (March 2007): 80–111.

42. Richard Antaramian, *Brokers of Faith, Brokers of Empire: Armenians and the Politics of Reform in the Ottoman Empire* (Stanford: Stanford University Press, 2020).

43. Suny, *"They Can Live in the Desert,"* 220–225.

44. The issue of minority rights emerged as a central aspect of what Holly Case calls "the age of questions" in the nineteenth century. Holly Case, *The Age of Questions* (Princeton: Princeton University Press, 2018).

45. The treaties that ended the Crimean War and the Russo-Turkish War had provisions that obliged Britain to protect the rights of Ottoman Christians. The 1878 Treaty of Berlin had the strongest provisions for Christian and Jewish minorities and put Britain in charge of enforcement. Carole Fink, *Defending the Rights of Others: The Great Powers, the Jews, and International Minority Protection, 1878–1938* (Cambridge: Cambridge University Press, 2004). On the Greek wars, see Mark Mazower, *The Greek Revolution: 1821 and the Making of Modern Europe* (New York: Penguin, 2021).

46. Tusan, *Smyrna's Ashes*; Davide Rodogno, *Against Massacre: Humanitarian Interventions in the Ottoman Empire* (Princeton: Princeton University Press, 2012); Gary Bass, *Freedom's Battle: The Origins of Humanitarian Intervention* (New York: Vintage, 2009); Der Matossian, *Horrors of Adana*.

47. Anderson, "Down in Turkey, Far Away."

48. Kieser, *Talaat Pasha*, 107–118.

49. Bedross Der Matossian, *Shattered Dreams of Revolution: From Liberty to Violence in the Late Ottoman Empire* (Stanford: Stanford University Press, 2014).

50. Ibid.

51. Ibid., 73–74.

52. Suny, *"They Can Live in the Desert"*; Akın, *When the War Came Home*; Hanioğlu, *Atatürk*.

53. Suny, *"They Can Live in the Desert,"* 281–282.

54. This question runs through Armenian Genocide survivor testimony. While not a complete list, see the following published memoirs: Avedis Albert Abrahamian,

Avedis' Story (2014); Aram Andonian, *Exile, Trauma and Death* (2012); Armen Anush, *Passage through Hell* (2007); Hagop Arsenian, *Towards Golgotha* (2011); Grigoris Balakian, *Armenian Golgotha* (2009); Kerop Bedoukian, *The Urchin* (1978) reprinted as *Some of Us Survived* (1979); Shahen Derderian, *Death March* (2008); Abraham H. Hartunian, *Neither to Laugh Nor to Weep* (1968); Ephraim K. Jernazian, *Judgment Unto Truth* (1990); Bertha Nakshian Ketchian, *In the Shadow of the Fortress* (1988); Ramela Martin, *Out of Darkness* (1989); John (Hovhannes) Minassian, *Many Hills to Climb* (1986); Hovhannes Mugrditchian, *To Armenians with Love* (1986); Thomas K. Mugreditchian, *The Diyarbekir Massacres and Kurdish Atrocities* (2013); Yervant Odian, *Accursed Years* (2009); Karnig Panian, *Goodbye, Antoura* (2015); Levon Shahoian, *On the Banks of the Tigris* (2012); Alice Muggerditchian Shipley, *We Walked, Then We Ran* (1983); John Yervant (Yervant Kouyoumjian), *Needles, Thread and Button* (1988).

55. Eventually, the villagers were rescued by a French ship and taken to a refugee camp in Port Said. See Chapter 3. Haroutune P. Boyadjian, *Musa Dagh and My Personal Memoirs* (Fairlawn, NY: Rosekeer Press, 1981).

56. Eastern Anatolia, the historic homeland of Armenians, had a long and problematic relationship to the imperial center. Yaşar T. Cora, et al., eds., *The Ottoman East in the Nineteenth Century: Societies, Identities and Politics* (London: I. B. Tauris, 2016).

57. Khatchig Mouradian, *The Resistance Network: The Armenian Genocide and Humanitarianism in Ottoman Syria* (East Lansing: Michigan University Press, 2021).

58. Lloyd George, *Truth about the Peace Treaties*, vol. II, 1257.

59. Bryce to White October 15, 1915. HM 66728, Bryce-White Papers, Huntington Library, San Marino, CA.

60. Ibid.

61. Bold in the original. Arnold Toynbee, *Armenian Atrocities: The Murder of a Nation* (London: Hodder and Stoughton, 1915), 117. German complicity in the massacres is still debated today. See, for example, Ihrig, *Justifying Genocide*; Anderson, "Down in Turkey, Far Away" and Margaret Anderson, "A Responsibility to Protest? The Public, the Powers and the Armenians in the Era of Abdülhamit II," *Journal of Genocide Research* 17, no. 3 (2015): 259–283; Bloxham, *Great Game of Genocide.*

62. British consulates had an established track record of performing aid work before the First World War in Adana and in the Russian–Ottoman borderlands. The newer consulates in eastern Anatolia owed their very existence to the need created during the Armenian massacres of the mid-1890s. This coupled with a vast network of mainly American missionary schools created a sizable Anglo-American relief work network in the Ottoman Empire that persisted during the war. Tusan, *Smyrna's Ashes*, 77, 89–92.

63. Balakian, *Burning Tigris*, 280.

64. Maude Mandel, *In the Aftermath of Genocide: Armenians and Jews in Twentieth-Century France* (Durham, NC: Duke University Press, 2003), 25, 33, 122, 133, 221 fn. 21; Tanielian, *Charity of War*, 240; Cabanes, *Great War and the Origins of Humanitarianism*, 171; Der Matossian, *Horrors of Adana*, 122, 136, 164–165.

65. Asya Darbinyan, "Russian Empire's Response to Armenian Genocide: Humanitarian Assistance to Armenian Refugees at the Caucasus Battlefront of the Great War (1914–1917)," Clark University dissertation, 2019, 37.

66. Ibid., 38–42.

67. The British Armenia Committee (BAC), formed during the Balkan Wars to support reforms in the Ottoman Empire, continued behind-the-scenes advocacy of Armenian issues in Parliament.

68. Lord Robert Cecil, "Eastern Committee Meeting," British Foreign Office, December 9, 1918. MSS Eur F112/274, Papers of the War Cabinet's Eastern Committee, India Office Records, British Library.

69. Thomas Laqueur, "Bodies, Details, and the Humanitarian Narrative," in Lynn Hunt, ed., *The New Cultural History* (Berkeley: University of California Press, 1989), 176–204.

70. Tanielian, *Charity of War*, 127.

71. Winston Churchill, *The World Crisis*, vol. V (New York: Scribner, 1963), 429. Some historians, even those who recognize the Armenian Genocide and in spite of evidence to the contrary, still use the disloyalty argument as an explanation for the mass killings. See Rogan, *Fall of the Ottomans*, chapter 7, "The Annihilation of the Armenians," 139–158.

72. "Visit of Boghos Nubar to Mr. Picot, with Messrs. Sykes, Mosditchian, and Malcolm" held in London on Oct. 27, 1916, in Vache Ghazarian, ed. and trans., *Boghos Nubar and the Armenian Questions, 1915–1918: Documents* (Waltham, MA: Mayreni Publishing, 1996), 393–397.

73. "Final Report of the Dardanelles Commission," 11.

74. Nikolas Gardner, *The Siege of Kut-al-Amara* (Bloomington: Indiana University Press, 2014).

75. "The Great War," *The Saturday Review*, May 6, 1916, 435–436.

76. Bouck White, "Beneath the Balkan Outburst," *Outlook*, October 20, 1915, 408.

77. Fawaz, *Land of Aching Hearts*, 65–69.

78. Das, "'Subalterns' at Mesopotamia," 134–149, 134.

79. "Brief for the Defence of the Mesopotamian Campaign," October 4, 1915. Mesopotamia Debate. Sir Austen Chamberlain Papers, Series Two, University of Birmingham Library.

80. Ibid.

81. Ibid.

82. Nikolas Gardner, "Charles Townshend's Advance on Baghdad," *War in History* 20, no. 2 (April 2013): 186. Gardner argues that he was looking for a better post on the Western Front.

83. "Brief for the Defence of the Mesopotamian Campaign," July 20, 1916. Mesopotamia Debate. Sir Austen Chamberlain Papers.

84. Gardner, "Charles Townshend's Advance on Baghdad," 187.

85. Report on Major-General Townshend's defence of Kut-Al-Amarah by Lieutenant-General Sir P. H. N. Lake. WO 106/907.

86. Gardner, "Charles Townshend's Advance on Baghdad"; J. Barker, *The Bastard War: The Mesopotamian Campaign of 1914–1918* (New York: Dial, 1967); Russell Braddon, *The Siege* (London: Jonathan Cape, 1969); Ronald Millar, *Kut: The Death of an Army* (London: Seeker and Warburg, 1969); David French, *British Strategy and War Aims, 1914–1916* (London: Allen and Unwin, 1986), 144–146; David French, "The Dardanelles, Mecca and Kut," *War & Society* 5 (1987), 45–61.

87. The battlefield was located fifteen miles southeast of Sidi Barrani. Rogan, *Fall of the Ottomans*, 251–252.

88. Ibid., 264.

89. Akin, *When the War Came Home*, 181.

90. Rogan, *Fall of the Ottomans*, 268.

91. Townshend describes his captivity which included lavish meals, hunting excursions and guided tours in *My Campaign in Mesopotamia* (London: Thornton Butterworth, 1920), 359–373.

92. Bryce's report on German soldiers' treatment of Belgian civilians was translated into twenty-seven languages and cast the German invasion as an indefensible crime against civilians in the context of the 1899 Hague Convention.

93. Michelle Tusan, "James Bryce's Blue Book as Evidence," *Journal of Levantine Studies* 5, no. 2 (Winter 2015): 9–24.

94. Response of Sykes to King's Speech: "Debate on the Address," HC, Deb (February 15, 1916), vol. 80, col. 41.

95. Ibid.

96. See, for example, "Sir Mark Sykes on the Realities," *Leeds Mercury*, February 16, 1916.

97. Mark Sykes sent a letter to Cox on August 21, 1916, asserting that with regard to the Middle East "our affairs suffer from a lack of policy, we don't seem to have any definite ideas as to what we are at." Sykes to Cox, August 21, 1916. DDSY2/4/107, Mark Sykes Papers, University of Hull and Sledmore House.

98. "First Report of the Dardanelles Commission."

99. Between January 4, 1917 and September 5, 1917, the Commission held sixty-eight meetings. "Final Report of the Dardanelles Commission."

100. "Final Report of the Dardanelles Commission," 33; 85.

101. Mesopotamia Debate, July 1916. MS, Sir Austen Chamberlain Papers.

102. It was released to the public on June 27, 1917. Sykes on Mesopotamia report, "Court of Inquiry," HC Deb (July 12, 1917), vol. 95, col. 2191.

103. Mesopotamia Debate, July 1916. MS, Sir Austen Chamberlain Papers.

104. Lord Curzon, "Memorandum," (secret) July 1917. Mesopotamia Debate, July 1917. MS, Sir Austen Chamberlain Papers.

105. "Dardanelles Commission," *Irish Times*, March 9, 1917.

106. "Northcliffe Assails Asquith's Old Gang," *New York Times*, March 10, 1917. Other responses included: "Investigation into Campaign at Dardanelles," *Christian Science Monitor*, March 8, 1917, 1; "Responsibility for Campaign at Dardanelles," *Christian Science Monitor*, March 9, 1917, 9; "Excisions from the Dardanelles Report Revealed," *Christian Science Monitor*, March 20, 1917, 1; "Dardanelles Commission Report," *Irish*

Times, March 17, 1917; "Dardanelles Commission's Report," *South China Morning Post*, March 19, 1917.

107. James Bryce, *The Treatment of the Armenians in the Ottoman Empire* (London: HMSO, 1916), 651–652.

108. Michael Reynolds, "The East's Eastern Front: The Ottoman–Russian Clash in the Great War and Its Legacies," *War in History* 28, no. 2 (2019): 333–358.

109. Tusan, "Crimes against Humanity," 62.

110. Tusan, *British Empire and the Armenian Genocide*, 137–143.

111. The memory of Gallipoli continued to cast a long shadow over British politics at home and in the empire. Macleod, *Gallipoli*.

112. Lord Hardinge, quoted in Berdine, *Redrawing the Middle East*, 50.

113. Sykes on Mesopotamia report, "Court of Inquiry," HC Deb (July 12, 1917), vol. 95, col. 2191.

114. "Evidence of Lieut.-Col. Sir Mark Sykes," War Committee Meeting, December 16, 1915. DDSY(2)/4/95, Mark Sykes Papers.

115. The failure of Gallipoli negated the agreement. D. Trudinger, "The Bear in the Room: Gallipoli, Russia, and the First World War," *War in History* 29, no. 1 (2022): 137–156.

116. Khoury, *Syria and the French Mandate*, 33–34.

117. Lt. Gen. George Macdonough, War Office military intelligence director, quoted in Berdine, *Redrawing the Middle East*, 81.

118. Grey to Cambon, May 16, 1916. F 204/3, David Lloyd George Papers, Parliamentary Archives, London.

119. Brecher, "French Policy toward the Levant," 642, 646.

120. Brecher, "French Policy toward the Levant," 646; Khoury, *Syria and the French Mandate*, 33–34, 39.

121. Brecher, "French Policy toward the Levant," 641.

122. Rogan, *Fall of the Ottomans*, 276.

123. Robson, *States of Separation*; Fraser, ed., *First World War and Its Aftermath*; Thompson, *Colonial Citizens*; M. Talha Çiçek, ed., *Syria in World War I: Politics, Economy and Society* (London: Taylor and Francis, 2015); Benjamin White, "Refugees and the Definition of Syria," *Past and Present* 235, no. 1 (May 2017): 141–178.

124. The report was published on June 30, 1915. Berdine, *Redrawing the Middle East*, 21.

125. Roger Adelson, *Mark Sykes* (London: Jonathan Cape, 1975).

126. Berdine, *Redrawing the Middle East*, 40, 46.

127. The original map that accompanied the agreement can be found in the National Archives, MPK 1/426.

128. "Meeting of Boghos Nubar with Mr. Picot," October 24, 1916, in Ghazarian, ed., *Boghos Nubar and the Armenian Questions*, 384.

129. Weizmann, quoted in Berdine, *Redrawing the Middle East*, 108.

130. "Memorandum," October 28, 1915. DDSY2/4/121, Mark Sykes Papers.

131. Berdine, *Redrawing the Middle East*, 86.

132. Imperial War Cabinet, 1917. Minutes. 1917. MS, Sir Austen Chamberlain Papers.

133. "Memorandum by Sir Mark Sykes on Mr. Nicholson's Note Regarding our Commitments," July 18, 1917. U DDSY2/4/151, Mark Sykes Papers.

134. Robson, *States of Separation*, 30–33.

135. White, *Emergence of Minorities in the Middle East*, 21–23.

136. This usage developed out of a liberal humanitarian ethos. Tusan, *Smyrna's Ashes*, 4-7.

137. "Memorandum," July 18, 1917. U DDSY2/4/151, Mark Sykes Papers.

138. Berdine, *Redrawing the Middle East*, 95.

139. Adelson, *Mark Sykes*, 212.

140. Tusan, *Smyrna's Ashes*, 40–41.

141. Berdine, *Redrawing the Middle East*, 137.

142. Minutes of the Mesopotamian Committee, Mark Sykes Papers. Berdine, *Redrawing the Middle East*, 134.

143. The original map used color-coded categories. The British sphere of influence was colored pink and the French sphere blue. The yellow area around Jerusalem was designated for international control but would go to the British as part of the Palestine mandate. Figure 1.1, "Sykes–Picot Map to Illustrate the Agreements of 1916" can be viewed in its original color at www.cambridge.org/TheLastTreaty.

144. Figure 1.2, Ethnographic Sykes–Picot map, can be viewed in its original color at www.cambridge.org/TheLastTreaty. Lawrence presented this to the War Cabinet Eastern Committee in November 1918. The original map can be found in the National archives MPI 1/720/1. He had been stationed in Cairo with the Arab Bureau earlier where he had a hand in creating regional maps. Satia, *Spies in Arabia*, 47–48.

145. "Tableau: Nations et Religions." FO 839/23.

146. Rogan, *Fall of the Ottomans*, 357.

147. Ibid., 309.

148. Figure 1.3, Allied military occupation map, 1918 can be viewed in its original at www.cambridge.org/TheLastTreaty.

149. He was pushed out of this position, most likely at Lloyd George's insistence, because he allowed his files on Arab dissidents to get into the hands of Ottoman officials. Brecher, "French Policy toward the Levant," 655–656.

150. Adelson, *Mark Sykes*.

151. Lloyd George, *Truth about the Peace Treaties*, vol. II, 1022–1023, 1026.

152. Lloyd George, *Truth about the Peace Treaties*, 1031, 1061; Brecher, "French Policy toward the Levant," 659, fn 44.

153. Elizabeth Thompson, *How the West Stole Democracy from the Arabs: The Syrian Arab Congress of 1920 and the Destruction of Its Historic Liberal–Islamic Alliance* (New York: Atlantic Monthly Press, 2020).

154. An agreement was reached in March 1916. Fawaz, *Land of Aching Hearts*, 72.

155. Picot ignored the advice of the American consul who urged him to destroy the files. Brecher, "French Policy toward the Levant," 655.

156. Rogan, Fall of the Ottomans, 291–295.

157. Salim Tamari, *Year of the Locust: A Soldier's Diary and the Erasure of Palestine's Ottoman Past* (Berkeley: University of California Press, 2011); Thompson, *Colonial Citizens*, 19–30; Najwa al-Qattan, "Fragments of Wartime Memories from Syria and Lebanon," in Çiçek, *Syria in World War I*, 130–149.

158. Tamari, *Year of the Locust*, 60.

159. Tanielian, *Charity of War*, 1; 23–26.

160. Akin, *When the War Came Home*, pp. 41–42.

161. Rogan, *Fall of the Ottomans*, 276.

162. Albert Hourani, *A History of the Arab Peoples* (Cambridge, MA: Harvard University Press, 1991), 333; 309–310.

163. Rogan, *Fall of the Ottomans*, 277–278.

164. "McMahon correspondence with Sharif of Mecca," letter from McMahon to Hussein, August 30, 1915. F 205/2–3, David Lloyd George Papers, Parliamentary Archives.

165. Thompson, *How the West Stole Democracy from the Arabs*.

166. Hussein negotiated Arab entry into the war based on the Damascus Protocol that set boundaries of a new Arab state and created a loosely defined economic and defensive alliance with Great Britain. Rogan, *Fall of the Ottomans*, 281.

167. Fawaz, *Land of Aching Hearts*, 74. Recruits first came from the Bedouin who lived in western Arabia and later officers and conscripts who had formerly served in the Ottoman army. Hourani, *History of the Arab Peoples*, 334.

168. Lloyd George, *War Memoirs*, vol. IV, 1811.

169. Rogan, *Fall of the Ottomans*, 315–316.

170. C. A. Bayly, *Empire and Information: Intelligence Gathering and Social Communication in India, 1780–1870* (Cambridge: Cambridge University Press, 1996).

171. Satia, *Spies in Arabia*.

172. Lloyd George, *War Memoirs*, vol. IV, 1811.

173. Satia, *Spies in Arabia*, 46–48.

174. Fawaz, *Land of Aching Hearts*, 73–74.

175. Fawaz discusses the debate in *Land of Aching Hearts*, 269. Rogan calls the Revolt "a distinct asset" in the Allied war effort (*Fall of the Ottomans*, 309).

176. The British used a similar tactic against Germany, dropping leaflets and encouraging desertion during the Gallipoli campaign. Fawaz, *Land of Aching Hearts*, 172.

177. Rogan, *Fall of the Ottomans*, 72–74.

178. The debate over the administration of Mesopotamia started early in the war. "Indian Moslems and the War," "Memorandum," October 28, 1915. Mark Sykes Papers, 4/ 120.

179. Rogan, *Fall of the Ottomans*, 308–309.

CHAPTER 2 THE MIDDLE EASTERN FRONT

1. Lloyd George, *War Memoirs*, vol. III.

2. As early as October 1915, Asquith wrote to Kitchener expressing fears that Lloyd George was trying to oust him from his leadership role. Asquith to Kitchener, October 17, 1915. PRO 30/57/76/25.

3. Lloyd George, *War Memoirs*, vol. II, 807.

4. The original War Cabinet included Lloyd George, Bonar Law, Lord Curzon, Arthur Henderson and Lord Milner. Sir Edward Carson and General Smuts joined the group in the middle of 1917. Henderson was replaced by George Barnes that August. Carson resigned in January 1918 and in April 1918 Austen Chamberlain replaced Milner, who moved to the War Office. David French, *The Strategy of the Lloyd George Coalition, 1916–1918* (Oxford: Clarendon, 2002), 17.

5. The military conducted internal investigations on specific failures including at Jutland, but debates during the war took place mostly outside of public view. Only after the war did broad questions about war failures begin to be raised as war memoirs by politicians – including Lloyd George and Churchill – and soldiers started being published. Heathorn, *Haig and Kitchener in Twentieth-Century Britain.*

6. Similar handwringing occurred after the defeat of Russia in the Russo-Japanese War in 1905. David Wells and Sandra Wilson, eds., *The Russo-Japanese War in Cultural Perspective, 1904–05* (Basingstoke: Macmillan, 1999).

7. According to David French, Britain fought the Ottoman Empire to stop the Germans from threatening its empire in the East. Victory here mattered only later in (re)establishing Britain at the head of the postwar order. French, *Strategy of the Lloyd George Coalition*, 3.

8. Ibid., 11.

9. Stacy Fahrenthold, "Former Ottomans in the Ranks: Pro-Entente Military Recruitment Among Syrians in the Americas, 1916–1918," *Journal of Global History* 11, no. 1 (2016): 88–112.

10. Lloyd George, *War Memoirs*, vol. III, 1084.

11. Lloyd George, *War Memoirs*, vol. IV, 1770–1775. The meeting included "representatives of the Dominions and Indian Empire."

12. Lloyd George, *Truth about the Peace Treaties*, vol. II, 1031. France had 185,000 soldiers in the Armée d'Orient at this time. Elizabeth Greenhalgh, *The French Army and the First World War* (Cambridge: Cambridge University Press, 2014), 176.

13. Elizabeth Greenhalgh, *Victory through Coalition: Britain and France during the First World War* (Cambridge: Cambridge University Press, 2005), 147. Conscription raised around 2.5 million men.

14. Stephen Constantine, *Lloyd George* (New York: Routledge, 1992), 55.

15. George Cassar, *Lloyd George at War, 1916–1918* (London: Anthem Press, 2009), 2.

16. Greenhalgh characterizes this alliance before Lloyd George premiership as "an imperfect, but nonetheless working, command relationship" (*Victory through Coalition*, 134).

17. France had over 2.8 million men on the Western Front. The British Expeditionary Force consisted of over 1.59 million men. Greenhalgh, *French Army and the First World War*, 176.

18. Greenhalgh, *Victory through Coalition*, 134–135, 152.

19. Jean-Jacques Becker argues that the French held out under these conditions because standards of living never sunk too low and that they feared German occupation more than the mishandling of the war by their leaders. *The Great War and the French People* (New York: St. Martin's Press, 1986).

20. Robert Doughty, *Pyrrhic Victory: French Strategy and Operation in the Great War* (Cambridge, MA: Harvard University Press, 2005), 355. Greenhalgh paints Nivelle in a more sympathetic light, arguing that as a relatively inexperienced commander who had a meteoric rise in the ranks he had to take account of the views of men who had once been his superiors as well as British aims in a period of tension and change (*French Army and the First World War*, 175–177).

21. The April offenses were undertaken under terrible circumstances. In addition to growing distrust between and among Allied forces, cold weather and the fact that Germany had a copy of French plan of attack for Arras further complicated things. The capture of Vimy Ridge was followed by over a month of terrible fighting resulting in 139,867 casualties. Greenhalgh, *Victory through Coalition*, 148–149.

22. Doughty, *Pyrrhic Victory*, 356. Though the word "mutiny" was used by French generals at the time, Greenhalgh calls the reactions to the failure of the Nivelle offensive that started in May a "crisis in the army" rather than a full-blown mutiny (*French Army and the First World War*, 208).

23. This was known as the Rapallo Pact.

24. "Joint Note to the Supreme War Council: 1918 Campaign," January 21, 1918. WO 106/729.

25. Lloyd George, *War Memoirs*, vol. IV, 1808–1811. The British Expeditionary Forces in Egypt and Palestine on February 1, 1917, comprised approximately 158,000 soldiers of which half were infantry.

26. "Note on the Prospect for 1918," January 5, 1918. AMEL 1/3/51, Leopold Amery Papers, Churchill Archives Centre, Cambridge.

27. Tusan, *Smyrna's Ashes*, 157.

28. Cassar, *Lloyd George at War, 1916–1918*, 2. Liberal criticisms of the Boer War are associated with journalist J. A. Hobson and his book *Imperialism*. Published in 1899, it was a seething critique of the Boer War as an imperial misadventure that only benefited a small group of capitalists and adventurers.

29. Michelle Tusan, "International Relations," in Tom Brooking and Todd Thompson, eds., *A Cultural History of Democracy in the Age of Empire* (London: Bloomsbury, 2021), 186.

30. Ian Packer, *Lloyd George* (New York: St. Martin's Press, 1998), 53.

31. This obligation dated back to the Treaty of Berlin which ended the Russo-Turkish War and was a hallmark of Liberal imperial foreign policy. Lloyd George, *War Memoirs*, vol. I, 2.

32. This explains why Ottoman Arabs were considered as part of this category despite their relative size. The idea of "small nationality" can be considered a predecessor to the conception of "minority" that Benjamin White identifies as developing out of the idea of nation-state in the mandate period (*Emergence of Minorities in the Middle East*, 37).

33. Tusan, *Smyrna's Ashes*, 66.

34. Lloyd George, *Truth about the Peace Treaties*, vol. I, 111.

35. Priya Satia, *Time's Monster: How History Makes History* (Cambridge, MA: Harvard University Press, 2020), 175–186.

36. Lloyd George, "Sowing the Winter Wheat," speech delivered at Carnarvon, Feb. 3, 1917, in *The Great Crusade: Extracts from Speeches Delivered during the War* (New York: George Doran, 1918), 102–103.

37. The British raised the question of supplying the Russian army with supplies after the March revolution due to fears that they might end up in German hands. Keith E. Neilson "The Breakup of the Anglo-Russian Alliance: The Question of Supply in 1917," *International History Review* 3, no. 1 (1981): 75.

38. Lloyd George, *War Memoirs*, vol. II, 802.

39. Kristian Ulrichsen, "The British Occupation of Mesopotamia, 1914–1922," *Journal of Strategic Studies* 30, no. 2 (2007): 350–351.

40. Kaushik Roy, *The Army in British India: From Colonial Warfare to Total War 1857– 1947* (London: Bloomsbury Publishing, 2014), 94.

41. Roy, *The Army in British India*, 103.

42. Ulrichsen, "The British Occupation of Mesopotamia," 351.

43. Roy, *The Army in British India*, 103.

44. Ibid., 94.

45. This organization later meet civil demands after the war. L. L. Fermor, "Thomas Henry Holland, 1868–1947," *Obituary Notices of Fellows of the Royal Society* 6, no. 17 (1948): 86.

46. Lloyd George, *War Memoirs*, vol. IV, 1767.

47. Berdine, *Redrawing the Middle East*, 1–3.

48. Memorandum by Mark Sykes on military situation in the Middle East, July 1916. DDSY2/4/105, Mark Sykes Papers.

49. Lloyd George, *War Memoirs*, vol. IV, 1816.

50. "Rapport," June 2, 1917. Le Fonds Andonian; H. Turabian to Boghos Nubar, August 17, 1917. Correspondence, Les archives de la Délégation nationale arménienne, Nubar Library, Paris.

51. A. P. Hacobian to Lloyd George, June 27, 1917. Correspondence, Les archives de la Délégation nationale arménienne.

52. Lloyd George, *War Memoirs*, vol. IV, p. 1820.

53. Lloyd George used his memoirs to settle scores and his earlier battles with Robertson about Western Front strategy clearly influenced his characterization of him in his memoirs. George Egerton, "The Lloyd George War Memoirs," *Journal of Modern History* 60, no. 1 (March 1988): 55–94.

54. Lloyd George, *War Memoirs*, vol. IV, 1825–1828.

55. Smuts became part of the War Cabinet after this time.

56. Michael Hynman Allenby was killed on July 29, 1917.

57. Lloyd George, *War Memoirs*, vol. IV, 1834–1835.

58. Faught, *Allenby*, 3–5, 13–15, 35–40.

59. Allenby to Mabel, August 20, 1917. 1/8/13, Edmund Allenby Papers, KCLMA.

60. Barkawi, *Soldiers of Empire*, 7, 84; Das, *India, Empire, and First World War Culture*, 239–273; Imy, *Faithful Fighters*, 9.

61. Allenby to Mabel, August 20, 1917. 1/8/10, Edmund Allenby Papers.

62. Allenby to Mabel, October 3, 1917. 1/8/15, Edmund Allenby Papers.

63. Allenby to Mabel, November 1, 1917. 1/8/17, Edmund Allenby Papers.

64. Edmund Allenby, *A Brief Record of the Advance of the Egyptian Expeditionary Force* (London: HMSO, 1919).

65. Lawrence James, *Imperial Warrior: General Allenby* (London: Weidenfeld and Nicolson, 1993), 141.

66. Allenby to Mabel, July 28, 1917. 1/8/7, Edmund Allenby Papers. On the British orientalist gaze, see Billie Melman, *Women's Orients: English Women and the Middle East, 1718–1918; Sexuality, Religion and Work* (Ann Arbor: Michigan University Press, 1992); Nancy Stockdale, *Colonial Encounters among English and Palestinian Women* (Gainesville: University of Florida Press, 2007); Eitan Bar-Yosef, *The Holy Land in English Culture 1799–1917: Palestine and the Question of Orientalism* (Oxford: Clarendon, 2005).

67. Allenby to Mabel, December 14, 1917. 1/8/33, Edmund Allenby Papers.

68. Sir Reginald's knowledge of Arabic allowed Allenby to conduct these interviews. Allenby to Mabel, November 10, 1917, 1/8/10 and November 20, 1917, 1/8/25. Edmund Allenby Papers.

69. While not as widespread as similar American and British institutions, Germany had an established network of Protestant missions and schools targeted by the Allied administration. The German Educational Institution Board, for example, was sent a letter informing it of the Allied takeover which included the administration of an orphanage called the Schneller Institute in Syria. "Memorandum for the German Educational Institution Board," n.d. Folder 7, Reel 157, American National Red Cross (ARC) Archives, Hoover Institution Library and Archives, Stanford University, CA.

70. James, *Imperial Warrior*, 122–124.

71. Allenby to Mabel, December 11, 1917. 1/8/32, Edmund Allenby Papers.

72. Ibid.

73. Allenby to Mabel, December 11, 1917. 1/8/38. Edmund Allenby Papers.

74. Allenby to Mabel, December 14, 1917. 1/8/33. Edmund Allenby Papers.

75. Britain established a consulate at Jerusalem in 1838. Alexander Schölch, "Britain in Palestine, 1838–1882: The Roots of the Balfour Policy," *Journal of Palestine Studies* 22 (1992): 39–56.

76. Abigail Green, "Intervening in the Jewish Question," in Brendan Simms and D. J. B. Trim, eds., *Humanitarian Intervention: A History* (Cambridge: Cambridge University Press, 2011), 139–158.

77. White, *Emergence of Minorities in the Middle East*; Ussama Samir Makdisi argues that religious affiliation emerged in nineteenth-century Lebanon as an important marker of identity in the Ottoman imperial context, "defining public and political characteristics of the modern subject and citizen." *The Culture of Sectarianism: Community, History, and Violence in Nineteenth-Century Ottoman Lebanon* (Berkeley: University of California Press, 2000), 8–12.

78. Eitan Bar-Yosef, *The Holy Land in English Culture 1799–1917: Palestine and the Question of Orientalism* (Oxford: Clarendon, 2000).

79. Leonard Stein, *The Balfour Declaration* (New York: Simon and Schuster, 1961), 7–9.

80. Schölch, "Britain in Palestine," 44–46; 51.

81. Tom Segev goes as far as to suggest that the Balfour Declaration was the product of "neither military nor diplomatic interests," *One Palestine, Complete: Jews and Arabs under the British Mandate*, trans. Haim Watzman (New York: Henry Holt, 1999), 33. See also, Jonathan Schneer, *The Balfour Declaration: The Origins of the Arab-Israeli Conflict* (New York: Random House, 2010).

82. J. Reinharz, "The Balfour Declaration and Its Maker: A Reassessment," *The Journal of Modern History* 64, no. 3 (1992): 455–499; Stein, *Balfour Declaration*.

83. This approach parallels critiques of reading the mandate system forward in order to find determinants for 1948 rather than in the context of the war. Martin Bunton cautions that such an approach risks an ahistorical treatment of the history of both the Palestine Mandate and Zionism. "Mandate Daze: Stories of British Rule in Palestine, 1917–48," *International Journal of Middle East Studies* 35, no. 3 (2003): 489. Penny Sinanoglou shows how the colonial project was connected to the wartime emergency and argues that British rule needs to be understood as more than a precursor to the birth of Israel. *Partitioning Palestine: British Policymaking at the End of Empire* (Chicago: Chicago University Press, 2019).

84. Stein, *Balfour Declaration*, 55–58. Segev argues that support for Zionism did not erase anti-Semitic thinking among many politicians (*One Palestine, Complete*, 33–39).

85. Robert Johnson understands this agreement as part of a wartime strategy rather than a plan for "long term occupation." "The de Bunsen Committee and a Revision of the 'Conspiracy' of Sykes–Picot," *Middle Eastern Studies* 54, no. 4, (2018): 611–637: 614.

86. This included the editor of the *Manchester Guardian*, C. P. Scott, a close friend of Lloyd George who had contact throughout the war with prominent Zionists. In fall 1918, Weitzmann met with Scott and lobbied him to get him an interview with Lloyd George. Diary, October 25/26, 1918. Add MS 50905, C. P. Scott Papers, British Library, London. A strong anti-Zionist sentiment also developed during this time led by Edwin Montagu. Stein, *Balfour Declaration*, 113, 131–135.

87. Stein, *Balfour Declaration*, 233.

88. Ibid., 234.

89. Weizmann first met Lord Balfour in 1905. Stein, *Balfour Declaration*, 141, 147.

90. Johnson, "The de Bunsen Committee," 612. Stein also sees the agreement as an attempt to "define war aims" (*Balfour Declaration*, 246).

91. Notes of a conference at 10 Downing Street to consider the instructions to Mark Sykes as Chief Political Officer, April 3, 1917, p. 2. DDSY2/12/6, Mark Sykes Papers.

92. Pascal Le Pautremat, "La mission du Lieutenant-colonel Brémond au Hedjaz, 1916–1917," *Guerres mondiales et conflits contemporains*, no. 221 (2006): 17–31.

93. This includes his four volumes of war memoirs and his two-volume *The Truth about the Peace Treaties*.

94. Edouard Brémond, *Le Hedjaz dans la Guerre mondiale* (Paris: Payot, 1931).

95. Sykes' conference speech, February 7, 1917, as quoted in Stein, *Balfour Declaration*, 373.

96. Sir Reginald Wingate to Graham, Telegram, December 14, 1917. DDSY(2)/11/82, Mark Sykes Papers.

97. Stein, *Balfour Declaration*, 270–271.

98. Ibid., 277.

99. Cecil, quoted in Stein, *Balfour Declaration*, 278.

100. Stein, *Balfour Declaration*, 388.

101. G. F. Clayton to Sykes, December 15, 1917, p. 4. DDSY (2)/11/83, Mark Sykes Papers.

102. Sykes to Sir Wingate (Cairo), December 11, 1917. DDSY(2)/11/79, Mark Sykes Papers.

103. Telegram Mark Sykes to Sir Reginald Wingate, November 17, 1917. DDSY(2)/11/73, Mark Sykes Papers.

104. Ibid.

105. Schneer, *The Balfour Declaration*, 174–175.

106. Reinharz, "The Balfour Declaration and Its Maker," 455.

107. This included a quieting of critics and official acknowledgments of the Zionist position such as a Labour Party pro-Zionist statement issued in August. Reinharz, "The Balfour Declaration and Its Maker," 461–466.

108. Lloyd George, *The Truth about the Peace Treaties*, vol. II, 1118.

109. Rogan, *Fall of the Ottomans*, 336–339.

110. Dimitrios Giannikopoulos, "Greece's Entry into the Great War," in Johnson and Kitchen, eds., *The Great War in the Middle East*, 86–87. China also entered the war on the Allied side that summer.

111. Reinharz, "The Balfour Declaration and Its Maker," 490–493.

112. The *Manchester Guardian* broke the story of Sykes–Picot at the end of November after foreign correspondents learned of its contents from the Soviet press. Cemal Pasha revealed the agreement to discredit the Arab Revolt in the days preceding the fall of Jerusalem. Though the revelation came as a relative surprise to Arab leaders, it did not break the alliance. It did, however, sow seeds of doubt about Allied intentions after the war. Rogan, *Fall of the Ottomans*, 357–358.

113. Borislav Chernev, *Twilight of Empire: The Brest-Litovsk Conference and the Remaking of Central Europe, 1917–1918* (Toronto: Toronto University Press, 2017).

114. Sykes quoted in Schneer, *The Balfour Declaration*, 349–350.

115. The first two battles of Gaza ended in failure in 1917 under the leadership of General Murray. Matthew Hughes, "General Allenby and the Palestine Campaign, 1917–18," *Journal of Strategic Studies* 19, no. 4 (1996): 59–88: 64.

116. The signing of Brest-Litovsk on March 3, 1918, restored Kars, Ardahan and Batum, lost in the Russo-Turkish War, to the Ottoman Empire.

117. Richard Hovannisian, *The Republic of Armenia*, vol. I: *The First Year, 1918–1919* (Berkeley: University of California Press, 1971), 29–38.

118. Rogan, *Fall of the Ottomans*, 371–373.

119. Robert Johnson, "British Strategy and the Imperial Axis in the Middle East, 1914–1918," in Johnson and Kitchen, eds., *The Great War in the Middle East*, 47–48.

120. Hughes, "General Allenby and the Palestine Campaign," 80–81.

121. "Progress of Allied Occupation" maps can be viewed in their original color at www .cambridge.org/TheLastTreaty.

122. J. Halstead, "Air Power and Allenby's Army: Combined Arms in Palestine 1917–1918," *War in History* 29, no. 1 (2022): 157–184.

123. Brig. Gen F. J. Moberly, *Official History of the War: Mesopotamia Campaign, 1914–1918*, vol. IV by Imperial War Museum Dept of Printed books (London: HMSO, 1925), i.

124. "Draft Treaty Discussion," August 7, 1919. FO 608/54/9.

125. Underline in original. Maurice Hankey, October 31, 1918, diary entry. HNKY 1/6, M. P. A. Hankey Papers, Churchill Archives Centre, Cambridge.

126. Tusan, *Smyrna's Ashes*, 27–30.

127. Article 44 applied to Jewish minorities and Article 61 codified British protection of Ottoman Christians. Fink, *Defending the Rights of Others*.

128. Tusan, "Crimes against Humanity," 64.

129. Confidential letter to Pollock from J. H. Morgan (War Office), October 29, 1918. Hanworth Papers, Bodleian, Oxford University.

130. "Minutes," October 31, 1918, War Cabinet 494A. CAB/23/14.

131. "Sir Somerset Gough Calthorpe," *The Times*, July 28, 1937, 16. He was made Admiral on July 31 upon his appointment at Portsmouth.

132. Another clause read, "In case of disorder in the six Armenian vilayets the Allies reserve to themselves the right to occupy any part of them."

133. "Minutes," October 31, 1918, War Cabinet 494A. CAB/23/14.

134. "Minutes," November 4, 1918, War Cabinet 496. CAB/23/8.

135. "Eastern Report," November 14, 1918, no. XCIV. CAB/24/145.

136. Ahmed Tevfik Pasha served as grand vizier four times between 1918–1922. Erik-Jan Zürcher, *Turkey: A Modern History* (London: I. B. Tauris, 2004), 404.

137. Talaat Pasha had resigned in early October along with Enver Pasha and Cemal Pasha. As the architects of Ottoman wartime policy, they did not want to be held responsible for the conditions of the peace.

138. "Eastern Report," November 28, 1918, no. XCVI. CAB/24/145.

139. "Eastern Report," December 5, 1918, no. XCVII. CAB/24/145.

140. Ibid.

141. Ibid.

142. Der Matossian, *Horrors of Adana*, 226–227.

143. "Eastern Report," January 23, 1919, no. CIV. CAB/24/145.

144. "Turkish Armistice Breeches," British High Commission communication from Calthorpe to Curzon, January 19, 1919. FO 608/82/10.

145. Tusan, "Crimes against Humanity," 67–68.

CHAPTER 3 CIVILIANS AT WAR

1. Lt. Gen. Sir Stanley Maude, "The Proclamation of Baghdad," March 19, 1917. IOR/L/PS/18/B253, India Office Records, British Library.
2. Baghdad was a city of around 250,000 before the war. L. W. Jones, "Rapid Population Growth in Baghdad and Amman," *Middle East Journal* 23, no. 2 (Spring 1969): 209–215.
3. Memorandum on Mr. Austen Chamberlain's amendment of the proposed Proclamation to the People of Baghdad, March 10, 1917. DDSY(2)11/32, Mark Sykes Papers.
4. When the French Syrian mandate came into force, aid work forged "transformative occupation" where humanitarian relief played a key role in facilitating governance. Simon Jackson, "Transformative Relief: Imperial Humanitarianism and Mandatory Development in Syria-Lebanon, 1915–1925," *Humanity* 8, no. 2 (Summer 2017): 247–268; Simon Jackson and Dirk Moses, "Transformative Occupations in the Modern Middle East," *Humanity* 8, no. 2 (Summer 2017): 231–246.
5. Benny Morris and Dror Ze'evi, *The Thirty-Year Genocide: Turkey's Destruction of Its Christian Minorities, 1894–1924* (Cambridge, MA: Harvard University Press, 2019); Suny et al., *A Question of Genocide*; Tusan, *Smyrna's Ashes*.
6. Watenpaugh, *Bread from Stones*; Branden Little, ed., *Humanitarianism in the Era of the First World War*, special issue of *First World War Studies* 5, no. 1 (2014); Cabanes, *Great War and the Origins of Humanitarianism*.
7. Aidan Forth, *Barbed Wire Imperialism: Britain's Empire of Camps* (Berkeley: University of California Press, 2017), 223.
8. Giorgio Agamben, *Homo Sacer: Sovereign Power and Bare Life*, trans. Daniel Heller-Roazen (Stanford: Stanford University Press, 1998), 133.
9. Officials understood the region as central to British power which could not be governed directly like "the Indian Empire." DDSY(2) 11/32, Mark Sykes Papers. Timothy C. Winegard, *The First World Oil War* (Toronto: University of Toronto Press, 2016), 14.
10. Watenpaugh, *Bread from Stones*, 2; Melanie Tanielian, "Politics of Wartime Relief in Ottoman Beirut," *First World War Studies* 5, no. 1 (2014): 69–82; Najwa al-Qattan, "Wartime Memory and the Language of Food in Syria and Lebanon," *International Journal of Middle East Studies* 46, no. 4 (November 2014): 719–736; Abigail Jacobson, "A City Living through Crisis: Jerusalem during World War I," *British Journal of Middle Eastern Studies* 36, no. 1 (April 2009): 73–92.
11. Cabanes, *Great War and the Origins of Humanitarianism*; Keith Watenpaugh, "The League of Nations' Rescue of Armenian Genocide Survivors and the Making of Modern Humanitarianism," *American Historical Review* 115, no. 5 (December 2010): 1315–1339; Jinks, "Marks Hard to Erase"; Andrekos Varnava and Trevor Harris, 'It is Quite Impossible to Receive Them': Saving the Musa Dagh Refugees and the Imperialism of European Humanitarianism," *Journal of Modern History* 90, no. 4 (December 2018): 834–862.
12. Forth, *Barbed Wire Imperialism*, 4–5.
13. In Britain, a network of camps developed over the course of the twentieth century to provide aid and refuge to foreigner subjects and British citizens alike. Jordanna Bailkin,

Unsettled: Refugee Camps and the Making of Multicultural Britain (Oxford: Oxford University Press, 2018), 6.

14. Peter Gatrell, *Whole Empire Walking: Refugees in Russia during World War I* (Bloomington: Indiana University Press, 2005), 8–10.

15. Stefan Manz and Panayi Panikos, *Enemies in the Empire: Civilian Internment in the British Empire during the First World War* (New York: Oxford University Press), 27. On the history of the concentration camp, see also Sybille Scheipers, "The Use of Camps in Colonial Warfare," *Journal of Imperial and Commonwealth History* 43, no. 4 (2015): 678–698; Iain R. Smith and Andreas Stucki, "The Colonial Development of Concentration Camps," *Journal of Imperial and Commonwealth History* 39, no. 3 (2011): 417–437; Jonathan Hyslop, "The Invention of the Concentration Camp: Cuba, Southern Africa and the Philippines, 1896–1907," *Southern African Historical Journal* 63, no. 2 (2011): 251–276; Jürgen Zimmerer, "Colonial Genocide: The Herero and Nama War in German South West Africa and its Significance," in Dan Stone, ed., *The Historiography of Genocide* (London: Palgrave Macmillan, 2008), 323–343; Jonas Kreienbaum, "Guerrilla Wars and Colonial Concentration Camps: The Exceptional Case of German South West Africa (1904–1908)," *Journal of Namibian Studies* 11 (2014): 83–101.

16. Forth, *Barbed-Wire Imperialism*; Heather Jones, *Violence against Prisoners of War in the First World War: Britain, France and Germany, 1914–1920* (Cambridge: Cambridge University Press, 2011); Panikos Panayi, *Prisoners of Britain: German Civilian and Combatant Internees during the First World War* (Manchester: Manchester University Press, 2012); Oliver Wilkinson, *British Prisoners of War in First World War Germany* (Cambridge: Cambridge University Press, 2017).

17. The terms "refugee camp" and "concentration camp" were often used interchangeably during the Boer War. Forth, *Barbed-Wire Imperialism*, 28, 152.

18. Isabel Hull, *Absolute Destruction: Military Culture and the Practices of War in Imperial Germany* (Ithaca, NY: Cornell University Press, 2013), 8, 152.

19. Aidan Forth, "Britain's Archipelago of Camps: Labor and Detention in a Liberal Empire, 1871–1903," *Kritika* 16, no. 3 (2015): 651–680; Omar Bartov, *Germany's War and the Holocaust: Disputed Histories* (Ithaca, NY: Cornell University Press, 2003); Bettina Greiner, trans., *Suppressed Terror: History and Perception of Soviet Special Camps in Germany* (New York: Lexington Books, 2014); Norman Naimark, *Stalin's Genocides* (Princeton: Princeton University Press, 2010); Peter Gatrell, *The Unsettling of Europe: How Migration Shaped a Continent* (New York: Basic Books, 2019).

20. Hull, *Absolute Destruction*, 189, 193.

21. Forth, *Barbed Wire Imperialism*, 11.

22. Manz and Panayi, *Enemies in the Empire*, 49; Bailkin, *Unsettled*, 24–25.

23. Forth, *Barbed Wire Imperialism*, 4.

24. Raymond Kévorkian, *The Armenian Genocide: A Complete History* (London: I. B. Tauris, 2011), 264.

25. Manz and Panayi, *Enemies in the Empire*, 28, 33–34.

26. "Concentration Camp Map," in Kévorkian, *The Armenian Genocide*, 264; Hull, "Routes of Deportation of Armenians in Turkey, 1914–1918 Map," in *Absolute Destruction*, 264.

27. The Hague Conventions of 1899 and 1907 attempted to protect "individual rights in wartime," which broadened the scope of agreements made regarding the treatment of combatants and non-combatants at Geneva in 1864 after the Crimean War. Cabanes, *Great War and the Origins of Humanitarianism*, 269–270; Caroline Shaw, *Britannia's Embrace: Modern Humanitarianism and the Imperial Origins of Refugee Relief* (Oxford: Oxford University Press, 2015), 209–210.

28. Hull, *Absolute Destruction*, 122.

29. On the rise of new bureaucratic attitudes toward solving hunger and state aid in the context of the British welfare state, see James Vernon, *Hunger: A Modern History* (Cambridge, MA: Harvard University Press, 2007) and Kevin Grant, *Last Weapons: Hunger Strikes and Fasts in the British Empire* (Berkeley: University of California Press, 2019), 17–18, 26–29.

30. The Nansen Passport system and 1933 and 1938 Refugee Conventions were key to this process. Claudina Skran, *Refugees in Interwar Europe: The Emergence of a Regime* (Oxford: Oxford University Press, 1995), 264.

31. Fink, *Defending the Rights of Others*.

32. Shaw, *Britannia's Embrace*, 39, 43.

33. Andrew Thompson, "The Protestant Interest and the History of Humanitarian Intervention, c. 1685–c. 1756," in Brendan Simms and D. J. B. Trim, eds., *Humanitarianism Intervention: A History* (Cambridge: Cambridge University Press, 2011), 67–88.

34. Tusan, *Smyrna's Ashes*, 14–15.

35. Rodogno, *Against Massacre*, 27–29.

36. Lloyd George, *Great Crusade*; J. Ellis Barker, "Germany and Turkey," *Fortnightly Review* 96 n.s. (December 1914), 1013.

37. Rogan, *Fall of the Ottomans*, 296–309. The term was used by an American Red Cross (ARC) worker to describe refugee camps where "Arabs or Syrians" were the majority inhabitants. Rosa E. Lee to Finley, September 23, 1918. Correspondence, ARC Archives, Hoover Library.

38. Satia, *Spies in Arabia*, 149–158.

39. Michel Foucault, *Birth of Biopolitics* (New York: Picador, 2010), 65.

40. Panayi, *Prisoners of Britain*, 77–83.

41. These are League of Nations' estimates immediately after the war. The Royal Institute of International Affairs estimated the number between 85,000 and 100,000 in 1938. "Armenian Refugees in Syria," *Refugee Survey 1937–1938*, vol. 11 (London: Royal Institute of International Affairs, 1938).

42. Agamben, *Homo Sacer*, 174.

43. P. Giaccaria and C. Minca, "Topographies/Topologies of the Camp: Auschwitz as a Spatial Threshold," *Political Geography* 30 (2011): 4–5. Agamben, *Homo Sacer*, 169–170.

44. Giaccaria and Minca, "Topographies/Topologies of the Camp," 5.

45. Kalliopi Nikolopoulou, "Review of *Homo Sacer: Sovereign Power and Bare Life*," *SubStance* 29, no. 3 (2000): 124–131.

46. Agamben, *Homo Sacer*, 166.

47. Kimberly Jensen, *Mobilizing Minerva: American Women in the First World War* (Urbana: University of Illinois Press, 2008); Susan Zeiger, *In Uncle Sam's Service: Women Workers with the American Expeditionary Force, 1917–1919* (Ithaca, NY: Cornell University Press, 1999).

48. These formal and informal camps are described in the *New Near East*, the official journal of Near East Relief.

49. Tanielian, *Charity of War*; White, "Refugees and the Definition of Syria"; Abigail Green, "Humanitarianism in Nineteenth-Century Context," *Historical Journal* 57, no. 4 (December 2014): 1157–1175.

50. Gen. H. H. Austin, *Baqubah Refugee Camp: An Account of Work on Behalf of the Persecuted Assyrian Christians* (Piscataway, NJ: Gorgias Press, 2006, repr.) 1, 4, 28, 39.

51. W. T. Stead, "Our Death Camps in South Africa," *Review of Reviews* (January 1902).

52. Criticisms of so-called "famine" and "plague" camps set up in India during the late nineteenth century may also have informed attempts to create "humane" spaces for internees at refugee, POW and civilian internment camps alike. Forth, *Barbed Wire Imperialism*, 71–72, 95–99. Panayi, *Prisoners of Britain*, 101. Hull suggests that British political culture, which encouraged oversight and critique of government action, also contributed (*Absolute Destruction*, 193).

53. Though death rates were relatively high when the camp opened, by the time of closing deaths were 3 per 1,000 and births at 200 per month at Baquba when compared to 146 deaths per 1,000 in South Africa in 1901. "Memorandum on the Armenian and Assyrian Refugees" (Baghdad, 1919), Appendix D. 39.7/4 (567), Imperial War Museum, London.

54. Bailkin, *Unsettled*, 5–6.

55. Austin, *Baqubah Refugee Camp*, 102.

56. "Publication Propaganda," Secret Political Department, Register no. P7105. Mr. Long to Secretary Montagu, November 7, 1919. IOR/L/PS/11/159, India Office Records, British Library; "Refugees in Mesopotamia," June 7, 1919, *Illustrated London News*.

57. *New Near East*, January 16, 1920.

58. Austin, *Baqubah Refugee Camp*, 72–73.

59. Michelle Tusan, "The Business of Relief Work: A Victorian Quaker in Constantinople and Her Circle," *Victorian Studies* 51, no. 4 (Summer 2009): 633–661.

60. Austin, "Baqubah Camp," 38–39.

61. A similar model was deployed by the Germans in POW camps where ethnic, national and racial groups were separated to try and bring internees over to their side. On German POW policy, see Wilkinson, *British Prisoners of War*, 47–53 and 56–57.

62. "Refugee Camps at Port Said and Baqubah," November 11, 1919. CAB/24/93.

63. Northcote to Mother, December 3, 1918. Add MS 57559, Northcote Papers, British Library, London.

64. Levon Shahoian, *On the Banks of the Tigris* (London: Gomidas Institute, 2012).

65. Ibid., 66.

66. Ibid., 56–57.

67. Austin, "Baqubah Camp," 43.

68. Zaven der Yeghiayan, *My Patriarchal Memoirs*, trans. Ared Misirliyan (Barrington, RI: Mayreni Publishing, 2002), 140.

69. Ibid., 164–166.

70. Letters from September 23 and 24, 1921. Add MS 57559, Northcote Papers.

71. Refugees flooded in at over 1,000 persons per day during extreme famine. Akaby Nassibian, *Britain and the Armenian Question, 1915–1923* (London: Croom Helm, 1984), 248–249.

72. Skran, *Refugees in Interwar Europe*, 65–78.

73. Shahoian, *Banks of the Tigris*, 83–84.

74. Rogan, *Fall of the Ottomans*, 280, 289–292.

75. On the Armenian case, see Richard Hovannisian, ed., *The Armenian People from Ancient to Modern Times*, vol. II (London: Palgrave Macmillan, 2004) and Razmik Panossian, *The Armenians: From Kings and Priests to Merchants and Commissars* (New York: Columbia University Press, 2006), 246–256; on Assyrians see David Gaunt, *Massacres, Resistance, Protectors: Muslim-Christian Relations in Eastern Anatolia during World War I* (Piscataway, NJ: Gorgias Press, 2006) and Saragon G. Donabed, *Reforging a Forgotten History: Iraq and the Assyrians in the Twentieth Century* (Edinburgh: Edinburgh University Press, 2015).

76. Lavinia Dock et al., *History of American Red Cross* (New York: Macmillan, 1922), 897. Dock recorded the often-anonymous sentiments of her fellow nurses in this firsthand history of the ARC.

77. Irwin, *Making the World Safe*, 2.

78. Ibid., 72–73, 139.

79. ARC had a large network of hospitals, clinics and auxiliary aid stations during the First World War which included Western and Eastern Europe in addition to the Middle East. Dock et al., *History of American Red Cross*; Irwin, *Making the World Safe*.

80. *History of the American National Red Cross Nursing* (New York: Macmillan, 1922), 891–893; "ARC Mission to Palestine," undated address by Capt. Carson. Reel 149, ARC Archives.

81. Tanielian, *Charity of War*, 51–63.

82. Rogan, *Fall of the Ottomans*, 275–309, 350–353.

83. "Memorandum," May 31, 1918. Folder 7, Reel 157, ARC Archives.

84. "American Red Cross Mission to Palestine" address by Capt. Carson of ARC, n.d. Reel 149, ARC Archives.

85. Watenpaugh, *Bread from Stones*, 16–19; Cabanes, *Great War and the Origins of Humanitarianism*, 280, 288.

86. Dock et al., *History of American Red Cross*, 890.

87. Ibid., 897.

88. Edward Fuller described Save the Children's use of images in the press to raise awareness and funds from the British public. *The Right of the Child Fuller: A Chapter in Social History* (Boston: Beacon Press, 1951), 92. Cabanes critiques the exploitative nature of these fundraising techniques in *Great War and the Origins of Humanitarianism*, 278.

89. Heide Fehrenbach, "Children and Other Civilians: Photography and the Politics of Humanitarian Image-Making," in Fehrenbach and Davide Rodogno, eds., *Humanitarian Photography: A History* (Cambridge: Cambridge University Press, 2015), 176–177.

90. Dock et al., *History of American Red Cross*, 892.

91. Ibid., 897.

92. ARC held the primary responsibility of enlisting military nurses during the war. Jensen, *Mobilizing Minerva*, 43.

93. Jensen, *Mobilizing Minerva*, 106; Zeiger, *In Uncle Sam's Service*, 78–80.

94. Gatrell, *Whole Empire Walking*, 123–124.

95. Rosa Lee, "First Report of Wadi Surar Education." Folder 16, Reel 155, ARC Archives.

96. Ibid.

97. Dock et al., *History of American Red Cross*, 902.

98. See, for example, correspondence between the Director of Medical Service and nursing staff in July and August 1918 over pay. Women earned $40 per month and $150 for uniforms, while men recruited to work for ARC were allowed to negotiate their salaries. ARC correspondence, ARC Archives.

99. Edward Kelsey to Commissioners, Jerusalem, July 23, 1918. Folder 16, Reel 155, ARC Archives.

100. Miss Edith Madeira to Miss Lillian Spelman, July 17, 1918. Folder 16, Reel 155, ARC Archives.

101. Dock et al., *History of American Red Cross*, 900–901.

102. These attitudes paralleled treatment of the so-called "deserving poor" in England during the Victorian period. Seth Koven, *Slumming: Sexual and Social Politics in Victorian London* (Princeton: Princeton University Press, 2004), 184–198.

103. Capt. Harry Carson, ARC engineer, report, August 24, 1918. Folder 18, Reel 155, ARC Archives.

104. Kelsey to Commissioners, August 24, 1918. Folder 17, Reel 155, ARC Archives.

105. Kelsey to Commissioners, August 17, 1918. Folder 17, Reel 155, ARC Archives.

106. Kelsey to Commissioners, August 24, 1918.

107. Rosa Lee to Col. Finley, September 23, 1918. Folder 17, Reel 155, ARC Archives.

108. Panayi, *Prisoners of Britain.*

109. Lee to Ward, July 28, 1918. Folder 16, Reel 155, ARC Archives.

110. Ibid.

111. Lee to Finley, September 23, 1918, ARC Archives.

112. Dock et al., *History of American Red Cross*, 902.

113. Ibid., 906.

114. Ibid., 902.

115. Kévorkian, *The Armenian Genocide*, pp. 799–800. Tusan, *British Empire and the Armenian Genocide*, 224–227.

116. Acting Commissioner to Brown, October 21, 1918. Folder 17, Reel 155, ARC Archives.

117. Vahram Shemmassian, "Armenian Genocide Survivors in the Holy Land at the End of World War I," *Journal of the Society for Armenian Studies* 21 (2012): 227–248.

118. "Refugee Camps Report," November 11, 1919, 2. Imperial War Museum.

119. Norman William Collins, Imperial War Museum interview, May 22, 1991, 12043.

120. Private Papers of C. H. Bond, 08/145/1, docs 16795, Imperial War Museum.

121. Tusan, *Smyrna's Ashes*, 30–35.

122. Varnava and Harris, "Saving the Musa Dagh Refugees," 835.

123. The army contributed 8,000 British pounds per month with the rest coming from ARC, the Egyptian government and private charity. "Refugee Camps Report," November 11, 1919, 1–2, Imperial War Museum.

124. Capt. Millikin to Commission, July 30, 1918; Director of Medical Service to Mr. Elder, August 1, 1918. Folder 18, Reel 155, ARC Archives.

125. Before the handover, the Egyptian government supplied food, shelter, sanitary arrangements, 1/3 the cost of schools, doctors and a head nurse; Armenian General Benevolent Union (AGBU) – 2/3 cost of schools; ARC, expenses of hospital, drugs and nurses; Friends of Armenia – salaries of sales agents; Armenian Red Cross and Armenian and Syrian Relief Committee – special diets. "Confidential Report," June 14, 1918. Folder 17, Reel 155, ARC Archives.

126. "Charity Reports: Armenian Refugee Camp, 1916–1917 and 1917–1918." Imperial War Museum.

127. This model of "self-help philanthropy" also was embraced by other humanitarian organizations. Tusan, "The Business of Relief Work," 645.

128. "The Refugee Camp, Port Said," *Friend*, August 17, 1917.

129. Francis Reed to Ward, December 30, 1919 [?]; Acting Commission to Francis Reed, December 16, 1918. Folder 11, Reel 149, ARC Archives.

130. "Charity Reports," 21.

131. Ibid.

132. Ibid.

133. The official address of the camp was changed from "Refugee Administration in Port Said" to "Armenian Refugee Camp" after the military changeover. Brown to Vance, September 13, 1918. Folder 18, Reel 155, ARC Archives.

134. Brown to Commission, September 15, 1918. Folder 17, Reel 155, ARC Archives.

135. Brown to Commission, October 9, 1918, Reel 155, Folder 17; Brown to Commission, September 15, 1918. Folder 17, Reel 155, ARC Archives.

136. Finley to Brown, August 13, 1918. Folder 18, Reel 155, ARC Archives.

137. Dikran Andreasian, trans. Stephen Trowbridge, "A Red Cross Flag that Save Four Thousand," American Red Cross Committee pamphlet (1916), 16.

138. Vahram Shemmassian, *Musa Dagh Armenians: A Socioeconomic and Cultural History 1919–1939* (Beirut: Haigazian University Press, 2015), 4–5.

139. "Refugee Camps at Port Said and Baqubah," November 11, 1919. CAB/24/93.

140. ARC sent five divisions, each serving 20,000 people. Luther Fowle, "Armenian and Syrian Relief," November 30, 1919. Folder 23, Reel 274, ARC Archives.

141. Armenia Committee Minutes, February 5, 1930. Library of the Society of Friends, Friends House, London.

142. Quoted in Shemmassian, *Musa Dagh Armenians*, 4.

143. On the support for relief campaigns in Britain after the war, see Tusan, *British Empire and the Armenian Genocide*, 151–183. For the French case see the collection of essays in Raymond Kévorkian et al., *Les Armeniens, 1917–1939: La quête d'un refuge* (Paris: Presses de L'Université Saint-Joseph, 2007).

CHAPTER 4 HOW WAR DIDN'T END

1. Eric-Jan Zürcher, *The Unionist Factor: The Role of the Committee of Union and Progress in the Turkish Nationalist Movement, 1905–1926* (Leiden: Brill, 1984). By late 1919, Kemal emerged as head of the anti-Entente movement and began to inherit Talaat's political role. A nationalist-led parliament was inaugurated in Ankara in April 1920. Kieser, *Talaat Pasha*, 319, 388, 393.

2. While the fate of Constantinople and plans to separate Armenia from the Ottoman Empire began at the Paris Conference, the determination of what this would look like evolved as battles with nationalists in Anatolia continued in late 1919 and 1920. Busch, *Mudros to Lausanne*; Michael Dockrill, and Douglas Goold, *Peace without Promise: Britain and the Peace Conferences, 1919–1923* (Hamden, CT: Archon Books, 1981); Salahi Ramadan Sonyel, *Turkish Diplomacy, 1918–1923: Mustafa Kemal and the Turkish Nationalist Movement* (London: Sage, 1975); Harry Howard, *The Partition of Turkey: A Diplomatic History, 1913-1923* (New York: Howard Fertig, 1966).

3. Arnold J. Toynbee, *Survey of International Affairs* (Oxford: Oxford University Press, 1928), 6–9.

4. Leonard Smith sees the Paris Conference as central to these overlapping conversations about peacemaking but considers the Lausanne Conference a departure because Turkey was treated as a "partner" rather than "defeated enemy" (*Sovereignty at the Paris Peace Conference*, 174). Macmillan includes discussions of individual treaties, ending with the breakdown of Sèvres but only briefly mentions Lausanne (*Peacemakers*).

5. In addition to Smith and Macmillan, on the Paris Peace Conference see Manela, *Wilsonian Moment*; Eric Weitz, "From the Vienna to the Paris System: International Politics and the Entangled Histories of Human Rights, Forced Deportations, and Civilizing Missions," *American Historical Review* 113, no. 5 (2008): 1313–1343; Marcus Payk and Roberta Pergher, *Beyond Versailles: Sovereignty, Legitimacy, and the Formation of New Polities after the Great War* (Bloomington: Indiana University Press, 2019); Mona Siegel, *Peace on Our Terms: The Global Battle for Women's Rights after the First World War* (New York: Columbia University Press, 2020). For a contemporary account, see Harold Nicolson, *Peacemaking 1919* (New York: Grosset and Dunlap, 1965).

6. Pedersen, *The Guardians*, 77–106.

7. Fromkin, *Peace to End All Peace*, 415–417, 424–455.

8. Leonhard, *Pandora's Box*, 848.

9. Manela argues that it ultimately failed to offer nations outside of Europe a place in the international order that Wilson's "Fourteen Points" had promised (*Wilsonian Moment*, 13).

10. Pedersen shows the importance of this process to the enacting of the mandate system (*Guardians*, 78–103).

11. Britain had over a million troops on Ottoman soil at the beginning of 1919 but began to draw down troops as early as that spring. By October that number was down to half a million. Lloyd George, *War Memoirs*, vol. VI, 3314; Macmillan, *Peacemakers*, 455.

12. Pedersen, *The Guardians*, 1.

13. Macmillan, *Peacemakers*, 386. The Ottoman delegations' presence was discussed at a meeting of the Supreme Council held on June 28, 1919. Woodward and Butler, eds., *Documents on British Foreign Policy*, vol. IV, 653.

14. Pedersen, *The Guardians*, 95.

15. Stein, *Balfour Declaration*, 659.

16. Ibid., 661–662.

17. Balfour to Lloyd George, June 26, 1919. Memorandum. Add MS 49752, Balfour Papers, British Library.

18. The case of Kurdistan was also widely discussed, but there were no prominent Kurdish leaders at the Paris Conference to plead the case for an independent state and participate in proceedings.

19. Macmillan, *Peacemakers*, 155.

20. They headed two separate Armenian delegations at the beginning of the conference. Eventually, they reconciled demands for the establishment of an Armenian state under Allied supervision. Hovannisian, *Republic of Armenia*, vol. I, 251–260.

21. Macmillan, *Peacemakers*, 388.

22. Her name is also spelled "Essayan." She penned articles in Armenian and French which included discussions of European feminism, the Woman Question and the role of Armenian women in social life and charitable work. Not long after marrying painter Dikran Yessayan in Paris in 1900, with whom she had two children, she returned to Constantinople to continue her writing career. She served on the humanitarian and fact-finding commission established by the Constantinople Patriarch to investigate massacres in the city of Adana in southern Anatolia in 1909. Her book *In the Ruins* chronicled her time as investigator and aid worker in Adana. Published in 1911, it cemented her reputation as intellectual, aid worker and activist. Victoria Rowe, "The 'New Armenian Woman': Armenian Women's Writing in the Ottoman Empire, 1880–1915," dissertation, University of Toronto, 9–13.

23. Yessayan to Boghos Nubar, Tehran, September 12, 1921. AGBU Archives, Nubar Library, Paris.

24. Lerna Ekmekçioğlu, "The Armenian National Delegation at the Paris Peace Conference" and "The Role of the Armenian Woman during the War."

25. Zabel Essayan, "Le rôle de la femme Arménienne pendant la guerre," *Revue des Études Arméniennes* 2, no. 1 (1922): 121–138.

26. Rebecca Jinks, "Marks Hard to Erase."

27. Note from Mme Essayan to Armenian National Delegation, Paris, March 8, 1919: "The Liberation of Non-Muslim women and Children in Turkey." AGBU Archives.

28. Ibid.

29. Robinson to Nubar, April 2, 1919. AGBU Archives.

30. Eugene Rogan, *The Arabs: A History* (New York: Basic Books, 2009), 156–158.

31. Macmillan, *Peacemakers*, 402.

32. Foreign Office documents from early 1919 suggest that Feisal was not given representative status by the French in part because of his communication with the British before the Paris conference. FO 608/97/24.

33. Macmillan, *Peacemakers*, 403.

34. Henry Chauvel memorandum, October 31, 1935. GB 165–0005, 1/2, Allenby Papers, Middle East Centre Archives, St. Antony's College, Oxford (MECA).

35. H. Chauvel's description of the meeting of Allenby and Feisal at the Hotel Victoria, Damascus on October 3, 1918, dated October 22, 1929. GB 165–0005, 1/2, Allenby Papers.

36. Allenby to Mother, [March 21?] 1919. 1/10/7, Edmund Allenby Papers, KCLMA.

37. Macmillan, *Peacemakers*, 405.

38. Samuel, quoted in Stein, *Balfour Declaration*, 559.

39. Stein, *Balfour Declaration*, 566.

40. Ibid., 637.

41. Ibid., 617–618.

42. Lloyd George, *Truth about the Peace Treaties*, 288–290.

43. Rogan, *The Arabs*, 212–213.

44. Sluglett, *Britain in Iraq*, 13–15; Bayly, *Empire and Information*.

45. Letter from Henry Chauvel describing his version of events to Director of the Australian War Memorial, Canberra, sent January 1, 1936, and dated October 31, 1935. GB 165–0005, 1/2, Allenby Papers, MECA.

46. Garabet Moumdjian, "Cilicia under French Administration," in Hovannisian, ed., *Armenian Cilicia*, 455–459.

47. The Eastern Committee was the successor to the Middle Eastern Committee and encompassed Russian and Persian affairs. Led by Curzon, it was now part of the Foreign Office rather than the War Cabinet and no longer included Mark Sykes. Berdine, *Redrawing the Middle East*, 209–210.

48. Satia, *Spies in Arabia*, 43.

49. Cecil to Balfour, July 20, 1918. 51071A, ff. 48, Robert Cecil Papers, British Library. Cecil suggested that the Foreign Office oversee the Eastern Committee because of the enormity of the task before it.

50. France had resisted an Armenian state that included Cilicia, hoping that this territory in southern Anatolia would be part of a French-controlled Syria. Hovannisian, *Republic of Armenia*, vol. I, 277–283.

51. Ibid., December 9, 1918.

52. Quoted in Lloyd George, *Truth About the Peace Treaties*, 1015.

53. General Milne, under General Franchet d'Espèrey, was the military commander of Constantinople and traveled to and reported on the situation along the Russia borderlands. War Cabinet, 516. January 1919, p. 2. CAB 23/9.

54. The last Allied troops left Constantinople in fall 1923.

55. Beth Baron, *The Orphan Scandal: Christian Missionaries and the Rise of the Muslim Brotherhood* (Stanford: Stanford University Press, 2014); Fahmy, *Ordinary Egyptians.*

56. Faught, *Allenby in Egypt,* 110.

57. Allenby to Mother, November 11, 1918. 1/9/17, Edmund Allenby Papers, KCLMA.

58. Faught, *Allenby in Egypt,* p. 117.

59. Allenby to Mother, March 31, 1919. 1/10/8, Edmund Allenby Papers, KCLMA.

60. He put Sykes on the side of the Arabs and Picot less so. Allenby to Mabel, December 10, 1918. 1/9/20, Edmund Allenby Papers, KCLMA.

61. Faught, *Allenby in Egypt,* 121.

62. *Ibid.,* 125.

63. Manela, *Wilsonian Moment,* 68–75.

64. Telegram from Allenby submitted by Calthorpe as part of the Eastern Report, February 9, 1919. Allenby arrived in Constantinople on February 7th. "Eastern Report," February 13, 1919. CAB 24/145.

65. Allenby to Mabel, December 10, 1919. 1/9/20, Edmund Allenby Papers, KCLMA.

66. Allenby to Mother, March 21, 1919. Edmund Allenby Papers, KCLMA.

67. Fahmy, *Ordinary Egyptians,* 135.

68. Baron, *The Orphan Scandal.*

69. Fahmy, *Ordinary Egyptians,* 136–138.

70. Siegel, *Peace on Our Terms,* 108–111.

71. Afaf, *History of Egypt,* 96.

72. Conditions included British say over matters of communication, defense, and the protection of minorities and foreign interests. This "sham independence" made Sultan Fuad King and longtime nationalist and politician Zaghlul Prime Minister under Allenby's close supervision. Richard Long, *British Pro-Consuls in Egypt, 1914–1929* (London: Routledge, 2005), 103.

73. Afaf, *History of Egypt,* 95.

74. Tamari, *Year of the Locust,* 15.

75. Sinanoglou, *Partitioning Palestine,* 19.

76. Andrew Patrick, *America's Forgotten Middle East Initiative: The King-Crane Commission of 1919* (London: I. B. Tauris, 2015), 34, 43, 65.

77. Letter to Peace Conference Secretariat from "The Hedjaz Delegates," signed MR Haidar and Aouni Abdul Hadi dated May 19, 1919. Item 8, Folder 6, Box 20, M. R. Montgomery Papers, Oberlin College Archives.

78. "Petitions," 1910. Folder 11, Box 1, Donald M. Brodie Misc. Papers, Oberlin College Archives.

79. Quoted in Sinanoglou, *Partitioning Palestine,* 199, n. 19. Rogan, *The Arabs,* 161–162.

80. Khalidi, *The Iron Cage,* 31–32; Campos, *Ottoman Brothers Muslims, Christians, and Jews,* 6–7.

81. Jacobson, *From Empire to Empire,* 177.

82. Bernard Wasserstein, "Herbert Samuel and the Palestine Problem," *English Historical Review* 91, no. 361 (1976): 753.

83. Allenby to Mother, June 1, 1920. 1/11/14, Edmund Allenby Papers, KCLMA.

84. Allenby to Mother, March 21, 1919. 1/11/12, Edmund Allenby Papers, KCLMA.

85. Tamari, *Year of the Locust*, 11.

86. Allenby to Mother, January 7, 1922. 1/13/1B, Edmund Allenby Papers, KCLMA.

87. Khalidi, *The Iron Cage*, 59–65.

88. Sinanoglou, *Partitioning Palestine*, 20.

89. Gelvin, *Divided Loyalties*, 31–35.

90. Sluglett, *Britain in Iraq*, 33.

91. De Caix and others associated with the so-called "colonial party" exercised outsized influence over French Middle Eastern policy despite Clemenceau's reluctance to take a larger role in Syria. Khoury, *Syria and the French Mandate*, 33–36.

92. Allenby sent the details of this meeting on to the Foreign Office "without comment." Allenby to Mother, July 22, 1920. 1/11/20, Edmund Allenby Papers, KCLMA.

93. Allenby to Mother, July 25 and 26, 1920, 1/11/22, Edmund Allenby Papers, KCLMA.

94. Khoury, *Syria and the French Mandate*, 44–50.

95. Gen. Henri Gouraud as high commissioner built a civil administration for France's mandated territories centered in Beirut which included relief work. Thompson, *Colonial Citizens*, 62–63.

96. This system at first was modeled on the system in British India. Sluglett, *Britain in Iraq*, 4, 12–41.

97. Sluglett describes it as the ultimate act of "perfidy to the Arabs" (*Britain in Iraq*, 20).

98. Henry Chauvel memorandum, October 31, 1935. GB 165–0005, Allenby Papers, MECA.

99. Revenue reports include discussions of resistance to taxation. FO 608/97/3.

100. The value of the oilfields was estimated to be around 50 million pounds. Sluglett, *Britain in Iraq*, 32.

101. "Mesopotamia Handbook," 46. Quote from Sir A. Lawley, "A Message from Mesopotamia," 1917, 33–35. FO 373/5/2.

102. Memorandum from Curzon to Balfour, February 20, 1919, FO 608/96/11. The French had an equally paternal view of the occupation in Syria under Gouraud. Thompson, *Colonial Citizens*, 39–43.

103. Sluglett describes the evolution of the British administrative system after the capture of Baghdad (*Britain in Iraq*, 12–15).

104. Ibid., 19.

105. Bell's report on the investigation of Turkish massacres, March 21, 1919. FO 608/247/3. The report is part of a dispatch to Balfour from Curzon who sent it to the Civil Commissioner at Baghdad. Bell, as part of small team of intelligence officers in Cairo in 1915 who comprised the Arab Bureau, worked as advisor on "tribal affairs" for military intelligence and helped devise the occupation plan after the capture of Baghdad. Gregg, *The Grand Strategy of Gertrude Bell*; Wallach, *Desert Queen*.

106. Telegram from Allenby to Balfour on May 30 [1919] at Cairo, including two telegrams from Feisal. Add MS 49752 ff1, Balfour Papers.

107. Memorandum, June 27, 1919. FO 608/97/5.

108. Sluglett, *Britain in Iraq*, 34.

109. Arab propaganda in Mesopotamia, December 3, 1919. FO 608/97/5.

110. He was chosen over his older brother, Abdullah, who was installed as the head of Transjordan. Rogan, *The Arabs*, 183–184.

111. The RAF officially took over surveillance activities in October 1922, although they already maintained a central role in Iraq after putting down the uprising. Satia, *Spies in Arabia*, 244.

112. Charles Baussan, "General Gouraud," *Studies: An Irish Quarterly Review* 7, no. 27 (1918): 400–415.

113. Lloyd George, *Truth about the Peace Treaties*, 1114.

114. Gaston Gaillard, *The Project Gutenberg Ebook of the Turks and Europe*, n.d. (originally publ. London: Thomas Murby and Co., 1921).

115. Internal response to letter from Zabel Yessayan, February 24, 1920. F/206/3/6, Lloyd George Papers.

116. Vahram Shemmassian, "The Repatriation of Armenian Refugees," in Hovannisian, ed., *Armenian Cilicia*, 419–456.

117. Internal response to letter from Zabel Yessayan, February 24, 1920.

118. Hovannisian, *Republic of Armenia*, vol. I, 21–38.

119. Memorandum, F/206/3/6. Lloyd George Papers.

120. Andrew Ryan, *The Last of the Dragomans* (London: Geoffrey Bles, 1951), 27.

121. Ibid., 123.

122. Ibid., 139.

123. Robert Graves, *Storm Centres of the Near East: Personal Memories 1879–1929* (London: Hutchinson, 1933), 325.

124. E. Paul to Andrew Ryan, Aleppo, June 18, 1919. File 4, Box IV, Ryan Papers, MECA.

125. Calthorpe was granted authority by Curzon to arrest, if possible, key suspects without the consent of the Turkish government. This included "Enver, Talaat and their leading confederates." War Cabinet, 516, January 15, 1919, 2. CAB 23/9.

126. Graves, *Storm Centres*, 324.

127. Taner Akçam, *The Young Turks' Crime against Humanity: The Armenian Genocide and Ethnic Cleansing in the Ottoman Empire* (Princeton: Princeton University Press, 2012).

128. "Eastern Report," April 16, 1919. CAB 24/145.

129. Ibid., 329.

130. Stein, *Balfour Declaration*, 653.

131. Ibid., 657.

CHAPTER 5 THE TREATY OF SÈVRES

1. De Robeck (Constantinople) to Earl Curzon, October 19, 1919, No. 1929 [146640/521/44] as reprinted in E. L. Woodward and R. Butler, eds., *Documents on British Foreign Policy, 1919–1939*, vol. IV (London: HMSO, 1952), 830.

2. Chernev, *Twilight of Empire*.

3. Mark Mazower, "Minorities and the League of Nations in Interwar Europe," *Daedalus* 126, no. 2 (1997): 47–63.

4. Lloyd George, *War Memoirs*.

5. Tarih Dergisi, "Discussions about the Invitation of the Ottoman Empire and Presentation Memorandums in the Paris Peace Conference," *Turkish Journal of History* 71 (2020/2021): 445–472.

6. "Memorandum Concerning the New Organisation of the Ottoman Empire" by the Ottoman delegation to the Peace Conference, in Woodward and Butler, eds. *Documents on British Foreign Policy*, vol. IV, 647–651.

7. Ottoman delegation "Memorandum," in ibid., 650–651.

8. "Answer to the Turkish Delegates," June 23, 1919, in ibid., 645–647.

9. "Notes of a Meeting Held at President Wilson's House in the Place des Etats-Unis," June 25, 1919, in ibid., 643.

10. This sentiment was shared by Balfour who wrote a memorandum to Lloyd George on June 26, 1919, asking why the Supreme Council members were leaving Paris before "the outlines of the Turkish settlement are more or less agreed to." He asked the Prime Minister to get them to wait until the "new arrangement" was settled in order to put aside "all petty jealousies and intrigues between these Allied Nations." Balfour to Lloyd George, June 26, 1919. Memorandum. Add MS 49752, Balfour Papers.

11. Hovannisian, *Republic of Armenia*, vol. I.

12. "Notes," June 25, 1919, in Woodward and Butler, eds., *Documents on British Foreign Policy*, vol. IV, 643–644.

13. Leonhard, *Pandora's Box*.

14. Peter Holquist, *Making War, Forging Revolution: Russia's Continuum of Crisis, 1914–1921* (Cambridge, MA: Harvard University Press, 2002).

15. This was emblematic of the shift to what Eric Weitz calls the "Paris system" which sought to create a peace settlement focused on the national aspiration of peoples and territories ("From the Vienna to the Paris System," 1313–1343).

16. "Notes of a Meeting Held in the Foyer of the Senate Chamber of the Chateau at Versailles," June 28, 1919, 5pm, and Damad Ferid Pasha's reply of June 30, 1919, in Woodward and Butler, eds., *Documents on British Foreign Policy*, vol. IV, 653–654.

17. W. F. Blaker, "Notes of the Journey of the Turkish Delegation from Versailles to Constantinople," sent by Admiral Calthorpe to Earl Curzon July 26, 1919, in ibid., 702–703.

18. Damad Ferid's reply to "Notes of a Meeting Held in the Foyer of the Senate Chamber of the Chateau at Versailles," June 30, 1919, 5 pm, in ibid., 654.

19. Calthorpe to Curzon, sent June 29, 1919 from Constantinople, in ibid., 657.

20. Webb to Sir R. Graham, June 28, 1919 (Constantinople), in ibid., 654–656.

21. De Robeck to Curzon, October 10, 1919 (Constantinople), in ibid., 809.

22. Mosul's status would be determined by the League of Nations after the Lausanne Conference. Sluglett, *Britain in Iraq*, 73.

23. Anand Toprani, *Oil and the Great Powers, Britain and Germany, 1914–1945* (Oxford: Oxford University Press, 2019), 43–44, 51, 59.

24. Calthorpe to Curzon (Constantinople) June 26, 1919, in Woodward and Butler, eds., *Documents on British Foreign Policy*, vol. IV, 651. See also documents relating to the Anglo-French negotiations, which included oil resources, in this same volume.

25. This was the rational given for dismissing the Ottoman delegation after the signing of the treaty with Germany on June 28, 1919. "Notes of a Meeting Held at President Wilson's House," June 27, 1919, in Woodward and Butler, eds., *Documents on British Foreign Policy*, vol. IV, 652.

26. Woodward and Butler make this argument in their introductory note to the "Memorandum by Balfour (Paris)," August 11, 1919 (Paris), in *Documents on British Foreign Policy*, vol. IV, 241, 340–349.

27. Woodward and Butler make this claim about the memorandum (ibid., 345–346). Balfour distanced himself from the statement claiming that he spoke "without any sort of authority" on this subject despite issuing the statement from Paris.

28. "Memorandum by Balfour," in ibid., 343.

29. Lord Curzon memorandum on Transcaucasia, January 10, 1920. FO 608/271/5.

30. Question mark and brackets in transcription. Admiral de Robeck (Constantinople) to Earl Curzon, February 4, 1920, in Woodward and Butler, eds., *Documents on British Foreign Policy*, vol. IV, 632.

31. De Robeck to Curzon, February 10, 1920, in ibid., 633.

32. "British Secretary's Notes of a Conference of Foreign Secretaries and Ambassadors," (Whitehall), February 28, 1920, in E. L. Woodward and R. Butler, eds., *Documents on British Foreign Policy, 1919–1939*, 3rd series, vol. VII (London: HMSO, 1954), 291–292.

33. De Robeck to Curzon, February 6, 1920, in Woodward and Butler, eds., *Documents on British Foreign Policy*, vol. IV, 1085.

34. See "Minutes of the First Meeting of an Anglo-French Conference," December 22, 1919; "Mr. Vansittart to Curzon" on draft of "Peace with Turkey," January 15, 1920, and "Letter from Forbes Adam to Phipps: Draft by Mr. Montagu," in Woodward and Butler, eds., *Documents on British Foreign Policy*, vol. IV, 938–989, 1016–1019, 1036–1039.

35. "Peace with Turkey." Translation of note communicated by Berthelot to Lloyd George on January 11, 1920. FO 608/272/7.

36. "Memorandum," in Woodward and Butler, eds., *Documents on British Foreign Policy*, vol. IV, 648.

37. "Answer to the Turkish Delegates," in ibid., 646–647.

38. Vansittart to R. H. Campbell (FO), British Delegation, Paris, May 13, 1920. FO 608/272/7.

39. A. E. Montgomery, "The Making of the Treaty of Sèvres of 10 August 1920," *Historical Journal* 15, no. 4 (1972): 779.

40. Pedersen, *The Guardians*, 21.

41. Montgomery, "Making of the Treaty of Sèvres," 780–783.

42. Ibid., 785.

43. Ibid., 786.
44. Ibid., 787.
45. The San Remo Conference ran from April 18–26, 1920.
46. "Notes of a Meeting of the Heads of British, French and Italian Delegations," April 18, 1920, in E. L. Woodward and R. Butler, eds., *Documents on British Foreign Policy, 1919–1939*, 3rd series, vol. VIII (London: HMSO, 1955), iv, 1.
47. "Draft Answer to American Note," April 19, 1920 (San Remo), in ibid., 31–35. Delegates included representatives of the British Empire led by Lloyd George, and those from France, Italy and Japan.
48. "British Secretary's Notes of Meeting of the Supreme Council," April 23, 1920 (San Remo), in ibid., 119–120.
49. "British Secretary's Notes of Meeting of the Supreme Council," April 22, 1920 (San Remo) and April 25, in ibid., 112–113, 179.
50. "Kurdistan," April 19, 1920 (San Remo), in ibid., 43–45.
51. As quoted in Gaillard, *The Turks and Europe*.
52. Montagu filed the memorandum which may have been written by Philip Kerr and based on material given to him by Forbes Adams at the San Remo conference. See "Memorandum," and Montagu to Curzon, May 10, 1920. FO 608/107/4.
53. Fink, *Defending the Rights of Others*.
54. "The Allied Case for the Turkish Treaty," n.d. FO 608/107/4.
55. The Ottoman sultans had claimed the title of Caliph starting in the sixteenth century. Nurullah Ardıç, *Islam and the Politics of Secularism: The Caliphate and Middle Eastern Modernization in the Early 20th Century* (New York: Routledge, 2012).
56. [R. Vansittart] to Curzon, August 11, 1920. FO 608/272/7.
57. Fromkin, *Peace to End All Peace*, 404.
58. "Conference Conclusions," held January 5, 1920, at Downing Street. CAB 23/37.
59. "Conflicting Aims in the Near East," de Robeck to Commander of Grand Fleet, November 13, 1919 [?]. De Robeck Papers, Churchill Archives Centre, Cambridge.
60. Roger Long and Ian Talbot, eds., "Introduction," in *India and World War I: A Centennial Assessment* (London: Routledge, 2018), 15–21.
61. "Conference Conclusions," held January 5, 1920, at Downing Street. CAB 23/37.
62. Kemal remained "vague" on the future of the Caliph when pressed in 1923. Gingeras, *Fall of the Sultanate*, 293. He faced little resistance, however, when he abolished the institution showing the already declining status of the institution as a symbol of unity in the Muslim world. Ardıç, *Islam and the Politics of Secularism*.
63. "Conference Conclusions," held January 5, 1920 at Downing Street. CAB 23/37.
64. Jason Knirck, *Imagining Ireland's Independence* (Lanham: Rowman and Littlefield, 2006); Will Hanley, *Identifying with Nationality: European, Ottoman, and Egyptians in Alexandria* (New York: Columbia University Press, 2018).
65. Kim Wagner, *Amritsar 1919: An Empire of Fear and the Making of a Massacre* (New Haven: Yale University Press, 2019).
66. C. F. Andrews, "India Today," *Manchester Guardian*, January 31, 1924.

67. Conference, January 5, 1920. CAB 23/37.
68. Ibid.
69. On the importance of Indian soldiers to the British army, see Barkawi, *Soldiers of Empire* and Imy, *Faithful Fighters.*
70. Imy, *Faithful Fighters*, 75–78.
71. Curzon, "The Peace with Turkey: Appendix," January 7, 1920. CAB 23/37.
72. This was a complaint made by Admiral Calthorpe and his successor Admiral Webb.
73. The March 23, 1919, report was also interested in the "German attitude towards these atrocities" and collecting the names of German officers deemed responsible. FO 608/ 97/21.
74. Response of April 10, 1919, to report listing Turkish offenders and transmitted to GHQ at Constantinople and GHQ Mesopotamian by the Foreign office. FO 608/247/3.
75. Akçam, *The Young Turks' Crime against Humanity.*
76. Response (C.J.B. Hower?), April 25, 1919, to Commission on Responsibility for the War, Peace Conference on "List of persons responsible for the massacres and deportation of Armenians," presented on April 22, 1919. FO 608/247/3.
77. Sir Henry Wilson, [Chief of Imperial Staff] to Winston Churchill, April 21, 1920. 16/46, Chartwell Collection, Churchill Archives Centre, Cambridge.
78. Sir Archibald Sinclair[?] to Churchill, relaying details of meeting with Williams. February 2, 1920. 16/44, Chartwell Collection.
79. Churchill, *World Crisis*, vol. V, 442.
80. "The French Agreement with the Turks," *Manchester Guardian*, November 18, 1921.
81. Yessayan to Nubar, September 21, 1918. Nubar Library, Paris.
82. Lord Curzon memorandum on Transcaucasia, January 10, 1920. FO 608/271/5.
83. Marash, January 21, 1920. File 1, Kerr Archive, Zoryan Institute, Toronto.
84. Diary of YMCA Secretary, C. F. H. Crathern, February 11, 1920, as published in Hovannisian and Payaslian, eds., *Armenian Cilicia*, 531.
85. Note from Yessayan in French on behalf of the Armenian Delegation from Alexandria. Written on 10 Downing Street Stationary, February 24, 1920. F/206/3/5, Lloyd George Papers.
86. Kerr to Family, April 4, 1920, File 107, Kerr Archive.
87. Balfour to Curzon, September 3, 1919, in Woodward and Butler, eds., *Documents on British Foreign Policy*, vol. IV, 748.
88. Ryan, *Last of the Dragomans*, 150–151.
89. Letters to Curzon, April 4, 1921. Mss Eur F112/221B, British Library.
90. T. P. O'Connor to Curzon, December 24, 1921. Mss Eur F112/221B.
91. Graves, *Storm Centres*, 147. The work of the AGS officially wound up at the end of January 1922.
92. Merih Erol, "Between Memories of Persecution and Refugee Experience," in Konstantinos Travlos, ed., *Salvation and Catastrophe: The Greek-Turkish War, 1919–1922* (New York: Lexington Books, 2020). On early Greek missionary work, see Merih Erol, "'All We Hope is a Generous Revival': The Evangelization of the Ottoman Christians in

Western Anatolia in the Nineteenth Century," *Osmanlı Araştırmaları/ The Journal of Ottoman Studies* 55 (2020): 243–280.

93. Graves had helped draft the minority sections of the Treaty of Sèvres (*Storm Centres*, 333–340).

94. Ibid., 236.

95. Ryan, *The Last of the Dragomans*, 130.

96. Cabanes, *Great War and the Origins of Humanitarianism*; Tanielian, *Charity of War*; Watenpaugh, *Bread from Stones*.

97. Baughan, *Saving the Children*; Ellen Boucher, "Cultivating Internationalism: Save the Children Fund, Public Opinion, and the Meaning of Child Relief, 1919–24," in Laura Beers and Geraint Thomas, eds., *Brave New World: Imperial and Democratic Nation-building in Britain between the Wars* (London: Institute for Historical Research, 2012), 169–188; Fuller, *Right of the Child*.

98. "Ann Mary Burgess Obituary." Temp. MSS 387, Ann Mary Burgess Papers, Friends Library.

99. Edward Annett, *Fifty Years among the Armenians: A Brief Record of the Work of Ann Mary Burgess* (London: Stanley Hunt, 1938), 24. Temp. MSS 387, Ann Mary Burgess Papers.

100. William Braithwaite, "Medical Mission among the Armenians," Friends Armenian Mission, London, 1896. Box 308/28, Friends Library.

101. Circular Letter to supporters, August 2, 1920. TEMP MSS 1030, Ann Mary Burgess Papers.

102. Burgess to (Miss Miller?), July 1, 1921. MSS 1030, Ann Mary Burgess Papers.

103. Letter to Miss Miller, January 30, 1921. MSS 1030, Ann Mary Burgess Papers.

104. Burgess to (Miller?), July 1, 1921. Ann Mary Burgess Papers.

105. Burgess reported annual sales of around 5,000 pounds. Burgess to (Miller?), November 25, 1922. Ann Mary Burgess Papers.

106. Letter to Yessayan, from the Armenian National Delegation, January 10, 1920. Nubar Library.

107. Emily Robinson to Nubar, July 22, 1918. Nubar Library.

108. Undated letter from G. M. Gregory to ?. Nubar Library.

109. Kévorkian et al., *Les Armeniens*, 73.

110. "Deportation of Women and Children in Turkey and Neighboring Countries," *League of Nations Journal*, April 11, 1921, Geneva. The League appointed a three-person commission of inquiry: Miss Emma Cushman, nominated by Roberts College, Constantinople; Dr, Kennedy, nominated by British High Commission; and Mdme Gaulis, nominated by the French representative.

111. Rowe, "New Armenian Woman," 13.

112. Burgess to Peckover, 1921 (no exact date). Ann Mary Burgess Papers.

113. Watenpaugh, *Bread from Stones*, 91–117; Nora Nercessian, *The City of Orphans: Relief Workers, Commissars and the "Builders of the New Armenia"* (Hollis, NH: Hollis Publishing, 2016); White, "A Grudging Rescue"; Jinks, "Marks Hard to Erase."

114. Moumdjian, "Cilicia under French Administration," 458. For exact numbers and where these refugees came from, see Vahram Shemmassian, "Repatriation of Armenian Refugees," in Hovannisian and Payaslian, eds., *Armenian Cilicia*, 440.

115. Hovannisian, *Republic of Armenia*, vol. I.

116. For Hovannisian, it spelled "an end to any French designs to maintain political control in Cilicia." "Postwar Contest for Cilicia," in Hovannisian and Payaslian, eds., *Armenian Cilicia*, 512.

117. Moumdjian, "Cilicia under French Administration," 481.

118. Ari Sekeryan, "Rethinking the Turkish-Armenian War in the Caucasus: The Position of Ottoman Armenians," *War in History* 27, no. 1 (2020): 81–105.

119. Robert Hewson, "Armenia Maritima," in Hovanissian and Payaslian, eds., *Armenian Cilicia*, 63. On the tensions of French/British relations in Cilicia, see William T. Dean, "The French in the Middle East in the Great War," *The Historian* 80, no. 3 (2018): 485–496.

120. "Eastern Report," March 27, 1919, no. CXL. CAB/24/145.

121. Repatriation efforts were stopped in late 1919, and deteriorating conditions led Georges-Picot, now an administrator in the region, to meet secretly in Ankara with Kemal to negotiate a solution. Moumdjian, "Cilicia under French Administration," 463, 486–487.

122. Vahe Tachjian, "Cilician Armenians and French Policy," in Hovannisian and Payaslian, eds., *Armenian Cilicia*, 543.

123. Moumdjian, "Cilicia under French Administration," 458–459.

124. Andrekos Varnava, "French and British Postwar Imperial Agendas," *Historical Journal* 57, no. 4 (2014): 997–1025.

125. "British Secretary's Notes of a Conference of Foreign Secretaries," February 28, 1920, in Woodward and Butler, eds., *Documents on British Foreign Policy*, vol. VII, 294.

126. Moumdjian, "Cilicia under French Administration," 486–489.

127. Tachjian, "Cilician Armenians and French Policy," 547.

128. As quoted in White, "A Grudging Rescue," 6.

129. Ibid., 14.

130. This figure includes 4,000 non-Armenian evacuees. Ibid., 12.

131. Curzon's response to Williams letter on Armenia, December 6, 1921. FO 286/879.

132. Churchill, *World Crisis*, vol. V, 432–433.

133. Letter from Vahan Portoukalian to Kourken Tahmazian, Adana, January 29, 1922. "La Cilicie (1909–1921) des massacres d'Ana au manda francais, deuxieme partie: la légion d'Orient, le mandat français et l'explusion des Arméniens, 1916–1929," *Revue d'histoire arménienne contemporaine* 3 (1999). www.imprescriptible.fr/rhac/tome3/.

134. "C.U.P. Maneuvers," *The Times*, July 21, 1919, 11; "Young Turks Again in Power," *The Times*, October 13, 1919: 11; "Grand Vizier Ousted," *The Times*, October 9, 1919, 9; "The Massacre of Armenians," *The Times*, February 28, 1920, 16; "Grand Vizier's Troubles," *The Times*, August 9, 1920: 9; "Damid Ferid Pasha," *The Times*, October 8, 1923, 11.

135. "Eastern Report," July 31, 1919, no. CXXXI. CAB/24/14.

136. Lord Curzon to Sir H. Rumbold (Constantinople), September 3, 1922, FO 141/580.

137. Secret telegram from Sir H. Rumbold, September 19, 1922. 8/258, Chartwell Collection.

138. Tusan, *Smyrna's Ashes*, 144–153.

139. Churchill, *World Crisis*, vol. V (New York: Charles Scribner's Sons, 1929), 434.

CHAPTER 6 HUMANITARIAN CRUSADES

1. Watenpaugh, *Bread from Stones*; Little, ed., special issue of *First World War Studies* 5, no. 1 (2014); Cabanes, *The Great War and the Origins of Humanitarianism*.

2. Lilie Chouliaraki, *The Ironic Spectator: Solidarity in the Age of Post-Humanitarianism* (Cambridge: Polity Press, 2013), 43.

3. Tusan, *Smyrna's Ashes*.

4. Watenpaugh, *Bread from Stones*.

5. Matthew Hilton, "Ken Loach and the Save the Children Film," *Journal of Modern History* 87 (2015), 357–394; Rodogno, *Night on Earth*.

6. Chouliaraki, *Ironic Spectator*, 44–45.

7. Simms and Trim, eds., *Humanitarian Intervention*; Rodogno, *Against Massacre*; Balakian, *Burning Tigris*.

8. Fuller, *Right of the Child*, 17.

9. Francis Jude, "Educating for Peace" (Society of Friends pamphlet, n.d.), 3.

10. Paul Rogers, "The Cinema and Peace Propaganda," *Friend*, August 18, 1922.

11. In addition to the films considered here dozens of now lost short and feature-length films were produced by affiliates of the International Committee of the Red Cross. Cabanas, *The Great War and the Origins of Humanitarianism*, 220.

12. Exact numbers are hard to determine since most have been lost. Films viewed for this article are held by the British Film Institute in London and the Armenian Film Foundation.

13. Rev. W. E. Orchard, "The Famine Film and the Future of Europe," *Save the Children Fund*, January 3, 1922. Other organizations similarly characterized film as having a power "infinitely greater than that of the press." John R. Freuler, "The Motion Picture as an Influence for Peace," *The World Court*, February 1917, 54–55.

14. Daniel Palmieri, "Humanitarianism on the Screen: The ICRC Films, 1921–1965," in Johannes Paulmann, ed., *Humanitarianism and Media, 1900 to the Present* (New York: Berghahn Books, 2019), 100.

15. "Friends Relief Work Cinema," *Friend*, February 23, 1923.

16. Freuler, "The Motion Picture as an Influence for Peace," 55.

17. *The League of Nations and Intellectual Cooperation*, Revised ed. Information Section, Geneva 1927, 43; "The Cinema in Public Health Education," *International Review of Educational Cinematography* 1, no. 2 (August 1929): 183.

18. Cabanes, *The Great War and the Origins of Humanitarianism*, 220. The ICRC produced sixteen films between 1921 and 1923 with ten focused on Greece. Palmieri, "Humanitarianism on the Screen," 91–92.

19. Quakers had been involved in the Near East since the 1860s where they started a medical mission and engaged in industrial work and philanthropic activities. Michelle Tusan, "The Business of Relief Work."

20. John Ormerod Greenwood, *Quaker Encounters*, vol. I (York: William Sessions, 1975), 194–195.

21. Baughan, *Saving the Children*; Sarah Fieldston, *Raising the World: Child Welfare in the American Century* (Cambridge, MA: Harvard University Press, 2015); Clare Mulley, *The Woman Who Saved the Children: A Biography of Eglantyne Jebb* (Oxford: Oneworld Publications, 2009); Kathleen Freeman, *If Any Man Build: The History of the Save the Children Fund* (London: Hodder and Stoughton, 1965); Fuller, *Right of the Child*; Dorothy F. Buxton and Edward Fuller, *The White Flame: The Story of the Save the Children Fund* (London: Weardale Press, 1931).

22. This cooperation was widely acknowledged at the time. As the final intertitle in the film *Salvage in Austria* (1922) read, "Save the Children Fund has spent over a quarter of a million pounds in saving Austrian and Hungarian children. A large portion of that has been administered by the Society of Friends" (BFI National Archive, London).

23. David McFadden and Claire Gorfinkel, *Constructive Spirit: Quakers in Revolutionary Russia* (Pasadena, CA: Intentional Productions, 2004). ARA also made a film. Paternaude, *Big Show in Bololand*, 505–507.

24. Fuller, *Right of the Child*, 95. Portrayals of neutral aid can be seen as a strategy for gaining influence over regions and populations outside of Britain as well as creating the illusion of aid as operating outside of politics. Matthew Hilton et al., *The Politics of Expertise: How NGOs Shaped Modern Britain* (Oxford: Oxford University Press, 2013). On Save the Children's imperial roots, see Emily Baughan, "'Every Citizen of Empire Implored to Save the Children!' Empire, Internationalism and the Save the Children Fund in Interwar Britain," *Historical Research* 86, no. 231 (2012): 116–137.

25. Pedersen, *The Guardians*, 18–27.

26. David Lloyd George, "Winning the War" (May, 1916), in *Great Crusade*, 23.

27. Clark, *Twice a Stranger*, xii–xiv.

28. Suzi Feay, "All Lively on the West End Front," *Financial Times*, February 9, 2014.

29. Dennis Gifford, *British Film Catalogue, 1895–1985* (New York: Facts on File, 1986). Wartime films had a distinct propagandistic purpose to support the war effort and make heroes of soldiers and politicians. These included titles, all produced in 1918, such as *Victory and Peace* produced by the National War Aims Committee; *Onward Christian Soldiers* and *The Life Story of David Lloyd George*.

30. Two notable exceptions were *Comradeship* (1919) about male bonding and *Warrior Strain* (1919) about a foiled German sabotage plot. British Instructional Films Company produced patriotic films. Christine Gledhill, *Reframing British Cinema, 1918–1928* (London: BFI, 2003), 58–59, 102–106.

31. The newsreel was launched in London in 1910 by Charles Pathé. It produced news images complete with intertitles of the Greco-Turkish War and the Russian famine for British audiences. The company began producing feature films in the 1930s. www .britishpathe.com.

32. Andrew Higson and Richard Maltby, eds., *Film Europe and Film America* (Exeter: University of Exeter Press, 1999).

33. That 1917 number was up from 7–8 million in 1914. Lez Cooke, "British Cinema: From Cottage Industry to Mass Entertainment," in Clive Bloom, ed., *Literature and Culture in Modern Britain*, vol. I: *1900–1929* (London: Longman, 1993), 167–188; *Picturegoer*, November 1921, 50.

34. "The Movies," *English Review*, May 1920.

35. Gledhill, *Reframing British Cinema*, 9.

36. Ibid., 38–41.

37. Peter Stead, *Film and the Working Class* (London: Routledge, 1989), 13.

38. Iris Barry, *Let's Go to the Movies* (New York: Chatto & Windus, 1926), 59, 187.

39. "Church-Film Data" and "Gathering the Flock," *Moving Picture Age*, September 1922. The Salvation Army started its own Cinematograph Department for similar reasons, "tempting people away from the music hall and pub." Colin Harding and Simon Popple, *In the Kingdom of Shadows: A Companion to Early Cinema* (Madison, NJ: Farleigh Dickinson University Press, 1996), 63–64.

40. Paolo Cherchi Usai, *Silent Cinema: A Guide to Study, Research and Curatorship* (London: BFI, 2000), 162.

41. F. K. Prochaska, *Women and Philanthropy in Nineteenth-Century England* (Oxford: Oxford University Press, 1980).

42. Ellen Ross, "A Tale of Two Sisters," unpublished paper delivered at the North American Conference on British Studies annual meeting, November 2014.

43. Stefan Moitra makes this point about the Miners' Institutes in Wales during the interwar years. "The Management Committee Intend to Act as Ushers: Cinema Operation and the South Wales Miners' Institutes in the 1950s and 1960s," in Daniel Biltereyst et al., eds., *Cinema, Audiences and Modernity: New Perspectives on European Cinema History* (London: Routledge, 2012), 102.

44. Leshu Torchin, *Creating the Witness: Documenting Genocide on Film* (Minneapolis: University of Minnesota Press, 2012), 40–43.

45. Glendhill traces the "fluid combination of live and film entertainment" in the late 1910s and early 1920s (*Reframing British Cinema*, 12–14).

46. Watenpaugh, *Bread from Stones*, 60–61.

47. Out of an estimated population of 1.9 million Armenians, 1 million were killed and the remaining two-thirds deported (Kévorkian, *Armenian Genocide*, 278).

48. The film was called *Auction of Souls* in Britain and *Ravished Armenia* in the United States.

49. Pierre Sorlin, "Cinema and the Memory of the Great War," in Paris, ed., *The First World War*, 5.

50. The book went through twenty-six printings and was read on both sides of the Atlantic. "Aurora Mardiganian in the Film Founded on the Book Ravished Armenia (Auction of Souls)," pamphlet. Toynbee Box, Bodleian, Oxford University.

51. These reports appeared in the urban and provincial press including *The Times, Manchester Guardian; Derby Daily Telegraph, Evening Telegraph and Post* (Dundee, Scotland); *Western Times* (Exeter, England); *Daily Mail* (Hull, England); *Aberdeen Daily Journal* (Aberdeen, Scotland); *Nottingham Evening Post; Courier and Argus* (Dundee, Scotland).

52. The film has been the subject of several studies: Leshu Torshin, "'Ravished Armenia': Visual Media, Humanitarian Advocacy, and the Formation of Witnessing Publics," *American Anthropologist* 108, no. 1 (2006): 214–220; Donna-Lee Frieze, "Three Films, One Genocide: Remembering the Armenian Genocide through Ravished Armenia(s)," in N. Eltringham and P. Maclean, eds., *Remembering Genocide* (New York: Routledge, 2014), 38–54; Valentina Calzolari-Bouvier, "L'American Committee for Armenian and Syrian Relief et l'instrumentalisation du témoignage d'Aurora Mardiganian (1918–1919)," *Relations Internationales* 3, no. 171 (2017): 17–30. Arsine Khanjian has staged a theater performance on memory and genocide based on the film.

53. Balakian, *Burning Tigris*, 313.

54. International Near East Relief was formed in 1923 and headquartered in Geneva. Vicken Babkenian, "Stories of International Goodness during the Armenian Genocide," *Genocide Prevention Now*. www.genocidepreventionnow.org/Portals/0/docs/International_goodness.pdf.

55. Helen McCarthy, *The British People and the League of Nations* (Manchester: Manchester University Press, 2011), 79.

56. "The Auction of Souls," *Daily Mail*, January 28, 1920.

57. C.R., "Turkish Horrors Filmed," *Daily Mail*, October 30, 1919.

58. Though Bryce supported the film, he claimed to have nothing to do with its production. Anthony Slide, *Ravished Armenia and the Story of Aurora Mardiganian* (Lanham, MD: Scarecrow Press, 1997), 207. The editor's acknowledgment in the book *Auction of Souls* struck a similar note: "For verification of these amazing things, which little Aurora told me . . . I am indebted to Lord Bryce, formerly British Ambassador to the United States, who was commissioned by the British Government to investigate the massacres." Aurora Mardiganian, *The Auction of Souls* (London: Harry Hardingham, 1934).

59. The cost of sponsoring the film represented approximately one-sixth of its cash on hand. The anti-war and pro-Armenian message justified the expense, according to a resolution passed in support of the film. "Financial Statement," LNU Executive Committee Minutes, March 4, 1920. LNU 2/2, LNU Archives, London School of Economics Library (LSE), Special Collections.

60. J. Richards, "British Film Censorship," in Robert Murphy, ed., *The British Cinema Book*, 3rd edn (London: Bloomsbury, 2009), 67–68.

61. "Turk Atrocity Film," *Daily Mail*, January 20, 1920.

62. Lord Curzon regretted that the "press dwells unduly on the religious aspect of the Armenian massacres and is calculated to give offence in India" and demanded that the BBFC make "alterations in the film itself . . . in order to prevent on the ground of public morals, the appearance of the film unless the producers are ready to submit to censorship." Letter sent on behalf of Lord Curzon, January 5, 1920. HO 45/10955/312971/92.

63. Though the actresses were not naked, their bodysuits made them appear so to the viewer. The Foreign Office believed that labeling the film obscene proved the strongest argument for censorship. "British Film Censorship," 67.

64. Shortt to Harris, (Prosecutions Department), n.d. HO 45/10955/312971/89.

65. Both Lord Bryce and Lord Gladstone expressed reservations over showing *Auction of Souls* to the general public after initially viewing the film in October 1919. HO 45/10955/31297.

66. On the war crimes tribunals, see Vahakn N. Dadrian and Tacer Akcam, *Judgment at Istanbul: The Armenian Genocide Trials* (New York: Berghahn Books, 2011); Gary Bass, *Stay the Hand of Vengeance: The Politics of War Crimes* (Princeton: Princeton University Press, 2000); Tusan, "Crimes against Humanity."

67. In Hull, the film initially was approved and "privately exhibited." Sixteen Armenian girls introduced the film when it opened to the public Easter week, 1920. A year later, a court in Middlesex County heard an unsuccessful appeal from the Council to convict theater owners for showing the film without proper approvals. "Film Censorship," *Daily Mail,* July 13, 1921.

68. How much of that went to humanitarian organizations is not entirely clear. One trade journal reported that the high $10 ticket cost helped NER meet its goal of raising $30 million. The film appears to have been more of a commercial than fundraising success in Britain due to Foreign Office restrictions which initially tied the hands of humanitarian organizations hoping to capitalize on the film. *Motion Picture World,* May 1919 and "News," *Moving Picture World,* April 22, 1922.

69. The edited subtitles with the censored parts still visible are included in a file entitled "Objectionable Films 1920" held in the National Archives. HO 45/10955/31297/98.

70. The LNU film sub-committee rejected a proposal to sponsor a so-called "super film" about the war in 1923. The LNU sponsored a feature film *The World War and After* in the late 1920s. LNU Minutes, May 16, 1923. LNU 3/8, LNU Archives, LSE, Special Collections.

71. Near East Relief appeal, n.d.

72. Edward Fuller approvingly describes the use of images in the press of "agonized, screaming women clutching to their breasts ghastly skeletons of children whom the British public were urged to save from otherwise certain death. The experiment, which made advertising history, was a success" (*Right of the Child,* 92).

73. Fehrenbach, "Children and Other Civilians," 176–177.

74. NER was incorporated in the United States by a special act of Congress in 1919.

75. *New Near East*, November 1921, 4.

76. "Alice in Hungerland," *New Near East*, November 1921, 4–5.

77. On the business and technology of the early film industry see Michael Chanan, "Economic Conditions of Early Cinema," in Thomas Elsaesser, ed., *Early Cinema: Space, Frame, Narrative* (London: BFI, 1990), 186–187. *Picturegoer* regularly advertised these services in the early 1920s.

78. *New Near East*, November 19, 1921.

79. *Sydney Morning Herald*, November 29, 1922.

80. "Church-Film Data," *Moving Picture Age*, September 1922.

81. Peterson, *Starving Armenians*.

82. James Barton, *Story of Near East Relief (1915–1930): An Interpretation* (New York: Macmillan, 1930).

83. Norma Talmadge, letter to the editor, *New Near East*, vii, January 1922, 8.

84. "Rabbi Wise Objects to Mrs. Duryea Adopting Jewish Refugee Seen in Movies," *New York Times*, April 28, 1922.

85. Other titles included *Seeing is Believing, Constructive Forces, Investment in Futures, One of these Little Ones, Stand by Them a Little Longer, A Great Achievement, Earthquake in Armenia, What the Flag Saw, Miracles from Ruins, Doorways to Happiness, Chautauqua Pageant, Caucasus Snap Shots, Romance of a Rug*, and *Making the Man*. Barton, *Near East Relief*, 391.

86. "Jackie Crusading," *Moving Picture World*, August 9, 1924.

87. "Jackie Coogan Decorated by Greek Government," *Moving Picture World*, October 25, 1924. As Coogan remembered it, The Pope "complimented me on my Near East Relief work and said he hoped I would always remember the little children who were in need." "Jackie Coogan's Diary," *Photoplay* (serialized starting in fall 1924).

88. "Jackie Coogan's Tour Abroad One Long Series of Welcomes," *Moving Picture World*, October 18, 1924. The tour benefited Coogan's own career and contributed to his status as an international celebrity with a conscience.

89. Rev. W. E. Orchard, "The Famine Film and the Future of Europe," *Save the Children Fund*, January 3, 1922.

90. Independent Ukraine's treaty with the Central Powers at Brest-Litovsk promised them "at least one million tons of foodstuffs," most of which had previously been promised to Russia. Though Germany had difficulty collecting the promised amount, Ukrainian food resources would have helped stabilize the Bolshevik regime especially in the midst of famine conditions. Chernev, *Twilight of Empire*, 137, 182.

91. Brian Winston, *Claiming the Real II* (London: Palgrave Macmillan, 2008), 12.

92. British Film Institute Archives holds both films.

93. Orlando Figes, *Peasant Russia, Civil War: The Volga Countryside in Revolution, 1917–1921* (Oxford: Claarendon, 1989), 20–21, 84, 268.

94. Greenwood, *Quaker Encounters*, I, 242.

95. Fuller, *Right of the Child*, 93.

96. Save the Children Annual Report, 1923, as quoted in Linda Manhood, *Feminism and Voluntary Action: Eglantyne Jebb and Save the Children, 1876–1928* (London: Palgrave, 2009), 177.

97. Patenaude, *Big Show in Bololand.*

98. G. H. Mewes, "Filming the Famine," *Record of Save the Children Fund*, January 15, 1922.

99. *Record of Save the Children Fund*, April 15, 1922.

100. Patenaude, *Big Show in Bololand.*

101. McFadden and Gorfinkel, *Constructive Spirit*, 58–66.

102. Mewes, "Filming the Famine," 138.

103. Rev. W. E. Orchard, "The Famine Film and the Future of Europe," *Record of Save the Children Fund*, March 1, 1922.

104. Ibid.

105. "Advertisement," *Friend*, February 23, 1923.

106. Tehila Sasson considers the case of the British response to the Russian famine as an example of what she calls "humanitarian governance." "From Empire to Humanity: The Russian Famine and the Imperial Origins of International Humanitarianism," *The Journal of British Studies* 55, no. 3 (2016): 519–537.

107. Wilkins traveled from Australia to England to work in the film industry in 1908. R. A. Swan, "Sir George Hubert Wilkins," *Australian Dictionary of Biography.* http://adb .anu.edu.au/biography/wilkins-sir-george-hubert-9099.

108. "New Worlds for Old (1923)," information sheet, Friends Library, London.

109. "Advertisement," *Friend*, March 23, 1923.

110. "Friends Relief Work Cinema," *Friend*, February 23, 1923.

111. "New Worlds for Old" was also the title of a socialist pamphlet published by H. G. Wells in 1919.

112. "New Worlds for Old," *Gloucester Citizen*, February 15, 1923.

113. "Quakers and the Aftermath of War," *Gloucester Citizen*, June 4, 1923, 5.

114. Aid workers spoke at Friends' Meetings about their experiences before screening the film and then would take a collection. "More Easter Gatherings," *Friend*, April 20, 1923; "Devon and Cornwall," *Friend*, April 27, 1923. "The Film," *Bulletin of the Society of Friends Relief Missions*, March 1923.

115. Friends 'Emergency and War Victims' Relief Committee Minutes, January 16, 1923; February 27, 1923. Friends Library, London. Individual Quakers were very interested in promoting the film. "New Worlds for Old" letter to editor, *Friend*, March 23, 1923.

116. On the first night 130 pounds were collected; 377 pounds for the entire month. "The Film," *Bulletin of the Society of Friends Relief Missions*, March 1923, 8.

117. "Friends Relief Film," *Aberdeen Journal*, March 19, 1923.

118. Income doubled between 1921 and 1922. *9th Report of the Emergency and War Victims' Relief Committee of the Society of Friends*, April 1922, British Library. The report stated that 18,524 British pounds of that amount was used for overheads with an additional 8,359 British pounds used for advertising.

119. Joice N. Loch, *A Fringe of Blue: An Autobiography* (London: John Murray, 1968), 218, 226.

120. Clark, *Twice a Stranger*, xii.

121. Hirschon, *Heirs of the Greek Catastrophe*, 1–10.

122. Fuller, *The Right of the Child*, 48.

123. *Tragedy of the Near East,* viewed at British Film Institute, London. May 2014.
124. "The Cinema Campaign," *World's Children,* April 1923, 149.
125. Flora Sturgeon, "The New Army of Helpers," *Quiver,* June 1923, 831.
126. "Our Schools," *World's Children,* July 1923, 199–200. The campaign raised 87 British pounds.
127. Ibid.
128. On self-help philanthropy, see Tusan, "Business of Relief Work," 634.
129. *9th Report of the Emergency and War Victims' Relief Committee of the Society of Friends,* April 1922, British Library.
130. The collaborative quality of these efforts could lead to inefficiencies. For example, Save the Children supported feeding children and the Imperial War Relief Fund supported feeding adults, presumably to keep the distinct missions of aid organizations working in the region clear in the minds of donors.
131. Fuller, *Right of the Child,* 95.
132. "Tragedy of the Near East," *Derby Daily Telegraph,* October 19, 1923.
133. This seems to be what happened with the Friends Relief campaigns in the Middle East where a scrapbook of images and print appeals make up the bulk of the archive on refugee resettlement after 1924. NER continued to raise money for refugee resettlement, as did Save the Children and the Quakers, which grew the amount and number of donors during this period for Armenia.
134. Ross, "A Tale of Two Sisters."
135. Save the Children started showing what it called a "composite film representing phases of the work ... in different countries" in the spring of 1923 but made no other feature-length humanitarian films until the 1950s. A few attempts at making films about the Middle East and the Spanish Civil war by Quaker filmmaker Cuthbert Wigham under the auspices of the Society of Friends started in the early 1930s, but Save the Children and NER seem to have stopped making films altogether. The LNU along with the League of Nations, which had started its own film bureau, sponsored the pro-peace film *The World War and After* only in the late 1920s. Information on the Wigham films are held at Friends House, London. The Near East Relief archive documents a renewal of film activity after the First World War.
136. Didier Fassin, *Humanitarian Reason: A Moral History of the Present* (Berkeley: University of California Press, 2012), 3.

CHAPTER 7 THE TREATY OF LAUSANNE

1. Ryan, *The Last of the Dragomans,* 198.
2. Harold Nicolson, *Curzon: The Last Phase* (London: Constable, 1934), 62.
3. Nicolson, *Peacemaking 1919,* 31–32.
4. Nicolson wrote this in 1933 (*Peacemaking,* 32).
5. Ryan accompanied Rumbold and attended both sessions of the Conference. At the Paris Peace Conference, Nicolson served on a number of Balkan committees under Sir Eyre Crowe. At the Lausanne Conference, his focus was Near and Middle Eastern

topics and he was the "chief expert" on the Eastern Question. T. G. Otte, "Nicolson, Sir Harold George (1886–1968), Diplomatist and Politician," *Oxford Dictionary of National Biography* (https://doi.org/10.1093/ref:odnb/35239).

6. As quoted in Nicolson, *Curzon*, 284.

7. Historiography on these different aspects of Lausanne include Smith, *Sovereignty at the Peace Conference*; Sevtap Demirci, *Strategies and Struggles: British Rhetoric and Turkish Response: The Lausanne Conference, 1922–1923* (Piscataway, NJ: Gorgias Press, 2010); Lerna Ekmekçioğlu, "Republic of Paradox: The League of Nations Minority Protection Regime and the New Turkey's Step-Citizens," *International Journal of Middle East Studies* 46, no. 3 (2014): 657–679; Erik Goldstein, "The British Official Mind and the Lausanne Conference, 1922–23," *Diplomacy & Statecraft* 14, no. 2 (2003): 201; Davison, "Turkish Diplomacy from Mudros to Lausanne"; George Kaloudis, "Ethnic Cleansing in Asia Minor and the Treaty of Lausanne," *International Journal on World Peace* 31, no. 1 (2014): 59–88; Orçun Can Okan, "The Treaty of Lausanne and the Construction of the Arab Middle East," *Journal of the Ottoman and Turkish Studies Association* 8, no. 1 (2021): 457–461; Ali Othman, "The Kurds and the Lausanne Peace Negotiations, 1922–23," *Middle Eastern Studies* 33, no. 3 (1997): 521; Jay Winter, *The Day the Great War Ended, 24 July 1923: The Civilianization of War* (Oxford: Oxford University Press, 2023); Jonathan Conlin and Ozan Ozavci, eds., *They All Made Peace – What Is Peace? The 1923 Lausanne Treaty and the New Imperial Order* (London: Gingko, forthcoming); Hans-Lukas Kieser, *When Democracy Died: The Middle East's Enduring Peace of Lausanne* (Cambridge: Cambridge University Press, forthcoming).

8. "Anonymous Account of the Burning of Smyrna," September 1922. Doc. 9483, Imperial War Museum, London.

9. Charles James Howes, "Smyrna 1922," p. 5. IWM 86/14/1 (2286), Private Papers of C. J. Howes, Imperial War Museum.

10. Tusan, *Smyrna's Ashes*; Giles Milton, *Paradise Lost: Smyrna 1922* (New York: Basic Books, 2008); Marjorie Housepian, *The Smyrna Affair* (New York: Harcourt Brace Jovanovich, 1971); George Horton, *The Blight of Asia* (Indianapolis: Bobbs Mererill, 1953); Edward Hale Bierstadt, *The Great Betrayal: A Survey of the Near East Problem* (New York: McBride, 1924).

11. "Anonymous Acccount of the Burning of Smyrna," September 1922. Doc. 9483.

12. The campaign against the Greek army began in earnest on August 26 at the battle of Afyon-Karahisar in the Anatolian interior. Michael M. Finefrock, "Atatürk, Lloyd George and the Megali Idea: Cause and Consequence of the Greek Plan to Seize Constantinople from the Allies, June–August 1922," *Journal of Modern History* 52, no. 1 (1980): 1047–1066. See also Clark, *Twice a Stranger*, 9–10.

13. Slobodan Markovich, "Eleftherios Venizelos, British Public Opinion and the Climax of Anglo-Hellenism," *Balcanica* (Beograd) 49 (2018): 125–155. This included mainly Greek, Armenian and Assyrian Orthodox Christians.

14. Telegram: Paris, Mr. Balfour to High Commissioner for Egypt, May 11, 1919. FO 141/580.

15. Daniel Joseph MacArthur, "Intelligence and Lloyd George's Secret Diplomacy in the Near East, 1920–1922," *Historical Journal* 56, no. 3 (2013): 707–728.

16. J. G. Darwin, "The Chanak Crisis and the British Cabinet," *History* 65, no. 214 (1980): 32–48.

17. Secret: Turko-Greek situation, no. 6 from September 3–4, 1922. F/207/1, Lloyd George Papers.

18. Secret: Turko-Greek situation, no. 6 from September 7–8, 1922. F/207/1, Lloyd George Papers.

19. Harington to War Office, September 7, 1922. F/207/1, Lloyd George Papers.

20. Secret: Turko-Greek situation, no. 6 from September 7–8, 1922. F/207/1, Lloyd George Papers.

21. Harington to War Office, September 8, 1922. F/207/1, Lloyd George Papers.

22. Harington to War Office, September 13, 1922. F/207/1, Lloyd George Papers.

23. This past is slowly being recovered. See Leyla Neyzi, "Remembering Smyrna/Izmir: Shared History, Shared Trauma," *History and Memory* 20, no. 2 (Fall 2008): 106–127 and Richard Hovannisian, ed., *Armenian Smyrna/Izmir: The Aegean Communities* (Costa Mesa, CA: Mazda Publishers, 2012).

24. Lord Curzon to Sir H. Rumbold, September 2, 1922. FO 141/580.

25. Foreign Office telegram to Rumbold, September 4, 1922. F208/1, Lloyd George Papers.

26. Harington to War Office, September 13, 1922. F207/1, Lloyd George Papers.

27. Cabinet Meeting, September 15, 1922. CAB 23/31/2.

28. John Ferris, "'Far Too Dangerous a Gamble'? British Intelligence and Policy during the Chanak Crisis, September–October 1922," *Diplomacy and Statecraft* 14, no. 2 (2003): 139–184.

29. The French, while not wanting to break the alliance, feared bolstering British power in the region and refused to send troops. A. L. Macfie, "The Chanak Affair (September–October 1922)," *Balkan Studies* 20, no. 2 (1979): 321–322.

30. Cabinet Meeting, September 15, 1922. CAB 23/31/2.

31. Conference Notes, September 11. CAB 23/31/9.

32. Cabinet Meeting, September 15, 1922. CAB 23/31/2.

33. Ibid.

34. John Darwin argues that this decision was not solely in the hands of Lloyd George and that support was broad based ("The Chanak Crisis").

35. Dora Sakayan, trans., *An Armenian Doctor in Turkey: Garabed Hatcherian: My Smyrna Ordeal of 1922* (Montreal: Arod Books, 1997), 38.

36. Rumbold to Foreign Office, October 8. F208/2, Lloyd George Papers.

37. Rumbold to Foreign Office, October 7. F208/2, Lloyd George Papers.

38. Cabinet Meeting, September 7, 1922. CAB 23/31/1.

39. Ibid.

40. Cabinet Meetings September 28 and 29, 1922. CAB 23/31/5.

41. This was a meeting of the Parliamentary Committee of the TUC on September 21. Cabinet Meeting, September 23, 1922. CAB 23/31/3.

42. Ibid.

43. Cabinet Meeting, September 30, 1922. CAB 23/31/5.

44. Appendix: "Revised Draft of Invitation to Angora Government," as suggested to Lord Curzon by the Cabinet on September 23, 1922. CAB 23/31/5.

45. Cabinet Meeting, September 23, 1922. CAB 23/31/3.

46. Actual financial contributions were relatively modest. Britain dedicated 50,000 pounds for refugee relief and the French pledged 100,000 francs.

47. Housepian, *Smyrna Affair*.

48. "Conclusions," September 20, 1922. CAB 23/31/3.

49. Macfie, "The Chanak Affair," 309–341.

50. Appendix: Harington to War Office, October 10, 1922. CAB 23/31/10.

51. Mr. Lindley [Sir Francis Oswald Lindley] writing from Athens, September 25, 1922. F208/3, Lloyd George Papers.

52. This conflict was at the root of the so-called "National Schism" in Greek politics. Basil Gounaris and Marianna D. Christopoulos, "Reassessing the Greek National Schism of World War I: The Ideological Parameters," *Historical Review* 15, no. 1 (2019): 234; Markovich, "Eleftherios Venizelos, British Public Opinion and the Climax of Anglo-Hellenism"; Gullu, "Ottoman Rums and the Venizelos."

53. Kitromilides, *Eleftherios Venizelos*; Michael Smith, *Venizelos: The Making of a Greek Statesman 1864–1914* (Oxford: Oxford University Press, 2021).

54. The war between Greece and Turkey in this moment has been called one of the major aftershocks of the First World War. Peter Jensen Kincaid, "The Greco-Turkish War, 1920–1922," *International Journal of Middle East Studies* 10, no. 4 (1979): 553–565.

55. According to Nicolson, the public viewed the Chanak Crisis as evidence of Lloyd George's recklessness regarding the war. On October 19, Bonar Law withdrew Conservative support for the coalition and forced Lloyd George to resign. Parliament was dissolved on October 26 and the General Election of November 15 put Conservatives in power under Law. Curzon was Secretary of State for Foreign Affairs (Nicolson, *Curzon*, 277–280). On Law's attitude toward the war, see his letters to Curzon during Lausanne: November 29, 1922; December 5, 1922; December 7, 1922; December 15, 1922; December 28, 1922; January 8, 1923. MSS Eur F112/282, G. N. Curzon Papers, British Library.

56. Lloyd George, *Truth about the Peace Treaties*, vol. II, 1350.

57. Winston Churchill, *World Crisis*, vol. IV, 337–338.

58. Rumbold to Curzon, November 11, 1922. FO 141/580.

59. Kemal's deposing of Sultan Mehmet VI and the resignation of the Ottoman cabinet on November 4 signaled the final collapse of the Ottoman state. Gingeras, *Fall of the Sultanate*, 293.

60. A. Hulme Beaman, "Lausanne and Its Lessons," *Nineteenth Century*, March 1923, 321.

61. Law to Curzon, January 8, 1923. MSS Eur F112/282, G. N. Curzon Papers.

62. The *Sphere*, quoting Mr. Scotland Liddell on the "fate of 400,000 Constantinople Christians," November 18, 1922.

63. Curzon to Lord Hardinge, October 13, 1922, in Medlicott et al., *Documents on British Foreign Policy, 1919–1939*, first series, vol. XVIII (London: HMSO, 1972), 194–195.

64. The opening ceremony and remarks delivered there were described in Foreign Office memoranda and coded telegrams. FO 839/5.

65. Curzon to Foreign Office, November, 20, 1922. FO 839/5.

66. Goldstein, "The British Official Mind and the Lausanne Conference," 201.

67. Housepian, *The Smyrna Affair*, p. 218.

68. Nicolson, *Curzon*, 324–325.

69. This happened on January 6 to the shock and objection of other conference delegates. Demirci, *Strategies and Struggles*, 60, 92–96.

70. Evans, *The Slow Rapprochement*, 69.

71. These included the status of Mosul, the capitulations that historically protected European privileges in the Ottoman Empire, minority safeguards along with the status of the Greek patriarch at Constantinople, prisoner exchange and the population exchange which would force Muslims living in Greece to trade places with Christians living in Turkey in order to create more ethnically and religiously homogeneous states.

72. Demirci, *Strategies and Struggles*, 75–108.

73. Curzon described the "painful and almost unbelievable scene" that accompanied his delayed departure in a letter to Mr. Lindsay on February 5, 1923. Medlicott et al., *Documents on British Foreign Policy*, vol. XVIII, 506.

74. Appointed in 1920 to the post, Rumbold as a longtime diplomat focused on Near Eastern affairs had worked in the Foreign Office earlier in the war as head of the Prisoner's Department. He served as Curzon's deputy at the first Lausanne Conference and took over as chief delegate at the second conference.

75. Andrew Ryan to Helm, July 21, 1923. FO 800/240/13.

76. "The Near East," *Manchester Guardian*, June 21, 1921.

77. Diplomatic correspondence. FO 800/240/4.

78. Henderson to Ryan, January 2, 1923. FO 800/240/13.

79. Henderson to Ryan, December 27, 1922. FO 800/240/13.

80. On the refugee crisis in Greece see Clark, *Twice a Stranger* and Hirschon, *Heirs of the Greek Catastrophe*.

81. The British government issued a Blue Book after the first conference which contained detailed information about the proceedings. British delegation at Lausanne (Ryan) to Henderson April 24, 1923. FO 800/240/5.

82. G. D. Clayton *Britain and the Eastern Question* (London: University of London Press, 1971), 235–239.

83. Ekmekçioğlu, "Republic of Paradox," 657–658.

84. Kieser, *When Democracy Died*, Part III.

85. Ekmekçioğlu argues that Lausanne further entrenched divisions between "Muslim" and "non-Muslim" populations in Turkey that continue today ("Republic of Paradox," 673–674).

86. "Territorial and Military Commission," Meeting of December 1, 1922. *Lausanne Conference on Near Eastern Affairs 1922–25: Records of Proceedings and Draft Terms of Peace with Map.* Cmd. 1814 (London: Stationery Office, 1923).

87. The term "unmixing" in this context has long been attributed to Curzon, but it seems that if he did indeed use it, he borrowed it from Nansen. I have not found a direct reference to Curzon using this term. On Nansen's use of the term, see J. Petropulos, "The Compulsory Exchange of Populations: Greek-Turkish Peacemaking," *Byzantine and Modern Greek Studies* 2, no. 1 (1976): 135–160.

88. Beaman, "Lausanne and Its Lessons," 324.

89. Nicolson, *Curzon*, 317.

90. Robson, *States of Separation.*

91. This shift is seen when comparing Treaty of Sèvres Articles 140–151 and Treaty of Lausanne Articles 37–45.

92. This process began in the wake of the Crimean War and was done largely through treaty agreements and humanitarian intervention. Tusan, *Smyrna's Ashes*, 10–21.

93. Prasenjit Duara, ed., *Decolonization: Perspectives from Now and Then* (New York: Routledge, 2004).

94. Defenders of the minority treaties self-consciously drew upon nineteenth-century precedent, tracing the history of minority protection to the Greek Wars of Independence and seeing the Treaty of Berlin as a watershed moment when new states created out of the Ottoman Empire's lands in Eastern Europe made such protection clauses necessary. Eyre A. Crowe, "The Treaties for the Protection of Minorities," in H. W. V. Temperley, ed., *A History of the Peace Conference of Paris*, vol. V: *Economic Reconstruction and Protection of Minorities* (London: Henry Frowde and Hodder & Stoughton, 1921).

95. This suggests that concerns for national rights in the twentieth century retained the religious character of the nineteenth century. Mazower, "Minorities and the League of Nations in Interwar Europe."

96. Mark Levene, "Harbingers of Jewish and Palestinian Disasters: European Nation-State Building and Its Toxic Legacies, 1912–1948," in Bashir Bashir and Amos Goldbert, eds., *The Holocaust and the Nakba* (New York: Columbia University Press, 2018), 53.

97. Ekmekçioğlu, "Republic of Paradox."

98. Kaloudis, "Ethnic Cleansing in Asia Minor and the Treaty of Lausanne."

99. Convention concerning the Exchange of Greek and Turkish Population signed at Lausanne, January 30, 1923, repr. from British Treaty Series, No. 16 (1923). It took well over a year for the process of exchange to unfold. Clark, *Twice a Stranger.*

100. Clark, *Twice a Stranger*, xii. As the passage of Nansen's plan became a foregone conclusion, Ryan and others began to worry about the details. A plan to abolish the Greek Patriarchate at Constantinople worried Ryan, who claimed that "the expulsion of the Patriarchate" would spark an emotional response by Anglicans in Britain and objections by the Archbishop of Canterbury.

101. Robson show how "by the end of the 1930s, the Middle East had become a space for a massive experiment in demographic engineering" (*States of Separation*, 6).

102. Skran, *Refugees in Interwar Europe*.

103. Part II: Report by Dr. Nansen on question of refugees in Greece and Asia Minor, n.d. FO 286/869.

104. Ibid.

105. Sir Charles Bentinck to Curzon Athens, January 31, 1923. See also dispatch no. 40, January 22, 1923. FO 286/869.

106. British Embassy communication to Ryan July 17, 1923. FO 800/240/14.

107. "Lausanne: Lord Curzon's Report," *Manchester Guardian*, February 7, 1923.

108. Mazower, *No Enchanted Palace*.

109. The reversal of the decision to grant Chester, an American company, the concession to build a railroad in Turkey five months after the signing of Lausanne was viewed as a victory for Britain, which believed the deal conflicted with its ambitions in Mosul. Sevtap Demirci, "Turco-British Diplomatic Manoeuvres on the Mosul Question in the Lausanne Conference, 1922–1923," *British Journal of Middle Eastern Studies* 37, no. 1 (2010): 57–71

110. A. L. Macfie, "The Straits Question: The Conference of Lausanne (November 1922–July 1923)," *Middle Eastern Studies* 15, no. 2 (1979): 211–238.

111. Darwin, "The Chanak Crisis and the British Cabinet."

112. Demirci, "Turco-British Diplomatic Manoeuvres," 59.

113. Richard Fogarty, "The French Empire," in Gerwarth, ed. *Empires at War* (Oxford: Oxford University Press, 2014), 109–129; Martin Thomas, *The French Empire between the Wars* (Manchester: Manchester University Press, 2005).

114. Nicolson, *Curzon*, p. 283.

115. See Curzon's correspondence with Mr. Lindsay on January 21, 22 and 24, 1923. FO 839/17. Darwin argues that the March 1922 conference was a dead letter because France was still involved in separate negotiations with Kemalists ("The Chanak Crisis and the British Cabinet").

116. Smith, *Venizelos*.

117. Communications, December 23, 1922, and January 4, 1923. FO 839/8.

118. "Note by Mr. Nicolson regarding a conversation with Venizelos," December 23, 1922. FO 839/8.

119. Hirschon, *Heirs of the Greek Catastrophe*, xvi.

120. See correspondence on Greece from May, 1923. FO 839/11.

121. Telegram to Sir E. Crowe from Curzon, November 22, 1922. FO 839/14.

122. Telegram to Sir E. Crowe (FO) from British Delegation to Lausanne, December 17, 1922. FO 839/26; Robert M. Hodgson, "George Chicherin," *Slavonic and East European Review* 15, no. 45 (1937): 698–703.

123. Nicolson, *Curzon*, 212, 222–223.

124. See correspondence from December 1 and 5, 1922, on the Armenian question. FO 839/12.

125. Bonar Law to Gen. Harington, December 5, 1922. FO 839/12.

126. Joseph Yacoub, *The Year of the Sword* (Oxford: Oxford University Press, 2016), 179–183.

127. "Assyrian Christians," November 23, 1922. FO 839/23.

128. Ali Othman, "The Kurds and the Lausanne Peace Negotiations, 1922–23," *Middle Eastern Studies* 33, no. 3 (1997): 521.

129. Protest by delegation, November 29, 1922–1923. FO 839/25.

130. Nicolson, *Curzon*, 329–330.

131. Law to Curzon, January 8, 1923. MSS Eur F112/282, G. N. Curzon Papers.

132. Demirci, "Turco-British Diplomatic Manoeuvres," 58.

133. British General Staff memorandum, October 19, 1922. Medlicott et al., *Documents on British Foreign Policy*, vol. XVIII, appendix II.

134. Goldstein, "The British Official Mind and the Lausanne Conference, 1922–23," 191, 202.

135. Curzon's speech on minorities; report of speech received on December 14, original speech given December 12, 1922. FO 286/827.

136. Curzon's speech on minorities; report of speech received on December 16, original speech given December 13, 1922. FO 286/827.

137. Demirci, "Turco-British Diplomatic Manoeuvres."

138. Curzon's speech on minorities, report of speech received on December 16, original speech given December 13, 1922. FO 286/827.

139. Rumbold, quoted in Goldstein, "The British Official Mind and the Lausanne Conference," 203.

140. Ryan, *Last of the Dragomans*, 198.

141. Andrew Crozier, "The Establishment of the Mandates System 1919–25," *Journal of Contemporary History* 14, no. 3 (1979): 483–513.

142. Ronald McNeill, undersecretary of state for foreign affairs, commenting on the Lausanne Treaty during the House of Commons Debate on August 2, 1923. FO 286/870.

143. The play was written in 1893 and was a hit, but the tour was cancelled when Wilde's trial commenced. It was made into a film in Britain in 1921.

144. Ryan, *Last of the Dragomans*, 218.

145. A search of terms related to the treaty in the press shows that only around fifty articles were published in the London *Times* about Lausanne between 1922 and 1930; even fewer appeared in the provincial and periodical press.

146. British Embassy communication to Ryan July 17, 1923. FO 800/240/14.

147. Shirley Komrower, "Out of the Diplomatic Bag," *Manchester Guardian*, February 14, 1958.

EPILOGUE

1. Balakian, *Armenian Golgotha*, 430.

2. Cabanes, *Great War and the Origins of Humanitarianism* and Watenpaugh, *Bread from Stones* both examine the wartime origins of the crisis in Europe and the Middle East respectively.

3. Tusan, "Crimes against Humanity."

4. Levene, "Harbingers of Jewish and Palestinian Disasters," 53.

5. Ihrig, *Ataturk in the Nazi Imagination*; Vanda Wilcox, ed., *Italy in the Era of the Great War* (Leiden: Brill, 2018).

6. At a Liberal Federation dinner, Lord Gladstone blamed Lloyd George for the decline of the Liberal fortunes, calling Labour the inheritor of liberal values and interests. "Mr. Lloyd George's Policy," *Manchester Guardian*, October 4, 1922.

7. Kieser sees Lausanne as crucial in the rise of fascism and "ultranationalism" in Europe. *When Democracy Died*, 7.

8. Weitz, "From the Vienna to the Paris System"; Smith, *Sovereignty at the Paris Peace Conference.*

9. Michelle Tusan, "War and the Victorians," *Victorian Studies* 58, no. 2 (Winter 2016): 324–331.

10. This has been shaped, in the case of the Paris Peace Conference, by reading Nicolson's disillusioned assessment of the attempt to enact the principles of peace in 1919. Few read Nicolson's even more dystopian assessment of Lausanne four years later.

Bibliography

ARCHIVES

Bodleian, Oxford University
  Hanworth Papers
  James Bryce Papers
  Toynbee Box
British Film Institute (BFI), London
  Salvage in Austria; Salvage in Hungary; World War and After; Tragedy of the Near East; New Worlds for Old; Syria; Famine: The Russian Famine of 1921
British Library, London
  Manuscripts:
    Balfour Papers
    C. P. Scott Papers
    G. N. Curzon Papers
    India Office Records (IOR)
    League of Nations Pamphlet Collection
    Map Collection
    Northcote Papers
    Robert Cecil Papers
Churchill Archives Centre, Cambridge
    Chartwell Collection
    De Robeck Papers
    J. H. Godfrey Papers
    Leopold Amery Papers
    M. P. A. Hankey Papers
Hoover Institution Library and Archives, Stanford University, CA
    American National Red Cross (ARC) Archives: Reels 149; 155–157; 159;
      185; 242
Huntington Library, San Marino, CA
    Bryce-White Papers
Imperial War Museum, London
    "Anonymous Account of the Burning of Smyrna"
    Private Papers of C. J. Howes

Private Papers of C. H. Bond; Private Papers of C. E. Temperley; Private
Papers of J. Coffey
King's College London: Liddell Hart Centre for Military Archives (KCLMA)
Alexander Keown-Boyd Papers
Archibald Percival Wavell Papers
Edmund Allenby Papers
Hubert Winthrop Young Papers
John Stuart Mackenzie Shea Papers
William Raine Marshall Papers
Library of the Society of Friends, Friends House, London
Ann Mary Burgess Papers
London School of Economics Library (LSE), Special Collections
League of Nations Union (LNU) Archives
Middle East Centre Archives, St. Antony's College, Oxford
Allenby Papers
Ryan Papers
The National Archives, Kew (UK)
Cabinet Papers (CAB): 23/8; 23/9; 23/14; 23/31/1–3; 23/31/5; 23/
31/9–10; 23/37; 24/14; 24/93/2; 24/93; 24/145
Foreign Office (FO): 141/580; 286/827; 286/869; 373/5/2; 608/54/
9; 608/82/10; 608/96/11; 608/97/3; 608/97/21; 608/97/24;
608/107/4; 608/271/5; 608/272/7; 608/247/3; 800/240/4;
800/240/5; 800/240/13; 800/240/14; 839/5; 839/8; 839/11;
839/12; 839/14; 839/23; 839/25; 839/26
Home Office (HO): 45/10955/31297/98; 45/10955/312971/89;
45/10955/312971/92
Public Records Office: PRO 30/57/76/25
War Office (WO): 106/729; 106/907
Nubar Library, Paris
AGBU Archives / Les archives de L'UGAB
Andonian Collection / Le Fonds Andonian
Archives of the Armenian National Delegation / Les archives de la
Délégation nationale arménienne
Parliamentary Archives, London
Lloyd George Papers
Zoryan Institute, Toronto
Stanley Kerr Archive

ARCHIVE DATABASES

British Library Newspapers Part IV
Chatham House Archive
Churchill Archive Online
Hansards Debates Online
House of Commons
House of Lords

King-Crane Commission Digital Collection, Oberlin College Archives
Mark Sykes Papers, University of Hull and Sledmere House
Sir Austen Chamberlain Papers, Series Two, University of Birmingham Library
UK Parliamentary Papers

PERIODICALS

Aberdeen Daily Journal (Aberdeen, Scotland)
Bulletin of the Society of Friends Relief Missions
Christian Science Monitor
Daily Mail
Daily Mail (Hull, England)
Derby Daily Telegraph
Evening Telegraph and Post (Dundee, Scotland)
Financial Times
Fortnightly Review
Friend
Gloucester Citizen
Illustrated London News
International Labour Review
Irish Times
League of Nations official publications, 1920–1940
Economist
Leeds Mercury
London Times
Manchester Guardian
Motion Picture World
Moving Picture Age
Moving Picture World
New Near East
New York Times
Nineteenth Century
Nottingham Evening Post
Orient magazine
Outlook
Photoplay
Picturegoer
Quiver
Saturday Review
Save the Children Fund
The Sphere
South China Morning Post
Sydney Morning Herald
The World Court

PUBLISHED PRIMARY AND SECONDARY SOURCES

Abou-Hodeib, Toufoul. *A Taste for Home: The Modern Middle Class in Ottoman Beirut.* Stanford: Stanford University Press, 2017.

Abrahamian, Avedis Albert. *Avedis' Story: An Armenian Boy's Journey.* London: Gomidas Institute, 2014.

Adams, R. J. Q. *Arms and the Wizard: Lloyd George and the Ministry of Munitions, 1915–1916.* College Station: Texas A&M University Press, 1978.

Adelson, Roger. *Mark Sykes.* London: Jonathan Cape, 1975.

Adjemian, Boris and Talin Suciyan, La construction mémorielle d'un espace communautaire: les orphelinats et le quartier arménien de Jérusalem dans les archives photographiques de la Bibliothèque Nubar, *Études arméniennes contemporaines*: 75–113.

Afaf, Marsot. *A History of Egypt.* Cambridge: Cambridge University Press, 2007.

Agamben, Giorgio. *Homo Sacer: Sovereign Power and Bare Life.* trans. Daniel Heller-Roazen. Stanford: Stanford University Press, 1998.

Ahmad, F. "Ottoman Perceptions of the Capitulations, 1800–1914," *Journal of Islamic Studies* 11, no. 1 (2000): 1–20.

Akçam, Taner. *From Empire to Republic: Turkish Nationalism and the Armenian Genocide.* London: Zed Books, 2004.

    Killing Orders: Talat Pasha's Telegrams and the Armenian Genocide. London: Palgrave Macmillan, 2018.

    A Shameful Act: The Armenian Genocide and the Question of Turkish Responsibility. New York: Holt, 2006.

    The Young Turks' Crime against Humanity: The Armenian Genocide and Ethnic Cleansing in the Ottoman Empire. Princeton: Princeton University Press, 2012.

Akçam, Taner and Ümit Kurt. *The Spirit of the Laws: The Plunder of Wealth in the Armenian Genocide.* New York: Berghahn, 2015.

Akin, Yiğit. *When the War Came Home: The Ottomans' Great War and the Devastation of an Empire.* Stanford: Stanford University Press, 2018.

Aksakal, Mustafa. "Holy War Made in Germany?" *War in History* 18, no. 2 (2011): 184–199.

    "The Ottoman Empire," in Robert Gerwarth and Erez Manela, eds., *Empires at War: 1911–1923.* Oxford: Oxford University Press, 2014, 17–33.

    "The Ottoman Proclamation of Jihad," in Erik-Jan Zürcher, ed., *Jihad and Islam in World War I.* Leiden: Leiden University Press, 2016, 53–65.

    The Ottoman Road to War in 1914: The Ottoman Empire and the First World War. Cambridge: Cambridge University Press, 2008.

Allen, W. and P. Muratoff, eds. *Caucasian Battlefields: A History of the Wars on the Turco-Caucasian Border, 1828–1921.* New York: Cambridge University Press, 1953.

Allenby, Edmund. *A Brief Record of the Advance of the Egyptian Expeditionary Force.* London: HMSO, 1919.

"The American Red Cross in the Land of the Philistines: Their Refugee Camps at Wady Surar," *Touchstone and the American Art Student Magazine,* January 1919, 280.

Anderson, Margaret. "Down in Turkey, Far Away: Human Rights, the Armenian Massacres, and Orientalism in Wilhelmine Germany," *Journal of Modern History* 79, no. 1 (March 2007): 80–111.

"A Responsibility to Protest? The Public, the Powers and the Armenians in the Era of Abdülhamit II," *Journal of Genocide Research* 17, no. 3 (2015): 259–283.

Andonian, Aram. *The Memoirs of Naim Bey: Turkish Official Documents Relating to the Deportations and Massacres of Armenians.* Intro by Viscount Gladstone. London: Hodder and Stoughton, 1920.

Exile, Trauma and Death: On the Road to Chankiri with Komitas Vartabed. London: Gomidas Institute, 2010.

Andreasian, Dikran. *A Red Cross Flag that Saved Four Thousand,* trans. Stephen Trowbridge. American Red Cross Committee, 1916?

Antaramian, Richard E. *Brokers of Faith, Brokers of Empire: Armenians and the Politics of Reform in the Ottoman Empire.* Stanford: Stanford University Press, 2020.

Anush, Armen. *Passage Through Hell: A Memoir.* Studio City, CA: Manjikian Publications, 2007.

Ardıç, Nurullah. *Islam and the Politics of Secularism: The Caliphate and Middle Eastern Modernization in the Early 20th Century.* New York: Routledge, 2012.

Arsan, Andrew. *Lebanon: A Country in Fragments.* London: Hurst, 2018.

Arsenian, Hagop. *Towards Golgotha: The Memoirs of Hagop Arsenian.* Beirut: Haigazian University Press, 2011.

Atkinson, Tacy. *The German, the Turk and the Devil Made a Triple Alliance.* Reading: Taderon Press, 2000.

Attabaki, Touraj, ed. *Iran and the First World War.* London: I. B. Tauris, 2006.

Attrep, Abe. "'A State of Wretchedness and Impotence': A British View of Istanbul and Turkey, 1919," *International Journal of Middle East Studies* 9, no. 1 (1978): 1–9.

Austin, General H. H. *Baqubah Refugee Camp: An Account of Work on Behalf of the Persecuted Assyrian Christians.* Piscataway, NJ: Gorgias Press, 2006. Repr.

Axworthy, Michael. *Empire of the Mind: A History of Iran.* New York: Basic Books, 2008.

Aydın, Cemil. *The Idea of the Muslim World: A Global Intellectual History.* Cambridge, MA: Harvard University Press, 2017.

Bailkin, Jordanna. *Unsettled: Refugee Camps and the Making of Multicultural Britain.* Oxford: Oxford University Press, 2018.

Balakian, Grigoris. *Armenian Golgotha: A Memoir of the Armenian Genocide.* New York: Knopf, 2009.

Balakian, Peter. *The Burning Tigris: The Armenian Genocide and America's Response.* New York: Perennial, 2003.

Barkawi, Tarak. *Soldiers of Empire: Indian and British Armies in World War II.* Cambridge: Cambridge University Press, 2017.

Barker, A. J. *The Bastard War: The Mesopotamian Campaign of 1914–1918.* New York: Dial, 1967.

Barker, J. Ellis. "Germany and Turkey," *Fortnightly Review* 96 n.s. (December 1914), 1013.

"Menace in the Near East," *Fortnightly Review* (December 1914), 994–1014.

Barkey, Karen. *Empire of Difference: The Ottomans in Comparative Perspective.* Cambridge: Cambridge University Press, 2008.

Barnett, Michael N. *The Empire of Humanity: A History of Humanitarianism.* Ithaca, NY: Cornell University Press, 2011.

Barr, James. *A Line in the Sand: The Anglo-French Struggle for the Middle East, 1914–1948.* New York: Norton, 2012.

Bar-Yosef, Eitan. *The Holy Land in English Culture 1799–1917: Palestine and the Question of Orientalism.* Oxford: Clarendon, 2000.

Baron, Beth. *Egypt as a Woman: Nationalism, Gender, and Politics.* Berkeley: University of California Press, 2005.

The Orphan Scandal: Christian Missionaries and the Rise of the Muslim Brotherhood. Stanford: Stanford University Press, 2014.

Barry, Iris. *Let's Go to the Movies.* London: Chatto & Windus, 1926.

Barton, James. *The Story of Near East Relief (1915–1930): An Interpretation.* New York: Macmillan, 1930.

Bartov, Omar. *Germany's War and the Holocaust: Disputed Histories.* Ithaca, NY: Cornell University Press, 2003.

Bashir Bashir and Amos Goldberg, eds. *The Holocaust and the Nakba: A New Grammar of Trauma and History.* New York: Columbia University Press, 2018.

Bass, Gary. *Freedom's Battle: The Origins of Humanitarian Intervention.* New York: Vintage, 2009.

Stay the Hand of Vengeance: The Politics of War Crimes (Princeton: Princeton University Press, 2000)

Baughan, Emily. *Saving the Children: Humanitarianism, Internationalism and Empire.* Berkeley: University of California Press, 2022.

"'Every Citizen of Empire Implored to Save the Children!' Empire, Internationalism and the Save the Children Fund in Inter-war Britain," *Historical Research* 86, no. 231 (2012): 116–137.

Baussan, Charles. "General Gouraud," *Studies: An Irish Quarterly Review* 7, no. 27 (1918): 400–415.

Bayly, C. A. *Empire and Information: Intelligence Gathering and Social Communication in India, 1780–1870.* Cambridge: Cambridge University Press, 1996.

Becker, Jean-Jacques. *The Great War and the French People.* New York: St Martin's Press, 1986.

Bedoukian, Kerop. *The Urchin: An Armenian Escape* (1978); repr. as *Some of Us Survived.* New York: Farrar Straus Giroux, 1979.

Beers, Laura and Geraint Thomas, eds. *Brave New World: Imperial and Democratic Nation-Building in Britain between the Wars.* London: Institute for Historical Research, 2012.

Berberian, Houri. *Roving Revolutionaries: Armenians and the Connected Revolutions in the Russian, Iranian, and Ottoman Worlds.* Berkeley: University of California Press, 2019.

Berdine, Michael D. *Redrawing the Middle East: Sir Mark Sykes, Imperialism and the Sykes–Picot Agreement.* London: Bloomsbury, 2018.

Bierstadt, Edward Hale. *The Great Betrayal: A Survey of the Near East Problem.* New York: McBride, 1924.

Biltereyst, Daniel, Richard Maltby and Philippe Meers, eds. *Cinema, Audiences and Modernity: New Perspectives on European Cinema History.* London: Routledge, 2012.

Bloom, Clive, ed. *Literature and Culture in Modern Britain,* vol. I. New York: Longman, 1993.

Bloxham, Donald. *The Great Game of Genocide: Imperialism, Nationalism, and the Destruction of the Ottoman Armenians.* Oxford: Oxford University Press, 2005.

Blumi, Isa. *Ottoman Refugees, 1878–1939.* London: Bloomsbury, 2013.

Bodenhamer, David J., John Corrigan and Trevor M. Harris, eds. *Deep Maps and Spatial Narratives.* Bloomington: Indiana University Press, 2015.

Boucher, Ellen. "Cultivating Internationalism: Save the Children Fund, Public Opinion, and the Meaning of Child Relief, 1919–24," in Laura Beers and Geraint Thomas, eds., *Brave New World: Democratic Nation-Building in Britain between the Wars.* London: Institute for Historical Research, 2012, 169–188.

Boyadjian, Haroutune P. *Musa Dagh and My Personal Memoirs.* Fairlawn, NJ: Rosekeer Press, 1981.

Braddon, Russell. *The Siege.* London: Jonathan Cape, 1969.

Brecher, F. W. "French Policy toward the Levant 1914–18," *Middle Eastern Studies* 29, no. 4 (1993): 641–663.

Brémond, Edouard. *Le Hedjaz dans la Guerre mondiale.* Paris: Payot, 1931.

Brief Record of the Advance of the Egyptian Expeditionary Force under the Command of General Sir Edmund H. H. Allenby July 1917 to October 1918. 2nd edn. London: HMSO, 1919.

Bryce, James. *The Treatment of the Armenians in the Ottoman Empire.* London: HMSO, 1916.

Bunton, Martin. "Mandate Daze: Stories of British Rule in Palestine, 1917–48," *International Journal of Middle East Studies* 35, no. 3 (2003): 485–492.

Busch, Briton. *Mudros to Lausanne: Britain's Frontier in West Asia.* Albany: State University of New York Press, 1976.

Buxton, Dorothy F. and Edward Fuller. *The White Flame: The Story of the Save the Children Fund.* London: Weardale Press, 1931.

Cabanes, Bruno. *The Great War and the Origins of Humanitarianism, 1918–1924.* Cambridge: Cambridge University Press, 2014.

Calzolari-Bouvier, Valentina. "L'American Committee for Armenian and Syrian Relief et l'instrumentalisation du témoignage d'Aurora Mardiganian (1918–1919)," *Relations Internationales* 3, no. 171 (2017): 17–30.

Campbell, Courtney J. "Space, Place and Scale: Human Geography and Spatial History," *Past and Present* 239, no. 1 (May 2018): 23–45.

Campos, Michelle U. *Ottoman Brothers Muslims, Christians, and Jews in Early Twentieth-Century Palestine.* Stanford: Stanford University Press, 2011.

Canton, William. *Dawn in Palestine.* 2nd edn. London: Pub. for Syria and Palestine Relief Fund by the Society for Promoting Christian Knowledge, 1918.

Captanian, Pailadzo. *Mémoires d'une déportée arménienne.* Paris: M. Flinikowski, 1919. http://gallica.bnf.fr/ark:/12148/bpt6k5609498b.

Case, Holly. *The Age of Questions.* Princeton: Princeton University Press, 2018.

Cassar, George. *Lloyd George at War, 1916–1918.* London: Anthem Press, 2009.

Chanan, Michael. "Economic Conditions of Early Cinema," in Thomas Elsaesser, ed., *Early Cinema: Space, Frame, Narrative*. London: British Film Institute, 1990, 174–188.

Chernev, Borislav. *Twilight of Empire: The Brest-Litovsk Conference and the Remaking of Central Europe, 1917–1918*. Toronto: Toronto University Press, 2017.

Child, W. J. *Across Asia Minor on Foot*. New York: Dodd, 1917.

Chouliaraki, Lilie. *The Ironic Spectator: Solidarity in the Age of Post-Humanitarianism*. Cambridge: Polity Press, 2013.

Churchill, Winston. *The World Crisis*, 6 vols. New York: Scribner, 1963.

Çiçek, M. Talha. *Negotiating Empire in the Middle East: Ottomans and Arab Nomads in the Modern Era, 1840–1914*. Cambridge: Cambridge University Press, 2021.

——— ed. *Syria in World War I: Politics, Economy and Society*. London: Taylor and Francis, 2015.

Clark, Bruce. *Twice a Stranger*. Cambridge, MA: Harvard University Press, 2006.

Clark, Christopher. *Sleepwalkers: How Europe Went to War in 1914*. New York: Harper Collins, 2013.

Clayton, G. D. *Britain and the Eastern Question*. London: University of London Press.

Clogg, Richard. *A Concise History of Greece*. 4th edn. Cambridge: Cambridge University Press, 2021.

Cohen, Deborah. *Last Call at the Hotel Imperial: The Reporters Who Took on a World at War*. New York: Random House, 2022.

Conference on Near Eastern Affairs. *Lausanne Conference on Near Eastern Affairs, 1922–1923: Records of Proceedings and Draft Terms of Peace*. London: HMSO, 1923.

Conlin, Jonathan and Ozan Ozavci, eds. *They All Made Peace – What Is Peace? The 1923 Lausanne Treaty and the New Imperial Order*. London: Gingko, forthcoming.

Constantine, Stephen. *Lloyd George*. New York: Routledge, 1992.

Cooke, Lez. "British Cinema: From Cottage Industry to Mass Entertainment," in Clive Bloom, ed., *Literature and Culture in Modern Britain*, vol. I. London: Longman, 1993, 167–188.

Cora, Yaşar T. Dzovinar Derderian and Ali Sipahi, eds. *The Ottoman East in the Nineteenth Century: Societies, Identities and Politics*. London: I. B. Tauris, 2016.

Crowe, Eyre A. "The Treaties for the Protection of Minorities," in H. W. V. Temperley, ed., *A History of the Peace Conference of Paris*, vol. V: *Economic Reconstruction and Protection of Minorities*. London: Henry Frowde and Hodder & Stoughton, 1921.

Crozier, Andrew. "The Establishment of the Mandates System 1919–25," *Journal of Contemporary History* 14, no. 3 (1979): 483–513.

The Cry of the Tormented. Intro. by Bedros Donabedian; ed. Mary Ellen Hewson; trans. Garabed Khachigian and Hewson, 2015. Originally in Armenian. Paris: Hagop Pouradian, 1922.

Dadrian, Vahakn N. *The History of the Armenian Genocide: Ethnic Conflict from the Balkans to Anatolia to the Caucasus*. 6th edn. New York: Berghahn Books, 2008.

——— *To the Desert: Pages from My Diary*. London: Gomidas Institute, 2020.

Dadrian, Vahakn N. and Taner Akçam. *Judgment at Istanbul: The Armenian Genocide Trials*. New York: Berghahn Books, 2011.

Dagi, Dogachan. "Balance of Power or Balance of Threat," *Open Political Science* 1 (2018): 143–152.

Darwin, John. *Britain, Egypt and the Middle East: Imperial Policy in the Aftermath of War 1918–1922*. London: Macmillan, 1981.

"The Chanak Crisis and the British Cabinet," *History* 65, no. 214 (1980): 32–48.

Das, Santanu. *India, Empire, and First World War Culture: Writings, Images, and Songs*. Cambridge: Cambridge University Press, 2018.

"'Subalterns' at Mesopotamia," in Roger Long and Ian Talbot, eds., *India and World War I: A Centennial Assessment*. London: Routledge, 2018, 134–149.

ed. *Race, Empire and First World War Writing*. Cambridge: Cambridge University Press, 2011.

Das, Santanu, Anna Maguire and Daniel Steinbach, eds. *Colonial Encounters in a Time of Global Conflict, 1914–1918*. Milton Park: Routledge, 2022.

Davies, Andrew. *Geographies of Anticolonialism: Political Networks Across and Beyond South India, c. 1900–1930*. Hoboken, NJ: Wiley, 2020.

Davison, Rodric. "Turkish Diplomacy from Mudros to Lausanne," in Gordon Craig and Felix Gilbert, eds., *The Diplomats*. Princeton: Princeton University Press, 1953, 172–209.

Dean, William T. "The French in the Middle East in the Great War," *The Historian* 80, no. 3 (2018): 485–496.

Der Matossian, Bedross. *The Horrors of Adana: Revolution and Violence in the Early Twentieth Century*. Stanford: Stanford University Press, 2022.

Shattered Dreams of Revolution: From Liberty to Violence in the Late Ottoman Empire. Stanford: Stanford University Press, 2014.

Derderian, Shahen. *Death March*. Studio City, CA: Manjikian Publications, 2008.

Délégation de la République arménienne. *L'Arménie et la Question Arménienne: Avant, pendant et depuis la guerre. Avec sept annexes et deux cartes hors texte*. Paris: H. Turabian, 1922.

Demirci, Sevtap. *Strategies and Struggles: British Rhetoric and Turkish Response: The Lausanne Conference, 1922–1923*. Piscataway, NJ: Gorgias Press, 2010.

"Turco-British Diplomatic Manoeuvres on the Mosul Question in the Lausanne Conference, 1922–1923," *British Journal of Middle Eastern Studies* 37, no. 1 (2010): 57–71.

Dergisi, Tarih. "Discussions about the Invitation of the Ottoman Empire and Presentation Memorandums in the Paris Peace Conference," *Turkish Journal of History* 71 (2020/2021): 445–472.

Dock, Lavinia L., Sarah Elizabeth Pickett, Clara Dutton Noyes, Fannie F. Clement, Elizabeth Gordon Fox and Ann R. Van Meter. *History of American Red Cross Nursing*. New York: Macmillan, 1922.

Dockrill, Michael and Douglas Goold. *Peace without Promise: Britain and the Peace Conferences, 1919–1923*. Hamden, CT: Archon Books, 1981.

Dockter, Warren. *Churchill and the Islamic World: Orientalism, Empire and Diplomacy in the Middle East*. London: I. B. Tauris, 2015.

Dolbee, Samuel. "The Desert at the End of Empire: An Environmental History of the Armenian Genocide," *Past & Present* 247, no. 1 (May 2020): 197–233.

Donabed, Saragon G. *Reforging a Forgotten History: Iraq and the Assyrians in the Twentieth Century*. Edinburgh: Edinburgh University Press, 2015.

Doughty, Robert. *Pyrrhic Victory: French Strategy and Operation in the Great War*. Cambridge, MA: Harvard University Press, 2005.

Duara, Prasenjit, ed. *Decolonization: Perspectives from Now and Then*. New York: Routledge, 2004.

Egerton, George. "The Lloyd George War Memoirs," *Journal of Modern History* 60, no. 1 (March 1988): 55–94.

Ekmekçioğlu, Lerna. *Recovering Armenia: The Limits of Belonging in Post-Genocidal Turkey*. Stanford: Stanford University Press, 2016.

"Republic of Paradox: The League of Nations Minority Protection Regime and the New Turkey's Step-Citizens," *International Journal of Middle East Studies* 46, no. 3 (2014): 657–679.

"The Armenian National Delegation at the Paris Peace Conference and 'The Role of the Armenian Woman during the War,'" https://blogs.commons.g eorgetown.edu/world-war-i-in-the-middle-east/seminar-participants/web-p rojects/lerna-ekmekcioglu-the-armenian-national-delegation-at-the-paris-p eace-conference-and-the-role-of-the-armenian-woman-during-the-war/.

Elliott, Wendy. *Grit and Grace in a World Gone Mad: Humanitarianism in Talas, Turkey, 1908–1923*. London: Gomidas, 2018.

Ellis, John and Michael Cox, eds. *The World War I Databook*. London: Aurum Press, 2001.

Erickson, Edward. *Defeat in Detail: The Ottoman Army in the Balkans, 1912–1913*. London: Praeger, 2003.

Erol, Merih. "'All We Hope Is a Generous Revival': The Evangelization of the Ottoman Christians in Western Anatolia in the Nineteenth Century," *Osmanlı Araştırmaları/ The Journal of Ottoman Studies* 55 (2020): 243–280.

"Between Memories of Persecution and Refugee Experience," in Konstantinos Travlos, ed., *Salvation and Catastrophe: The Greek-Turkish War, 1919–1922*. New York: Lexington Books, 2020, 341–368.

Essayan, Zabel. "Le rôle de la femme arménienne pendant la guerre," *Revue des études arméniennes* 2 (1922): 121–138.

Evans, Stephen. *The Slow Rapprochement: Britain and Turkey in the Age of Kemal Ataturk, 1919–38*. Tallahassee, FL: Eothen Press, 1982.

Fahmy, Ziad. *Ordinary Egyptians: Creating the Modern Nation through Popular Culture*. Stanford: Stanford University Press, 2011.

Fahrenthold, Stacy. *Between the Ottomans and the Entente: The First World War in the Syrian and Lebanese Diaspora, 1908–1925*. New York: Oxford University Press, 2019.

"Former Ottomans in the Ranks: Pro-Entente Military Recruitment Among Syrians in the Americas, 1916–18," *Journal of Global History* 11, no. 1 (2016): 88–112.

Falls, Cyril and A. F. Becke. *Official History of the Great War: Military Operations Egypt & Palestine from June 1917 to the End of the War*, Part I. London: HMSO, 1930.

Fantauzzo, Justin. *The Other Wars: The Experience and Memory of the First World War in the Middle East and Macedonia.* Cambridge: Cambridge University Press, 2020.

Fassin, Didier. *Humanitarian Reason: A Moral History of the Present.* Berkeley: University of California Press, 2012.

Faught, C. Brad. *Allenby: Making the Modern Middle East.* London: I. B. Tauris, 2020.

Faulkner, Neil. *Empire and Jihad: The Anglo-Arab Wars of 1870–1920.* New Haven: Yale University Press, 2021.

Fawaz, Leila. *A Land of Aching Hearts: The Middle East in the Great War.* Cambridge, MA: Harvard University Press, 2014.

Fehrenbach, Heide. "Children and Other Civilians," in Heide Fehrenbach and Davide Rodogno, *Humanitarian Photography.* Cambridge: Cambridge University Press, 2015, 165–199.

Feldman, David. *Englishmen and Jews.* New Haven: Yale University Press, 1994.

Fermor, L. L. "Thomas Henry Holland. 1868–1947," *Obituary Notices of Fellows of the Royal Society* 6, no. 17 (1948): 83–114.

Fernea, Elizabeth Warnock, ed. *Remembering Childhood in the Middle East.* Austin: University of Texas Press, 2002.

Ferris, John. "'Far Too Dangerous a Gamble'? British Intelligence and Policy during the Chanak Crisis, September–October 1922," *Diplomacy and Statecraft* 14, no. 2 (2003): 139–184.

Fieldston, Sarah. *Raising the World: Child Welfare in the American Century.* Cambridge, MA: Harvard University Press, 2015.

Figes, Orlando. *Peasant Russia, Civil War: Peasant Russia, Civil War: The Volga Countryside in Revolution, 1917–1921.* Oxford: Clarendon, 1989.

"The Final Report of the Dardanelles Commission," Cmd 371, *Parliamentary Papers.* London: HMSO, 1919.

"The First Report of the Dardanelles Commission," *Parliamentary Papers.* London: HMSO, 1917.

Finefrock, Michael M. "Atatürk, Lloyd George and the Megali Idea: Cause and Consequence of the Greek Plan to Seize Constantinople from the Allies, June–August 1922," *Journal of Modern History* 52, no. 1 (1980): 1047–1066.

Fink, Carole. *Defending the Rights of Others: The Great Powers, the Jews, and International Minority Protection, 1878–1938.* Cambridge: Cambridge University Press, 2004.

Finkel, Caroline. *Osman's Dream: The History of the Ottoman Empire.* New York: Basic Books, 2005.

Finley, John. "The Red Cross in Palestine," *Asia: Journal of the Asiatic Association* 19, no. 1 (January 1919): 10–15.

Fisher, H. A. L. *James Bryce*, 2 vols. New York: Macmillan, 1927.

Fogarty, Richard. "The French Empire," in Robert Gerwarth and Erez Manela, eds., *Empires at War: 1911–1923.* Oxford: Oxford University Press, 2014, 109–129.

Race and War in France: Colonial Subjects in the French Army. Baltimore: Johns Hopkins University Press, 2008.

Forth, Aidan. *Barbed-Wire Imperialism: Britain's Empire of Camps.* Berkeley: California University Press, 2017.

"Britain's Archipelago of Camps: Labor and Detention in a Liberal Empire, 1871– 1903," *Kritika: Explorations in Russian and Eurasian History* 16, no. 3 (2015): 651–680.

Foucault, Michel. *Birth of Biopolitics: Lectures at the Collège de France, 1978–1979,* ed. Michel Senellart, trans. Graham Burchell. New York: Picador, 2010.

Fraser, T. G., ed. *The First World War and Its Aftermath: The Shaping of the Middle East.* London: Gingko Library, 2015.

Freeman, Kathleen. *If Any Man Build: The History of the Save the Children Fund.* London: Hodder and Stoughton, 1965.

French, David. *British Strategy and War Aims, 1914–1916.* London: Allen and Unwin, 1986.

"The Dardanelles, Mecca and Kut: Prestige as a Factor in British Eastern Strategy, 1914–1916," *War & Society* 5 (1987): 45–61.

The Strategy of Lloyd George Coalition, 1916–1918. Oxford: Clarendon, 2002.

Frieze, Donna-Lee. "Three Films, One Genocide: Remembering the Armenian Genocide through Ravished Armenia(s)," in N. Eltringham and P. Maclean, eds., *Remembering Genocide.* New York: Routledge, 2014, 38–54.

Fromkin, David. *A Peace to End All Peace: Creating the Modern Middle East, 1914– 1922.* New York: Henry Holt, 1989.

Fuller, Edward. *The Right of the Child: A Chapter in Social History.* Boston: Beacon Press, 1951.

Fussell, Paul. *The Great War and Modern Memory.* New York: Oxford University Press, 2013.

Gaillard, Gaston. *The Project Gutenberg Ebook of the Turks and Europe,* n.d. (originally publ. London: Thomas Murby and Co., 1921). www.gutenberg.org/files/5 1761/51761-h/51761-h.htm#IV.

Gardner, Nikolas. "Charles Townshend's Advance on Baghdad," *War in History* 20, no. 2 (April 2013): 182–200.

The Siege of Kut-al-Amara. Bloomington: Indiana University Press, 2014.

Garo, Armen. *Bank Ottoman: Memoirs of Armen Garo,* trans. Haig Partizian. Detroit: Armen Topouzian, 1990.

Gatrell, Peter. *The Unsettling of Europe: How Migration Reshaped a Continent.* New York, Basic Books, 2019.

Whole Empire Walking: Refugees in Russia during World War I. Bloomington: Indiana University Press, 2005.

Gaunt, David. *Massacres, Resistance, Protectors: Muslim-Christian Relations in Eastern Anatolia During World War I.* Piscataway, NJ: Gorgias Press, 2006.

Gelvin, James L. *Divided Loyalties: Nationalism and Mass Politics in Syria at the Close of Empire.* Berkeley: University of California Press, 1998.

Geppert, Dominik, William Mulligan and Andreas Rose, eds. *The Wars before the Great War.* Cambridge: Cambridge University Press, 2016.

Gerwarth, Robert. *The Vanquished: Why the First World War Failed to End.* London: Penguin Books, 2017.

Gerwarth, Robert and Erez Manela, eds. *Empires at War: 1911–1923*. Oxford: Oxford University Press, 2014.

Ghazarian, Vache, ed. & trans. *Boghos Nubar and the Armenian Questions, 1915–1918: Documents*. Waltham, MA: Mayreni Publishing, 1996.

Giaccaria, P. and C. Minca, "Topographies/Topologies of the Camp: Auschwitz as a Spatial Threshold," *Political Geography* 30 (2011): 1–12.

Giannikopoulos, Dimitrios. "Greece's Entry into the Great War," in Robert Johnson, ed., *The Great War in the Middle East: A Clash of Empires*. London: Routledge, 2019, 74–96.

Gifford, Dennis. *British Film Catalogue, 1895–1985*. New York: Facts on File, 1986.

Gingeras, Ryan. *Eternal Dawn: Turkey in the Age of Atatürk*. Oxford: Oxford University Press, 2019.

   Fall of the Sultanate. Oxford: Oxford University Press, 2016.

   The Last Days of the Ottoman Empire, 1918–1922. London: Allen Lane, 2022.

Ginio, Eyal. *The Ottoman Culture of Defeat: The Balkan Wars and Their Aftermath*. New York: Oxford University Press, 2016.

Gledhill, Christine. *Reframing British Cinema, 1918–1928*. London: BFI, 2003.

Glenny, Misha. *The Balkans: Nationalism, War & the Great Powers, 1804–1999*. New York: Penguin, 2001.

Goldstein, Erik. "The British Official Mind and the Lausanne Conference, 1922–23," *Diplomacy & Statecraft* 14, no. 2 (2003): 185–206.

Gorman, Anthony and Sossie Kasbarian, eds. *Diasporas of the Modern Middle East: Contextualising Community*. Edinburgh: Edinburgh University Press, 2015.

Gounaris, Basil C. and Marianna D. Christopoulos. "Reassessing the Greek National Schism of World War I: The Ideological Parameters," *Historical Review* 15, no. 1 (2019): 237–270.

Grandy, Christine. *Heroes and Happy Endings*. Manchester: Manchester University Press, 2014.

Granick, Jaclyn. *International Jewish Humanitarianism in the Age of the Great War*. Cambridge: Cambridge University Press, 2021.

Grant, Kevin. *A Civilised Savagery: Britain and the New Slaveries in Africa, 1884–1926*. London: Routledge, 2005.

   Last Weapons: Hunger Strikes and Fasts in the British Empire. Berkeley: University of California Press, 2019.

Gratien, Chris. "The Sick Mandate of Europe: Local and Global Humanitarianism in French Cilicia, 1918–1922," *Journal of the Ottoman and Turkish Studies Association* 3, no. 1 (2016): 165–190.

Graves, Robert. *Storm Centres of the Near East: Personal Memories 1879–1929*. London: Hutchinson, 1933.

Grayzel, Susan R. *Women's Identities at War: Gender, Motherhood, and Politics in Britain and France during the First World War*. Chapel Hill: University of North Carolina Press, 1999.

Graziosi, Andrea and Frank Sysyn, eds. *Genocide: The Power and Problems of a Legal and Ethical-Political Concept*. Montreal: McGill-Queen's University Press, 2022.

Green, Abigail. "Humanitarianism in Nineteenth-Century Context," *Historical Journal* 57, no. 4 (December 2014): 1157–1175.

"Intervening in the Jewish Question," in Brendan Simms and D. J. B. Trim, eds., *Humanitarian Intervention: A History.* Cambridge: Cambridge University Press, 2011, 139–158.

Greenhalgh, Elizabeth. *The French Army and the First World War.* Cambridge: Cambridge University Press, 2014.

Victory through Coalition: Britain and France during the First World War. Cambridge: Cambridge University Press, 2005.

Greenwood, John Ormerod. *Quaker Encounters,* vol. I: *Friends and Relief.* York: William Sessions, 1975.

Gregg, Heather S. *The Grand Strategy of Gertrude Bell: From the Arab Bureau to the Creation of Iraq.* Carlisle: US Army War College Press, 2022.

Greiner, Bettina, trans. *Suppressed Terror: History and Perception of Soviet Special Camps in Germany.* New York: Lexington Books, 2014.

Gullace, Nicoletta. *"The Blood of Our Sons": Men, Women and the Renegotiation of British Citizenship during the Great War.* London: Palgrave, 2004.

"Sexual Violence and Family Honor: British Propaganda and International Law during the First World War," *American Historical Review* 102, no. 3 (1997): 714–747.

Gullu, Ramazan Erhan. "Ottoman Rums and the Venizelos – Constantine Conflict after the Armistice of Mudros: The Election of Meletios Metaxakis as Patriarch," *Middle Eastern Studies* 57, no. 4 (2021): 499–515.

Guoqi, Xu. *Asia and the Great War.* Oxford: Oxford University Press, 2016.

Gurney, John. "Legations and Gardens, Sahibs and Their Subalterns," *Iran* 40 (2002): 203–232.

Hall, Richard. *The Balkan Wars 1912–1913: Prelude to the First World War.* London: Taylor & Francis, 2000.

Halo, Thea. *Not Even My Name: A True Story.* New York: Picador, 2000.

Halpern, Paul. *A Naval History of World War I.* Annapolis: Naval Institute Press, 1994.

ed. *The Mediterranean Fleet, 1919–1929.* London: Ashgate, 2011.

Halstead, J. "Air Power and Allenby's Army: Combined Arms in Palestine 1917–1918," *War in History* 29, no. 1 (2022): 157–184.

Hanioğlu, M. Şükrü. *Atatürk: An Intellectual Biography.* Princeton: Princeton University Press, 2017.

Hanley, Will. *Identifying with Nationality: European, Ottoman, and Egyptians in Alexandria.* New York: Columbia University Press, 2017.

Harding, Colin and Simon Popple. *In the Kingdom of Shadows: A Companion to Early Cinema.* Madison, NJ: Fairleigh Dickinson University Press, 1996.

Harootunian, Harry. *The Unspoken as Heritage: The Armenian Genocide and Its Unaccounted Lives.* Durham, NC: Duke University Press, 2019.

Hart, Peter. *Gallipoli.* Oxford: Oxford University Press, 2014.

Hartunian, Abraham H. *Neither to Laugh Nor to Weep: A Memoir of the Armenian Genocide.* Boston: Beacon Press, 1968.

Hassiotis, Ioannis K. "The Armenian Genocide and the Greeks," in Richard Hovannisian, ed., *The Armenian Genocide: History, Politics, Ethics.* New York: St. Martin's Press, 1992, 129–151.

Heathorn, Stephen. *Haig and Kitchener in Twentieth-Century Britain: Remembrance, Representation and Appropriation.* London: Routledge, 2016.

Heazell, F. N. *The Woes of a Distressed Nation: Being an Account of the Assyrian People from 1914–1934.* London: Faith Press, 1934.

Hellot-Bellier, Florence. *Chroniques de massacres annoncés: Les Asyro-Chaldéens d'Iran et du Hakkari face aux ambitions des empires, 1896–1920.* Paris: Geuthner, 2014.

Helmreich, Ernst. *The Diplomacy of the Balkan War, 1912–1913.* New York: Russell and Russell, 1969.

Helmreich, Paul. *From Paris to Sevres: The Partition of the Ottoman Empire at the Peace Conference of 1919–1920.* Columbus: Ohio University Press, 1974.

Hewson, Robert. *Armenia: A Historical Atlas.* Chicago: University of Chicago Press, 2001.

"Armenia Maritima," in Richard Hovanissian and Simon Payaslian, eds., *Armenian Cilicia.* Costa Mesa, CA: Mazda Publishers, 2008.

Higson, Andrew and Richard Maltby, eds. *Film Europe and Film America.* Exeter: University of Exeter Press, 1999.

Hilton, Matthew. "Charity and the End of Empire: British Non-Governmental Organizations, Africa, and International Development in the 1960s," *American Historical Review* 123, no. 2 (1 April 2018): 493–517.

"Ken Loach and the Save the Children Film," *Journal of Modern History* 87 (2015): 357–394.

Hilton, Matthew, James McKay, Nicholas Crowson and Jean-Francois Mouhot. *The Politics of Expertise: How NGOs Shaped Modern Britain.* Oxford: Oxford University Press, 2013.

Hirschon, Renee. *Heirs of the Greek Catastrophe* Oxford: Clarendon, 1989.

Hodgson, Robert M. "George Chicherin," *Slavonic and East European Review* 15, no. 45 (1937): 698–703.

Holquist, Peter. *Making War, Forging Revolution: Russia's Continuum of Crisis, 1914–1921.* Cambridge, MA: Harvard University Press, 2002.

Holton, Sandra. *Quaker Women: Personal Life, Memory and Radicalism in the Lives of Women Friends, 1780–1930.* New York: Routledge, 2007.

Horne, John and Alan Kramer. *German Atrocities: A History of Denial.* New Haven: Yale University Press, 2001.

Horton, George. *The Blight of Asia.* Indianapolis: Bobbs Mererill, 1953.

Hourani, Albert. *A History of the Arab Peoples.* Cambridge, MA: Harvard University Press, 1991.

Housepian, Marjorie. *The Smyrna Affair.* New York: Harcourt Brace Jovanovich, 1971.

Hovannisian, Richard. "Postwar Contest for Cilicia," in Richard Hovannisian and Simon Payaslian, eds., *Armenian Cilicia.* Costa Mesa, CA: Mazda Publishers, 2008, 539–555.

The Republic of Armenia, vol. I: *The First Year, 1918–1919.* Berkeley: University of California Press, 1971.

ed. *Armenian Smyrna/Izmir: The Aegean Communities.* Costa Mesa, CA: Mazda Publishers, 2012.

ed. *The Armenian Genocide: History, Politics, Ethics.* New York: St. Martin's Press, 1992.

ed. *The Armenian People from Ancient to Modern Times,* vol. II: *Foreign Dominion to Statehood: The Fifteenth Century to the Twentieth Century.* London: Palgrave Macmillan, 2004.

Hovannisian, Richard and Simon Payaslian, eds. *Armenian Cilicia.* Costa Mesa, CA: Mazda Publishers, 2008.

Howard, Harry N. *The Partition of Turkey: A Diplomatic History, 1913–1923.* New York: Howard Fertig, 1966.

Hughes, Matthew. "General Allenby and the Palestine Campaign, 1917–18," *Journal of Strategic Studies,* 19, no. 4 (1996): 59–88.

Hull, Isabel. *Absolute Destruction: Military Culture and the Practices of War in Imperial Germany.* Ithaca, NY: Cornell University Press, 2013.

Hurewitz, J. C., ed. *The Middle East and North Africa in World Politics: A Documentary Record,* 2 vols. New Haven: Yale University Press, 1979.

Hyslop, Jonathan. "The Invention of the Concentration Camp: Cuba, Southern Africa and the Philippines, 1896–1907," *Southern African Historical Journal* 63, no. 2 (2011): 251–276.

Ihrig, Stefan. *Ataturk in the Nazi Imagination.* Cambridge, MA: Harvard University Press, 2014.

Justifying Genocide: Germany and the Armenians from Bismarck to Hitler. Cambridge, MA: Harvard University Press, 2016.

Imy, Kate. *Faithful Fighters: Identity and Power in the British Army.* Stanford: Stanford University Press, 2019.

Irwin, Julia. *Making the World Safe: The American Red Cross and the Nation's Humanitarian Awakening.* Oxford: Oxford University Press, 2013.

"The Disaster of War: American Understandings of Catastrophe, Conflict, and Relief," *First World War Studies* 5, no. 1 (2014): 17–28.

Jackson, Simon. "Transformative Relief: Imperial Humanitarianism and Mandatory Development in Syria-Lebanon, 1915–1925," *Humanity* 8, no. 2 (2017): 247–268.

Jackson, Simon and A. Dirk Moses. "Transformative Occupations in the Modern Middle East," *Humanity* 8, no. 2 (2017): 231–246.

Jacobsen, Maria. *Diaries of a Danish Missionary: Harpoot, 1907–1919.* Princeton: Taderon Press, 2001.

Jacobson, Abigail. *From Empire to Empire: Jerusalem between Ottoman and British Rule.* Syracuse: Syracuse University Press, 2011.

"A City Living through Crisis: Jerusalem during World War I," *British Journal of Middle Eastern Studies* 36, no. 1 (April 2009): 73–92.

James, Lawrence. *Imperial Warrior: General Allenby.* London: Weidenfeld and Nicolson, 1993.

Jensen, Kimberly. *Mobilizing Minerva: American Women in the First World War.* Urbana: University of Illinois Press, 2008.

Jernazian, Ephraim K. *Judgment unto Truth: Witnessing the Armenian Genocide.* New Brunswick, NJ: Transaction Publications, 1990.

Jinks, Rebecca. "'Marks Hard to Erase': The Troubled Reclamation of 'Absorbed' Armenian Women, 1919–1927," *American Historical Review* 123, no. 1 (February 1, 2018): 86–123.

John, Angela. *War and Journalism and the Shaping of the Twentieth Century.* London: I. B. Tauris, 2006.

Johnson, Robert. "British Strategy and the Imperial Axis in the Middle East, 1914–1918," in Robert Johnson and James E. Kitchen, eds., *The Great War in the Middle East: A Clash of Empires.* London: Routledge, 2019, 47–48.

"The de Bunsen Committee and a Revision of the 'Conspiracy' of Sykes–Picot," *Middle Eastern Studies* 54, no. 4 (2018): 611–637.

Johnson, Robert and James E. Kitchen, eds. *The Great War in the Middle East: A Clash of Empires.* London: Routledge, 2019.

Jones, Heather. *Violence against Prisoners of War in the First World War: Britain, France and Germany, 1914–1920.* Cambridge: Cambridge University Press, 2011.

Jones, L. W. "Rapid Population Growth in Baghdad and Amman," *Middle East Journal* 23, no. 2 (Spring 1969): 209–215.

Jones, Marian Moser. *The American Red Cross from Clara Barton to the New Deal.* Baltimore: Johns Hopkins University Press, 2013.

Kaiser, Hilmar. *At the Crossroads of Der Zor: Death, Survival, and Humanitarian Resistance in Aleppo, 1915–1917.* Princeton: Gomidas Institute, 2002.

Kaloudis, George. "Ethnic Cleansing in Asia Minor and the Treaty of Lausanne," *International Journal on World Peace* 31, no. 1 (2014): 59–88.

Kamouzis, Dimitris. *Greeks in Turkey: Elite Nationalism and Minority Politics in Late Ottoman and Early Republican Istanbul.* London: Routledge, 2021.

Kapikian, Garabed. *Story of Genocide: An Account of the Deportation and Massacres of the Armenians of Sebastia and Lesser Armenia.* Abridged by Arakel Badrig and trans. Aris Sevag. New York: Pan-Sebastia Rehabilitation Union, 1978.

Kaplan-Weinger. "Testimonies of Jewish Holocaust Survivors," in Viktoriïa Khiterer, Ryan Barrick and David Misal, eds., *The Holocaust: Memories and History.* Newcastle upon Tyne: Cambridge Scholars Publishing, 2014, 106–132.

Katouzian, Homa. "The Campaign against the Anglo-Iranian Agreement of 1919," *British Journal of Middle Eastern Studies,* 25, no. 1 (1998): 5–46.

Kayali, Hasan. "The Ottoman Experience of World War I," *Journal of Modern History* 89, no. 4 (December 2017): 875–907.

Keddie, Nikki. *Roots of Revolution: An Interpretative History of Modern Iran.* New Haven: Yale University Press, 1981.

Kerr, Stanley. *The Lion of Marash: Personal Experiences with Near East Relief.* Albany: State University of New York Press, 1973.

Ketchian, Bertha Nakshian. *In the Shadow of the Fortress: The Genocide Remembered.* Cambridge, MA: Zoryan Institute, 1988.

Kévorkian, Raymond. *The Armenian Genocide: A Complete History.* London: I. B. Tauris, 2015.

L'Extermination des déportés Arméniens Ottomans dans les camps de concentration de Syrie-Mesopotamie, 1915–1916. Paris: Bibliothèque Nubar de l'Ugab, 1998.

Kévorkian, Raymond, Levon Nordiguian and Vahe Tachjian. *Les Armeniens, 1917–1939: La quête d'un refuge.* Beirut: Presses de l'Université Saint-Joseph, 2007.

Khalidi, Rashid. *The Iron Cage: The Story of the Palestinian Struggle for Statehood.* Boston: Beacon Press, 2006.

Khalil, Osamah F. "The Crossroads of the World," *Diplomatic History* 38, no. 2 (2014): 299–344.

Khoury, Philip. *Syria and the French Mandate: The Politics of Arab Nationalism, 1920–1945.* Princeton: Princeton University Press, 1987.

Kieser, Hans-Lukas. *Talaat Pasha: Father of Modern Turkey, Architect of Genocide.* Princeton: Princeton University Press, 2018.

When Democracy Died: The Middle East's Enduring Peace of Lausanne. Cambridge: Cambridge University Press, forthcoming.

Kincaid, Peter Jensen. "The Greco-Turkish War, 1920–1922," *International Journal of Middle East Studies* 10, no. 4 (1979): 553–565.

Kitchen, James, ed. *The Great War in the Middle East: Clash of Empires.* London: Routledge, 2019.

Kitromilides, Paschalis M. *Eleftherios Venizelos: The Trials of Statesmanship.* Edinburgh: Edinburgh University Press, 2006.

Knightly, Phillip and Colin Simpson. *The Secret Lives of Lawrence of Arabia.* London: Nelson, 1969.

Knirck, Jason. *Imagining Ireland's Independence.* Lanham: Rowman and Littlefield, 2006.

Kouyoumjian, John. Needle, *Thread and Button.* Cambridge, MA: Zoryan Institute, 1988.

Koven, Seth. *Slumming: Sexual and Social Politics in Victorian London.* Princeton: Princeton University Press, 2004.

Kreienbaum, Jonas. "Guerrilla Wars and Colonial Concentration Camps: The Exceptional Case of German South West Africa (1904–1908)," *Journal of Namibian Studies* 11 (2014): 83–101.

Kriegel, Lara. *The Crimean War and Its Afterlife.* Cambridge: Cambridge University Press, 2022.

Kulischer, E. M. *Europe on the Move: War and Population Changes 1914–1917.* New York: Columbia University Press, 1948.

Laqueur, Thomas. "Bodies, Details, and the Humanitarian Narrative," in Lynn Hunt, ed., *The New Cultural History.* Berkeley: University of California Press, 1989, 176–204.

Lausanne Conference on Near Eastern Affairs, 1922–25. Records of Proceedings and Draft Terms of Peace with Map. London: Stationery Office, 1923. Cmd. 1814.

Le Pautremat, Pascal. "La mission du Lieutenant-colonel Brémond au Hedjaz, 1916–1917," *Guerres mondiales et conflits contemporains,* no. 221 (2006): 17–31.

Lefebvre, Henri, trans. Donald Nicholson-Smith. *The Production of Space.* Oxford: Blackwell, 1991.

Leonhard, Jörn. *Pandora's Box: A History of the First World War.* Cambridge, MA: Belknap, 2018.

Levene, Mark. "Harbingers of Jewish and Palestinian Disasters: European Nation-State Building and Its Toxic Legacies, 1912–1948," in Bashir

Bashir and Amos Goldberg, eds., *The Holocaust and the Nakba: A New Grammar of Trauma and History*. New York: Columbia University Press, 2018, 45–65.

Lewis, Mark. *The Birth of the New Justice: The Internationalization of Crime and Punishment, 1919–1950*. Oxford: Oxford University Press, 2014.

Little, Branden, ed. *Humanitarianism in the Era of the First World War*, special issue of *First World War Studies* 5, no. 1 (2014).

Lloyd George, David. *The Great Crusade: Extracts from Speeches Delivered during the War*. New York: George Doran, 1918.

The Truth about the Peace Treaties, vols. I–II. London: Gollancz, 1938.

War Memoirs, 6 vols. London: Ivor, Nicholson and Watson, 1933.

Loch, Joice. *A Fringe of Blue*. London: John Murray, 1968.

Long, Richard. *British Pro-Consuls in Egypt, 1914–1929*. London: Routledge, 2005.

Long, Roger and Ian Talbot, eds. *India and World War I: A Centennial Assessment*. London: Routledge, 2018.

Low, Michael Christopher. *Imperial Mecca: Ottoman Arabia and the Indian Ocean Hajj*. New York: Columbia University Press, 2020.

Low, Michael Christopher, Kent F. Schull and Robert Zens. *The Subjects of Ottoman International Law*. Bloomington: Indiana University Press, 2020.

Lust-Okar, Ellen. "The Failure of Collaboration: Armenian Refugees in Syria," *Middle Eastern Studies* 32, no. 1 (1996).

MacArthur, Daniel Joseph. "Intelligence and Lloyd George's Secret Diplomacy in the Near East, 1920–1922," *Historical Journal* 56, no. 3 (2013): 707–728.

MacArthur-Seal, Daniel-Joseph. *Britain's Levantine Empire, 1914–1923*. Oxford: Oxford University Press, 2021.

Macfie, A. L. "The Chanak Affair (September– October 1922)," *Balkan Studies* 20, no. 2 (1979): 309–341.

"The Straits Question: The Conference of Lausanne (November 1922– July 1923)," *Middle Eastern Studies* 15, no. 2 (1979): 211–238.

Macleod, Jenny. *Gallipoli: Great Battles*. Oxford: Oxford University Press, 2015.

Macmillan, Margaret. *Peacemakers: The Paris Conference of 1919 and Its Attempt to End War*. London: John Murray, 2001.

McCarthy, Helen. *The British People and the League of Nations*. Manchester: Manchester University Press, 2011.

McFadden, David and Claire Gorfinkel. *Constructive Spirit: Quakers in Revolutionary Russia*. Pasadena, CA: Intentional Productions, 2004.

McGrew, William *Educating across Cultures: Anatolia College in Turkey and Greece*. New York: Rowman and Littlefield, 2015.

McMeekin, Sean. *Berlin to Baghdad Express: The Ottoman Empire and Germany's Bid for World Power*. Cambridge, MA: Harvard University Press, 2010.

The Ottoman Endgame: War Revolution and the Making of the Modern Middle East. New York: Allen Lane, 2015.

Mack, John. *A Prince of Our Disorder: The Life of T. E. Lawrence*. Boston: Little Brown, 1976.

Mardiganian, Aurora. *The Auction of Souls*. London: Harry Hardingham, 1934.

Maguire, Anna. *Contact Zones of the First World War: Cultural Encounters across the British Empire*. Cambridge. Cambridge University Press, 2021.

"'I Felt Like a Man': West Indian Troops Under Fire during the First World War," *Slavery & Abolition* 39, no. 3 (2018): 602–621.

Makdisi, Ussama Samir. *The Culture of Sectarianism: Community, History, and Violence in Nineteenth-Century Ottoman Lebanon.* Berkeley: University of California Press, 2000.

Mandel, Maude. *In the Aftermath of Genocide: Armenians and Jews in Twentieth-Century France.* Durham, NC: Duke University Press, 2003.

Manela, Erez. *The Wilsonian Moment: Self-Determination and the International Origins of Anticolonial Nationalism.* Oxford: Oxford University Press, 2007.

Manhood, Linda. *Feminism and Voluntary Action: Eglantyne Jebb and Save the Children, 1876–1928.* London: Palgrave, 2009.

Manz, Stefan and Panikos Panayi. *Enemies in the Empire.* Oxford: Oxford University Press, 2020.

Manz, Stefan, Panikos Panayi and Matthew Stibbe, eds. *Internment during the First World War: A Mass Global Phenomenon.* London: Routledge, 2019.

Markovich, Slobodan G. "Eleftherios Venizelos, British Public Opinion and the Climax of Anglo-Hellenism (1915–1920)," *Balcanica (Beograd),* no. 49 (2018): 125–155.

Marrus, Michael. *The Unwanted: European Refugees in the Twentieth Century.* Oxford: Oxford University Press, 1985.

Martin, Ramela. *Out of Darkness.* Cambridge, MA: Zoryan Institute, 1989.

Masters, Bruce. *The Arabs of the Ottoman Empire, 1516–1918.* Cambridge: Cambridge University Press, 2013.

Mazower, Mark. *The Greek Revolution: 1821 and the Making of Modern Europe.* New York: Penguin, 2021.

"Minorities and the League of Nations in Interwar Europe," *Daedalus* 126, no. 2 (1997): 47–63.

No Enchanted Palace. Princeton: Princeton University Press, 2013.

Medlicott, W. N, Douglas Dakin and M. E. Lambert, eds. *Documents on British Foreign Policy, 1919–1939, first series,* vol. XVIII. London: HMSO, 1972.

Melman, Billie. *Women's Orients: English Women and the Middle East, 1718–1918.* Ann Arbor: Michigan University Press, 1992.

Mentzel, Peter. *Transportation Technology and Imperialism in the Ottoman Empire, 1800–1923.* Washington, DC: Society for the History of Technology and the American Historical Association, 2006.

Millar, Ronald. *Kut: The Death of an Army.* London: Seeker and Warburg, 1969.

Miller, Donald and Lorna Touryan Miller. *Survivors: An Oral History of the Armenian Genocide.* Berkeley: University of California Press, 1993.

Milton, Giles. *Paradise Lost: Smyrna 1922.* New York: Basic Books, 2008.

Minassian, John. *Many Hills to Climb: Memoirs of an Armenian Deportee.* Santa Barbara, CA: J. Cook, 1986.

Minohara, Tosh and Evan Dawley, eds. *Beyond Versailles: The 1919 Moment and a New Order in East Asia.* New York: Lexington Books, 2021.

Moberly, Brig. Gen F. J. *Official History of the War: Mesopotamia Campaign, 1914–1918,* vols. III and IV by Imperial War Museum Dept. of Printed Books. London: HMSO, 1925.

Moitra, Stefan. "The Management Committee Intend to Act as Ushers: Cinema Operation and the South Wales Miners' Institutes in the 1950s and 1960s," in Daniel Biltereyst et al., eds., *Cinema, Audiences and Modernity: New Perspectives on European Cinema History.* London: Routledge, 2012, 99–115.

Montgomery, A. E. "The Making of the Treaty of Sèvres of 10 August 1920," *Historical Journal* 15, no. 4 (1972): 775–787.

Morris, Benny and Dror Ze'evi. *The Thirty-Year Genocide: Turkey's Destruction of Its Christian Minorities, 1894–1924.* Cambridge, MA: Harvard University Press, 2019.

Moses, A. Dirk. *The Problems of Genocide.* Cambridge: Cambridge University Press, 2021.

Moumdjian, Garabet. "Cilicia under French Administration," in Richard Hovannisian and Simon Payaslian, eds., *Armenian Cilicia.* Costa Mesa, CA: Mazda Publishers, 2008, 455–459.

Mouradian, Khatchig. *The Resistance Network: The Armenian Genocide and Humanitarianism in Ottoman Syria.* East Lansing: Michigan University Press, 2021.

Moyd, Michele. *Violent Intermediaries: African Soldiers, Conquest and Everyday Colonialism in German East Africa.* Athens: Ohio University Press, 2014.

Mugerditchian, Thomas K. *The Diarbekir Massacres and Kurdish Atrocities.* London: Gomidas, 2013.

Mugrditchian, Hovhannes. *To Armenians with Love* [1986]. Hobe Sound, FL: Paul Mart, 1996.

Mulley, Clare. *The Woman Who Saved the Children: A Biography of Eglantyne Jebb.* Oxford: Oneworld Publications, 2009.

Murphy, Robert, ed. *The British Cinema Book.* 3rd edn. London: Bloomsbury, 2009.

Naimark, Norman. *Fires of Hatred: Ethnic Cleansing in Twentieth Century Europe.* Cambridge, MA: Harvard University Press, 2002.

Stalin's Genocides. Princeton: Princeton University Press, 2010.

Nalbandian, Louise. *The Armenian Revolutionary Movement.* Berkeley: University of California Press, 1963.

Nassibian, Akaby. *Britain and the Armenian Question, 1915–1923.* London: Croom Helm, 1984.

Nasson, Bill. *Springboks on the Somme: South Africa in the Great War.* New York: Penguin, 2008.

Neilson, Keith E. "The Breakup of the Anglo-Russian Alliance: The Question of Supply in 1917," *International History Review* 3, no. 1 (1981): 62–75.

Nercessian, Nora. *The City of Orphans: Relief Workers, Commissars and the "Builders of the New Armenia."* Hollis, NH: Hollis Publishing, 2016.

Neyzi, Leyla. "Remembering Smyrna/Izmir: Shared History, Shared Trauma," *History and Memory* 20, no. 2 (Fall 2008): 106–127.

Nicolson, Harold. *Curzon: The Last Phase.* London: Constable, 1934.

Peacemaking 1919. New York: Grosset and Dunlap, 1965.

Nikolopoulou, Kalliopi. "Review of *Homo Sacer: Sovereign Power and Bare Life,*" *SubStance* 29, no. 3 (2000): 124–131.

Odian, Yervant. *Accursed Years: My Exile and Return from Der Zor, 1914–1919.* London: Gomidas, 2009.

Okan, Orçun Can. "The Treaty of Lausanne and the Construction of the Arab Middle East," *Journal of the Ottoman and Turkish Studies Association* 8, no. 1 (2021): 457–461.

Olson, Stanley, ed. *Harold Nicolson: Diaries and Letters, 1930–1964.* New York: Atheneum, 1980.

Othman, Ali. "The Kurds and the Lausanne Peace Negotiations, 1922–23," *Middle Eastern Studies* 33, no. 3 (1997): 521–534.

Ozavci, Ozan. *Dangerous Gifts: Imperialism, Security and Civil Wars in the Levant, 1798–1864.* Oxford: Oxford University Press, 2021.

Özsu Umit. *Formalizing Displacement.* Oxford: Oxford University Press, 2015.

"Ottoman Empire," in Bardo Fassbender and Anne Peters, eds., *The Oxford Handbook of the History of International Law.* Oxford: Oxford University Press, 2012, 429–448.

Özsu, Umit and Thomas Skouteris. "International Legal Histories of the Ottoman Empire: An Introduction to a Symposium," *Journal of the History of International Law/Revue d'histoire du droit international* 18, no. 1 (2016): 1–4.

Packer, Ian. *Lloyd George.* New York: St. Martin's Press, 1998.

Palabıyık, M. "International Law for Survival: Teaching International Law in the Late Ottoman Empire (1859–1922)," *Bulletin of the School of Oriental and African Languages* 78, no. 2 (2015): 271–292.

Palmieri, Daniel. "Humanitarianism on the Screen: The ICRC Films, 1921–1965," in Johannes Paulmann, ed., *Humanitarianism & Media, 1900 to the Present.* New York: Berghahn, 2019, 90–106.

Panayi, Panikos. *Prisoners of Britain: German Civilian and Combatant Internees during the First World War.* Manchester: Manchester University Press, 2012.

Panian, Karnig. *Goodbye, Antoura: A Memoir of the Armenian Genocide.* Stanford: Stanford University Press, 2015.

Panossian, Razmik. *The Armenians: From Kings and Priests to Merchants and Commissars.* New York: Columbia University Press, 2006.

Paris, Michael, ed. *The First World War and Popular Cinema.* New Brunswick, NJ: Rutgers University Press, 2000.

Parry, Jonathan. *Promised Lands: The British and the Ottoman Middle East.* Princeton: Princeton University Press, 2022.

Patenaude, Bertrand M. *The Big Show in Bololand: The American Relief Expedition to Soviet Russia in the Famine of 1921.* Stanford: Stanford University Press, 2002.

Patrick, Andrew. *America's Forgotten Middle East Initiative: The King-Crane Commission of 1919.* London: I. B. Tauris, 2015.

Paulmann, Johannes, ed. *Humanitarianism and Media: 1900 to the Present.* New York: Berghahn Books, 2019.

Payk, Marcus M. and Roberta Pergher. *Beyond Versailles: Sovereignty, Legitimacy, and the Formation of New Polities after the Great War.* Bloomington: Indiana University Press, 2019.

Pedersen, Susan. *The Guardians: The League of Nations and the Crisis of Empire.* Oxford: Oxford University Press, 2015.

Permanent Bureau of the Turkish Congress Lausanne. "Inquiries in Anatolia" (pamphlet), 1919.

Petropulos, J. "The Compulsory Exchange of Populations: Greek-Turkish Peacemaking, 1922–1930," *Byzantine and Modern Greek Studies* 2, no. 1 (1976): 135–160.

Piller, Elisabeth. "American War Relief, Cultural Mobilization and the Myth of Impartial Humanitarianism, 1914–17," *The Journal of the Gilded Age and Progressive Era* 17, no. 4 (2018): 619–635.

Porter, Stephen R. *Benevolent Empire: US Power, Humanitarianism and the World's Dispossessed.* Philadelphia: University of Pennsylvania Press, 2016.

Prochaska, F. K. *Women and Philanthropy in Nineteenth-Century England.* Oxford: Oxford University Press, 1980.

Provence, Michael. *The Last Ottoman Generation and the Making of the Modern Middle East.* Cambridge: Cambridge University Press, 2017.

Pugsley, Christopher. *The Anzac Experience: New Zealand, Australia and Empire in the First World War.* Auckland: Reed Publishing, 2004.

al- Qattan, Najwa. "Fragments of Wartime Memories from Syria and Lebanon," in M. Talha Çiçek, *Syria in World War I: Politics, Economy and Society.* London: Taylor and Francis, 2015, 130–149.

"When Mothers Ate Their Children: Wartime Memory and the Language of Food in Syria and Lebanon," *International Journal of Middle East Studies* 46, no. 4 (2014): 719–736.

Quataert, Donald. *The Ottoman Empire, 1700–1922.* Cambridge: Cambridge University Press, 2005.

Rappard, William. *International Relations as Viewed from Geneva.* New Haven: Yale University Press, 1925.

Rawlinson, Lt. Col. A. *Adventures in the Near East 1918–1922.* New York: Dodd, Mead, 1924.

Refugee Survey 1937–1938, vol. 11. London: Royal Institute of International Affairs, 1938.

Reinharz, J. "The Balfour Declaration and Its Maker: A Reassessment," *The Journal of Modern History* 64, no. 3 (1992): 455–499.

Reynolds, Michael A. *Shattering Empires: The Clash and Collapse of the Ottoman and Russian Empires, 1908–1918.* Cambridge: Cambridge University Press, 2011.

"The East's Eastern Front: The Ottoman–Russian Clash in the Great War and Its Legacies," *War in History* 28, no. 2 (2019): 333–358.

Richards, J. "British Film Censorship," in Robert Murphy, ed., *The British Cinema Book.* 3rd edn. London: Bloomsbury, 2009, 66–77.

Riegg, Stephen Badalyan. *Russia's Entangled Embrace: The Tsarist Empire and the Armenians, 1801–1914.* Ithaca, NY: Cornell University Press, 2020.

Robson, Laura. *States of Separation: Transfer, Partition, and the Making of the Modern Middle East.* Berkeley: University of California Press, 2017.

Rodogno, Davide. *Night on Earth: A History of International Humanitarianism in the Near East.* Cambridge: Cambridge University Press, 2021.

Against Massacre: Humanitarian Interventions in the Ottoman Empire. Princeton: Princeton University Press, 2012.

Rogan, Eugene. *The Arabs: A History.* New York: Basic Books, 2009.

The Fall of the Ottomans. New York: Basic Books, 2015.

Romirowsky, Asaf and Alexander H. Joffe. *Religion, Politics, and the Origins of Palestine Refugee Relief.* London: Palgrave Macmillan, 2013.

Roy, Kaushik. *The Army in British India: From Colonial Warfare to Total War 1857–1947.* London: Bloomsbury, 2014.

Ryan, Andrew. *The Last of the Dragomans.* London: Geoffrey Bles, 1951.

Sakayan, Dora, trans. *An Armenian Doctor in Turkey: Garabed Hatcherian: My Smyrna Ordeal of 1922.* Montreal: Arod Books, 1997.

Sasson, Tehila. "From Empire to Humanity: The Russian Famine and the Imperial Origins of International Humanitarianism," *Journal of British Studies* 55, no. 3 (2016): 519–357.

Satia, Priya. *Spies in Arabia: The Great War and the Cultural Foundations of Britain's Covert Empire in the Middle East.* Oxford: Oxford University Press, 2008.

Time's Monster: How History Makes History. Cambridge, MA: Harvard University Press, 2020.

al-Sayyid-Marsot, Afaf Lutfi. *A History of Egypt: From the Arab Conquest to the Present.* Cambridge: Cambridge University Press, 2007.

de Schaepdrijver, Sophie. *Bastion: Occupied Bruges in the First World War.* Veurne: Hannibal Publishing, 2014.

Schatkowski, Schilcher, L. "The Famine of 1915-1918 in Greater Syria," in John Spangnolo, ed., *Problems of the Modern Middle East in Historical Perspective.* Oxford: MECA, 1992, 229–258.

Scheipers, Sybille. "The Use of Camps in Colonial Warfare," *Journal of Imperial and Commonwealth History* 43, no. 4 (2015): 678–698.

Schneer, Jonathan. *The Balfour Declaration: The Origins of the Arab-Israeli Conflict.* New York: Random House, 2010.

Schölch, Alexander. "Britain in Palestine, 1838–1882: The Roots of the Balfour Policy," *Journal of Palestine Studies* 22 (1992): 39–56.

Segev, Tom. *One Palestine, Complete: Jews and Arabs under the British Mandate.* trans. Haim Watzman. New York: Henry Holt, 2000.

Sekeryan, Ari. "Rethinking the Turkish-Armenian War in the Caucasus: The Position of Ottoman Armenians," *War in History* 27, no. 1 (2020): 81–105.

Shahoian, Levon. *On the Banks of the Tigris.* London: Gomidas Institute, 2012.

Shaw, Caroline. *Britannia's Embrace: Modern Humanitarianism and the Imperial Origins of Refugee Relief.* Oxford: Oxford University Press, 2015.

Shemmassian, Vahram. "Armenian Genocide Survivors in the Holy Land at the End of World War I," *Journal of the Society for Armenian Studies* 21 (2012): 227–248.

The Musa Dagh Armenians: A Socioeconomic and Cultural History 1919–1939. Beirut: Haigazian Press, 2015.

"The Repatriation of Armenian Refugees," in Richard Hovannisian and Simon Payaslian, eds., *Armenian Cilicia.* Costa Mesa, CA: Mazda Publishers, 2008, 419–456.

Shipley, Alice Muggerditchian. *We Walked, Then We Ran.* Phoenix: A. M. Shipley, 1984.

Shirinian, George. *Genocide in the Ottoman Empire: Armenians, Assyrians and Greeks, 1913–1923.* New York: Berghahn Books, 2017.

Siegel, Mona L. *Peace on Our Terms: The Global Battle for Women's Rights after the First World War.* New York: Columbia University Press, 2020.

Simms, Brendan and D. J. B. Trim, eds. *Humanitarian Intervention: A History.* Cambridge: Cambridge University Press, 2011.

Simpson, John Hope. *The Refugee Problem.* London: Oxford University Press, 1939.

Sinanoglou, Penny. *Partitioning Palestine: British Policymaking at the End of Empire.* Chicago: Chicago University Press, 2019.

Sjöberg, Erik. *The Making of the Greek Genocide: Contested Memories of the Ottoman Greek Catastrophe.* New York: Berghahn Books, 2017.

Skran, Claudena. *Refugees in Interwar Europe: The Emergence of a Regime.* Oxford: Clarendon, 1995.

Slide, Anthony. *Ravished Armenia and the Story of Aurora Mardiganian.* Lanham, MD: Scarecrow Press, 1997.

Sluglett, Peter. *Britain in Iraq: Contriving King and Country.* 2nd edn. London: I. B. Tauris, 2007.

Smiley, Will. *From Slaves to Prisoners of War: The Ottoman Empire, Russia, and International Law.* Oxford: Oxford University Press, 2018.

Smith, Charles D. *Palestine and the Arab-Israeli Conflict.* Boston: Bedford/St. Martin's, 2021.

Smith, George Adam. *The Historical Geography of the Holy Land.* New York: AC Armstrong and Son, 1896.

Smith, Iain R. and Andreas Stucki. "The Colonial Development of Concentration Camps," *Journal of Imperial and Commonwealth History* 39, no. 3 (2011): 417–437.

Smith, Leonard. *Sovereignty at the Paris Peace Conference.* Oxford: Oxford University Press, 2018.

Smith, Michael Llewellyn. *Venizelos: The Making of a Greek Statesman 1864–1914.* New York: Oxford University Press, 2021.

Somakian, Manoug. *Empires in Conflict: Armenian and the Great Powers, 1895–1920.* London: I. B. Tauris, 1995.

Sonyel, Salahi Ramadan. *Turkish Diplomacy, 1918–1923: Mustafa Kemal and the Turkish Nationalist Movement.* London: Sage, 1975.

Sorlin, Pierre. "Cinema and the Memory of the Great War," in Michael Paris, ed., *The First World War and Popular Cinema.* New Brunswick, NJ: Rutgers University Press, 2000, 5–26.

Speed, R. *Prisoners, Diplomats, and the Great War: A Study in the Diplomacy of Captivity.* New York: Greenwood Press, 1990.

Stafford, R. S. *The Tragedy of the Assyrians.* London: Allen and Unwin, 1935.

Stead, Peter. *Film and the Working Class.* London: Routledge, 1989.

Steel, Nigel and Peter Hart. *Defeat at Gallipoli.* London: Papermac, 1995.

Stein, Leonard. *The Balfour Declaration.* New York: Simon and Schuster, 1961.

Stein, Sarah Abrevaya. *Extraterritorial Dreams: European Citizenship, Sephardi Jews, and the Ottoman Twentieth Century.* Chicago: University of Chicago Press, 2016.

Stockdale, Nancy. *Colonial Encounters among English and Palestinian Women.* Gainesville: University of Florida Press, 2007.

Stone, Norman. *The Eastern Front, 1914–1917.* New York: Penguin, 1998.

Stuga, Glenda. *The Nation, Psychology, and International Politics, 1870–1919.* Basingstoke: Palgrave, 2006.

Suny, Ronald. *"They Can Live in the Desert but Nowhere Else": A History of the Armenian Genocide.* Princeton: Princeton University Press, 2017.

Suny, Ronald, Fatma Müge Göçek, and Norman Naimark, eds. *A Question of Genocide: Armenians and Turks at the End of the Ottoman Empire.* New York: Oxford University Press, 2011.

Sykes, Mark. *Through Five Turkish Provinces.* London: Bickers, 1900.

Tachjian, Vahe. "Cilician Armenians and French Policy, 1919–1921," in Richard Hovannisian and Simon Payaslian, eds., *Armenian Cilicia.* Costa Mesa, CA: Mazda Publishers, 2008, 539–556.

Daily Life in the Abyss. New York: Berghan Books, 2017.

La France en Cilicie et en Haute-Mésopotamie: aux confins de la Turquie, de la Syrie et de l'Irak, 1919-1933. Paris: Karthala, 2004.

Tamari, Salim and Ihsan Salih Turjman. *Year of the Locust: A Soldier's Diary and the Erasure of Palestine's Ottoman Past.* Berkeley: University of California Press, 2011.

Tanielian, Melanie. *The Charity of War: Famine, Humanitarian Aid and World War I in the Middle East.* Stanford: Stanford University Press, 2017.

"Politics of Wartime Relief in Ottoman Beirut," *First World War Studies* 5, no. 1 (2014): 69–82.

Taylor, A. J. P., ed. *Lloyd George: Twelve Essays.* London: Atheneum, 1971.

Temperley, H. W. V., ed. *A History of the Peace Conference of Paris,* vol. V: *Economic Reconstruction and Protection of Minorities.* London: Henry Frowde and Hodder & Stoughton, 1921.

Thomas, Martin. *The French Empire between the Wars.* Manchester: Manchester University Press, 2005.

Thompson, Andrew. "The Protestant Interest and the History of Humanitarian Intervention, c. 1685–c. 1756," in Brendan Simms and D. J. B. Trim, eds., *Humanitarianism Intervention: A History.* Cambridge: Cambridge University Press, 2011, 67–88.

Thompson, Elizabeth. *Colonial Citizens: Republican Rights, Paternal Privilege and Gender in French Syria and Lebanon.* New York: Columbia University Press, 2000.

How the West Stole Democracy from the Arabs: The Syrian Arab Congress of 1920 and the Destruction of Its Historic Liberal–Islamic Alliance. New York: Atlantic Monthly Press, 2020.

Toprani, Anand. *Oil and the Great Powers, Britain and Germany, 1914–1945.* Oxford: Oxford University Press, 2019.

Torchin, Leshu. *Creating the Witness: Documenting Genocide on Film.* Minneapolis: University of Minnesota Press, 2012.

"'Ravished Armenia'": Visual Media, Humanitarian Advocacy, and the Formation of Witnessing Publics," *American Anthropologist* 108, no. 1 (2006): 214–220.

Torossian, Sarkis. *From Dardanelles to Palestine.* Boston: Meador Publishing Company, 1929.

Townshend, Charles. *My Campaign in Mesopotamia*. London: Thornton Butterworth, 1920.

Toynbee, Arnold J. *Armenian Atrocities: The Murder of a Nation*. London: Hodder and Stoughton, 1915.

Survey of International Affairs. Oxford: Oxford University Press, 1920.

Travlos, Konstantinos, ed. *Salvation and Catastrophe: The Greek Turkish War, 1919–1922*. New York: Lexington Books, 2020.

Trudinger, D. "The Bear in the Room: Gallipoli, Russia, and the First World War," *War in History* 29, no. 1 (2022): 137–156.

Tusan, Michelle. *The British Empire and the Armenian Genocide: Humanitarianism and Imperial Politics from Gladstone to Churchill*. London: I. B. Tauris, 2017.

"The Business of Relief Work: A Victorian Quaker in Constantinople and Her Circle," *Victorian Studies* 51, no. 4 (2009): 633–661.

"'Crimes against Humanity': Human Rights, the British Empire, and the Origins of the Response to the Armenian Genocide," *American Historical Review* 119, no. 1 (2014): 47–77.

"International Relations," in Tom Brooking and Todd Thompson, eds., *A Cultural History of Democracy in the Age of Empire*, vol. V. London: Bloomsbury, 2021, 185–202.

"James Bryce's Blue Book as Evidence," *Journal of Levantine Studies* 5, no. 2 (Winter 2015): 9–24.

Smyrna's Ashes: Humanitarianism, Genocide, and the Birth of the Middle East. Berkeley: University of California Press, 2012.

"War and the Victorians" *Victorian Studies* 58, no. 2 (Winter 2016): 324–331.

Ulrichsen, Kristian. "The British Occupation of Mesopotamia, 1914–1922," *Journal of Strategic Studies* 30, no. 2 (2007): 349–377.

The First World War in the Middle East. London: Hurst, 2014.

Usai, Paolo Cherchi. *Silent Cinema: A Guide to Study, Research and Curatorship*. London: BFI, 2000.

Van den Boogert, M. *The Capitulations and the Ottoman Legal System: Qadis, Consuls and Beraths in the 18th Century*. Leiden: Brill, 2005.

Varnava, Andrekos. "French and British Postwar Imperial Agendas," *Historical Journal* 57, no. 4 (2014): 997–1025.

Varnava, Andrekos and Trevor Harris. "'It Is Quite Impossible to Receive Them': Saving the Musa Dagh Refugees and the Imperialism of European Humanitarianism," *Journal of Modern History* 90, no. 4 (December 2018): 834–862.

Veidlinger, Jeffrey. *In the Midst of Civilized Europe: The Pogroms of 1918–1921 and the Onset of the Holocaust*. New York: Henry Holt, 2021.

Vernon, James. *Hunger: A Modern History*. Cambridge, MA: Harvard University Press, 2007.

Wagner, Kim. *Amritsar 1919: An Empire of Fear and the Making of a Massacre*. New Haven: Yale University Press, 2019.

Wallach, Janet. *Desert Queen: The Extraordinary Life of Gertrude Bell, Adventurer, Adviser to Kings, Ally of Lawrence of Arabia*. New York: Doubleday, 1996.

Wasserstein, Bernard. "Herbert Samuel and the Palestine Problem," *English Historical Review* 91, no. 361 (1976): 753–775.

Watenpaugh, Keith. *Being Modern in the Middle East: Revolution, Nationalism, Colonialism, and the Arab Middle Class.* Princeton: Princeton University Press, 2006.

　Bread from Stones: The Middle East and the Making of Modern Humanitarianism. Berkeley: California University Press, 2015.

　"The League of Nations' Rescue of Armenian Genocide Survivors and the Making of Modern Humanitarianism, 1920–1927," *American Historical Review* 115, no. 5 (2010): 1315–1339.

Wavell, Archibald. *Allenby: A Study in Greatness.* New York: Oxford University Press, 1941.

Weitz, Eric D. A. "From the Vienna to the Paris System: International Politics and the Entangled Histories of Human Rights, Forced Deportations, and Civilizing Missions," *American Historical Review* 113, no. 5 (2008): 1313–1343.

　World Divided: The Global Struggle for Human Rights in the Age of Nation-States. Princeton: Princeton University Press, 2019.

Wells, David and Sandra Wilson, eds. *The Russo-Japanese War in Cultural Perspective, 1904–05.* Basingstoke: Macmillan, 1999.

White, Benjamin. "A Grudging Rescue: France, the Armenians of Cilicia, and the History of Humanitarian Evacuations," *Humanity* 10, no. 1 (2019): 1–27.

　The Emergence of Minorities in the Middle East. Edinburgh: Edinburgh University Press, 2012.

　"Refugees and the Definition of Syria," *Past and Present* 235, no. 1 (May 2017): 141–178.

Wilcox, Vanda, ed. *Italy in the Era of the Great War.* Leiden: Brill, 2018.

Wilkinson, Oliver. *British Prisoners of War in First World War Germany.* Cambridge: Cambridge University Press, 2017.

Williams, W. "Armenia and the Partition of Asia Minor," *Fortnightly Review* (November 1915).

Wilson, Jeremy. *Lawrence of Arabia: The Authorized Biography of T. E. Lawrence.* London: Heinemann, 1989.

Winegard, Timothy C. *The First World Oil War.* Toronto: University of Toronto Press, 2016.

　Indigenous Peoples of the British Dominions and the First World War. Cambridge, Cambridge University Press, 2012.

Winston, Brian. *Claiming the Real II: Documentary: Grierson and Beyond.* London: Palgrave Macmillan, 2008.

Winter, Jay, ed. *America and the Armenian Genocide.* Cambridge: Cambridge University Press, 2003.

　The Day the Great War Ended, 24 July 1923: The Civilianization of War. Oxford: Oxford University Press, 2023.

Wolff, Larry. *Woodrow Wilson and the Reimagining of Eastern Europe.* Stanford: Stanford University Press, 2020.

Woodward, David. *Hell in the Holy Land: World War I in the Middle East.* Lexington: University of Kentucky Press, 2006.

Woodward, E. L. and R. Butler, eds. *Documents on British Foreign Policy, 1919–1939*, vol. IV. London: HMSO, 1952.

    eds. *Documents on British Foreign Policy, 1919–1939*, 3rd series, vol. VII. London: HMSO, 1954.

    eds. *Documents on British Foreign Policy, 1919–1939*, 3rd series, vol. VIII. London: HMSO, 1955.

Yacoub, Joseph. *The Year of the Sword*. Oxford: Oxford University Press, 2016.

Yeghiayan, Zaven Der. trans. Ared Misirliyan. *My Patriarchal Memoirs*, Barrington, RI: Mayreni Publishing, 2002.

Yervant, John. *Needle, Thread and Button*. Cambridge, MA: Zoryan Institute Press, 1988.

Yessayan, Zabel, trans. Jennifer Manoukian. *The Gardens of Silihdar*. Boston: AIWA Press, 2014.

    trans. G. M. Goshgarian. *In the Ruins: The 1909 Massacres of Armenians in Adana, Turkey*. Boston: AIWA Press, 2016.

Yilderim, Onur. *Diplomacy and Displacement: Reconsidering the Turco-Greek Exchange of Populations, 1922–1934*. London: Routledge 2006.

Yosmaoğlu, İpek. *Blood Ties: Religion, Violence, and the Politics of Nationhood in Ottoman Macedonia, 1878–1908*. Ithaca, NY: Cornell University Press, 2014.

Zahra, Tara. *The Lost Children: Reconstructing Europe's' Families after World War II*. Cambridge, MA: Harvard University Press, 2011.

    The Great Departure. New York: W. W. Norton, 2016.

Zeiger, Susan. *In Uncle Sam's Service: Women Workers with the American Expeditionary Force, 1917–1919* Ithaca, NY: Cornell University Press, 1999.

Zimmerer, Jürgen. "Colonial Genocide: The Herero and Nama War in German South West Africa and Its Significance," in Dan Stone, ed., *The Historiography of Genocide*. London: Palgrave Macmillan, 2008, 323–343.

Zimmern, Alfred. *The Prospects of Democracy*. Freeport, NY: Books for Libraries Press, 1968 (repr. 1929).

Zirinsky, Michael P. "Imperial Power and Dictatorship: Britain and the Rise of Reza Shah, 1921-1926," *International Journal of Middle East Studies* 24, no. 4 (1992): 639–663.

Zürcher, Erik-Jan. *Jihad and Islam in World War I: Studies on the Ottoman Jihad on the Centenary of Snouck Hurgronje's "Holy War Made in Germany."* Leiden: Leiden University Press, 2015.

    Turkey: A Modern History. London: I. B. Tauris, 2004.

    The Unionist Factor: The Role of the Committee of Union and Progress in the Turkish Nationalist Movement, 1905–1926. Leiden: Brill, 1984.

    Young Turk Legacy and Nation Building: From the Ottoman Empire to Atatürk's Turkey. London: I. B. Tauris, 2014.

THESIS

Darbinyan, Asya. "Russian Empire's Response to Armenian Genocide: Humanitarian Assistance to Armenian Refugees at the Caucasus

Battlefront of the Great War (1914–1917)," Clark University dissertation, 2019.

Grieve-Laing, Jenny. "Russian Refugee Relief Aid in Inter-war Europe: The Case of Constantinople, 1920–1922," University of Aberdeen dissertation, 2016.

Morea, Gary J. "Angels of Armageddon: The Royal Air Force in the Battle of Megiddo," MA thesis, US Army Command and General Staff College, Fort Leavenworth, Kansas, 2007.

Rowe, Victoria. "The 'New Armenian Woman': Armenian Women's Writing in the Ottoman Empire, 1880–1915," University of Toronto dissertation, 2000.

Index